Off the Page

Off the Page
Screenwriting in the Era of Media Convergence

DANIEL BERNARDI AND JULIAN HOXTER

University of California Press

University of California Press, one of the most distinguished university presses in the United States, enriches lives around the world by advancing scholarship in the humanities, social sciences, and natural sciences. Its activities are supported by the UC Press Foundation and by philanthropic contributions from individuals and institutions. For more information, visit www.ucpress.edu.

University of California Press
Oakland, California

© 2017 by The Regents of the University of California

Library of Congress Cataloging-in-Publication Data

Names: Bernardi, Daniel, author. | Hoxter, Julian, author.
Title: Off the page : screenwriting in the era of media convergence / Daniel Bernardi and Julian Hoxter.
Description: Oakland, California : University of California Press, [2017] | Includes bibliographical references and index.
Identifiers: LCCN 2017005898 (print) | LCCN 2017008436 (ebook) | ISBN 9780520285644 (cloth : alk. paper) | ISBN 9780520285651 (pbk. : alk. paper) | ISBN 9780520961043 ()
Subjects: LCSH: Motion picture authorship. | Motion picture plays. | Screenwriters—United States. | Television writers—United States. | Hollywood (Los Angeles, Calif.)
Classification: LCC PN1996 .B467 2017 (print) | LCC PN1996 (ebook) | DDC 808.2/3—dc23
LC record available at https://lccn.loc.gov/2017005898

Manufactured in the United States of America

24 23 22 21 20 19 18 17
10 9 8 7 6 5 4 3 2 1

Contents

Acknowledgments ix

INTRODUCTION: SCREENWRITING OFF THE PAGE 1

1. MILLENNIAL MANIC: CRISIS AND CHANGE IN THE BUSINESS OF SCREENWRITING 27

2. ATOP THE TENTPOLE: HOLLYWOOD SCREENWRITING TODAY 62

3. RUNNING THE ROOM: SHOWRUNNING IN EXPANDED TELEVISION 102

4. NEW MARKETS AND MICROBUDGETS: "INDEPENDENT" STORYTELLERS 139

5. SCREENWRITER 2.0: THE LEGITIMATION OF WRITING FOR VIDEO GAMES 182

CONCLUSION: SCRIPTING BOUNDARIES 217

Notes 245

Index 273

*We dedicate this book to our partners
for feeding us ideas and challenging our assumptions . . .*

Helen (Daniel)
SL (Julian)

Acknowledgments

We were ably assisted in our research for this book by the professional and always collegial staff at the Academy of Motion Picture Arts and Sciences' Margaret Herrick Library in Beverly Hills. The Herrick's archive of screenplays and other materials is a wonderful resource for film scholars, and no matter how often we visit, we continue to find new and important insights there.

The support of other friends, colleagues, and talented students in San Francisco State University's School of Cinema has also been invaluable during the development of this project. In particular we are grateful to our research assistant, Allyce L. Ondrika, for her excellent work pulling together and parsing material on feature and story development at Marvel and DC and to our friend and colleague Aaron Kerner, for his sage commentary on an early draft of the material on online content creation.

We are also grateful to our undergraduate and graduate students, specifically those in Julian's CINE 568 Creating Story Worlds class, with whom we field-tested the chapter on writing for video games. Their in-depth knowledge of and thoughtful engagement with the contemporary ludisphere was invaluable to the further development of the chapter—if your parents tell you playing video games is a waste of time, show them this book!

We are most grateful to the screenwriters, filmmakers, online content creators, and film scholars who contributed their time, thought, and material support to this project, whether officially or unofficially, and in various capacities. The list is long, and it includes a number of friends and colleagues whose valuable input remains anonymous but no less important than the subjects of our prominent case studies. Particular gratitude goes out, inter alia, to Pamela Gray, Robert Moreland, Travis Mathews, Michael Grais, Scott Sublett, Scott Boswell, Bryan Darling, Gary Whitta, Denise R. Mann, Shawn

Ryan, Karen and Lisa Alkofer, Mike Stabile, Sam Hamm, Richard Walter, Kevin Sandler (his early work with Daniel on *The Shield* was invaluable to this project), Lloyd A. Silverman, Joseph McBride, William Tyler Smith, Michael Whalen, Cheryl Valenzuela, Sarah Dunham, Ariel Sinelnikoff, David Carson, Andy Horton, Will Frampton (a.k.a. Quickybaby), and Joshua Grannell (a.k.a. Peaches Christ). Any errors and omissions are ours alone.

Finally, many thanks are due our editors at the University of California Press: Mary Francis who fostered the project from its inception, and Raina Polivka, her able replacement after Mary left to take up her new post as editorial director of Michigan Publishing. Their enthusiasm for the project throughout its development, combined with sage advice and considerable patience, is greatly appreciated.

Introduction
Screenwriting off the Page

The product of the dream factory is not one of the same nature as are the material objects turned out on most assembly lines. For them, uniformity is essential; for the motion picture, originality is important. The conflict between the two qualities is a major problem in Hollywood.

HORTENSE POWDERMAKER[1]

A screenplay writer, screenwriter for short, or scriptwriter or scenarist is a writer who practices the craft of screenwriting, writing screenplays on which mass media such as films, television programs, comics or video games are based.

Wikipedia

In the documentary *Dreams on Spec* (2007), filmmaker Daniel J. Snyder tests studio executive Jack Warner's famous line: "Writers are just schmucks with Underwoods." Snyder seeks to explain, for example, why a writer would take the time to craft an original "spec" script without a monetary advance and with only the dimmest of possibilities that it will be bought by a studio or producer. Extending anthropologist Hortense Powdermaker's 1950s framing of Hollywood in the era of Jack Warner and other classic Hollywood moguls as a "dream factory," *Dreams on Spec* profiles the creative and economic nightmares experienced by contemporary screenwriters hoping to clock in on Hollywood's assembly line of creative uniformity.

There is something to learn about the craft and profession of screenwriting from all the characters in this documentary. One of the interviewees, Dennis Palumbo (*My Favorite Year*, 1982), addresses the downside of the struggling screenwriter's life with a healthy dose of pragmatism: "A writer's life and a writer's struggle can be really hard on relationships, very hard for your mate to understand. Your ups and downs, the fact that you're spending all of these hours doing something that doesn't seem to have a tangible reward. Not to mention the financial strain. Because for most writers they have to take day jobs that don't bring them the kind of money and security that their mate would want, particularly if children start coming into the equation."[2] Palumbo reminds us that many professional screenwriters struggle to make ends meet, a fact exacerbated by often-stark familial realities that undercut the aspirational myth of the economy of screenwriting.

As *Dreams on Spec* suggests, screenwriters have never had it easy in the hierarchy of cinema preproduction. They have always lived at the bottom of the Hollywood totem pole, their director and actor colleagues habitually eclipsing them in the cultural and economic discourse. Equally problematic, the creative freedom of the contemporary Hollywood screenwriter has been increasingly constrained in recent years as the list of genres and stories that studios deem fundable shrinks to an unprecedented low. The major studios are operating with greatly reduced production slates, making little more in-house than a few high-budget "tentpole" movies, or potential financial blockbusters, a scattering of teen and romantic comedies, and the occasional prestige drama often strategized as awards bait or to pacify important talent and their agents. The budgets of their shrinking development departments have been slashed, and so have the project pipelines that used to offer the possibility of funding for aspiring and established screenwriters alike, even if the movies they worked on never got made. As a consequence, the average feature screenwriter's family is more likely to go hungry today than it is to bask in prestige and associated riches.

THE SCREENWRITING FACTORY

Hollywood is buying very few original screenplays, in part because it is producing more and more of its films for an expanding global market. Character-driven drama, once a mainstay of studio and independent production, has increasingly been moved away from the movie theater to smaller screens. Production in the largely co-opted "prestige independent" sector has also shrunk from the boom it experienced in the early 1990s. On the one hand, microbudget production, fueled by digital technology and reduced production costs, is booming; yet it is far from easy for a successful microbudget screenwriter, who often doubles as a project's director and triples as its producer, to make a living from no-to-low-budget moviemaking. On the other hand, making a mark at microbudget is one way she or he may be discovered.

In the last two decades the industrial context for a screenwriter's labor has been changing faster than at any time since the coming of sound. For almost the entire history of cinema, Jack Warner's schmuck, or what we might now call the traditional screenwriter—or, to borrow from the lexicon of the tech industry, "screenwriter 1.0"—wrote either for the big screen of the movie theater or, after its introduction, for the small screen of television. Today's writer—"screenwriter 2.0"—writes in the era of media convergence, an era that foreshadows the end of cinema as we think we know it. This new or convergent screenwriter is likely to practice her craft in new media and across multiple screens. Markets and media are changing and with them the craft and careers of those who write for those transforming industries and platforms. All is not lost, therefore, for the craft of screenwriting, despite the unprecedented reduction of opportunities to hit it rich with a spec script. Opportunities abound for writers willing and able to think off the page.

Dreams on Spec both understands the histories of the dream factory's own crafts and tells their stories through a well-established mix of "how to break in" stories and, once in, "war stories" of exploitation. For example, Snyder's documentary tells a compelling story about the struggles of aspiring screenwriters from within what film scholar Steven Maras calls the "practitioner" and "business" frames of industry discourse. "The practitioner frame," Maras writes, "tends to be about advice, experience, and the so-called creative process." The "business frame," in contrast, tends to be about industrial activities such as deal making and pitching.[3] Screenwriting professionals, along with the screenwriting paraindustry gurus (people and businesses that sell the hidden value of screenwriting to aspiring writers), typically address their craft uncritically from within these practitioner and business frames. They circumscribe the self-reflexive discourse through which screenwriting practice is framed within the industry. Missing from Snyder's otherwise provocative documentary, for instance, is an exploration of the effects of media convergence on both contemporary writers and the conglomerate studios that simultaneously drive and are driven by the craft of screenwriting. Missing, too, is how the screenwriters' trade union, the Writers Guild of America (WGA), functionally accedes in the propping up of an increasingly modernized assembly line that needs fewer and fewer original writers. The WGA's de facto stance is, in part, due to the narrow self-interest of its established membership and, in part, because its influence has been marginalized by and within the new media industries.

Hollywood limits the opportunities for aspiring writers while enhancing the viability of the few established writers who can write to contemporary tentpole formulas. It also co-opts the efforts of the WGA, which is obliged to focus much of its work within the default employment formula presented by the studios and producers. Snyder's documentary, like much of the paraindustry, offers valuable insights into the business frame of screenwriting yet fails to address explicitly the conundrum of the studio/guild complex.

As we show in chapters 1 and 5, the wider the definition of professional screenwriting becomes, the harder it has been for the WGA to spread its jurisdictional umbrella to cover the new creative and industrial contexts in which professional screenwriters now strive to make a living. Even the writers' strike of 2007–8, which was fought over the economic implications of media convergence for the craft, centered less on increasing membership and thus expanding the ranks to different kinds of writers than on ensuring its established members remained economically viable as studios spread their interest across new delivery platforms. As a result, the new convergent screenwriter is less likely to be a member of the guild or even to aspire to join it.

To tackle the contemporary world of screenwriters and the screenwriting economy, we engage critically with Maras's practitioner and business frames through an analysis of a range of industrial texts such as the media trade press, craft guild publications, paraindustrial testimonials of all kinds, online outlets for screenwriters' discussions, and other records of and responses to the guild's collective action. We also look at scripts and production documents such as studio notes, as well as fiction films and documentaries. As professor-types, we also engage extant film and media scholarship; however, we are always keen to work between the registers of the paraindustrial and scholarly discourses that frame the craft of screenwriting for different purposes and for different audiences. We look at all—and employ all—critically and, we hope the reader will find, creatively.

Our work in chapters 2, 3, and 4 is also underpinned by interviews with working screenwriters from all sectors of the industry. Some of these interviews were conducted as background research and remain anonymous at the request of the subject. At the same time, we also offer several substantial interview-based case studies of prominent writers such as Pamela Gray (*Conviction*, 2010) and Shawn Ryan (*The Shield*, 2002–8) and others who are perhaps less well known but are navigating professional challenges that illustrate and bring into focus important aspects of the state of the screenwriting craft today. These interviews are intended to explore the attitudes unique and common to screenwriters in the contemporary moment, with an emphasis on current craft and trade practices, to illustrate the effects that broader corporate practices are having on the careers of working writers.

To be sure, interviews with professional screenwriters are also texts that require critical interpretation. In the research context they function as both primary and secondary evidence: evidence that either goes directly to a specific point, perhaps revealing industrial discourse, or that helps contextualize a broader point. Nonetheless, the subjects of these interviews are just as embedded in culture—and, at times, the paraindustry—as those who sell the dreams of screenwriting via the usual "how to" and "war stories." Traditional screenwriters are well practiced in selling themselves, their industry, their experiences, and their ideas. Indeed, this kind of practiced self-promotion is a core professional skill among members of all the major Hollywood crafts. We are thus always careful to relate our interviews to wider issues and debates in contemporary screenwriting, as well as to the scholarly field that sees these types of texts as one of many forms of evidence. In this way the personal stories of our subjects should be taken to be illustrative and contextual rather than definitive.

We can say the same about our use of the myriad texts that make up the screenwriting paraindustry. One need only search Google for "how to sell a blockbuster screenplay" to find a host of reputable and not-so-reputable institutions and individuals selling the hidden method to creative success, as well as screenwriting professors professing a winning "practitioner" formula and the associated dreams that will come true for those undergraduates and graduate students who learn how to write to formula. As we will discuss in more detail in our conclusion, film schools, even the most competitive and prestigious like UCLA, USC, NYU, and AFI, still market traditional screenwriting curricula with the aim of attracting students through the implied promise of Hollywood success. High demand from potential students and the economic imperatives of modern higher education have also ensured that, when there is insufficient space in their prestigious screenwriting programs, aspiring students that are not admitted can nonetheless secure the imprimatur of the institutions by taking screenwriting classes through their online or extension programs. Indeed, paraindustrial discourses—the selling of dreams of success, of the narrative of "breaking in" to share in Hollywood's riches—are now helping to meet the revenue needs of both public and private higher education.

The trade book market is equally rich with "how to make it as a screenwriter" books; a simple search of Amazon.com offers an algorithmic library of options to the buyer in search of Hollywood originality by way of the screenplay page. Hence, this dimension of the paraindustry, from how-to websites and books to formal and informal film education, is in the business of marketing the fantasy of "breaking in" from the perspective of Maras's third "story and structure frame." Here Maras refers to accounts of the nuts and bolts of writing a screenplay, viewed through an empirical lens. Execute carefully, the narratives of the story and structure frame advise, assemble with precision according to previously blueprinted formulae, and understand how the industry came to work as it does, and the student screenwriter in and outside academe might just sell that spec script.

This educational dimension of the paraindustry also provides us with primary and secondary evidence. Screenwriting manuals, for example, offer blueprints for screenplay design that, in effect, sell variant narratives of success through conformity rather than innovation. From the perspective of film and media studies it is easy to dismiss these manuals and textbooks on the grounds of a long list of scholarly and perspectival limitations. Viewed through the discourses that give some texture to the screenwriting profession, however, many of these manuals offer sound practical advice and self-reflexive insights that shouldn't be dismissed or marginalized on the grounds of scholarly antipathy to Hollywood orthodoxies alone or, for that matter, scholarly debates that seek to limit evidence to textual analysis, critical theory, and, of course, canonical methods. We take them seriously yet engage with them critically.

Whether screenwriters and screenwriting professors like it or not, their profession is engaged in one of the most rule-bound forms of creative writing. Many of these rules—such as a prevailing three-act screenplay form that requires specific dramatic developments to happen at specified moments—are practical accretions that speak to the collaborative history of the medium and apply to many innovative independent features as much as they do to the most formulaic genre stories. It is precisely because of the particular kind of insight that they offer and because of the work they do in propagating and sustaining the realities and myths of the screenwriting profession that the paraindustry is worthy of critical attention, both as complex discourse and as primary evidence. As we hope to show in this book, success in screenwriting trades directly on the ability of the writer to work creatively within the multiple accreted constrictions of her or his chosen profession. And that includes the parlance of a diverse paraindustry. We take it that our readers will bring their own critical judgment to our use of manuals, interviews, textbooks, and related paraindustry artifacts.

We also trust that they will do the same in parsing the attitudes of screenwriting professionals among whom there exists both a fair amount of critical insight and a commitment to a brand of industrial spin. UCLA screenwriting professor Richard Walter, for example, offers a good reason why his students would do well not to focus too hard too soon on the aspect of their careers that we could place within Maras's business frame. Although he doesn't use that kind of scholarly language, Walter is all in on the practitioner and story and structure frames because he has recognized that focusing on the business frame will only sway an aspiring screenwriter either to focus on riches over story or to give up entirely. The prominent professor in effect tells his students that one needs to be a bit of a schmuck to enter the screenwriting profession. He encourages aspiring screenwriters to focus on story, character, thematic development—the stuff of a good Hollywood script—and to live with a degree of poverty. Indeed, many of the points we make in this book from our own historical and critical perspectives elucidate the harsh reality of the craft and industry that prompts and underpins his position as a screenwriting teacher.

So do the many insights offered by scholars in such diverse disciplinary fields as textual analysis, industry studies, and production culture studies. Here scholars such as John Thornton Caldwell figure in our story. A pioneer of production studies who draws on Powdermaker's important anthropological fieldwork of several decades earlier, Caldwell encourages research that helps ground a scholarly enterprise focused on the "here, now and how" of Hollywood. Discussing Caldwell in greater detail later in this chapter, we treat his work and the work of other scholars much the same way we treat manuals, interviews, WGA rhetoric, and other paraindustry texts: both critically and creatively. Hence, we're interested in more than a synthesis of the craft-centric frames of the screenwriting profession today, engaging also with Maras's fourth frame, the frame of screenwriting as "discourse." At the same time, we rely broadly on the production-studies method to help us foreground the ways in which today's screenwriters write both on and off the page—that is, how they work in and out of the production process today.

Professional screenwriters, like the moviegoers they serve, are not merely dupes alienated by the false ideologies of a conglomerate industry. Those who have come to understand the ever-shifting complexities of the movie business are still able to navigate and adapt to it with some success. Their brand of industrial spin provides us with diffuse entry points to this aspect of cinema's convergent turn. At the same time, of course, today's working screenwriter is being asked to put new syntax to tried-and-true formulas designed to improve the economic performance of the studio's parent company. The days of Hollywood studios being independent corporate entities concerned primarily with making movies are long gone, as the screenwriter Billy Ray (*The Hunger Games*, 2012; *Captain Phillips*, 2013) noted in a recent polemical piece titled "A Warning for Our Next Great Screenwriters":

> When I started writing there were still a few mavericks out there; a few gunslingers who ran studios.

These were people who went with their guts and would make a movie just because they believed in it.

But that's not the process anymore.

Today, before a studio chair can green-light a movie, that movie must also be blessed by the head of marketing, the head of foreign sales, and the head of home video.

It must be subjected to a process called "running the numbers," which means that the movie's cost—or, downside—is compared against its potential value because of its cast and what it might do in foreign markets.

This process takes into account every variable except the variable which actually matters—the one that can't possibly be gauged by any sort of calculus—which is whether or not the movie's going to be any good.

And yet the process continues.[4]

Professor Walter's advice points to another trend, if only at the margins, that either rationalizes hope or suggests a path out of the rhetoric of the tentpole paradigm: where there is creative will and talent, and perhaps some luck to go along with pluck, today's working screenwriter can find opportunities to tell other kinds of stories. And this is more than hinted at in the broad definition of the word *screenwriter* offered in the reference from *Wikipedia* with which we opened this introduction. This so-called nonspecialist resource is aptly suggesting that the contemporary screenwriter might be writing "screenplays" for comics and video games as much as for movies and television. In other words, *Wikipedia*'s definition speaks to the transformative expansion of the screenwriting profession in the flattening era of media convergence.

And this is a key concern of this book. For students, film enthusiasts, and aspiring screenwriters to understand the new screenwriter, they, like us, have to rethink the two constituent words that have combined to delimit the traditional screenwriter: *screen* and *writer*. Today's screenwriters can write for a panoply of screens, pushing and at times exploding tried-and-true formulae. They also collaborate in the broader *scripting* processes—to deploy another insightful term borrowed from Maras—of syncretistic media texts with professionals from other crafts. In so doing, they require us to expand our definition of writing beyond the simple inscription of words on a page and to think of the scripting of a project as a collaboration that may extend authorship far beyond the traditional boundaries of the craft of screenwriting. This begs the question: how has the craft of screenwriting changed to accommodate those screens and those convergent collaborations?

Off the Page: Screenwriting in the Era of Media Convergence explores how both the craft and the industrial context of screenwriting are changing to accommodate new forms of writing on new platforms in a new millennium and how we got to this point of dramatic change. Of course, many established Hollywood screenwriters continue to do what they have always done: they write movies and television shows. Yet those writers are now working on conglomerate assembly lines that exert particular commercial and creative pressures on their labor. As old markets and opportunities contract, new generations of writers—and some established writers—are expanding the profession, moving it away from media familiar to previous generations of screenwriters and engaging with new markets, new media forms, and new technologies in their search for creative opportunity and economic security. These "new" screenwriters do not merely stand on the shoulders of fellow schmucks; they also walk where there are few if any giant footprints to follow.

The episodic and serial narratives of comics and the less linear and more interactive stories found in many of today's video games have become lucrative arenas for the screenwriters who increasingly work across platforms. Television drama and comedy storytelling, which still have a well-established apprenticeship model, are alive and well on HBO, Showtime, FX, and even the old major broadcast networks (some would argue in ways that are more interesting than big-screen storytelling). And then there's the online world of expanded television (Netflix, Amazon, and Hulu, inter alia), independent features, and short films. There is creative opportunity for screenwriters and independent writer-directors in the complex, converging business of show business, though perhaps not so much in many studio executives' offices.

Although providing some opportunities for screenwriters, the issue of transmedia storytelling is more complex than that of comics, video games, and television. For clarification, we see a narrow distinction between transmedia storytelling as an (always) emerging practice for the creative development of story worlds and storytelling and corporate transmedia as more or less straightforward synergistic cross-platform marketing strategies. In the former context the development of an intellectual property (IP) or a story world that can be explored across subtly interacting narrative and expositional frameworks in different media, often without a conventional ending, let alone a clear act structure, offers unique opportunities for writers to engage with the limits of contemporary digital and online culture. A famous example of this was the creative extrapolation of the *Matrix* "universe" from movies, through different kinds of video games, including a

Massively Multiplayer Online Role Playing Game (MMORPG), to comics, to animated shorts (*The Animatrix*).[5] In the latter context conglomerate Hollywood is simply able to maximize the monetization of IP by marketing and spinning off products across media in ways that do not necessarily deepen the storytelling potential of the material or open up opportunities for working screenwriters at the margins of economic success and industrial cachet. The new starship designs, characters, troop types, and combat scenarios seen in the science fiction war movie *Rogue One: A Star Wars Story* (2016) will soon make their appearance across the tabletop product line of licensee Fantasy Flight Games in games such as *X Wing, Star Wars: Armada, Star Wars: Destiny,* and *Star Wars: Imperial Assault,* for example.

Hollywood has experimented with more creative transmedia marketing. At its most innovative this involves elements of complex interactive storytelling and gaming, as with the yearlong, Internet-driven "Why So Serious" teaser puzzles anticipating the release of the Batman movie *The Dark Knight* in 2008. To date, and as the WGA strike of 2007–8 foreshadowed, the investment of marketing resources at this level is disproportionate to its effect on the box office. Given its limited impact on the corporate bottom line, creative transmedia marketing of this type does not appear likely to become commonplace anytime soon.[6]

We engage these constraints through the range of texts, or evidence, we introduce above, revealing the repercussions of conglomeration, globalization, and union co-optation; we then turn to the creative ways writers are working through all attempts to, in the political philosopher Antonio Gramsci's conception of ideology, coerce them into consenting to the Hollywood matrix.[7] For Gramsci, advanced capitalism works to establish hegemony, or temporary domination, that seeks the "consent" of labor through the "coercive" forces, the give and take, of ideology. For the screenwriter outsider, this consent manifests itself around the narratives of breaking in and persevering in the hope of selling a script and becoming rich and popular. For the Hollywood insider it is manifested in an acceptance by the creative worker of coercive, underhanded, and adhesive practices on the part of employers. When the most egregious of these practices are resisted, through collective action and even the withdrawal of labor, it is with the expectation of limited gains weighed against the fear of losing the dubious privilege of continuing to occupy the spot at the base of the conglomerate totem pole. The subordination of the screenwriter to the studio system, the narrative of the duped schmuck, has helped to produce a hegemonic "common sense" that successful Hollywood screenwriting is about conforming to a particular kind of storytelling.

We frame this ideological reading within the larger corporate and cultural trends that inform the industry. We analyze the recent history of the Hollywood studio development paradigm alongside different iterations of "independent" screenwriting, including "microbudget" and expanded-screenwriting practices, theories, and microeconomic models. Our goal is to write critically about the American screenwriting profession, to engage with its current industrial state, and to contextualize the commonsense discourses of the academic and paraindustries in an effort to offer a creative analysis. Equally important, we engage in the close textual analysis of screenplays, considering them as historical documents that communicate much more than story. Indeed, screenplays and similar texts reveal a great deal about the industry for which they are written through their format, through how their prosodic styles are implemented by their writers to target implied readers, and through how they are read within the industry. Recent examples of screenplay form and content also reveal how the screenwriter's labor is, in some measure, adapting to technological developments both within and outside their own craft and to new modes of onscreen storytelling. In this turn of the enterprise some of these scripts demonstrate creative resistance to conglomeration and ideology in the working world of the screenwriter. In grounding our readings in this way, we attempt to avoid, or at least to minimize, the kind of critical self-indulgence that can diminish the value of close textual analysis.

How do corporate interests, union struggles, and paraindustrial myths frame today's screenwriting profession? What is the current state of Hollywood's tentpole paradigm, and how has it solidified the opportunities of a few screenwriters to the exclusion of others and reinforced economic hierarchies within the craft? What role does teamwork play in television and even video game writing? Where are writers now turning to express their ideas in words, to create different worlds through story, to engage audiences in meaningful ways, and to make a living? More abstractly, in what ways do the radical changes in the mediated work of storytelling portend screenwriter 2.0?

In addressing these questions, the following chapters will consider the potential of new technologies and platforms (including interactivity and the Internet) that are transforming the screenwriter's understanding of character, plot, and structure. They also consider the role of the screenwriting industry: from the conglomerates to social media companies and festivals. The early chapters set the stage with our own additions to the business frame long-fetishized by the paraindustry, considering the industrial context and labor relations of the tentpole era of Hollywood screenwriting, where the latest iteration of the blockbuster holds up the financial interests of multinational media companies. Later chapters reveal the opportunities and practices in independent and convergent media that are transforming the labor of screenwriting, as well as our collective understanding of the profession. Our conclusion pushes the definition of the screenwriter firmly past its conventional and preconvergent boundaries while reflecting on how those obsolete boundaries are nonetheless being solidified in today's film schools.

But first, and given the discussion about evidence and method above as critical to our project, we position *Off the Page* in the context of the scholarly models that have been applied to the academic study of screenwriting. We, too, follow in the footsteps of giants.

THE SCHOLARSHIP FACTORY

Of all the major craft disciplines involved in the production of motion pictures, screenwriting has been, until recently, the least studied and theorized within film and media studies. The academic literature on directing, acting, editing, cinematography, and sound is generally better established. With few exceptions the screenwriting profession is rarely mentioned outside introductory film production or history textbooks—"outside," to use the language of film theory and criticism, auteur, star, style, and, until recently, industry studies. When film and media studies engage with the question of story, the focus is typically on narration and discourse as it is manifest in finished films; also writing and development threaten to get in the way of auteur theory.[8] As a result, with few exceptions, the primary structuring text for what we see on the screen, the screenplay, slips past scholarly scrutiny. Historically, we academics have not been doing our part to challenge the common sense of screenwriting practice and the profession.

An instructive example can be found in the otherwise admirable standard history of Hollywood in the 1980s, Stephen Prince's *A New Pot of Gold: Hollywood under the Electronic Rainbow, 1980–1989*.[9] In his chapter on the filmmakers of the period, Prince is rightly keen to acknowledge the importance of creative contributions beyond stars and directors. He makes space for sections assessing the most influential "below the line" talent, or cinematographers, production designers, and editors, among others, who have "rates" but whose salaries are not fixed and can vary depending on actual work performed. Prince acknowledges that screenwriters should be grouped with "above the line" talent, or those receiving residuals, like the directors, producers, and stars, whose salaries are negotiated and fixed in the budget. Prince, however, gives screenwriters no section of their own and focuses entirely on the other "craft" professions. This oversight notwithstanding, every film made by Hollywood is based on a screenplay that was written by one or more screenwriters.

Recent interventions within what film and media scholars call "industry studies" have begun to expand our understanding of the discourses, labor, and ideology of the craft. Notable contributions include the work of the Screenwriting Research Network; Kevin Alexander Boon's *Script Culture and the American Screenplay;* Steven Maras's *Screenwriting: History, Theory, and Practice;* Steven Price's *The Screenplay: Authorship, Theory and Criticism;* the collection edited by Jill Nelmes, *Analyzing the Screenplay;* and Bridget Conor's *Screenwriting: Creative Labor and Professional Practice.*[10] All have been published in the last decade or so. We believe that industry studies, along with the related field of production culture studies, offers the greatest promise for developing an in-depth critical approach to the screenwriting profession and the major role it has played and continues to play in Hollywood mythmaking.

Of particular note is Miranda Banks's *The Writers: A History of American Screenwriters and Their Guild,* which provides a rich, rigorous, and critically insightful analysis of the historical role screenwriters and the WGA have played in Hollywood filmmaking and attendant discourses since the turn of the millennium.[11] Banks also considers contemporary production culture—the conditions of preproduction and production filmmaking informing the working life of screenwriters—in ways that are both critical and instructional. Banks's analysis of the WGA's ambivalent role in both supporting screenwriter rights and limiting membership in the profession is particularly insightful and undergirds our analysis of "tentpole" cinema in chapter 2.

For all of its insightful points, Banks's work—and the work of many of the aforementioned industry studies texts—does not engage fully with the complexity of the screenplay text, its format, and its prose since the turn of the century. No single book can cover all dimensions of a complex phenomenon like screenwriting, but Banks's work is the best sustained historical analysis of American screenwriting yet published. Few academic books actually engage in close analysis of the style, format, and tropes—in short, the textuality—of screenplays as a way to reveal how the widgets of the professional writer, the results of her labor, articulate both story and power dynamics.

When they do address the screenplay-as-text, analyses are usually broad and the points illustrative but general. Nelmes's edited collection, *Analyzing the Screenplay,* is a case in point. It offers a broad, international perspective on script analysis and its related industrial practices. Borrowing from both film historiography and theory, *Analyzing the Screenplay* looks at the screenplay as an industrial form rather than screenwriting as a set of creative and institutional practices or as a locus of debate within larger shifts occurring in the culture of filmmaking, script reading, and film viewing. Contributors to Nelmes's collection tend to reinforce the orthodox notion that the screenplay is the default object of screenwriting studies and, in so doing, fail to accept the challenge offered by the emerging and, in many cases, already proven arenas in which writers have seen their words transformed into moving pictures.

Andrew Horton and Julian Hoxter's coedited collection, *Screenwriting*, focuses on the history of screenwriting as a craft and thus offers a sort of history to *Off The Page*.[12] Their book offers broad historical insights in terms of Maras's "practitioner," "story and structure," "business," and "discourse" frames. But because the focus of the contributors to Horton and Hoxter's collection is largely on the history of screenwriting before the turn of the present century, its coverage of the contemporary industrial moment is narrower and far less substantial than what we aim to cover here. The same could be said of Steven Price's otherwise admirable *A History of the Screenplay*, which also falls short of engaging at length with the broader contemporary moment of conglomeration and convergence.[13] In focusing on the contemporary moment, we hope to offer deeper analysis of a more tightly focused set of issues immediately relevant to today's reader: what is the current state of the screenwriting profession, how did it come to be, and where is it heading?

Contrary to its coverage in the field of film and media studies in the academy, screenwriting as craft and practice is without a doubt the most overtheorized craft in the paraindustrial market treating with the movie industry. With a high degree of what John Thornton Caldwell calls industrial self-reflexivity,[14] the screenwriting industry looks positively on itself as a way to extend, or spin, its share of the more "rigorous" self-help market. That market has, in fact, exploded over the last three decades as writing a spec screenplay has increasingly been seen—and marketed—as an accepted route by which the Hollywood outsider can break into the business. Many working in academia have, in fact, given it even greater legitimacy. There may be some modest credibility to that claim, since it appears far more difficult for producers, directors, and actors to sell what they do on "spec" (the audition process notwithstanding).

It is important to reinforce the point we made earlier that some paraindustrial texts grounded in a kind of research do influence the Hollywood industrial mind-set. Famously, Syd Field's 1979 how-to manual, *The Screenplay*, popularized the notion of a three-act, post-Aristotelian structure for mainstream movies. As prominent film historian David Bordwell notes, it went on to become the default shorthand for story development in studios and has remained a prominent resource ever since.[15] Importantly, Field filled a gap left by more critically minded scholars at a time when film studies was yet to be widely accepted by the academy. Similarly, the trajectory from Joseph Campbell's Jungian (and après Vladimir Propp) notion of a heroic monomyth, expounded in his book *The Hero with a Thousand Faces*, was influential among Hollywood filmmakers like George Lucas. Subsequently it has become another version of development shorthand after being adapted explicitly into screenwriting terms by Christopher Vogler in *The Writers Journey: Mythic Structure for Writers*.[16]

Fortifying this growing body of how-to texts is the proliferation of for-profit screenwriting workshops, screenwriting competitions, and story consultants with advanced degrees. The expansion of the *Writers Store* from a single West Los Angeles storefront in 1982 that offered computer packages for screenwriters to an expanded online operation replete with an online journal *(Script Magazine)* and an educational and training entity calling itself Screenwriters University is indicative of the health of the paraindustry. Similarly, the publisher of *Final Draft*, the industry standard formatting software for screenplays and related media that is used and taught at many film schools, now runs its own major screenwriting competition *(Final Draft Big Break)*, capitalizing on the aspirational message that keeps it in business by offering incentives and spec dreams for purchase. After all, *Final Draft* and similar products would not be profitable if they only sold their software to working professional screenwriters and educators alike.[17]

The paraindustry extends and pretends to scholarly theories, extrapolating rules and guidance from established models of storytelling and recodifying and reselling that guidance back to the established craft, as well as to its aspirants. Specifically, the paraindustry has retooled the long legacy of Aristotle's *Poetics* and, as noted above, a broadly Jungian model of narrative archetypes and repressions inspired by Joseph Campbell (who has been appropriated by the screenwriting paraindustry as the acceptable theoretical complement to Aristotle) to inform many popular screenplay manuals and workshops.[18] Yet the appropriation of Campbell's Jungian theory remains largely unchallenged by either scholars or practicing screenwriters despite the fact that it actually influences, if not dictates, the structure of many blockbuster movies.

Bringing with it a rigid conception of a three-act story structure paying off in a generalized and entirely desacralized iteration of Aristotle's catharsis—

referred to more simply as the "redemptive ending"—the paraindustry's informal screenplay theory sits at the heart of industrial debates around genre: from action to science fiction to horror and comedy. This is what Ken Dancyger and Jeff Rush in *Alternative Screenwriting: Beyond the Hollywood Formula* see as the often repressive impulses in mainstream movies: "The pattern of transgression, recognition and redemption," they argue, "makes the restorative three-act structure a very comforting form.... But to find a way to respond to the arbitrariness and indifference of the contemporary world, we have to look elsewhere."[19] In short, what we see is a reductive application of Aristotle's work—sometimes combined with a totalizing appropriation of Jung's theories of psychoanalytic-derived archetypes, mixed in with a practitioner's commonsense guide to self-help from screenwriting experts, infused with genres as marketing vehicles—that looks toward blockbuster redemption and teasing an entry into the dream factory as an explicit happy ending.

The critical impulse of Dancyger and Rush notwithstanding, there is very little scholarly work on the new avenues of professional practice pursued by today's new convergent screenwriter. Yet writers in the ever-shifting arena of independent filmmaking have repeatedly tested the boundaries of conventional storytelling and, thus, the attendant theories that inform the craft. The availability of affordable digital production technologies, the post–Sundance Film Festival boom, and the relative democratization of certain kinds of Internet-based distribution mechanisms have encouraged a new generation of filmmakers to rethink the work of screenwriting, just as new approaches to transmedia storytelling have been offered up by scholars such as Henry Jenkins and Lev Manovich.[20] Where there is a paradigm, a kind of one-way-fits-all model, there is a writer seeking to undermine it in favor of other creative pathways.

The script and screenplay text remains critical to this endeavor, as well as an investigation of the relationship between screenwriters and screenplay buyers. This task is easier said than done, as the fields of industrial and textual analysis of screenplays is far less developed than, as we noted above, the published analysis of directing, producing, or production studies. Although we are unconvinced that a united approach benefits the field (scholars, like screenwriters, should and must argue across and against paradigms), the divides, particularly those involving the theoretical underpinnings of multiple fields, pose particular challenges for one fundamental reason: they often replicate the divides that reframe old debates in the major intellectual movements of the last one hundred plus years—from Marxism to deconstruction—and thus reify the very paradigms that are being challenged. At this point, and to be fair to our colleagues, we think a little meta-analysis might be in order.

THE FILM STUDIES FACTORY

Scholars that rely on political economy, a benchmark Marxist model, tend to focus on macrolevel questions concerning conglomeration as a mode of production, regulation as democratic contradiction, and texts as ideologies supporting the structure of the conglomerate and its capitalist interests. Often unable to avoid circular arguments and universalizing tenets ironically equivalent to "it's the economy, stupid," political economy often neglects the cultural processes that contextualize media production; the range of diverse and competing decision-makers involved in creating film, television, and other works; the complexity of the texts themselves; and the creative activity of viewers. Instead, approaches to film and media studies based in political economy often posit that media ownership rests in the hands of a small, "elite" collection of capitalists that, by definition, produces a one-way flow of communication from monolithic media industries to passive receivers. As a result, they simplify the creative work of production, reduce the complexity of the text to capitalist ideology, and essentialize the viewer, or reader, as a passive receptacle of those ideologies. We saw something quite different in the course of our research, though, to be sure, we also saw the work of late capitalism.

Despite our obvious affection for it, textual analysis represents yet another potential critical pitfall. In film and media studies, textual analysis is a well-defined method that underpins approaches from formalism, or neoformalism, through semiotics, to content analysis, to name a few. Scholars working within these models emphasize the text's narratological and discursive features often at the expense of broader socioeconomic factors. As such, the text is closely analyzed for its meaning-making codes and related formal systems. Yet scholars that rely on textual analysis, like those that rely on political economy, also implicitly replicate the divides found in the larger intellectual movements that underpin their work.

As we suggested above, a common charge is that close textual analysis tends to be self-indulgent in the way its proponents focus on film and media discourse at the expense of historico-industrial factors (including the work of producers, network executives, and their various industrial structures and cultures of production). Moreover, scholars who rely too much on textual analysis can be relativistic or prefer to describe codes and signs outside of a consideration of dominant forces such as capitalism, racism, homophobia, and misogyny. Their studies can also produce a kind of viewer utopia when they stretch the conclusion that texts are infinitely polysemic, as prominent television scholar John Fiske has argued, such that viewers can thus read them outside or in opposition to dominating formulas like capitalism or the interplay between social formations.[21] In this model the reader is not a passive receptacle but rather an ahistorical and, ironically, essential figure. As Gregory Curry asks: "To what extent is cinematic meaning a construction of the viewer rather than something the viewer finds in the work?"[22] We think the latter, though admittedly it is almost impossible to prove the composite versatility of script reading—given also the provisos of accreted industrial and craft rules in screenplay form—let alone film viewing.

Yet there is great value in political economy and textual analysis, and film and media scholars have attempted to synthesize these approaches. Douglas Kellner calls for an approach that addresses both macrolevel structures offered by political economy and the microlevel practices offered by cultural studies. Critical of what he sees as an overemphasis in the field of textual analysis in the formalist model, Kellner argues that the traditional gap between empirical, social science–based approaches of mass communication and the humanities-based textual analysis approach creates an artificial bifurcation within the field.[23] Instead, he argues, film and media scholars should explore the interconnections between the production of culture, its political economy, and textual complexity:

> Political economy grounds its approach within empirical analysis of the actual system of media industry operation, investigating the constraints and structuring influence of the dominant capitalist economic system and a commercialized cultural system dominated by powerful corporations. Inserting texts into the system of culture within which they are produced and distributed can help elucidate features and effects that textual analysis might miss or downplay. Rather than being antithetical approaches to culture, political economy can contribute to textual analysis and critique. The system of production often determines what types of artifacts will be produced, what structural limits there will be as to what can and cannot be shown, and what kind of audience effects cultural artifacts may generate.[24]

Kellner wants to engage the capitalist dimensions of Hollywood from a Marxist perspective to show how labor—and one can extend that to screenwriting labor—is alienated from the means of production.

By synthesizing political economy and textual analysis via cultural studies, film and media studies can analyze texts such as screenplays, institutional practices such as conglomeration and convergence, and labor relations such as strikes within existing networks of power and creative expression. In so doing, the scholar is able to locate the forces that make up the circuit of culture in media studies and the forces for resistance, of thinking outside the screen, that complete that circuit. After all, states Kellner, the media industries are not "innocent" and "inherent bastions of enlightenment, creativity and abundance."[25] They legitimize the dominant organization of society and idealize social norms. Yet there are forces, or "players" in the 1990s vernacular, made up of committed screenwriters and filmmakers very much aware of the social and economic structures they inhabit and that constrain their work. They are no more dupes than readers and viewers.

Kellner's reference to the notion of the "circuit of culture," elaborated by Birmingham Centre scholar Richard Johnson, provides scholars like us with a useful lattice on which to build a more encompassing approach to studying the art and business of writing for the entertainment industry. Specifically, Johnson's approach emphasizes the need for scholars to study the interdependent circuit of media production, textuality, and consumption in specific cultural contexts. Johnson places particular emphasis on the analysis of the capitalist conditions of production quite differently from practitioners of political economy. Scholarship, suggests Johnson, not only must understand how the material means of production and the organization of labor are structured by capitalist imperatives but how the production sphere creates texts from "a stock of already existing *cultural* elements drawn from the reservoirs of lived culture or from the already public fields of public discourse."[26] As practicing screenwriters, as well as academics, we agree: only by studying production culture in relation both to economics and to texts made by individuals, specifically the means by which a diverse cadre of creative decision-makers exercise cultural power within the confines of industry common sense, can scholars more fully conceptualize the state of the screenwriting profession.

Scholars have been grappling with the solutions proposed by Kellner and Johnson. In the introduction to their edited collection, *Media Industries: History, Theory, and Method,* Jennifer Holt and Alisa Perren put forward a solution to the divide between macrolevel political economy and microlevel textual analysis by arguing that media scholars should approach cultural production as "sites of struggle, contestation, and negotiation between a broad range of stakeholders," from the screenwriter to the studio executive, whose texts are produced for a diverse global audience across a multitude of media platforms.[27] More specifically, Holt and Perren urge scholars to embrace more culturally based theories that explore the nuances and contradictions of various genres, series, and episodes at what cultural theorist

Stuart Hall calls the "encoding" stage: how players exercise cultural power and engage in decision-making that produces texts like scripts and films within larger media structures.[28] Such an approach, they conclude, further challenges top-down, linear models of communication advanced by academics applying political economy and embraces Johnson's "circuit of culture" model, reifying the give-and-take of script writing and selling, that integrates analyses of production, text, and sociohistorical context.

Caldwell's ethnographic model advanced in *Production Culture* is especially useful in this regard, as it provides a method for studying the various dimensions of production to include the degree to which, in our case, screenwriters are coerced into consenting to the ideology of the tentpole paradigm. Focused on what is left out of macro- and microlevel approaches, Caldwell also studies trade and worker publications and artifacts. He moves beyond the paraindustry to the industrial trade. Following Powdermaker's lead, Caldwell also engages in ethnographic fieldwork by embedding himself in production spaces (the set, editing rooms, etc.), as well as professional gatherings like industry conferences and workshops. He does this within the context of industrial analysis and, at least in past books like *Televisuality*, close textual analysis of style, representation, and narrative discourse or the product this labor produces.[29]

Richly detailed and expansive in scope, *Production Culture* makes the case "that the social performance of show making itself must also be considered to fully understand film and television form. Taking this approach means considering how media creators function as industrial actors in a large ensemble of creative workers."[30] In short, Caldwell considers the complexity of the production environment in a way that works against the political economic tendency of oversimplifying it or reducing it to a singular cause (the economic base of late capitalism). We hope to follow suit.

Since 2008 several academic books and journal articles have been published by scholars who have studied under or with Caldwell in an effort to advance what is emerging as a production-cultures emphasis within industry studies. In addition to *Production Culture* and *Media Industries*, Timothy Havens, Amanda D. Lotz, and Serra Tinic provide a general framework for examining the media industries in their essay "Critical Media Industry Studies: A Research Approach."[31] For these scholars, creative forces interpret and redirect the economics of media institutions. Vicki Mayer, Banks, and Caldwell offered the field a second edited collection in 2009, *Production Studies: Cultural Studies of Media Industries*, which also attempts to traverse the divide between political economic approaches to the industry and textual analytic approaches by focusing on production cultures. "Production studies," they note, "borrow theoretical insights from the social sciences and humanities, but, perhaps most importantly, they take the lived realities of people involved in media production as the subjects for theorizing production as culture."[32]

Many of the methodological insights offered in these and other works of industry studies helped us to better understand the business of screenwriting today. Yet in the course of our work we discovered that our attempt to link close analysis of screenplays to the conditions of production requires emphasis on the decisions made by screenwriters—how their consent materialized in terms of form and how resistance resisted form. And here we had to take some care as to how we account for and incorporate "industrial spin," as Mayer, Banks, and Caldwell call it, offered by screenwriters and studio executives, not to mention screenwriting educators like ourselves during our interviews or with the interviews we quote. Yet perhaps, like some of the writers in *Dreams on Spec*, we are not blinded by our own self-interest. We are, in addition to being academics, working screenwriters, aspiring, like all the other shmucks, to sell scripts on spec.

The main challenge that Mayer, Banks, and Caldwell, as well as those working more prominently in industry studies, find in accessing above-the-line decision-making is the fact that producers, directors, and writers tend to hold the process, procedures, and documents they use to produce media close to the proverbial vest. And they are not always forthcoming in interviews, preferring instead to rely on what Timothy Havens calls "industry lore."[33] Just as studios would never reveal their "ultimates" (the final accounting statements of an individual movie's profitability), save for when they are hacked (as happened to Sony), so Hollywood development keeps the granular secrets of story sausage-making top secret. As Caldwell notes: "Fieldwork for a study of this sort is complicated by the fact that film and media today reflect obsessively back upon themselves and invest considerable energy in over-producing and distributing this industrial self-analysis to the public."[34] Caldwell concludes that interviews with below-the-line workers, people with less (or no) stake in the back-end profits generated by Hollywood texts, tend to offer less industrial self-reflexivity, less lore, in their interviews. Caldwell is nonetheless self-conscious about this assumption: "'Naive ethnography,'" he writes, "proves to be as problematic as naive textualism in accounting for cultures of media production. Having access, and informants, and backstory information on industry may by itself position the industry scholar as a 'text' being written by the industry."[35] Our point is more than cursory: below-the-line interviews and observations need to be approached by the scholar with the same degree of skepticism as above-the-line interviews. They, too, tell stories.

There is also an important hierarchy within and between the above-the-line crafts and professions. Our own case studies for this book focus on above-the-line subjects working in an above-the-line craft, as well as other subjects for whom the distinction is largely irrelevant; however, with the exception of the showrunner Shawn Ryan and the recent producing work of the animation writer Robert Moreland, their credit status does not necessarily imply empowerment within the development process. Indeed, they often explicitly argue the reverse. In the old media, screenwriters are employed and credited per WGA rules, but they do not share the influence of their producing and even directing peers even as they do their above-the-line status. Screenwriters working in new media such as video games are employed according to the practices of individual producer entities, and their status varies widely, as does the visibility of their credit.

All this to lead to the value in using interviews as evidence: we seek to contextualize what screenwriters, producers, and executives tell us in print and on camera. But we must admit that an analysis of screenwriting in the era of media convergence must live with an ironic level of industry lore and thus our own participation in the paraindustry. Hence, the interview material we use is supported and challenged by primary research to include analysis of scripts, related production documents (e.g., WGA policies and reports), and, of course, industrial data to include box-office figures and ratings reports. The intention here is to substantiate the conventional grids of critical and industrial analysis with concrete examples that include the diverse voices of today's working players.

OUR FACTORY

Each of the following chapters addresses particular dimensions of the contemporary screenwriting profession. They are all divided into linked sections, each of which critically interrogates an aspect of industrial and creative screenwriting practice or a cognate analog. Chapter 1, "Millennial Manic: Crisis and Change in the Business of Screenwriting," provides a detailed critical introduction to American screenwriting since 2000. Building on Banks's work specifically, and the larger field of industry studies, it assesses the impact of the transformation of the studio model in the 1980s on the freelance screenwriting paradigm, as well as on the film school and paraindustry models. Acting as a kind of preface to the chapters that follow, it considers the impact of digital and high-speed network technologies on the style, the format, the practice, the distribution, and the exhibition of screenwriting since the highpoint of the "spec boom" in the late 1980s and early 1990s. It also considers the import of the 2007–8 WGA strike on the status of screenwriting today.

In chapter 2, "Atop the Tentpole: Hollywood Screenwriting Today," we focus on the latest shift toward franchise series, comedies, and big-budget spectacular movies such as *Harry Potter*, *The Hangover*, and *Transformers* as this affects Hollywood screenwriters. The screenwriter of the 1989 version of *Batman*, Sam Hamm, suggests that to understand the current status of studio screenwriting we must first acknowledge that "genre won."[36] The postconglomerate Hollywood studios are more focused than ever on producing big-budget movies that play to "four-quadrant" audiences, the male/female and young/old masses, and thus have easy international appeal as well as ancillary market potential (e.g., toys, video games, amusement park rides, etc.). And yet most of the genre movies that are still green-lighted by major Hollywood studios—notably spectacular science fiction and adventure films, raunchy and romantic comedies, and thrillers of different kinds—are less diverse and less challenging in their content than broadly equivalent productions were in previous decades. The entrance into the tent for the writers of spec scripts is clearly getting smaller, more exclusive, and in many ways less interesting to navigate, amid a carnival of emerging, if not odd, attractions. Finally, chapter 2 begins our attempt at the close textual analysis of screenplays.

In chapter 3, "Running the Room: Screenwriting in Expanded Television," we focus on the way complex dramas have been successfully reimagined away from the big screen, first on pay cable *(The Sopranos)*, then on basic *(The Shield)*, and, finally, both online *(House of Cards)* and, at a point in the circuit, on network television *(Hannibal)*. This chapter addresses screenwriters telling prestige stories both for prestige small-screen networks and for formally insignificant broadcasters that remade themselves on the backs of innovative drama series. We examine, in particular, the role of the television showrunner as an empowered writer-producer. Chapter 3 considers the recent work of Aaron Sorkin on HBO and looks more closely at the influence on the transformation of basic cable drama series of Shawn Ryan, formerly the showrunner of *The Shield* (FX), who also played a prominent role in the 2007–8 WGA strike.

Chapter 4, "New Markets and Microbudgets: 'Independent' Storytellers," considers what happened to the promise of a strong independent sector after the "indie boom" of the late 1980s and 1990s. Here we begin our attempt to show how practicing screenwriters are both obliged and able to find new alternatives for screen storytelling and income generation in the era of media convergence. Although the indie boom bore early fruit, we suggest that in recent years the prestige independent film has become little more than a niche genre sold through corporate festivals such as Sundance and Cannes or developed by the remaining prestige arms of studios such as Fox Searchlight. Nonetheless, it remains the dominant aspirational model taught at progressive film schools and espoused in paraindustry texts.

Our extended interview case studies in this chapter focus on screenwriters who are struggling with the contraction of traditional markets for independent screenplays (Pamela Gray), creating their own commercial markets in emerging screens and through entrepreneurialism (Robert Moreland), and working at the microbudget level, outside of the conventional Hollywood and independent structures and institutions (Travis Mathews). Indeed, the microbudget scene has revitalized American independent filmmaking in the last decade, encouraging experimentation and opening up opportunities for new and younger filmmakers led by a ripple rather than a wave of "mumblecore" naturalism from filmmakers like Joe Swanberg *(Nights and Weekends)*, Lena Dunham *(Tiny Furniture)*, Lynn Shelton *(Humpday)*, and the Duplass Brothers *(Baghead)*. Microbudget production opportunities have also increased for minority and women filmmakers, some of whom are able to take risks with their storytelling and representations in ways that would not have been possible without the budget savings of digital production and the distribution potential of the Internet and the regional festival circuit. Again, we offer comparative close textual analysis of screenplays as a way to complete an analysis of the indie market.

Chapter 5, "Screenwriter 2.0: The Legitimation of Writing for Video Games," focuses on where many of today's young (and not so young) screenwriters are heading when they can't sell scripts to the studios. Given the retrenchment in Hollywood and the decline of the spec market for freelance screenwriters, many writers are looking to other platforms to provide regular employment or the kind of proof-of-concept that will attract studios to their intellectual properties. At the same time, studios are increasingly looking to adapt story- and spectacle-driven product originated in the comics and video gaming industries with built-in audience recognition and fan bases in the all-important youth sector. In some ways, in fact, the big screen has become an ancillary market for video game and comic book "studios," including Electronic Arts and Marvel respectively, as well as social media companies like Facebook. With the emergence of new markets and media for screenwriting come new challenges for the WGA. This was true of the emergence of television in the late 1940s, and it has proved to be equally true of the video games industry in the last decades. This chapter focuses on how the WGA has worked to legitimize writing for video games for its membership through its practices and publications in expanding its definition of craft, in outreach to producers and writers, and in attempting to establish jurisdiction. The almost complete failure of the guild to cover convergent scripting in the video games industry reveals much about the nature of employment and production in the converging media.

We wrap *Off the Page* with a postscript of sorts: "Conclusion: Scripting Boundaries" reviews the key critical points raised in preceding chapters, while also imaging the emerging cultural trends informing the scripting of unconventional screen stories in newly convergent forms. In particular we examine the diversity of online content creation and consider how far one can push the definition and boundaries of screenwriting before they break. In the process our conclusion also wraps up our discussion of the state of screenwriting education in film schools and the paraindustry, mapping out the antipodal directions in which the craft of screenwriting is going at the end of cinema.

As Hoxter notes in *Screenwriting*, there is an inevitable "'to-be-transcended-ness' that circumscribes the work of the professional screenwriter."[37] That work is both present and absent—always structuring yet always already moved beyond—in media texts. *Off the Page* attempts to transcend the textual and cultural instability of the products of screenwriting across contemporary media, to elucidate and make sense of the creative practices that underlie that work and the shifting economic contexts, industrial imperatives, and production cultures from which it emerges or against which it strives.

1. Millennial Manic

Crisis and Change in the Business of Screenwriting

The most important person in the motion picture process is the writer, and we must do everything in our power to prevent them from ever realizing it.

IRVING THALBERG

Strike action, also called labor strike, labour strike, on strike, greve (of French: *grève*), or simply strike, is a work stoppage caused by the mass refusal of employees to work. A strike usually takes place in response to employee grievances.

Wikipedia

The classic opening sequence of Robert Altman's *The Player* (1991), script by Michael Tolkin, follows fictional studio executive Griffin Mill (Tim Robbins) as he navigates his way through a morning's work spent hearing movie pitches from screenwriters. In the course of the sequence Griffin brushes off unwanted contact from an aspiring writer, listens to a ridiculous proposal for *The Graduate, Part II*—from the original movie's screenwriter, Buck Henry, in a cameo—and another for a movie that promises to be "kind of like *The Gods Must Be Crazy* except the Coke bottle is now an actress... sort of like *Out of Africa* meets *Pretty Woman*." Grist for his mill, Griffin pays the writers only marginal attention. Meanwhile, other characters snipe behind Griffin's back, reminding the audience that the career of a Hollywood dream master is only as secure as his last hit at the box office.

Hollywood metanarratives like *The Player* give us a particular kind of insight—limited, of course, but useful—into prevalent attitudes to craft and industry at the time of their production. To this end, the opening sequence of *The Player* is also engaging with the enduring myth of the desperate postclassical Hollywood screenwriter. Equally tagged by the success or failure of their latest screenplay, screenwriters in *The Player* perform their story ideas like court jesters before a bored monarch whose entire focus is on avoiding being dethroned. With their pitches the screenwriters are attempting to sell, rather than tell, stories. They are presented as objects of ridicule, despite all their conjuring in a shorthand dream factory production culture sociolect that mixes and matches past films in a feeble attempt to break the barrier between the seemingly distinct worlds of originality on one side and uniformity on the other, which we discussed in our introduction. The humiliations for one ingratiating screenwriter continue when Mill inquires about casting options for the characters. The Hollywood executive's response to story is immediately to consider marketability—to consider the star "attachments" that might make any movie idea, no matter how unlikely or preposterous, worthy of development. In this way the divergent priorities of the two professions, the screenwriter who writes scripts and the executive who buys them, are lampooned in an almost surreal process, replete with intimations of its creative futility. In Hollywood, *The Player* is telling us, screenwriters pitch stories to executives who have no interest in them *as stories*.

These instances of linguistic shorthand and of industrial performance art, to borrow another term once more from John Thornton Caldwell, present the Hollywood screenwriter as a powerless, dismissible figure. The portrayal prevents them or the audience, as the Irving Thalberg comment opening this chapter acknowledges, from realizing their importance. As another film and media studies scholar, Bridget Conor, reminds us, the profession of screenwriting is often distinguished in popular media—and in the popular imagination—from similar occupations, such as playwriting, by the invisibility and powerlessness of its practitioners. Screenwriters, she writes, are "framed as 'hired hands' or replaceable cogs in the capitalist-intensive entertainment industries. Unlike auteur directors, they are not the subjects of retrospectives at film festivals and they are not viewed as creating fully autonomous art forms. Instead they are viewed as blueprint generators, or in extreme cases, as formula-driven 'hacks.'"[1] *The Player* duly plays into that mythical construction, offering a satirical yet self-conscious view of the parlous position of the Hollywood screenwriter. Tolkin's script for *The Player* tells a good story from within Maras's "business" and "practitioner" frames of industry discourse. Yet missing from this Hollywood film, of course, is an exploration of the conglomerate studio model that—already in 1991—was the force behind the limiting of opportunities for aspiring writers that accelerated after that period. In other words there are more powerful players involved in the transformation of Hollywood development toward the tentpole than mere studio executives.

The Player came out at a time in which, against all established industrial probability, some Hollywood screenwriters were experiencing a moment in which it seemed as if finally their status in the industry was rising. A few writers, notably Shane Black *(Lethal Weapon)* and Joe Eszterhas *(Basic Instinct),* were becoming famous for the multimillion-dollar sales their action and erotic thriller screenplays were achieving. The studios were also investing more in development and hence buying more screenplays. The late 1980s and early 1990s "spec boom" marks a short-lived golden age for Hollywood screenwriters. As we will examine in this chapter, the industrial relationships that now characterize screenwriting during the era of media convergence make the satire in Tolkin and Altman's film seem rather prescient.

This brief moment in screenwriting history raises several interesting questions for the profession of screenwriting today. First, we should ask, how has the conglomeration of Hollywood studios impacted the craft of writing? A second question emerges directly from the first: what is the impact of globalization on the art and business of Hollywood screenwriting? In that changing environment, we should also ask: how has the screenwriter's union, the Writers Guild of America (WGA), fared at ensuring that the studios and the public know that the screenwriter is, in fact, the most important person in the moviemaking process? Or, more succinctly, what has the guild done to support the new convergent screenwriters of the twenty-first century, the era of ubiquitous screens of all sizes and in all parts of the wired world?

In addressing these questions, this chapter aims to set up the story we tell in later chapters—to offer a "prehistory," in the academic vernacular, or "backstory," in screenwriting parlance. Our goal is to show how Hollywood screenwriters, fresh from the boom of the early 1990s, returned to being cogs in the wheel of today's dream factory. Rather than open up new pathways for screenwriters, both already in and aspiring to be in the Hollywood tent, we argue that conglomeration and consolidation have limited the creative and economic possibilities of the Hollywood screenwriter. Ironically, a gradual process of craft-labor retrenchment was facilitated—sometimes with misguided good intentions and sometimes by dint of negotiated circumstance—by a kind of ideological collusion with the Writers Guild of America. How this came to be is, for us and we hope the reader, an interesting story.

THE BIG PICTURE

To appreciate the industrial and creative contexts in and for which Hollywood screenwriters are now working, we need first to explore the current economic state of the industry that inflects the market priorities of the studios. The best place to start is with the summer 2014 reports from the US popular and trade presses, the stuff Hollywood players sometimes actually read, that presented two contradictory takes on the economic health of the movie industry. On the one hand, the headlines reported a continuing decline in domestic box-office revenues. On the other hand, the international box office was booming. On the domestic front, sales of movie tickets in the US summer market had declined by 30 percent year on year. No summer movie made more than $300 million domestically for the first time in thirteen years. Overall annual ticket sales were also declining.[2] Even the latest installments in well-established tentpole franchises performed below industry expectations. For example, *Transformers: Age of Extinction*, script by Ehren Kruger, made approximately $245 million domestically for Paramount, a 35 percent decline on the performance of the previous entry in the series, *Transformers: Dark of the Moon*, also written by Kruger, released three years before.

Industry analysts have noted that 2014 was a relatively fallow year in terms of major franchise releases. Competition from the World Cup and from other television attractions also seemed to have had a negative impact on moviegoing in the summer of 2014. Nevertheless, the figures do confirm Hollywood's struggle to maintain a substantial North American audience for big-screen movie exhibition. According to the official reporting of the Motion Picture Association of America (MPAA), the lobbying organization funded by and representing the major studios, domestic box office did increase from $7.75 billion in 2000 to $10.6 billion in 2010 before starting to decline. The actual number of tickets sold, however, decreased from 1.57 billion in 2002 to 1.34 billion in 2010.

Throughout the last decade, domestic and international box-office revenues have been sustained largely by the introduction of premium pricing for digital 3-D exhibition. In 2013 the MPAA reported that more than 80 percent of the world's approximately 135,000 screens now use digital projection systems; two years later, few can project 35 mm. Moreover, in that year 31 percent of the US/Canada population viewed at least one movie in 3-D. For context, between 2006 and 2013, the share of the domestic box office returned from 3-D exhibition grew around 70 percent. The number of movies released annually in 3-D rose in that period from eight to forty-five.[3] This economic reality has increased the pressure on studios to produce more 3-D movies. Consequently, these pressures have also had a direct impact on how more and more tentpole movies are written and developed through script and previsualization to accommodate the needs of 3-D.

Fewer North Americans have been going out to the movies or, better said, going to see movies in movie theaters, but those who do are being channeled into watching a more limited range of genres, many of which are being reworked to be ever more spectacular. As a consequence, studio movies are increasingly expensive to produce, justifying the increase in the dollar cost of the moviegoing experience. Indeed, despite recent developments in online distribution, which allows access to movies and television on demand and thus away from theaters, recent studio production has been oriented more and more toward sustaining what remains of the distribution patterns of *The Player* era.[4] The big-budget movie is being deployed to keep seats filled in the domestic multiplexes much like it did in the 1950s with CinemaScope and early 3-D, when viewers were increasingly turning to television.[5]

Today's big-budget movie, almost always made and projected with high-definition digital technologies, is also intended to increase audience attendance in international markets, which have now eclipsed US domestic exhibition in terms of total revenue generation. In 2010 the MPAA reported that international box-office receipts made up 67 percent of revenues for first-run cinema exhibition. According to the association's statistics, in 2013 the global box office had risen 4 percent, year-on-year, to $35.9 billion. In the last decade much of this growth came in the Asian market. As the MPAA reported: "In 2013, the Asia Pacific region ($11.1 billion) surpassed EMEA [Europe, the Middle East, and Africa], and became the top region in international box office."[6]

Chinese demand for spectacular Hollywood movies appears insatiable. After only two weeks of its summer 2014 release, US media were reporting that *Transformers: Age of Extinction* had become the most successful movie in the history of Chinese cinema exhibition, pushing *Avatar* into second place. In mid-July the *Los Angeles Times* noted that the movie's take in China alone was outpacing revenues from domestic US distribution.[7] Its success was driven in part by the production's well-publicized, if at times fractious, coproduction and product-placement deals with Chinese companies, the location of major sequences in China, and the casting of well-known Chinese actors like Li Bingbing in supporting roles. Produced as much for the Chinese market as for the American market, *Transformers: Age of Extinction* also benefited from the rapid expansion in the Chinese exhibition sector during the last decade. The number of Chinese cinema screens increased from thirteen hundred in 2002 to more than thirteen thousand in 2012.[8] The movie's international take, as of this writing, is estimated at $841,965,423, for a total of $1,087,404,499.[9]

As a consequence, when today's Hollywood screenwriter pitches an idea to the conglomerate studios or the production houses that sell to the studios, the writer has to cut his or her creative cloth according to international as well as domestic tastes as never before. As the producer Lynda Obst *(Sleepless in Seattle; The Fisher King)* observes: in contemporary Hollywood "pictures are not chosen on gut as in Sherry [Lansing's] day—or David O. Selznick's for that matter—but on whether they are properties that can be marketed into international franchises."[10] Screenwriters today are taught this lesson multiple times and in multiple contexts: by film schools, by the paraindustry, by agents and managers, and by their potential employers in studio development. For example, UCLA's Richard Walter recently reported that his school is coming under increasing pressure from students to structure their screenwriting MFA program explicitly around franchise trends and genre adaptation.[11] The economic importance of the international box office has begun to eclipse that of the domestic one in terms of development decisions major Hollywood studios are making, and many aspiring tentpole screenwriters are eager to retool their craft education toward mastering the current widget.

In 2014 the economic power of the international box office effectively green-lit its first tentpole sequel. In 2013 *Pacific Rim*, script by Travis Beacham and Guillermo del Toro, combining a variant on the giant robot (mecha) trope with the giant monster (kaiju) and alien invasion tropes, failed to meet domestic revenue expectations against its budget level. Nevertheless, it is getting a second installment based on the success of the film in Asia. The sequel is scheduled for release in 2017. As *Forbes* reported in June of 2014, *Pacific Rim* "was a wholly original film, intended to be a franchise-starter, which basically bombed in America. Yet thanks almost exclusively to the strength of its overseas box office, it's getting a sequel along with an animated episodic television series to boot."[12] The movie made $111 million from Chinese audiences alone.

Given the targeting of its subject matter, influenced by Japanese popular cultural texts such as *Mobile Suit Gundam* and *Gojira*, the relative success of *Pacific Rim* in Asia is perhaps unsurprising despite the cultural and political tensions across the region. It is clear that, as the domestic market "softens," as the *Hollywood Reporter* likes to describe a weakening market, increasing pressure is being placed on producing spectacles that can appeal to international audiences.[13] It is not simply that this latest iteration of the globalization of American popular culture has arrived—like many preceding iterations—thanks in no small measure to the hegemony of Hollywood; rather, conglomerate Hollywood understands that, under its tentpole paradigm, the continued ability to control the changing marketplace for cinema necessitates a reorientation of product toward international taste publics. To sell that spec script or get attached to a script in development, and thus to help the industry maintain its global hegemony, today's screenwriter must also be able to navigate the entertainment needs of multiple cultures and also have some appreciation of their textual practices.

Dialogue- and character–driven drama, once a staple of studio production, is a much harder fit than action for these increasingly important global markets. *Transformers: Age of Extinction* and *Pacific Rim* are examples of the kind of special-effects heavy, attraction-driven movie that Hollywood is now privileging in the hope of expanding its global sales. This is the result of a major reorientation of the entire Hollywood industry toward new markets and distribution systems that accelerated from the first years of the new century. Linda Obst describes it as akin to being "swept up in gale forces that weren't unlike the tornado that took Dorothy to Munchkinland. For us in the movie business, we landed not in little Munchkinland, for sure, but in giant Franchiseland. The New Abnormal."[14]

Obst acknowledges that Hollywood's industrial practices have never been conventional or straightforward. To tease out her epigrammatic analysis of the recent history of the movie industry, before the "New Abnormal" emerged, in the last decades there was a long established "Old Abnormal" in Hollywood. And the "Old Abnormal" was at its time "new," of course, as Hollywood has always shifted its norms to meet new economic opportunities while addressing threats to its hegemony. Obst is pointing to a new business model, an aspect of what we call millennial manic, in which the range of movies that can now be made by Hollywood studios—the range of stories and genres that screenwriters can now work with—has shrunk.

The causes of this shift in focus and production are multiple, but notable among them has been the continuing collapse of the home video market (latterly DVD) that provided the studios with significant and, most importantly, reliable income for decades. In her memoir Obst refers to this loss of DVD revenue as "The Great Contraction," and as the statistics given elsewhere in this chapter indicate, its impact should not be underestimated. Equally important, however, is the parallel contraction of the domestic movie*going* (as distinct from the movie-*viewing*) audience occurring simultaneously to the expansion of international cinema markets. We know this as one aspect of globalization.

The recent iteration of spectacular franchise filmmaking was critiqued by film critic Terrence Rafferty in 2008: "Action movies are, over all, a good deal snappier than they were 30 years ago, but they also tend to be a good deal less intelligible. They skimp on the exposition and go straight for sensation, as if cutting to the chase were not a metaphor but literally the cardinal rule of filmmaking."[15] To critics like Rafferty, these movies are simply the overtechnologized digital descendants of the formulaic action movies that were drawing fire in the 1990s. "Gone are the suspense-filled thrills, memorable characters and infectious charm of *Die Hard*, the original *Speed*,

Raiders of the Lost Ark, and the early James Bond films," writes film critic Annabelle Villanueva. "In their place," she continues, "is a veritable army of mega-stupid mega-movies—loud, bloated ActionChaseExplodoRamas brimming with Unabomber-style subtlety and all the wit and character development of a *Simon and Simon* episode."[16]

Like their antecedents, today's tentpole blockbusters represent a kind of manic cinema, defined by overall narrative acceleration and featuring a succession of special-effects highs punctuated by storytelling lows.[17] Hollywood screenwriters recognize this manic acceleration of tentpole narratives as the major change to studio genre screenwriting in the last two decades. For example, Michael Grais, writer of the original *Poltergeist* (1982), argues that, unlike in the 1980s, the imperative for screenwriters to lead their screenplays with action is now present from the start: "No longer can you spend the first act building character in a genre film like *[Poltergeist]*, or [a] thriller or action adventure. . . . The action has to be almost immediate as the audience's minds are tuned to video games and such and don't have patience."[18] In 2005 the *Hollywood Reporter* also framed the change as the embrace of spectacle at the expense of narrative: "Studios innovate on eye-popping visuals, not mind-bending screenplays."[19] A tentpole film today is designed from script to screen to be more akin to a global digital amusement park ride than ever before.

The approach to manic cinema evidenced in films like *Transformers: Age of Extinction* and *Pacific Rim* has been the particular target of popular opprobrium. David Denby, movie critic of the *New Yorker,* argues that the movies in the *Transformers* franchise generate a kind of numbing kinetic affect: "dark, whirling digital masses slam into each other, or thresh their way through buildings, cities, and people, and the moviegoer, sitting in the theater, feels as if his head were repeatedly being smashed against a wall."[20] The film critic Roger Ebert agreed, describing the third installment in the franchise, *Transformers: Dark Side of the Moon* (2009), as an exercise in poor technical filmmaking and redundant storytelling. The film, he writes in his irreverantly titled book, *A Horrible Experience of Unbearable Length: More Movies That Suck,* "has long stretches involving careless and illogical assemblies of inelegant shots. One special effect happens, and then another special effect happens, and we are expected to be grateful that we have seen two special effects."[21]

For Denby this is what makes the *Transformers* films exemplars of a recent trend in studio moviemaking that he calls "conglomerate aesthetics." This style, he argues, is a particular distillation of action genres, privileging dynamic movement over narrative, character, and emotion. Manic action is tasked with carrying the "entire burden of the movie's pleasure. . . . The audience has been conditioned to find the absence of emotion pleasurable."[22] *Transformers* screenwriter Ehren Kruger acknowledges that his franchise's priorities are oriented toward delivering a particular understanding of spectacle at the expense of narrative cohesion:

> At moments it is quasi-experimental, yes. You have to understand, with a big summer movie like this, especially this franchise, [the director, Michael Bay] doesn't quite look at it like competing with movies. He looks at it like "should I go see *Transformers*, or spend a day at Six Flags?" There's a big spectacle quality to it that he is promising, and that is one of the things that makes this franchise different than your *X-Men*, *Spider Man*, or *Planet of the Apes* films. It's something this series does that is its own style. That is all part of the package. Some days, it's like writing a *Cirque du Soleil* show.[23]

The connection to Cirque du Soleil might be a bit too far off the nose, but Kruger's candid insight into the writerly implications of the *Transformers* business and story and structure frames suggests a self-conscious understanding of and commitment to the generation of spectacle over story, and of Bay's—and by extension his own—commitment to the haptic thrill ride as the epitome of film viewing. His surprising use of the term *experimental* to describe the visual style of the franchise is, in fact, strangely apposite in accounting for the way affect is generated by these spectacular texts and how it is inscribed into the screenplay and into the broader scripting process at several points (as we will explore in our discussion of tentpole screenplay style and format in the next chapter). In short, Kruger's "experimental" practice doubles down on the manic intent of the contemporary tentpole movie by embracing excess, or what the psychoanalyst and philosopher Julia Kristeva calls the "stupid," at the expense of narrative coherence.

Kristeva argues that movies (including those in "poor taste") that emphasize form over content can generate a kind of catharsis from an excess of affect: "the *stupider* it is, the better," Kristeva argues, "for the filmic image does not need to be intelligent: what counts is that the specular presents the drive—aggression—through its directed signified (the object or situation represented) and encodes it through its plastic rhythm (the network of lektonic elements: sounds, tone, colors, space, figures), which can come back to us from the other without response and which consequently has remained uncaptured, unsymbolized, unconsumed."[24] The key term here is *lektonic*, referring to a signifier without a signified. In terms of the *Transformers* franchise we can experience the "plastic rhythms" of lektonic representation in a range of stylistic choices including the radically fluctuating deployment of scale that alternatively evokes the sublime through immensity and then abandons and undercuts that immensity with manic and confused close-ups that abstract themselves and are divorced from clear narrative meaning. In Hollywood terms this is indeed "experimental" because at times it radically displaces visual and narrative continuity as the sine qua non of commercial moviemaking. The end result is an exaltation of the spectacle of excess. Arguably it is precisely because the visual style of *Transformers* is scripted to be manically "stupid" that, on its own terms, it works almost perfectly.

It is important to recognize that this relegation of conventional narrative structure to secondary status in the *Transformers* and *Pacific Rim* franchises is not typical, even among contemporary big-budget action movies. The mainstream counters are the aspirational, middlebrow tentpole films establishing original story worlds *(Inception, Interstellar)* or digging into already established story worlds from media such as comics with a fan's obsession and a "smarter" play of story thematics. Some recent blockbusters have even dialed back the action in favor of character drama *(The Amazing Spiderman 2)*. Narrative acceleration, in the way screenwriter Michael Grais describes it, is still present—or even dominant—in most tentpole cinema, especially in superhero stories and the comic book movie genre more broadly, but its attractions are often rather better integrated into narrative than those of the clinically manic, or "stupid," franchise. A case in point is the fact that the most successful contemporary tentpole producers in Hollywood, notably Marvel Studios *(The Avengers, Captain America)*, are paying very close attention to deep plotting and efficient genre-character development across titles as they develop complex, interweaved franchises extrapolated over multiple movies that are based on multiple heroes from the same story world but with very different story backgrounds.

The calculation for the studios is about how the equation of story versus special effects drives ancillary market monetization—the markets of video games, toys, and the like. Even character-driven franchise films must have tie-ins if they are to be green-lit. These films are also written strictly to budget, often requiring screenwriters to add an understanding of the basics of visual effects costing to all their other craft skills, as computer graphics supervisor Ron Brinkman *(Contact, The Ghost and the Darkness)* reminded the readers of the WGA's house magazine, *Written By*, in 1998: "If a writer doesn't know approximate costs they'll just put in stuff that seems interesting. We go through and come up with a dollar amount, and sometimes that's outrageous."[25]

Tentpole screenwriters may be asked to rewrite spectacle multiple times until their manic action sequences conform to the budgetary analysis of the studio's financial departments. Sam Hamm (*Batman*, 1989) had exactly this experience working (uncredited) on drafts of the first iteration of the *Fantastic Four* franchise for Fox. The project had been given a specific and immovable green-light budget point from the studio head, and the writers worked and reworked the screenplay until it was deemed to have hit that mark. Pages would be returned from finance, Hamm recalls, marked up with green or red stamps indicating whether the scenes were estimated to be at or over budget.[26] Today's screenwriter must not only be transculturally astute but also able to anticipate the corporate obsession with multiple markets in ways that project dollars to spectacle.

Manic aesthetics is still primary to story, but in movies like the *Avengers*, written by former television writer and producer-turned-big-screen writer and director Joss Whedon, the attraction for hard-core fans and the general audience alike is also to see the development of characters that have long been engrained in American popular culture. In these films story is important. Indeed, the Marvel franchises, as well as some recent DC comic book movies such as Christopher Nolan's *Batman* trilogy, treat their characters with a level of seriousness and naturalism that surpasses previous iterations of the franchise. This latest tonal approach to the writing of story and character has been successful enough times for the comic book movie to have become the tentpole's exemplar genre and to dominate the box office for a number of years. The first *Avengers* film earned Disney $1.5 billion at the box office, for example.[27]

The Avengers also holds a specific place within the long-term franchise development program at Marvel Studios. The story brought to a close the first phase of the Marvel Comics Universe (MCU), as the superhero characters who had been introduced and explored individually in their own movie franchises—Iron Man, Captain America, Thor, and The Hulk—were brought together in a super team. Subsequently, the MCU was further developed through a second and emergent third phase of interlinked movies.

Television is not the only ancillary or cross-platform market. Conglomerate media now self-fertilizes in all directions. For example, Marvel Comics plans to revise a series from the 1980s, *Secret Wars*, to extend its cross-platform strategy into a yearlong event. Reportedly the story rides on the coattails of events playing out in the *Avengers* and *New Avengers* lines of comic books, and it is anticipated that the *Secret Wars* narrative will feed back again from the comics into future movies. The industrial spin on the series is neither shameless nor modest: "However massive you think this is," Tom Brevoort, the executive editor assigned to the comic series, noted, "let me assure you it is bigger than that."[28]

Comic book franchises are being rebooted after ever-shorter gaps, primarily as technological reimaginings with new-generation special effects to tell the same "origin" stories over and over. In the last decade *Superman, Batman,* and *Spiderman* franchises have all been the subjects of rapid sequence series rebooting. Compounding this creative reality is the fact that the studios hire writers well versed in the franchises' canonical story worlds. Given the proliferation of these fantasy readaptations, the qualifications for being a contemporary tentpole screenwriter now include a deeper knowledge of comic books, video games, and other platforms—and the complex iterations of those stories and their fan bases—than at any time in the history of motion pictures.

In addition to action, superhero, science fiction, and fantasy blockbusters Hollywood studios are, of course, still buying and producing romantic (*Trainwreck*, 2015), character (*Bridesmaids*, 2011), and adolescent comedies (*Superbad*, 2007). They are also investing in or distributing thrillers (*Taken*, 2008 and its franchise sequels) and various iterations of the crime drama (*Zodiac*, 2006), often at a lower budgetary level. And they still produce and distribute a limited number of "prestige" dramatic films each year, from *42* (2013) to *Unbroken* (2014). Lower-budget genre pictures such as horror movies are also being picked up for distribution or produced through affiliates and subsidiaries (*Mama*, 2013). Studios mitigate their investments in these films, however, by partnering with numerous production companies and also leveraging film festival selections and social media for marketing.

What gets displaced in the numerical and creative contraction of moviemaking today and in all this discussion of cross-platform storytelling is the professional screenwriter. The work of a movie and television screenwriter in the new century is circumscribed by continuities with the industrial relations and creative practices of past eras of production as much as by new conditions. On the one hand, the organization of labor for established screenwriters under the post-1950s freelance paradigm can be viewed as post-Fordist—or, to use Conor's term: "flexibly specialized"—but, on the other hand, it also falls under the auspices of a distinctly Fordist form of unionization.[29] This is what Hortense Powdermaker identified as the "assembly line" versus originality problem in her classic 1951 ethnographic study of Hollywood labor, *Hollywood, the Dream Factory: An Anthropologist Looks at the Movie-Makers.*[30]

THE PLOT

Established screenwriters are members of the WGA, the craft union that operates as something like a closed shop in terms of its master-contract relationships with studios and networks. Since the modern WGA was formed in 1954, it has worked to maximize and protect its members' rights and benefits through negotiation and contract enforcement within a changing industry. And it has done so with considerable success. For example, it has increased the economic viability of its writers by regulating the money studios spend on script ideas, spec and assigned scripts, cowritten scripts, script doctoring, and, with some failings, associated royalties. Yet in the light of media convergence and the emergence of an ever-expanding array of new media platforms and attendant viewing patterns, it has done little to expand its ranks given the proliferation of writing opportunities across media platforms.

While the revenue of its most successful members has risen to enviable heights, the guild has not done much to broaden opportunities for women and minority screenwriters. According to its own statistics, the membership of the WGA is still largely middle-aged, white, and male (writers ranging from forty-one to fifty years old claim the largest share of employment in film and television).[31] The most recent of the guild's semiannual *Writers Reports* notes, for example, that women occupy only 27 percent of unionized television sector writing posts. In television, women are at least holding their own (modest) position. In feature films, however, they have been losing what little ground they once occupied. In 2012, women accounted for just 15 percent of sector employment, down from 17 percent in 2009. As of this writing, a cluster of successful white male writers are sitting in the narrowing WGA tent.

The picture for minority screenwriters is much worse. Although numbers have increased recently in expanded and convergent television, where opportunities for diverse storytelling are currently less restricted than they are in feature films, minority writers make up a mere 11 percent of the sector. In feature films minority writers account for only 5 percent. In a modest attempt to spin the numbers, the WGA West's press release quotes its report's author, UCLA professor of sociology Darnell M. Hunt: "The good news is that, since the last report published in 2011, there appears [sic] to have been small gains for women and minorities in television employment and earnings—though both groups still have quite a way to go to reach parity with their white male counterparts. The story for film, unfortunately, is not so good. Since the last report, there has been no progress for either group. Indeed, relative to white males, women and minorities have lost ground in the sector."[32] Evidently the tent that the studios erect for their conglomerate owners has, to mix our metaphors, a glass ceiling.

In addition to the established marketing and green-lighting priorities of the studios, the underrepresentation of women and minorities in the industry has had an impact on the number and kinds of roles that are being written for them (at least outside the usual stereotypes). For example, the journalist Anne Thompson cites a 2012 University of Southern California Annenberg School for Communication and Journalism study that placed female representation in popular movies at its lowest level in five years: "Among the highest-grossing movies at the U.S. box office in 2012, the USC study reported, 28 percent of speaking characters were female. That marked a drop from 32.8 percent three years ago."[33] As the WGA's figures suggest, the situation is somewhat more positive in television (and, anecdotally, in independent film), but the fact remains that "there are fewer movies made for women, written by women, or starring women in the lead role. It's a vicious cycle."[34]

Women screenwriters have always been obliged to work within a male-centric industry. As the writer and scholar J. Madison Davis notes of the early history of screenwriting, "Almost from the beginning, women had played important roles in the development of the film business, but gradually they were replaced—not so much as a policy, but as an indication that the movie business was now a serious business, and should, in the thinking of the time, therefore, be male."[35] In terms of access to and employment within the professional craft of screenwriting, therefore, the circuit of culture is still keeping the gender and racial norms of Hollywood fully charged.

Those women writers who persevere with studio pictures in the conglomerate era have adopted various strategies to survive and thrive. Genre writers such as Kathryn Bigelow can, in Marsha McCreadie's words, "successfully borrow or steal a male form" or turn a genre story, as with *Thelma and Louise* (1991), script by Callie Khouri, from a simple reliance on physical action to an emphasis on what Khouri calls "emotional action."[36] The need for women writers to be able to "play with the boys"—even while rewriting some of the rules on a case-by-case basis—is as important in conglomerate Hollywood as it was in the 1950s, when Howard Hawks spoke of Leigh Brackett (who wrote John Wayne's character in *Rio Bravo* [1959], written by Jules Furthman and Leigh Brackett) thus: "She writes like a man—she writes good." Gramsci's notion of coercion and consent applies to women and men equally. As McCreadie notes, Brackett never responded publicly, other than saying in a conference at San Francisco State University that Hawks's characters fit her style because "the women are all, by God, people, with independent lives and thoughts of their own, capable of being comrades and mates but always of their own free choice and as equals with men—an earned quality. Men have to earn it. So do they."[37]

Brackett's eloquent evocation of the strong female character could be viewed as the prototype for many of the interventions contemporary women screenwriters are able to make within mainstream Hollywood stories. When they are given the opportunity, many women find—indeed, have always found—ways to accommodate creatively and to work dynamic and progressive female roles (and other tropes) into conventionally masculine genres. Leslie Dixon did this effectively for Rene Russo in the remake of *The Thomas Crowne Affair* (1999), script by Leslie Dixon and Kurt Wimmer, for example. Alternatively, they work to rescue the characterization of women from stereotype and cliché, as Audrey Wells did in writing Uma Thurman's character in *The Truth about Cats and Dogs* (1996). The creative success of these and other individual instances of women's screenwriting notwithstanding, even those women screenwriters who are still being employed in mainstream Hollywood feature writing only earn an average of ninety-two cents on the male dollar for their labor.

A recent snapshot of the overall economic health of unionized Hollywood screenwriting labor can be found in the WGA West's *Annual Financial Report* of 2014.[38] In that document the WGA noted a total of 4,745 guild writers (across movies and television) reporting new earnings for the year 2013, a decline on the previous year of 0.5 percent. Their total earnings amounted to $1,012.5 million, also a decline of 6.4 percent. The report further breaks down the earnings from television (3,681 writers earning $668.5 million) and "screen" or movies (1,595 writers earning $331 million), noting both sets of figures as a decline on relatively strong 2012 numbers. For the same period, the WGA West reported that it had collected record income from residuals (fees for the replay and purchase of movies and television shows in and through ancillary markets) of $373.8 million (an increase of 7.2 percent over 2012) on behalf of its members. While the DVD market continued to shrink (by 8.2 percent year by year), the most notable increase was in what the report calls "New Media." In 2013, New Media residuals paid to guild screenwriters increased by 47.2 percent to $15.9 million. Pay TV residuals were also increasing strongly (up 34.4 percent), whereas residuals from feature films grew a modest 3 percent to $140.08 million.

These figures reveal that the economics of Hollywood screenwriting are in something of a manic low as the proliferation of screen stories is soaring. Indeed, while writers in movies and television still receive primary income from their current contracts, the structure of their residuals payments is changing as media convergence and digital downloads begin to transform and drive the ancillary markets for their employers' products. Specifically, the DVD market is on the decline as digital is in the process of monetizing. The figures for 2013 also offer a partial snapshot accounting of the aftermath of the most significant event in Hollywood labor relations in the new century: the strike called by the WGA in 2007, following the breakdown of contract negotiations with their employers. The "New Media" residuals noted above are due to screenwriters because of an important concession won from the studios and networks by the craft guilds during that dispute. It was an important victory for WGA members that, though hard-fought, also had long-lasting negative effects that rippled across the industry and did little to open the tent to more writers.

This brings us to the 2007–8 writers' strike. To date, this industrial dispute has been the most significant and most public crisis for professional Hollywood screenwriters in the new millennium. The strike is worthy of extended analysis because its impact resonates throughout the chapters that follow. The causes of the strike illustrate the influence of the fraught history of movie-industry labor relations on the WGA's current internal debates, official policies, and institutional strategies; its conduct demonstrates to what extent the current generation of the WGA's membership and leadership had learned from that history and from broader changes in Hollywood and the media since the previous round of major industrial disputes in the 1980s; and its resolution set the agenda for the current post-strike economic and ideological relationship between screenwriters and their industry. In short, the strike provides immediate context for understanding the current politics and paradigms of professional Hollywood screenwriting and sets the stage for our detailed discussion of the industry in which the new or convergent screenwriter works.

BEHIND THE SCENES

The 2007–8 strike offers an insight into the class tensions that exist within the professional screenwriting craft. There has always been an internal dichotomy between the middle-class rank-and-file WGA members and their wealthy A-list and showrunner colleagues that also transcends the traditional film and television media lines. These tensions have been the cause of historical splits in the union over the perceived and vested interests of the two screenwriter classes. Indeed, the resolution of past strikes has been precipitated by fractures in membership solidarity precisely along the fault line of this bourgeois class split.

In the dispute of 2007–8 the internal class structure within the WGA was tested once again. In this case the guild remained unified because making an accommodation with convergence affected the bottom line of the traditional screenwriter just as it played to the concerns of the new screenwriter. Since the strike, this class tension has been further replicated and exacerbated by the latest iterations of movie development practiced by the ever more budget-conscious conglomerate studios. Of course, many of the increasingly unfavorable contractual terms under which most Hollywood screenwriters now work predated the strike. Nonetheless, the dispute certainly accelerated the process.

There is a cliché in military history that poor generals are always guilty of refighting the last war. The strike of 2007–8 certainly saw both sides falling into the traps of battle plans from the past, but it also saw new insurgent tactics being employed by a younger generation of writers who worked to bring the themes of the dispute out from behind the scenes to a wider public. In so doing, they attempted to outflank the Maginot Line of habitual industrial discourse by controlling the storytelling of the strike to win the hearts and minds of moviegoers. The writers staged their militancy in plain sight, but their efforts were a direct result of simmering long-term resentment about poor deals from the past and a fear those deals would be repeated once again as the uncertain economics of a converging industry became inscribed in a new craft contract. This time around, their battle plan played out tactically to the benefit of the writers, as media coverage of their efforts put pressure on studios and their executives to compromise. Although the strike was resolved by decidedly old-school backroom dealing, it is unlikely that such a deal would have been made without the studios having lost the propaganda war decisively.

The hard-fought and often bitter strike lasted from November 2007 to February 2008. The dispute was followed, coincidentally but closely, by the global economic crisis later that year. In combination these events contributed to a further contraction in Hollywood spec script sales while simultaneously exacerbating the current iteration of the de facto "class system" among movie screenwriters.[39] They also illustrate the perceptions held by working writers and management of the present state and future development of a transforming industry at a specific point in time. Importantly, the strike was also a moment in which writers at all levels of the industry were motivated to speak, some even eloquently, about their sense of worth and place in a changing media world. In this way it offers a unique snapshot of deeply held emotional and political attitudes from working screenwriters that likely would not have been revealed in public under normal circumstances. Both directly and indirectly, however, in the longer term the strike adversely impacted the working conditions of middle-class screenwriters, and for the most part the issues that prompted it are still working through the Hollywood industry a decade or so later.

The strike was not a peacekeeping effort to widen the tent that houses and welcomes working writers, although that was one of its ideological messages. It was an effort to ensure that current writers had access to revenue generated from changing ancillary markets. As Miranda Banks notes, the 2007–8 dispute fits a pattern established by previous strikes:

> It should come as no surprise that Hollywood's creative labor strikes have occurred at critical moments of technological change within the industry. Once every generation, enough technological shifts happen within the industry that the old systems of compensation for labor need to readjust to keep pace. Just looking at the WGA strikes since the inception of television makes this clear. In 1960, television writers went to the picket lines and established the residual system that has since ensured that television writers would see a profit from the rerun. In 1988, the WGA failed in their attempt to secure fair residuals from the sales of film and television on VHS. In part, what led to the WGA giving up their fight was that television writers saw no reason to care about VHS residuals—at the time they could not imagine the future success of TV DVD sales. Now, in this latest technological cycle, the WGA is hoping to make up for what they lost in 1988.[40]

Banks's historical view contextualizes the struggle between middle-class and wealthy writers, the quasi union that represents them, and the conglomerates expanding their cross-platform strategies facilitated by new technologies and corporate globalization.

Most significant, in 2007 writers in the WGA were looking to get ahead of the digital curve by establishing a basis for fair remuneration for the exploitation of their work in the emerging new-media theater. Foreshadowing the economic reality of media convergence, they wanted a deal on digital residual payments that protected their future interests as the revenue streams from ancillary markets shifted. As we have noted, at the time of the dispute sales of DVDs were already declining, and it was becoming clear that the long-term economic impact of Blu-ray would be limited.[41] Accessing movies and TV shows via streaming and digital download, while not yet established as the commonplace it has become since 2008, was already being recognized in the industry as an onrushing distribution shockwave.

That a dispute should have arisen in late 2007 was, in part, a simple consequence of the regular schedule of contract negotiations between the craft guilds and their employers. Every three years the WGA East and West, the organizations that make up the WGA, renegotiate their master contract with the Alliance of Motion Picture and Television Producers (AMPTP), representing the studios and networks.[42] This master contract, known as the Minimum Basic Agreement (MBA), locks in minimum levels of remuneration for writers working in most areas of feature film and television production, as well as rates for residual payments from the rebroadcast of movies and shows on network and cable, from DVD sales, and from the exploitation of scripted product through other media and in other ancillary markets. The MBA also sets rates for employer pensions and for health and medical benefit contributions. Although the relationship between the two branches of the WGA had not always been easy, during the dispute of 2007–8 the WGA East, led by its president Michael Winship and executive director Mona Mangan, supported the strategy and leadership of its larger West Coast partner.

The negotiations over the renewal of the agreement in 2007 escalated into a strike in large part because of the legacy of fraught labor relations that had existed between the craft guilds and the AMPTP. Hollywood writers in the WGA held on to a deep and lingering resentment over the outcomes of prior negotiations and industrial disputes dating back to the 1980s. Many writers believed strongly that they had been denied fair deals on residual payments when previous ancillary markets emerged (such as home video). There was also an increasing consensus within the guild that its previous negotiating tactics, and the close relationship between prior WGA leadership teams and the studio executives representing the employers, had contributed to this continuing failure.

In the years following the contract negotiations of 2004, the WGA West changed leadership and took steps to professionalize its preparations for possible strike action in advance of the next round of negotiations in 2007. In so doing, the WGA learned to campaign more in the style of a traditional labor union than a Hollywood craft guild. Its newly asynchronous tactics, including most impressively the leveraging of social media to spread the word of its members' insurgency, would win in the court of public opinion.

At WGA West the changes were initiated under the auspices of a new, more labor-conscious leadership team. In 2005 Patric Verrone, a comedy writer known for his work on *The Simpsons* (1989), *Futurama* (1999), and *The Critic* (1994), was elected as the guild's president on a platform that promoted harder bargaining and better internal organization and discipline. More of the guild's educational and financial resources were directed toward strike preparation. Moreover, Verrone and the WGA West's board proceeded to remove some of the more moderate "old guard" figures from senior management positions. The highest profile casualty of this exercise in house cleaning was executive director John McLean. McLean had led the WGA in previous negotiations in 2001 and 2004 but was seen by the new regime as being too close to the AMPTP. Howard Rodman summed up the dissatisfaction many in the guild felt toward McLean's 2004 negotiating tactics in *Deadline Hollywood* in 2009: "It was during the 2004 negotiations that our then-Executive Director John McLean negotiated against his own Guild. Far more than he was willing to negotiate against his old pals in the conglomerates. Again and again he maintained that we'd be 'laughed out of the room' if we asked for the things we asked for.... During some of the dismal, dispiriting, and astonishingly long Negotiating Committee meetings, some of us began to pass notes. And to hum, under our breath, 'Which Side Are You On.'"[43] McLean was positioned as a traitor.

David Young, an experienced textile-union organizer who would be the principal architect of the guild's strike effort in 2007–8, duly replaced McLean. As a direct consequence of the guild's improved strike education and internal organization, when the dispute did eventually escalate into a strike, the WGA was better prepared and more unified than it had been at any time during or since the last round of strikes back in the 1980s. Conversely, the AMPTP underestimated the political and organizational skills of the new WGA West leadership team and, more importantly, the solidarity of its rank and file. Initially, the AMPTP was unprepared to respond to the creative tactics the WGA employed on the streets, on picket lines, at staged events, and on social media and other demonstration platforms (discussed later). The Neo-Marxist Antonio Gramsci would have been impressed, as the guild also consistently out-maneuvered or, more aptly, out-wrote the other side.

An additional consequence of the adoption of more assertive strike tactics by the WGA was to further polarize the negotiations both before and during the strike. Antagonistic statements from both sides made the chances of constructive communication between the guild's negotiating committee and the AMPTP's labor relations executives very unlikely. This situation was exacerbated by errors both of tactics and tone, especially during the prestrike negotiations, made by the AMPTP's negotiating team, led by its president, Nicholas Counter. Counter and the AMPTP had noted the changes in the WGA's leadership and the increasing stridency of its public statements since 2005. As a result, they approached the negotiations in 2007 on the assumption that the guild intended to strike no matter the outcome. Confident in their ability to pressure the WGA into accepting only minor concessions, they proceeded to try and set the agenda from the start. From the perspective of many writers, both their tone and the unrealistic opening proposals they offered seemed calculated to push the WGA toward taking such action.

Initially, the AMPTP offered two proposals, one addressing the contentious issue of residuals from digital distribution and the other proposing a radical overhaul of the overall structure of "recoupment" in the movie and television industry. The first proposal advocated maintaining the status quo regarding digital residuals for the duration of the next contract, while studying the economic potential of the new-media market. The second was to restructure the entire deal on residuals in all media, creating a two-tier system based on the initial success of the movie or show: "This framework ran completely counter to decades of industry practice, and it would ensure that only a small percentage of productions would generate residuals for writers, actors and directors in a timely manner."[44] Both proposals were deemed unacceptable by the WGA; instead, they were viewed as provocation. In return the WGA offered its own, twenty-six-point proposal. It included a formula for digital residuals based on 2.5 percent of the distributor's gross. This proposal, in turn, was viewed as entirely unacceptable by the employers' side. The two sides would not be moved from these positions for almost the entire duration of the strike, causing a temporary yet, for the most part, unnoticeable shortage in the circuit of culture.

The AMPTP also attempted to marginalize the WGA's new leadership in its public statements, portraying them as outsiders, too radical, and out of touch both with the realities and the traditions of the entertainment industry. They sought to cause division within the guild's membership, a tactic that had been successful in previous disputes but that singularly failed in 2007–8, in the face of solidarity from the WGA. By all accounts the AMPTP's tactics only served to anger and alienate the WGA's membership and helped further unite the guild behind Verrone and Young's leadership and strategy.[45]

An early and significant manifestation of this solidarity within the WGA was the formation of the United Showrunners group, following a meeting of leading television showrunners, the writer-producers responsible for managing story and production development in television shows, at the Sheraton Universal Hotel, on November 3, 2007. In 2007 showrunners were in a uniquely complex position, being both writers and producers. Because they were responsible for the delivery of entire television shows, their professional duties extended well beyond story development in their writers' rooms. As we discuss in greater detail in chapter 3, the showrunner is the major creative and managerial force behind a television show, having risen through the ranks of writers and then writer-producers on other shows in what is still in many ways a writer's medium. Some showrunners are relatively unknown to the wider public while others develop a public prominence beyond the relatively tight circle inhabited by fans of their shows. Recent examples of well-known television showrunners include David Chase *(The Sopranos)*, David Simon *(The Wire)*, Joss Whedon *(Buffy* the Vampire Slayer; Firefly), and Shonda Rhimes (Grey's Anatomy; Scandal).

The hyphenate status of television showrunners, having broad responsibility for story development as well as production management, gave them the right to continue working on the aspects of their job that did not relate directly to screenwriting during a WGA strike. In past disputes, however, some showrunners had been suspected of breaking the terms of strikes by continuing to work on scripted material. Moreover, in the strike of 1988 it had been a public split by showrunners that had finally forced the WGA to settle the dispute to its disadvantage. Given this history, there was considerable pressure on showrunners to take a principled and public-leadership role in the 2007 strike. This pressure came from within the WGA, but also from allied unions, notably the Teamsters, who also resented that some showrunners had continued to work in 1988 while their members lost wages.

In its coverage of the 2007–8 dispute, the *Independent* newspaper noted that "during the last writers' strike, in 1988, the showrunners kept working, which both prolonged the dispute—it went on for 22 weeks—and made it that much harder for the writers to get what they wanted."[46] Because of the divisive precedent set by this history, some showrunners were vocal and explicit about their personal responses to the strike. On November 5, 2007, Shawn Ryan, showrunner on the FX show *The Shield* and the primary case study in chapter 3, published an email outlining the actions he proposed to take.

> At the Showrunners Meeting it became very clear to me that the only thing I can do as a showrunner is to do nothing. I obviously will not write on my shows. But I also will not edit, I will not cast, I will not look at location photos, I will not get on the phone with the network and studio, I will not prep directors, I will not review mixes. These are all acts that are about the writing of the show or protecting the writing of the show, and as such, I will not participate in them. I will also not ask any of my writer/producers to do any of these things for me, so that they get done, but I can save face.[47]

Ryan's statement encouraged the more prominent cadre of showrunners to align with the WGA, their country of origin, rather than the networks and studios, their country of citizenship.

Contrary to their practice in previous disputes, in 2007 the members of the United Showrunners group took the unprecedented step of closing down all production on their shows during the strike. Their action formed part of the WGA's Pencils Down campaign. In closing down their shows, the showrunners demonstrated their willingness to take significant financial and professional risks—including the potential cancellation of their shows—in its support. Indeed, some shows did not survive the strike, and many established television writers also lost their lucrative "overall deals" with networks and studios. The actions of the United Showrunners, among the best paid, highest profile, and most influential members of the WGA, sent a powerful signal to the AMPTP of the guild's unity and seriousness of intent.

With showrunners on its side the WGA fought for a wide range of issues at the start of the dispute, but the twenty-six-point proposal presented to the AMPTP as an opening position for the negotiations included objectives that were put on the table for internal political reasons but with little expectation of adoption. Some of the issues were uncontroversial, while others, such as a large percentage increase in home video / DVD sales and rentals, were obviously unrealistic. This approach was typical of the positional documents that are proffered by both sides in guild negotiations. In other words, some issues were core, and others, like the home video increase, were only included so that they could be waived later as public gestures of goodwill and compromise.

The critical issue for the striking screenwriters in 2007 was the impact of media convergence and digital technologies on the distribution chain for movies and scripted TV shows, the guild anticipating the stable monetization of a distribution mechanism that had already arrived. Both sides in the dispute understood that a formula for digital residuals would eventually have to be included in all of the guild master contracts, but they viewed the status of digital distribution—both actual and potential—very differently. In this regard the timing of the 2007 contract negotiations occurred at a moment in the industry's response to the convergence of media in which the writers' own understanding of the potential importance of digital and online distribution for the future prosperity of the guild's existing members was running well ahead of the appreciation, to say nothing of the actual monetization, of digital assets by the studios and networks.

In 2007 the revenue streams from limited digital distribution were only beginning to generate income. The studios and, more importantly, the TV networks were still experimenting with downloading and streaming. Netflix, Hulu, and Amazon, which now produce original content as well as distributing extant media, were far from the new media powerhouses they are as we are writing this book. Fears of piracy and uncertainties about the market led most of the major Hollywood institutions to remain hesitant about making recently screened and broadcast material available online.[48] Early adopters such as Disney and its subsidiaries, who moved into download-on-demand in a serious way through a deal with Apple on the release of the video iPod, were very much the exception. In other words, the potential of online markets was evident, but the economics of such models and the distribution practices that could maximize revenue generation had yet to firm up. But both sides saw it coming.

This led to a situation in which the AMPTP was loath to establish potentially costly precedents regarding remuneration before it fully understood how digital would pay out. As film scholar Dina Smith argues, "Producers were investing in and acknowledging the changing infrastructure yet delaying outlay and short-changing labor for as long as possible in order to see how consumption patterns and the industry would shift. The WGA strike goals came down to acknowledging a present and foreseeing a future that producers wished to avoid."[49] From the writers' perspective, this reticence also spoke of another attempt to pull the wool over their eyes and force them into an unfavorable deal, such as the WGA had been obliged to swallow on home video residuals back in the 1980s. In 1985 the employers had negotiated to pay writers a low rate on home video based on what is known in the industry as the "80/20" formula. Under this provision the studios take 80 percent of revenues off the top and the writer gets a base 1.5 percent residual calculated only from the remaining 20 percent—the so-called "producer's gross."[50]

This formula had been negotiated originally on the principle that home video was still a developing market and that more time was needed to understand how it would pay out in the longer term. Once 80/20 was in the MBA, however, it proved impossible to negotiate away when DVD replaced home video. And, of course, a key proposal in the opening position of the AMPTP in 2007 was that digital residuals should be tabled for three years pending further research, repeating the corporate stance from the video negotiation back in the 1980s. The WGA had learned its lesson, however, and greeted the proposal with staged outrage by its membership. Indeed, studio executives later acknowledged that its introduction had been a major tactical error because it played directly into the WGA's public-relations narrative of a history of unfair deals. For example, the WGA's chief negotiator, John Bowman, quipped: "According to Hollywood accounting, 'The Simpsons' is not in profits. How can we trust that kind of bookkeeping?"[51] The fact that the employers had something of a case to make regarding the current monetization of digital did nothing to convince the writers—and their public—that history wasn't repeating itself, to their economic and ideological disadvantage.

WGA members were determined not to lose out now that the next significant transformation of ancillary markets had begun.[52] Fueled by video games and, of course, the Internet, they saw the writing on the digital wall. In the negotiations that followed, one of the most important demands from the WGA was that whatever formula was agreed for the calculation of residuals from digital, it would not be based on the "producer's gross." Rather, the new deal must be calculated from the "distributor's gross," or 100 percent of the revenue generated by the project. The AMPTP resisted discussion of this proposition until its negotiation with the Directors Guild of America (DGA) near the end of the strike.

The WGA won the public-relations battle over the issue, presenting it, again, as a simple matter of fairness. In November of 2007 *Variety* conducted a survey of its subscribers, finding a majority (54 percent) in favor of the strike and an even larger number of respondents (69 percent) supporting the WGA's position as being "honest and forthright."[53] But the WGA had not adequately researched the state of the digital marketplace and did not have concrete evidence of the current economic situation. As the movie producer Obst writes: "In truth, the value of the revenue stream had not been definitively evaluated by either TV or films at that point. There were guesses, estimates, based on models pulled out of models. It was 2008, and deals of consequence are just now, in 2012, being made—and they are still not predictable enough to be projected onto any profit-and-loss statement. But who believed this then? Not the writers."[54] Perhaps unsurprisingly, given the results of previous contract negotiations and well-established traditions of sharp practice in Hollywood accounting, the WGA's argument was based more on past precedent and endemic distrust than on current realities. The WGA's position assumed that significant money was already being made from digital distribution and, if unchecked, proven cheaters would continue to cheat.

The 2007–8 dispute was a writers' strike in more than just name. WGA members at all levels of the profession directed their creativity toward promoting their struggle in the press and in wordsmithing their experience of the dispute in blogs and social media. In this way a strike about the economic potential of the Internet was also fought on the Internet. As the writer and strike blogger John Aboud noted in an interview in 2008: "The very tools that were the basis of the dispute in the strike were the tools that were used to wage the strike. . . . The strike itself was a demonstration of the change that is sweeping through the business."[55] The writers' informal and semiofficial social media campaigns did much to maintain sympathy for their position among their peers in the other crafts and in the wider public arena. It also helped to shore up solidarity among guild membership as the duration of the strike extended from weeks into months.

One of the most influential contributions to this new-media activity was a blog started by a group of WGA strike captains including John Aboud and Alan Berman. Called *United Hollywood,* in an attempt to demonstrate the relevance of the WGA's campaign for all Hollywood artists and craft workers, the blog became the nexus of online activity for writers. The blog's introduction articulated clearly that Hollywood writers believed they were fighting for a collective future at a time of unprecedented institutional and technological change: "United Hollywood advocates for working people in the entertainment industry facing the digital revolution."[56] During the strike, *United Hollywood* acted as a forum for writers to comment personally and individually on the developing situation but also as a space for publishing critiques of media reporting, campaign videos, links to news and other organizational and logistical information. As Littleton notes, "*United Hollywood* and other Internet-driven communications during the WGA strike proved to be a groundbreaking model for organized labor in any sector. Never before had union members been afforded such instantaneous access to news and information germane to the dispute."[57]

The adoption of social media campaigning tactics during the strike also reflected a growing activist mentality among a younger generation of writers more closely aligned with Verrone (who was, like most of the WGA's rank-and-file members, a middle-class working writer and not an influential television showrunner or A-list Hollywood movie screenwriter). Alongside the more traditional strike experiences of picketing and public protest, participating in social media activity did much to bond screenwriters of all kinds into a sense of common identity. David Latt acknowledged this unity in a piece he wrote for *United Hollywood* in January of 2008: "Walking on the picket line last week, there wasn't any question that writers feel a stronger sense of community and purpose than ever before in the history of the Guild."[58]

United Hollywood became a vehicle for strong opinion, as did the comments section for Nikki Finke's increasingly influential website, DeadlineHollywoodDaily.com (subsequently Deadline.com). Unlike traditional trade publications *Variety* and the *Hollywood Reporter,* DeadlineHollywoodDaily.com was seen by many writers as sympathetic to the goals of the strike and to labor in general. But even though in formal public discourse the strike maintained a solid front, the internal debate became increasingly strident as the dispute moved into 2008. This debate played out in the public comments sections of the blogs. As the economic consequences of the strike hit the entertainment economy harder, unofficial arguments raged among fellow writers and among WGA members and members of other guilds and unions—notably below-the-line International Alliance of Theatrical Stage Employees (IATSE) crew—over the handling of the dispute and even the definition of unions and unionism. Observing from the sidelines, Obst reflected that "the politics got baffling. It was much like the Stalinist-vs.-Trotskyite years, as my grandfather explained them to me: the narcissism of small differences."[59] One contribution from Whedon to *United Hollywood* toward the end of the strike summed up the anger and frustration of his peers not only about the current dispute but also of working with the institutions of conglomerate Hollywood: "The studios are inefficient, power-hungry, thieving corporate giants who have made the life of the working writer harder from decade to decade. They are run by men so out of touch with basic humanity that they would see Rome burn before they would think about the concept of fair compensation. I maintain that they have never revealed their true agenda in the causing and handling of this strike, and to expect them to now is cock-eyed optimism of the most dangerous kind."[60] Whedon was speaking with passion, of course, something one does not see often from a Hollywood player. Yet in the aftermath of the strike it was arguably the studios and networks that—once again—benefited most from the dispute. In fact, the AMPTP members were able to leverage the dispute to shift the ground on screenwriters in ways that had nothing to do with the WGA's demands.

The writers' strike played out in an extended public duel over the moral high ground, in competing versions of industrial spin. It was also a kind of intramural class conflict for an elite yet small (and mostly white male) cadre of bourgeois writers. Meanwhile, behind the scenes, negotiations between the WGA and the AMPTP stalled. Experienced negotiators attempted to moderate the impact of some of the more fractious personalities on both sides but to little immediate effect. Attempts were also made by some writers to bypass the stalled formal negotiations and talk informally but directly with studio and network CEOs in search of pragmatic solutions. These maneuvers represented an attempt to reassert the familiar terms under which negotiations had been conducted in the past. The studio and network bosses, sitting silently behind the AMPTP's Maginot Line, were evidently concerned that the Old Hollywood relationship-driven culture of dispute resolution had failed in the face of the guild's new professionalism and increased militancy on one side and the AMPTP's failed bullying strategy on the other. For the negotiations the result of all of this was a retreat into intransigence.

The other two major Hollywood craft guilds, the DGA and the Screen Actors Guild (SAG), both of which also negotiate master contracts for members with the AMPTP, were concerned with the looming issue of residuals from digital distribution. As the bargaining process began, however, the WGA took the lead because its contract expired eight months before those of the DGA and SAG (both June 30, 2008). The assumption was that whatever deal the WGA reached with the employers would be used as a template for renewing the master contracts of the other guilds, so DGA and SAG members were paying close attention to the progress of the negotiations. And they were getting nervous.

Relationships between the Hollywood craft guilds have historically been fractious, in particular that between the WGA and the DGA. In particular, the directors already had a reputation in the other crafts as being too ready to accommodate the employer. It therefore came as no surprise to the wider Hollywood community that during the strike of 2007–8 SAG lined up strongly behind the WGA, whereas the DGA stayed largely on the sidelines during most of the dispute and followed a different strategy in pursuing its own interests.

The writers' strike was finally resolved when the DGA opened secret and, by all accounts, largely amicable discussions with the AMPTP in parallel with the WGA's negotiation. The DGA succeeded in negotiating its own deal on digital residuals, and that agreement did indeed serve subsequently as a blueprint for all three master contracts. In her persuasive account of the dispute, Cynthia Littleton argues that, on the one hand, the DGA would not have been in a position to make the deal it did with the AMPTP if the WGA's strike had not proved solid. On the other hand, by late 2007 the AMPTP was also more inclined to deal with the DGA as a way of punishing the WGA for its stridency and temerity: "The CEOs knew they had erred by vastly underestimating the WGA's ability to wage war under David Young's leadership. After being knocked on their heels in November, the CEOs were determined to ensure that the studios got their act together in December starting with the push to marginalize the WGA by negotiating with the DGA."[61] In typical Hollywood fashion, then, the writers wrote the script, and the directors carried it out without much regard to the writers' intent.

If the resolution of the writers' strike can be viewed as an instance of Old Hollywood deal making, its causes speak clearly to the present tense of conglomerate Hollywood. In order to have a stake in the future economic model of the industry, screenwriters asserted the collective power of their labor, taking their fight to the public via social and traditional media and thus exposing some aspects of the conditions of production prevalent in Hollywood's dream factory. By taking extended strike action and putting significant economic pressure on the networks and studios, the WGA risked nothing less than disrupting and permanently altering the paradigm of movie and television development and production. What the guild won and lost in 2007–8—both directly and in the multiple subtle and often unexpected ways that the conduct and outcome of the strike altered the employment culture for writers in Hollywood—illustrates exactly how high those stakes were for the working conditions, opportunities, and potential wealth for screenwriters.

AN (IM)PERFECT PACKAGE

The writers' victory did not pay off entirely for WGA members. It merely helped to further entrench the new abnormal. Unlike the WGA, the DGA had gone to considerable expense to commission its own independent studies assessing the monetization of digital distribution in anticipation of the next round of contract negotiations. Their research led them to better appreciate the AMPTP's position because the results of their own studies fell more closely in line with the conglomerate studios' assessment of the present economic reality of digital distribution than with that of the WGA. This would prove to be the common ground that contributed to a breakthrough in the DGA's parallel negotiations with the AMPTP. Yet, as we discuss in the next few chapters, the breakthrough foreshadowed a different end from what screenwriters imagined, tightening the job market and the structure of deals for writers and accelerating the transformation of the television industry.

Lost was the weak pitch the WGA made to broaden its representation of working writers in the motion picture and television industries, notably by expanding its coverage of writing into the arenas of reality television and animation production. Despite the stridency and, from the WGA's perspective, the logic of their pitch, neither of these goals were ever likely to be achieved. Expanding into reality television was not a welcome proposition for some guild members who looked down on the form, also resenting how these cheaper-to-produce shows were taking more and more broadcast slots away from traditionally scripted programming. They also worried that the association with reality television would cheapen their craft, and thus the limited cachet in the industry that screenwriters still enjoyed. Finally, they were concerned that a significant expansion of guild membership from lower-waged reality TV writers might undermine the value of their pension and health benefits over time. Unlike more traditional unions, many Writers Guild members were not all that interested in expanding their base unless they had a vested interest in employment in or revenues from the new medium. We discuss the WGA's recent attitude to jurisdictional expansion and its approach to the legitimation of new media for screenwriters in more detail in chapters 2 and 5.

From the studios' perspective a jurisdictional expansion by the WGA into reality television in particular would also have required both an acknowledgment that these so-called unscripted shows were indeed substantially "written" and an acceptance of changed budgetary and working practices that would have dented the profitability of reality shows. The producers won this struggle. During the period of the strike and shortly thereafter, TV networks duly commissioned more reality programs as cover for the broadcast hours previously filled by the scripted shows that were not being produced during the dispute. As Susan Murray and Laurie Ouellette note, the twenty-two-week WGA strike back in 1988 did not affect the earlier generation of reality programs. Moreover, the strike had the effect of delaying the start of the fall TV season that year and gave producers and networks "the impetus to develop future shows that did not depend on writing talent."[62] In 1988 the writers underestimated the networks' willingness to write off the season and replace scripted shows with reality TV. "The networks claimed they could live without crucial showrunners through reality programming, 'unscripted television' that was cheap to produce," Linda Obst recalled. "Reality TV wasn't taken seriously at the time, and the creative community pooh-poohed the networks' strategy."[63] In a similar vein, Littleton reports that part of the ongoing legacy of the dispute of 2007–8 was a predictable move by the networks to look "for more unscripted reality shows for their prime-time schedules."[64] Over time the pendulum has swung back toward the commissioning of scripted shows for a range of small screens, but the conflict certainly strengthened the justification for the networks to make significant investments in reality programming.

Also lost was the attempt to bring other forms of writing under the WGA's remit. Since the 1950s the representation of many animation writers had come under the auspices of IATSE locals, not the WGA. For this reason an attempt by the guild to bring animation writing under the terms of its contract was seen as muscling in on another union's turf. Indeed, IATSE president Thomas Short would become one of the most vocal critics of the WGA's leadership ("a huge clown car that's only missing the hats and horns"), of its strike tactics in general, and of its "unethical poaching" of IATSE members during the course of the strike.[65] Hollywood labor did not, therefore, have uncontested solidarity during the strike.

On the much more positive side of the equation, the DGA was able to negotiate an agreement that established initial benchmarks for residual payments on a range of digital download options and rates for productions intended for the Internet. In a press release dated January 17, 2008, Gil Cates, chair of the guild's Negotiations Committee and former dean of the School of Theater, Film and Television at UCLA, trumpeted their success: "Two words describe this agreement—groundbreaking and substantial."[66] Most important, the deal calculated residual payments from digital distribution on an agreed interpretation of the controversial distributor's gross. "The deal more than doubled the traditional home video rate of pay for popular television programming, and it marked an 80 percent improvement for feature films."[67] Going forward, however, the challenge for the WGA of accounting revenues from digital would prove to be considerable. In 2013 the *New York Times* quoted Liesl Copland, a digital media specialist from the William Morris Endeavour Entertainment agency: "There is still no uniform reporting system that aggregates all data on, say, a film or documentary across all of its platforms."[68] The suspicion that sharp accounting practices were still taking place also prompted agenda items in subsequent MBA negotiations.

One issue on which there had been no movement was the initial residual-free window of seventeen days (with some exceptions) for streaming that the studios had insisted was necessary to allow them to promote a show or movie online. As most viewings of streamed material take place within this initial window of availability—and given that the studios were selling advertising with the streams, thus making a profit during that residual free period—the crafts had campaigned for it to be included in the calculation of residuals. The AMPTP would not move on this, and it remained excluded until the contract of 2014. Nevertheless, the intervention of the DGA into the WGA's dispute had helped to break the deadlock on the guild's key demand.

The WGA also won the right to have unprecedented access to documentation regarding the deals AMPTP members were making over new media. As Littleton argues, this concession to transparency was unprecedented in the occluded history of creative Hollywood accounting and came in large part as a consequence of AMPTP members' "frustration at the perception in the creative community that the studios were profiting hand over fist from new media licensing and exhibition, when in fact digital distribution seemed to have a mostly corrosive effect on traditional business models."[69]

The studios prepared for the possibility of industrial action by stockpiling screenplays and diverting development and production resources into reality television and away from scripted shows that might be shut down, strategic preparation for the strike seen as a Gramscian war of position. As John

Hazelton suggested in 2011, it also did much to encourage studios to change the terms of their contracts with individual screenwriters. "While the 100-day strike certainly produced some gains for writers particularly in the area of payments for new-media exploitation," he wrote, "the script stockpiling which preceded it helped foster the one-step deal trend."[70] The increase in one-step deals after the strike and more draconian pronouncements on the enforcement of delivery dates for first draft screenplays, from Warner Bros. in particular, pushed the guild to meet with the studio in order to obtain a promise that they would be phased out.[71] From all reports, the one-step deal is still commonplace for new writers and most spec sales. As we will explore in chapters 2 and 4, it now underpins the development model for much prestige independent as well as tentpole and other studio screenwriting.

As film and media scholar Henry Jenkins argues, convergence is an ongoing phenomenon. Media do not suddenly converge and then stop converging.[72] Rather, the term seeks to illustrate the ways in which different media forms continually renegotiate their interactions over time as technology, markets, patterns of consumption, and even post facto fan creation variously respond to change and become its vanguard. Similarly, "digital" is not a single ancillary market, nor is it indicative of a single technological interface. Digital distribution outlets for streaming and download include free formats such as YouTube and, for the gaming community, Twitch, as well as a range of monetized formats through cable and the Internet such as Pay Per View, Premium Video on Demand, and, most recently, Subscription Video on Demand (SVOD) outlets such as Netflix. The industry continues to redraw and be redrawn by the map of convergence and, as it does so, the AMPTP and the craft guilds seek to keep up with the drafts and to anticipate future developments. Unsurprisingly, the 2008 MBA did not resolve all of the issues inherent and implicit in digital and new media for writers. The deal that emerged, following the DGA talks in 2008, set important precedents, yet the industry continued to change, and digital residuals were revisited in the negotiations of 2011 and again in 2014.

In the 2011 negotiations the issue at stake in terms of digital media was primarily enforcing adherence by AMPTP signatories to the terms of the 2008 contract. In 2014 the WGA's summary of the proposed MBA returned its focus to a digital-industrial mediascape that had changed once again in the interim. This MBA highlighted the importance of setting rates for content created specifically for "High Budget" SVOD platforms, which had not been an issue in 2008.[73]

In contrast to the drawn-out process in 2007, the 2011 round of negotiations between the WGA and the AMPTP was remarkably swift: "The writers and studios shocked everyone by reaching an agreement in a mere two weeks, which was six weeks prior to the existing MBA's expiration date."[74] One reason for this was that there was little appetite on either side to rehearse the damage caused to the industry by the previous dispute. During the strike, on December 19, 2007, a hearing called by the housing, community, and economic development committee of Los Angeles City Council heard evidence that the strike had already cost the region upward of $220 million in discretionary spending, as well as ten thousand jobs. Littleton records that WGA members had lost approximately $120 million in wages by mid-December, and other crafts and unions, including the Teamsters, had also suffered. Assuming those figures were accurate, the totals by the end of the strike would have been much higher.[75] In 2011 the new WGA West leadership, under its president, John Wells, was certainly influenced by the expressed determination of the membership to avoid another strike and by the deals already reached between the AMPTP and both SAG and the DGA.

The priorities had shifted to some extent to repairing the damage done by the financial crisis of 2008 to members' pensions and health benefits. Nevertheless, the WGA also argued that in many cases the employers had not abided by the provisions of the 2007–8 contract in paying writers the new-media residuals that had been agreed on. Dustin Lance Black, the screenwriter of *Milk* (2008), spoke for many WGA members in 2011 when he said, "We have to keep a very close eye on residuals because what we're getting residuals from is changing so rapidly now. Who wants residuals from DVDs anymore?"[76] The mistrust between the parties was still in evidence, and the WGA felt the need to engage, once again, in limited positional bargaining to establish its strength at the start of the process, as much for the benefit of its own membership as to impress the AMPTP.

In the 2011 MBA writers obtained an increase in pension contributions and a modest increase in pay television residuals, historically set at a lower rate than for network rebroadcast. They failed to get an increase in basic cable residuals, however. In return, they agreed to a three-year freeze in prime-time residuals, a major and controversial concession for many guild members. Despite the gains, many writers thought the agreement simply rubber-stamped the AMPTP's position. They expected more from a negotiation undertaken during an improving economy and at a time when, as Nikki Finke wrote in *Deadline Hollywood*, "nearly all writers are wringing their hands and hanging by their fingernails to maintain their livelihoods under the studio and network cutbacks."[77]

By 2014, the MBA negotiation was picking away at details, including a 0.5 percent increase in pension-fund contributions, raising residuals for ad-supported streaming, increasing script minimums for one-hour basic cable by 5 percent, doubling the fee for theatrical script publication, and generally avoiding rollbacks. Perhaps most significant, in terms of the legacy of unresolved issues from the 2008 agreement, the window for free streaming was reduced from seventeen days to seven days for the first seven episodes of a television series.[78] The guild ratified its new contract a day before the deadline. Nonetheless, *Deadline Hollywood* headlined the very low percentage of participation in the ratification ballot: "Of the 8,218 eligible WGA voters, only 1,193 valid votes were cast. That's just 14%. Of those actually voting, there were 1,175 'Yes' votes and 18 'No' votes, according to the union. Last time round in 2011, 1,952 votes were cast with 90.7% voting in favor of the agreement."[79] This compares to a vote total of 3,492 in favor of ending the 2008 strike (and 283 against). Higher participation in guild ballots during industrial disputes is hardly surprising, but the 2014 figures do suggest that guild members viewed their major battles as variously won and lost, for the short term at least.

CONCLUSION

If, to use Obst's eloquent catchphrases, the Great Contraction led—among other factors—to the New Abnormal in Hollywood, then, despite the gains won by the WGA, the writers' strike of 2007–8 was "The Catastrophe" that accelerated that trajectory. The strike simultaneously secured for established screenwriters a slice of the emerging digital pie and yet facilitated the breakdown of old business relationships and helped ensure that, in the short term at least, fewer screenwriters would be working on studio movies. Meanwhile, beleaguered drama writers who had little hope of regular studio employment in the tentpole era learned another of the unexpected lessons of the strike that also spoke to a much broader transformation of the media sphere: "As movies had been getting dumber, television had been getting smarter. As movies constricted their parameters, television's parameters were growing exponentially. HBO and cable had helped push what was possible, and longtime TV writers picked up the mantle and ran into brilliant uncharted territory. Feature writers felt the creative action happening in TV, and an exodus began. There was a blooming, booming business in this business—a way out of Egypt into a tempting, changing new land."[80]

Movie screenwriters who did continue to work beneath the tentpoles often did so under more restrictive terms of employment. There were now more opportunities for new—for which read *cheaper*—writers to grasp some of the increasingly scarce studio assignments; however, their chances of being kept on the projects they wrote for were far less than in previous decades. As we will see, the hierarchy among Hollywood screenwriters was further polarized after the strike by fear-driven business practices from budget-strapped studio development departments whose fear and frugality are both direct manifestations of the tentpole development paradigm.

To use a cinematic illustration, with an eye on both the subtler and the more brutal aftereffects of the writers' strike, we will now pull our shot back from its close-up on the front lines of industrial conflict to encompass a panoramic view of the current state of screenwriting and script development in Hollywood studios. Our master shot will track alongside the development of the conglomerate studios since the 1980s, capturing their move to a tentpole model of development and production and revealing how the transformation of the corporate and business models of the Hollywood industry has impacted both the creative practice and working conditions of the professional screenwriters who pitch to and write for the studios. In so doing, we are reminded of a line delivered by the studio boss Jack Lipnick to the aspiring screenwriter Barton Fink in the Coen brothers' film that sums up both the creative expectations placed on the writer and the ease by which the terms of his deal might be changed:

> LIPNICK
> We're only interested in one thing, Bart. Can you tell a story? Can you make us laugh? Can you make us cry? Can you make us want to break out in joyous song? Is that more than one thing? Okay!

2. Atop the Tentpole
Hollywood Screenwriting Today

> Screenwriting is the most prized of all the cinematic arts. Actually, it isn't, but it should be.
>
> HUGH LAURIE

> A tent-pole or tentpole is a program or movie that supports the financial performance of a movie studio or television network. A tent-pole movie may be expected to support the sale of tie-in merchandise.
>
> Wikipedia

In another Hollywood metanarrative, *Barton Fink* (1991), scripted and directed by Joel and Ethan Coen, left-wing playwright Barton Fink is hired out of New York to write a wrestling screenplay for a major studio in 1940s Hollywood. This is not the kind of art he was used to writing in the Big Apple, but for Fink, something of an analogue to the actual 1940s playwrights-turned-screenwriters Clifford Odets and George S. Kaufman, it is paid work, and he needs the money. Inevitably, in the process of attempting to write this genre piece, poor Fink "discovers the hellish truth of Hollywood."[1] Screenwriting is not a prized cinematic art.

A kind of horror-noir-Künstlerroman hybrid, *Barton Fink*'s exposition offers some biographical connectivity to the careers of its East Coast storytellers, New York University film school graduate Joel Coen and Princeton University philosophy graduate Ethan Coen, who made their own way out west to Hollywood. The Coen brothers, responsible for such films as *Fargo* (1996), *The Big Lebowski* (1998), and *No Country for Old Men* (2007), among many others, not only produce and direct but also write their own films. Yet unlike Fink, they have earned themselves a very particular niche on the edges of conglomerate Hollywood. In current parlance we would call them "Indiewood" filmmakers, notable beneficiaries of the 1990s expansion of the major studios into the arena of independent production and distribution.

In quintessential Hollywood fashion Fink's dramatic story is about how he is buffaloed by writer's block and how he tries to overcome it. All the while, studio executives work to transform his uniqueness as a writer—his

"Barton Fink feeling," in the film's terms—into B-movie filament. In developing this theme, the Coen brothers are apparently reflecting on the writer's block they experienced crafting *Miller's Crossing* (1990). Yet they are also reflecting on the culture of the American movie industry—on its penchant for self-reflexivity, for telling stories about its storytelling apparatus, and for laying the blame for all that is wrong with Hollywood at the feet of studio bosses. In this way *Barton Fink* is a story about the Hollywood we think we know. It also has much to say about the status of the writer within that corporate world about which we should know.

The Coen brothers spare no feelings. Fink, having moved to Los Angeles, meets up with his studio executive, Jack Lipnick (Michael Lerner) of Capitol Pictures. The writer's place in the corporate order of things is presented in prescient dialogue:

> LIPNICK
>
> The writer is king here at Capitol Pictures. You don't believe me, take a look at your paycheck at the end of every week — that's what we think of the writer.

One cannot help but see the reference to Marxist intellectualism behind the Coens' choice to name the studio "*Capitol* Pictures," an obvious homonym for *capital* and an institution where a worker's salary defines and circumscribes his or her human value. Perhaps equally straightforward is the sarcastic cliché "the writer is king," which is still very much with us in popular lore but much less so in praxis.

In offering an industrial metanarrative, the Coen brothers are being "very Hollywood." Their story articulates myths that cinephiles hold in common about the classical studio era. Yet at the same time, as we have suggested, their story is revelatory. It is, after all, a period piece that—like most good period pieces—speaks most eloquently to the moment of its creation. In *Barton Fink* the Coens speak to the increasingly formulaic films that are sucking most of the creative air from Hollywood story development. Their script hits it on the nose in this exchange between Fink and his studio-hired muse, Audrey (Judy Davis), a wise old pro:

> BARTON
>
> Well I have to come up with — an outline, I'd guess you call it. The story. The whole goddamn story. Soup to nuts. Three acts. The whole goddamn-
>
> AUDREY
>
> It's alright, Barton. You don't have to write actual scenes?

A few lines later, Audrey goes on to explain to the playwright how Hollywood genre stories actually work, beginning with the soup:

> AUDREY
>
> Well, usually, they're . . . simply morality tales. There's a good wrestler, and a bad wrestler whom he confronts at the end. In between, the good wrestler has a love interest or a child he has to protect. Bill would usually make the good wrestler a backwoods type, or a convict. And sometimes, instead of a wife, he'd have the wrestler protecting an idiot manchild. The studio always hated that. Oh, some of the scripts were so . . . spirited!

And then the nuts:

> AUDREY
>
> Look, it's really just a formula. You don't have to type your soul into it. We'll invent some names and a new setting. I'll help you and it won't take any time at all. I did it for Bill so many times —
>
> Barton's pacing comes up short.
>
> BARTON
>
> Did what for Bill?
>
> Guardedly:
>
> AUDREY
>
> Well . . . THIS.
>
> BARTON
>
> You wrote his scripts for him?

Like the Coens' Fink, today's working screenwriter is asked to rework established, and profitable, story formulas to boost the performance of the conglomerate as well as the industrial cachet of studio executives. As Robert Iger, chairman and chief executive officer of the Walt Disney Company, advises: "One way to rise above the din and the competition is with a big film—not just big-budget but big story, big cast, big marketing behind it."[2] Yet today the B-movie formulas with which Fink is struggling to earn his crust in the fictional 1940s are the antecedents of the A-movie formulas that completely dominate the production slates of conglomerate studios like Disney. Once again, the screenwriter Sam Hamm, is right: in Hollywood, genre has won. Hollywood studios used to call these big films *blockbusters;* now they call them *tentpole movies.* As the uncredited writers of the *Wikipedia* entry that leads off this chapter define it, a tentpole movie is designed to be big enough in terms of its potential profitability that it "supports the financial performance of a movie studio or television network."

In this chapter we begin by exploring the current tentpole paradigm of studio production in some detail in order to establish proper context for our exploration of TV, independent, animation, video games, microbudget, and online writing in the chapters that follow. To get there, we ask three linked questions about the recent development of the Hollywood screenwriting craft. First, how do changes to the craft and style of screenplay writing reflect the longer-term adaptation of Hollywood's movie development process toward the tentpole paradigm? Second, how has the acceleration of technological transformation, notably into digital special effects (and thus the manic aesthetics identified in chapter 1), also impacted the writing style that successful tentpole screenwriters employ in their work? Third, and perhaps most important, how has the tentpole paradigm affected the working lives of Hollywood screenwriters?

In addressing these questions, we show that, for screenwriters who work for the tentpole-driven studios, the pressure to pitch projects and produce specs that fit easily within today's contracted and meager definition of Hollywood cinema has never been higher. The conglomerate studios simply understand moviemaking at budgetary levels that make them more risk-averse and less likely to speculate on unproven intellectual properties with relatively low shareholder value. Indeed, studios no longer produce large slates of pictures in the way they did in the 1940s and 1950s. As a consequence, every green-light decision represents a much larger proportional investment of the institution's economic viability from year to year than in previous eras. To make this case, we continue the industry studies approach undertaken in chapter 1 and support it by close readings of recent scripts to reveal the intersection of manic form and manic content that exemplifies the "new spec format" of tentpole screenplay writing.

THE BASE

Hollywood movie production is dominated by six major studios: Warner Bros., Sony Pictures Entertainment, Walt Disney Pictures, 20th Century Fox, Paramount Pictures, and Universal Pictures. There is also a small and fluctuating group of what are referred to loosely as "mini-major" studios, the largest of which is currently Lionsgate, a subsidiary of Lions Gate Entertainment. But the six majors generate approximately 80 percent of the domestic box office every year, despite releasing relatively few movies. In 2014 this revenue pool was derived from only 136 studio pictures, a slight year-by-year increase, according to the Motion Picture Association of America's own statistics.[3] Representing the six major studios listed above, the MPAA ensures the dominance of its members—members that control, either directly or through their market power, most of the domestic and international distribution and exhibition networks.

But despite their dominance of the market and the diligence of the MPAA's lobbyists and negotiators, the studios are no longer the powerful independent entities they once were. Gone are the days of the "independent" studio bosses, the Jack Lipnicks of the world. Starting in the 1980s, successive waves of mergers and acquisitions have transformed the studios into relatively minor divisions within much larger conglomerate structures. The majors still wield power within the movie industry itself, but they are increasingly beholden to these larger corporate and thus shareholder interests. For the screenwriters who work—or who aspire to work—for them, the pressure to generate significant and consistent profit for their parent institutions now largely circumscribes the kind of movies they hire screenwriters to write. In short, to the conglomerates, small projects—and their small profit margins—no longer add up.

The current corporate status of the majors is the result of three extended periods of acquisitions and mergers spread over the last forty years, with some studios being bought and resold more than once during each of these rounds. The primary motivation behind most, if not all, of these acquisitions was to achieve economic *synergies* among the products and services produced by divisions of the same conglomerate, to perfect a post-Fordist iteration of the vertical integration of production, distribution, and exhibition that once defined the classical studio system. In corporate terms synergy is seen as an opportunity to increase profitability through a kind of intrainstitutional cross-pollination. In this way synergies are understood to exist between digital hardware and associated software, between production and distribution, from connectivity to exhibition, through the exploitation of products across divisions of the same corporation (movies, television, music, etc.), and through the development and exploitation of ancillary markets (video games, toys, theme parks, etc.).

Throughout this extended process of corporate reorganization, the late capitalist grail of synergy has been variously defined and prioritized, as the lessons of previous rounds of conglomeration were learned, ignored, or forgotten. For example, many of the first-round mergers in the 1980s involved foreign investors buying into Hollywood as News Corporation,

Sony, and Matsushita sought product to broadcast or software to generate and secure sales for the home video equipment (VCRs) they manufactured.[4] A number of the second round of mergers in the 1990s were motivated by the desire to link movie product with cable distribution. For example, Viacom merged with Paramount Communications in 1993. After the Federal Communications Commission (FCC) rescinded the Financial Interest and Syndication Rules (fin-syn) in 1993, television networks also became merger targets for similar synergistic reasons. Walt Disney, for example, bought Capital Cities/ABC and Viacom bought CBS in 1999.

The third round of mergers began in the following decade and often linked the Internet with established media in different combinations. The most famous deal was the disastrous, at least from a shareholder perspective, AOL–Time Warner merger, but Comcast also bought Universal in 2011. In many cases the assumption that the hoped-for synergies would generate significant long-term profit proved to be more fiction than documentary.

Since the 1980s, the prosperity of the majors was ensured as much by the exploitation of its product in new distribution markets, specifically home video and DVD sales, as by first-run cinema exhibition. The toy, video game, and theme park markets also emerged as significant revenue streams, perhaps best symbolized by superhero, young adult, and science fiction franchises and, with respect to theme parks, by Universal and especially Disney. With the music industry as a possible exception, the larger entertainment industry was able to adapt to new technologies throughout the 1990s. The VHS format gave way to DVDs and then Blu-ray. These formats are now giving way, in their turn, to streaming and on-demand distribution. SVOD services like Netflix are now becoming players in a newly and hugely expanded television industry, investing in producing original content (e.g., *House of Cards*), as is Amazon.com through Amazon Studios (e.g., *The Man in the High Castle*). The proliferation of cable channels and streaming services like Netflix and Amazon also provide additional revenue streams for studios to exploit for both new programming and to maximize the profit potential of their intellectual property vaults.

The DVD market has shrunk significantly along with cinema ticket sales, and as the strike of 2007–8 illustrated, the monetization of new digital distribution channels has not yet risen to match the lost revenues. The industry took a further hit from the great recession of 2008, from which it, like the broader US economy, took time to recover. Moreover, the broader economic conditions put more pressure on the studios to generate profits for their struggling corporate parents, and this, in turn, cemented a kind of creative paralysis into Hollywood movie development. As film scholar Tino Balio notes, "Such pressures are combined with substantial anxieties about new technologies, piracy and the erosion of theatrical ticket sales. All of this has engendered significant changes in industry strategy, practice and output. Today the studios focus almost exclusively on tentpoles and franchises, leaving lower-budget productions to their partners and independents."[5] The majors are now making ever fewer films, in fewer genres, and employing fewer creative professionals to do so. In 2013, for example, the MPAA member studios released a total of 114 movies.[6] This represented an 11 percent drop on the previous year and a whopping 36 percent decline since 2004. This contraction means there are far fewer opportunities for big-screen screenwriters in Hollywood than in previous decades. David Steinberg, one of four writers credited with *American Pie 2* (2001), lamented the state of the market in 2010: "If I was going to break into the business now, I don't know if I could do it because there are so few opportunities to sell a script or get an assignment."[7] Moreover, those who do still get work with the studios often find the terms of their employment less advantageous and their freedom to exercise and develop their craft ever more restricted. We discuss this in greater detail later.

The contemporary tentpole represents the latest stage in a longer process of reorienting the studios toward a new notion of the mainstream in genre production. Before the 1980s, science fiction and action films, and particularly the crime and western films most popular in the 1950s and 1960s, were largely considered B movies, receiving lower production and publicity budgets. They were and often still are also considered less "artistic" despite the fact that many B movies of the era have become classics. Yet the new blockbuster and now tentpole films are the direct descendants of the B movie science fiction and action movies of previous generations. These genres now dominate domestic and international markets.

The success of Steven Spielberg's *Jaws* (1975), script by Peter Benchley and Carl Gottlieb, and of George Lucas's *Star Wars* (1977), scripted by Lucas, prompted the studios to redefine the potential value of once-marginal genres like science fiction in an attempt to replicate the success of what were thought, before they broke, to be unlikely blockbusters. The success of the toy and video game market for these two films, but particularly *Star Wars*, also raised corporate eyebrows and later peaked conglomerate interest. As *Forbes* noted in 2007: "Sales of games and toys have made up the bulk of *Star Wars* revenue over the last three decades. Of its total revenue, only $6.68 billion has been generated at the box office. The largest chunk, more than $9 billion, has been shared by toy companies like Kenner and Hasbro, who feed the *Star Wars* fan base with action figures and other toys. And according to analysts at NPD Fungroup, $1.6 billion has come from videogames developed by LucasArts, the gaming branch of Lucasfilm."[8] In many ways Lucas's *Star Wars* and its universe of sequels and spin-offs set the stage for conglomeration as studios and parent companies tracked its galactic reach across ancillary markets in all territories.

Disney's 2012 purchase of Lucasfilm ensures that the *Star Wars* megafranchise will be exploited in an effort to meet the profit needs of a conglomerate well into the future. The lessons learned from the development of Marvel's megafranchise of superhero films are already being applied more broadly to Lucasfilm's own siloed intellectual property. Different iterations of the *Star Wars* universe are currently playing across several animated TV shows, and the story world on which it draws has just begun to spawn its own second franchise of individual spin-off tentpole movies with plotting adjacent to the core franchise story line but with new characters, starting with *Rogue One: A Star Wars Story*, story by John Knoll and Gary Whitta and screenplay by Chris Weitz and Tony Gilroy.

Successful theatrical exhibition is typically understood to be a function of producing genre movies that will appeal to four-quadrant audiences at present and into the future. Failing that, the core audience at which Hollywood product is still targeted has been the boys and young men who are assumed to be the core of genre fandom and thus the prime consumers of synergized spin-off product like toys and video games. The video games industry's official statistics for 2015 show, however, that the average age of gamers is currently thirty-five and that at least 44 percent of video game players are female.[9] This targeting of young male audiences also flies in the face of Hollywood's own statistics that show, since 2009, that the majority of moviegoers have been women. In 2013 female moviegoers, many of whom are, of course, also genre fans, also slightly "outperformed" their demographic percentage (51 percent) in terms of their movie attendance. The success of *The Hunger Games: Catching Fire* (2013), script by Simon Beaufoy and Michael Arndt, which came in second place at the domestic box office in 2013, also suggests that female audiences for the domestic run (59 percent) can sustain box office for tentpole movies with female leads and more "female-driven" genre stories. The first of the two-part series conclusion, *The Hunger Games: Mockingjay, Part 1* (2014), script by Peter Craig and Danny Strong, made around $242 million domestically and $271 million internationally by mid-2014. The domestic audience demographics skewed even more strongly female (60 percent).[10]

Women also helped drive the four-quadrant animated movie *Despicable Me 2* (2013), script by Cinco Paul and Ken Daurio, by 53 percent to third place in domestic box office that year. And they drove *Monsters University* (2013), which has six writers credited, by 52 percent to fifth place. There is some evidence that it is the mothers that make up a portion of these audiences who are buying up the toys that are spun off from the films—and DVDs—for their children of the new millennium. These audience figures notwithstanding, contemporary spectacular incarnations of the old B-movie genres are deemed to be the most likely to attract the young male audience members the studios still cultivate today. In short, the young male quadrant (and the parents who buy for that market) is still, in the conglomerate commonsense calculus, always already much larger than the others.

What makes Lynda Obst's New Abnormal distinct from the previous blockbuster model is that now the studios are making little else. The old balance between the production of big-budget genre movies and lower-budget dramas, more appealing to older audiences, has finally been broken. The metaphor of the tentpole was first used to suggest that the success of a few big-budget movies would hold up the "tent" of economic security to allow the studios to make a wider range of cheaper but less "global," less easily synergized, and less directly commercial product. In practice studio development has moved almost entirely toward the tentpole and away from mid-budget moviemaking. Why take those risks, the logic goes, when the exhibition market seems to require only spectacular tentpole blockbusters to drive up the parent corporation's earnings? In manic fashion Hollywood puts up a lot of tentpoles, but it isn't interested in hanging the canvas to cover the cost of producing a greater diversity of films.

Writing in *Screen International* in 2011, the film critic John Hazelton noted that "the studios' focus on branded, globally appealing tentpole films has arguably elevated the status of stars and directors while it has marginalized screenwriters more used to scripting adult-oriented thrillers and dramas."[11] As a partial consequence of this shift, many of the leading drama screenwriters have sought work in expanded television on shows like HBO's *The Wire* (2002–8), FX's *The Shield* (2002–8), Netflix's *House of Cards* (2013–), and Amazon Studios' *Goliath* (2016). "It's no coincidence," film critic Patrick Goldstein wrote in the *Los Angeles Times* back in 2001, "that most of the writers who've migrated to TV specialize in adult-oriented dramas, a genre nearly extinct in Hollywood except for a handful of star-driven vehicles released during Oscar season. Most studios have little room for personal stories or ambiguous characters.... Much of the difference is physical: The big screen lends itself to spectacle; the small screen is better

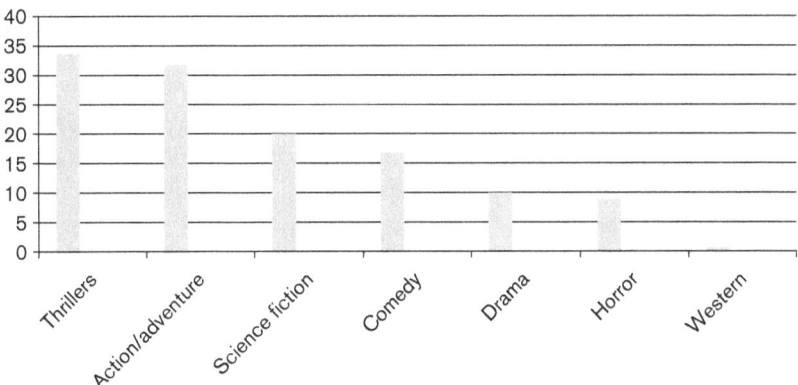

FIGURE 1. Spec screenplay sales in 2013 by genre. Statistics from *The Scoggins Report*.

suited to intimate drama."[12] The irony for screenwriters, of course, is that in the previous era the move in the search for artistic credibility and relative creative freedom was always away from television and toward the movies.

According to the industry script sales tracker *The Scoggins Report*, 124 agented spec screenplays were bought (but not necessarily produced) in the Hollywood market in 2013, down 6 percent on the previous year.[13] Of these, thirty-four were classified as thrillers, thirty-two as action/adventure, twenty as science fiction, seventeen as comedy, ten as drama, nine as horror, and one a western. Tracking these numbers since 2009, there has been a steady increase in action/adventure and thriller purchases, a drop in comedy, and the other genres have bumped along at broadly consistent levels (see fig. 1).

Tentpole movies are major investments, and the temptation to mitigate risk by capitalizing as many times as possible on already-established brands that bring an extant audience with them is significant. The list of studio pictures released in 2015 gives a clear snapshot of the current status of sequels, adaptations, and remakes in Hollywood development. The following franchises were continued, relaunched, remade, or initiated: *The Avengers, Star Wars, The Terminator, Fast and Furious, Jurassic Park, The Fantastic Four, Mad Max, The Man from U.N.C.L.E., Poltergeist,* and *Minions* (a spin-off from the *Despicable Me* animated films). All share these common tentpole characteristics: they have recognized brands with proven and thus (the studio wagers) relatively predictable records; they feed multiple ancillary markets that need to remain in the popular consciousness if the parent company is to maintain high margins; they are action-driven films, mostly science fiction with a mix of horror and animation.

Equally important, most of these films were written by multiple writers, in discrete moments of development rather than in collaboration. Indeed, the tendency to use more than one writer—or many additional writers—in the development of tentpole movies speaks eloquently to the prevalent corporate neurosis over the scale of investment involved in each green-light decision. This pervasive atmosphere of insecurity manifests in specific business strategies that both maintain and manipulate a "class system" or hierarchy among Hollywood screenwriters.

The trend toward multipart productions is also a consequence of economic rather than creative decision-making. For the major studios that invest heavily in adapted franchises and have come to rely on them to prop up their profit margins, the problem is that eventually they run out of source material. The decisions to split the final *Harry Potter*, *Twilight*, and *Hunger Games* franchise "conclusions" into two parts, for example, certainly increased the profit potential of each series. Arguably, the storytelling in the *Harry Potter* (2010 and 2011) movies benefited from the split in a way that *The Hunger Games: Mockingjay* (2014 and 2015) and *Twilight: Breaking Dawn* (2011 and 2012) did not. The *Hollywood Reporter*'s review of *The Hunger Games: Mockingjay, Part 1* did not mince words and summed up the popular critical response to the profit-driven division of the final novel into two movies effectively: "Unfortunately, *Mockingjay—Part 1* has all the personality of an industrial film. There's not a drop of insolence, insubordination or insurrection running through its veins; it feels like a manufactured product through and through, ironic and sad given its revolutionary theme."[14]

Distributors deploy the kinds of attractions that have been intrinsic to the appeal of cinema since its invention yet were often sidelined in critical discourse during the long preeminence of drama in cinema history.[15] These attractions are designed to pull large audiences to a movie's opening weeks through spectacle, not to develop such audiences through limited release and word of mouth. In 2011 Walt Disney Animation Studios chief technical officer Andy Hendrickson spoke bluntly at SIGGRAPH (Special Interest Group on Graphics and Interactive Techniques) about the economic and creative priorities of the studio tentpole production model: "People say 'It's all about the story,'" he said. "When you're making tentpole films, bullshit." Hendrickson went on to show a chart of the top twelve all-time domestic grossers and noted that every one is a spectacle film. Of his own studio's *Alice in Wonderland* (2010), script by Linda Woolverton, he said:

"The story isn't very good, but visual spectacle brought people in droves. And Johnny Depp didn't hurt." These same principles did not apply to *The Lone Ranger*, as we will see, but the paradigm nonetheless remains a central tenet of conglomerate Hollywood ideology, or common sense in its Gramscian definition.

THE SUPERSTRUCTURE

Not all tentpole films perform equally, including those built on decades of cultural memories with built-in cross-platform and ancillary market capability. In August of 2013, Jay Rasulo, the chief financial officer of Walt Disney Studios, reported to shareholders that the studio expected to lose between $160 million and $190 million on the new *Lone Ranger* (2013), featuring Johnny Depp as Tonto, Jerry Bruckheimer as producer, Gore Verbinski as director and no fewer than six (credited) screenwriters. Disney was reminded that establishing new franchises from old story worlds was not a sure thing. The year before, the studio also lost a small fortune on its $250 million tentpole gamble *John Carter* (2012). That movie has fewer writers earning credit, but even the novelist Michael Chabon's rewrites (*Wonder Boys*, novel) couldn't rescue director John Stanton's script. Their efforts were also undermined by a woefully misdirected marketing campaign that "got rid of the most commercial element of the project by trimming the title *John Carter of Mars*."[16]

The studios—or perhaps their parent companies—are still committed to the tentpole strategy despite the astronomical cost of big movie failures like *John Carter*. The reason for this is also rather straightforward: despite a culture of fear prevalent at lower levels of the studio development hierarchy, the wins still generate far too great a revenue upswing across markets to warrant too much fear of the risks associated with "failures." Disney's profits from its theme parks, ESPN, animated films, and Marvel partnerships are sufficient for the conglomerate despite multimillion-dollar losses on a few films. As the *Wall Street Journal* reported in 2013: "Parks and resorts revenue increased 7% to $3.7 billion as Disney reaped the rewards of investments such as the new Cars Land attraction at the Disney California Adventure resort and an expansion of the Magic Kingdom at Walt Disney World in Florida. Operating income rose 9% to $689 million."[17]

The one recent and somewhat accidental excursion from the tentpole paradigm has been the relatively successful release slate of Universal Pictures in 2014, when, as Universal CFO Michael Angelakis aptly predicted at the time, "We will have the most profitable year in the . . . history of Universal."[18] The studio's slate of movies that year included *Lucy, A Walk among the Tombstones, A Million Ways to Die in the West,* and *Ride Along.* All were lower-budget offerings, under $70 million, from diverse genres, including science fiction, western, and comedy. Despite the likelihood that Universal would have preferred to have been able to put out more franchise movies, the overall financial success of its accidentally modest 2014 slate points to the viability of alternative strategies to the tentpole but not to the actual demise of the strategy year-to-year. The reason, once again, is the conglomerate commitment to synergy. Nonfranchised movies, however successful they might be at the box office, do not produce the kind of product tie-in or theme park revenues we see from the contemporary tentpole paradigm.

Tracking the recent history of Disney, Universal, or almost any Hollywood studio shows how a manic industry affects the economic status, the creative freedom, and the day-to-day working conditions of its workforce, despite the occasional "big" loss or an accidental slate of lower-budget films. Owing to a combination of the history of its source medium, the nature of the international marketplace, and the expansion of its core fan base, the most powerful tentpole genre is currently the superhero fantasy. The model for the successful deployment of this kind of megafranchise is the Disney subsidiary Marvel Studios, and—unlike its comics rival DC—it has achieved its dominance in the genre in large part through the strict control of story.

As both a prop for and a testament to the perceived strength of the market for core tentpole genres like the superhero movie, Marvel is locking scripts into production pipelines many years ahead. This is a strategic attempt to control story and characters across its microfranchises and, in so doing, to game the circuit of culture. As the writers John August and Craig Mazin note in their influential *Scriptnotes* screenwriting podcast, the exploitation of superhero properties from Marvel and (until recently to a much lesser extent) DC, and the complex, arcing narratives that link many of them, are planned out a decade ahead. In their November 4, 2014, episode, August and Mazin track the cross-studio and cross-franchise slate of superhero tentpoles as far ahead as 2020.[19] This long-term control of story development not only locks in potential security for the studio in terms of profitability and synergy but also speaks to the kind of collaborative work screenwriters in that genre are expected to embrace.

Transcending the potential of the limited cycles, such as Warner Bros.' *Harry Potter* movies and Lionsgate's *The Hunger Games,* the Marvel Comics Universe (MCU) is the perfect tentpole property for the economics of the conglomerate studios because it is potentially inexhaustible, as long as the global box office returns support the budgetary outlay.[20] The unique flexibility of the MCU is built principally around the fact that it is Marvel's superhero characters that define the franchise, not just specific canonical stories. As a consequence, Marvel's many superheroes are endlessly (re) deployable. That is at least in part a direct legacy of the publishing history of American superhero comic books, in which characters have been rebooted for new generations of readers, have had their origin stories retold multiple times, and have even been recast across race and gender. Comic book fans accepted this potential for intracanonical recreation a long time ago, and general audiences have evidently taken their cue from the acquiescence of fan culture and learned not to care.

Although in harder times the main source of profitability for Marvel Comics came from licensing its superhero franchises for movies, in recent years Marvel Studios has worked hard to bring its licensed properties back in-house. The studio has strategized its slate into the future based on its ability to braid microfranchise story strands into the developed master narrative of the MCU. Indeed, through 2015 and 2016 Disney moved to consolidate story control at Marvel even more firmly into the hands of Marvel's president, Kevin Feige.

Until recently, control of story at the studio was divided between Feige and Marvel's "Creative Committee," consisting of Alan Fine (president of Marvel Entertainment), comics writer Brian Michael Bendis *(Secret War; Age of Ultron)*, Marvel Comics publisher Dan Buckley, and Joe Quesada (Marvel chief creative officer). The Creative Committee's primary purpose was to keep the MCU coherent and true to the original comics, an important part of the studio's overall strategy of franchise control. Increasingly, however, the committee moved beyond its primary brief as the "lorekeeper" and involved itself more and more with the granular discourses of movie development, offering its own notes and directives to screenwriters on story structure and character arcs. Importantly, the members of the committee came principally from the comic book publishing arm of Marvel, and their script notes were sometimes criticized and resented by cinema professionals for a lack of fluency with the craft of movie screenwriting. In addition, the group was often criticized for being slow in its turnaround time with notes on scripts, and for creating soulless, commercialized products, cleaved too closely to the formulas of paraindustrial screenwriting manuals, as media commentator Devin Faraci notes: "Over the years I've heard many stories of the Creative Committee giving notes that are pedestrian, motivated by 'save the cat' story logic and sometimes a drag on creativity. One Marvel creative talked ... about battles with the Creative

Committee where they focused on details of nit-picky science that ignored the general tone of the script itself."[21]

For genre screenwriters another knock to the reputation of story development under the Creative Committee at Marvel Studios was that it removed much of the overall creative license from its screenwriters. Of course, this is also a charge sometimes laid at the door of Kevin Feige, who is typically credited with being the most important creative mind behind keeping the MCU cohesive. In addition, Marvel is famous for paying its entire filmmaking talent relatively low wages, even when they are signed to multipicture deals. (The extreme example is Samuel L. Jackson, who signed a nine-picture deal to play Nick Fury across future MCU pictures in 2009.) In response, Marvel's contention, often expressed, is that the true stars of the Marvel movies are its superhero characters, not the actors, writers, and directors who bring those characters to life.[22] Under this logic, and no matter their popularity and talent, the actors, writers, and directors employed by Marvel do not drive their franchises (one need only think back to the number of actors that have played Spiderman in the last ten years). All of this has caused resentment among screenwriters, often expressed more publicly by their agents and managers. Many reports link the replacement of Edgar Wright *(Shaun of the Dead; Hot Fuzz)* as writer and director on *Ant Man* in 2014 with his dissatisfaction over script changes mandated by the Creative Committee. "They don't want you to speak up too much or have too much vision," IGN.com reported in 2014.[23]

Following the fallout from Wright's departure from *Ant Man*, the committee was disbanded. The date commonly reported was September 2, 2015, though as of this writing there are conflicting reports about whether the committee has been dissolved entirely or if it will now focus on Marvel's television properties *(Marvel's Agents of S.H.I.E.L.D.; Marvel's Daredevil; Luke Cage;* etc.) and have minimal input into the films.[24] However the future of the committee plays out, the immediate result has been to centralize the control of Marvel's story development even more firmly in the hands of Kevin Feige. In a linked move, Feige now reports directly to Alan Horn, of Disney Studios, though previously he answered to the eccentric Isaac "Ike" Perlmutter, of Marvel, with whom he is known to have had a fractious relationship.[25]

In comparison, until recently story control in the competitor DC Comics Universe (DCCU), located at Warner Bros., has been placed more directly in the hands of talent. But the notion that DC is "talent driven" should not be interpreted to imply true artistic independence from the usual strictures of Hollywood studio development. Nevertheless, the writers and directors of recent and current iterations of DCCU franchises, such as Christopher

Nolan (*Batman Begins*, etc.), have reportedly been given more latitude to develop story within the general boundaries of character and canon. Unlike the Marvel tentpole model, the DC story universe has not operated as coherently across its cinematic microfranchises. For example, iterations of the same character franchises also operate simultaneously in different media. Thus the Batman franchise offers a teenage Bruce Wayne within the TV series *Gotham*, while a middle-aged Batman is featured in *Batman vs. Superman*. The Batman franchise story world is also explored in *Suicide Squad* and in the forthcoming *Justice League* (DC's "*Avengers*") movie. Different actors play all. There is a kind of market logic at play, of course, as these films are early evidence of DC attempting to combine franchises and link characters across story lines.

Within the cross-media expansions of the DC universe, microfranchises in different media with very distinct approaches to tone and audience also have to relate—such as *Teen Titans Go* on Cartoon Network and the Christopher Nolan *Batman* films. Therefore, another downside of this relative creative freedom has been a lack of tonal unity and conceptual focus within the DC brand, unlike with the generally lighter and funnier Marvel brand. Even though, as we noted above, DC is now attempting to bring more of its franchises together, its strategy is in an early phase and has yet to prove as creatively or financially successful as Marvel's. The much-publicized rewriting and reshooting of *Suicide Squad* to lighten the tone of the film is a notable manifestation of the corporate uncertainty surrounding the branding and development of the DC tentpole franchises in general.

After the removal of Zach Snyder from an oversight position, DC-Warner brought in Geoff Johns (chief creative officer of DC Comics) as the continuity lead to take on the strategic story development on its tentpole movie franchises. His appointment is a clear attempt to stop the rot of poorly received films like *Batman vs. Superman* and *Suicide Squad*. Warner Bros. and DC have also received a terrible reputation within the screenwriting community (and the world of superhero fandom more broadly) from their recent story development practices under Snyder and others. According to the *Hollywood Reporter*, producer Charles Roven initially asked screenwriter Kelly Marcel to write the script for *Wonder Woman* (2017), but she declined because of concerns about both the number of people involved with the project and her clash of vision for the film with that of then-director Michelle MacLaren (MacLaren has since been replaced by Patty Jenkins).[26] At one point, five different screenwriters were commissioned separately to write treatments (and, according to some reports, first acts) of the *Wonder Woman* screenplay, with the writers competing against each other for the final assignment. One anonymous source told the *Hollywood Reporter* that the process "felt like they were throwing shit against the wall to see what stuck."[27] Despite the involvement during earlier stages of development of Jason Fuchs, who won that first act sweepstakes pitching "bake off," and at least one other unnamed writer, the writing credits on *Wonder Woman* have since been awarded to Alan Heinberg and Geoff Johns, with an additional story credit for Zach Snyder. In 2017 *Wonder Woman* passed the first box office test for the Johns story regime at DC.

Sweepstakes pitching and parallel development of the kind seen in the development of both *Wonder Woman* and the forthcoming *Aquaman* (2018) are now increasingly common practices in Hollywood. These development strategies are not just confined to the superhero genre. Sony Pictures, for example, is reported to have commissioned three screenplays for its upcoming live-action *Barbie* movie (2017). *Deadline Hollywood* reports that the first draft was written by Jenny Bicks, but Diablo Cody took over writing duties in March 2015, and now Lindsey Beer is further developing Cody's work, while Bert Royal and Hilary Winston are both providing their own independent screenplay drafts.[28]

Despite the otherwise divergent practices of "story control" seen in a comparison of the DC and Marvel franchises, the megabudget tentpole paradigm exists in parallel with a significant contraction of development budgets at Hollywood studios. As we have tried to show, while studios are investing in costly franchise movies, they are feeling the economic pinch at a corporate and divisional level. As a partial consequence, there is less work for screenwriters, and more restrictions are being placed on the work of those screenwriters who do get assignments. Yet those who do are making increasingly higher salaries, and those who can doctor a script share in its creative production and return to the scene of studio production time and again to make a very good living from their often-uncredited writing.

ALIENATION

The economic downturn of 2008, the collapse of the DVD market, questions about the nature and viability of "long tail" revenue streams from digital, and an ongoing contraction of the domestic box office (at least in terms of numbers of tickets sold) have resulted in economic uncertainty in Hollywood.[29] The major studios are under increased pressure to generate profits, and they have cut the cloth of their tents accordingly, in terms both of the size and the content of their development and production slates and in otherwise cutting costs across the board.

For screenwriters this parsimonious approach from their employers has created its own economic anxieties and, as we have noted, has encouraged many writers to seek opportunities in cable television and other media. Film and media scholar Susan Christopherson notes that "for much of the workforce ... this period of industry expansion has been marked by heightened anxiety over their income expectations, and anger over a loss of creativity and pressure to produce too much too fast. Even in this historically high-risk industry, the recent period has been one in which the rewards of working in media entertainment are more elusive than ever."[30] Feature screenwriters have never been more alienated, to use the Marxist vernacular, working in the New Abnormal of the tentpole paradigm that circumscribes Hollywood production in the new millennium.

Changes to movie development prompted by these new conditions have also further polarized movie writers within the employment hierarchy. These changes have contributed to increasingly fewer screenwriters getting assignments from the studios and to an increase in the number of writers assigned to one script; they have also influenced the kinds of remuneration deals writers are being offered, as well as the shared or back-end revenue they can now expect to receive. Of course, there has always been a hierarchy of talent in Hollywood screenwriting. A-list writers, those who win major awards and can attract talent to their work, or who craft studio-friendly spec scripts, or who are considered safe pairs of hands for in-house assignments or rewrites, have always been paid more for their work and are often employed more consistently.

The box-office return of the movies they write is also an important factor in determining contractual status. But given the relative impotence of writers in terms of the corporate and creative decision-making that drives development as well as the cultural (and thus economic) assignment of low value to certain crafts in terms of movie authorship within Hollywood and in the public arena, it is less important than for stars and directors. William Goldman is not expected to "open" a movie, for example, whereas Steven Spielberg and Tom Cruise still are. Partly as a consequence of this lack of status, in today's Hollywood the studios act directly to manipulate the existing hierarchy among screenwriters to the point that it has become an issue of industrial relations for the Writers Guild of America as we saw in the previous chapter.

The proliferation of industry practices such as signing writers to one-step deals, pitting them against each other in sweepstakes pitching for studio assignments, and pressuring them to undertake free drafts and "prewrites" has certainly contributed to this atmosphere of anger and unease among screenwriters.[31] From the perspective of Hollywood screenwriters, these abuses of their labor became even more prevalent after the writers' strike of 2007–8, but one-step deals were already becoming commonplace before that dispute. The cumulative effect was to further marginalize screenwriters within the creative development process of studio production and, we argue, to undermine their ability to offer their best and most innovative work. To borrow Denby's term once more: one-step deals helped to lock in conglomerate aesthetics as the default style of Hollywood screenwriting.

One-step deals have changed the terms on which scripts are purchased or on which writers are brought in to work on projects in development. Dave McNary and Paul F. Duke outlined the change in *Variety* back in 2000: "Unlike the usual agreement for a guaranteed treatment, draft and two revisions, with the writer getting paid in increments at each step, the so-called one-step deals promise the writer only the first draft. Whether the script continues in the development process is entirely up to the studio."[32] For this reason the deal puts great pressure on the screenwriter to deliver a draft that is acceptable to the studio if she wants to continue working on the project. It also comes with the expectation that other writers will work on the script, thereby minimizing a unique voice and typically splitting above-the-line residuals. From the perspective of writers and their agents (who most often earn 10 percent of the total salary for each of their writer clients) these deals run counter to the creative process of collaborative experimentation that is often necessary for "breaking a story." *Variety* quotes an unnamed agent: "With the one-step deal, the writer's goal is purely to please the studio so that he can get paid for the next draft. Doing something fresh becomes much more frightening. It results in formulaic writing."[33]

Writers see one-step deals as a risk-averse corporate strategy to save money in the expectation of failure. In 2011 Jim Kouf, the first of six writers credited for *National Treasure* (2004), suggested that deals of this kind reveal the fear and job insecurity prevalent inside contracting studio development departments: "Most people have forgotten how to work with writers. A lot of the give and take that we used to see doesn't seem to be there anymore.... Everyone's afraid to spend money and nobody trusts writers to deliver so nobody wants to take a chance on anything more than a first step."[34] Scott Burns, the first of five writers credited with *The Bourne Ultimatum* (2007), echoed this sentiment in relation to the challenge of unpacking the notes studio executives give on screenplay drafts: "A lot of times you have to find the note behind the note.... You get notes from studios which are completely based on fear and you have to listen to those and not damage your movie in an attempt to make someone feel safer."[35]

For screenwriters navigating conglomerate Hollywood, understanding the immediate pressures on the individuals and departments with whom they are working—in short the psychology of executives—is even more vital as JC Chandor, who wrote and directed *Margin Call* (2011), explained to *Screen International:* "You have to go back and look at the power structures for the executives giving the notes. What are they hearing that day? They've got jobs that are pretty tenuous, so what's making them try to steer you towards something?"[36]

From the perspective of the studios, one-step deals and similar measures represent an attempt to get value for the increasingly meager development budgets they have to spend without blowing up above-the-line costs attributed to writers. Most development projects are never green-lit, so, as an unnamed development executive remarked to *Variety:* "Why should the studio pay for another draft when we can tell from the first draft that it's simply not going to work?" He continued with requisite disingenuous industrial spin: "Frankly, the less we spend on rewrites of bad scripts, the more we can spend on that little script that seems marginal but has a shot."[37] Producers Guild of America president Marshall Herskovitz attempted to provide additional perspective in 2010: "It's a reflection of the studios feeling like they aren't getting enough for what they paid for. The studios tend to view that money as wasted development rather than the price that they have to pay for getting the really amazing stories into production." He goes on to point to the moment: "There's so little development going on that I'd rather see someone at least get hired, even if it's only for one step, because the whole process forces writers to work on spec, which is what the studios want."[38]

At the same time that they are limiting many screenwriters to one-step deals, studios are also demanding what is considered, in terms of standard WGA contracts, unpaid work. There has always been some mutually accepted play at the edges of contracts, as former WGA West president Daniel Petrie Jr., the first writer credited on *Beverly Hills Cop* (1984), acknowledges: "When I joined the guild, there was an unspoken understanding among many writers that after a script went to the producer but before it went to the studio or network, we'd do a short courtesy pass as a favor to the producer—and as a favor to ourselves, since it was also understood that a writer didn't make any changes he or she didn't agree with."[39] In our period, however, the courtesy pass has often expanded to major uncompensated rewrites: "It's commonly accepted," *Variety* reported in 2010, "that scribes do seven drafts but get paid for two or three."[40]

This can lead to an opposite effect, where that single draft becomes an overdeveloped text without a clear voice or meaningful thematic development. As

Craig Mazin suggested on the *Scriptnotes* podcast in 2012, some one-step deals also cede stages of development to producers, where they control what gets submitted as the one-step draft: "The producer—knowing now that they only have one shot because there's only one draft that's going to be turned in and they don't make money unless the movie gets made—will grind that writer down to a nub. They won't just write one script. They'll have to probably write three or four drafts for this producer who is obsessive about polishing this thing to a shine before they turn it in, because they only get one shot.... So, what you're getting is an overworked, committee-ized piece of crap."[41] Mazin argues that forcing new writers into one-step deals also has the side effect of denying them the learning experience that comes from the creative negotiations at the heart of the development process. In so doing, this argument goes, the studios are saving very little money—because new writers get paid less in Hollywood terms—which sets up problems developing writers for future projects. In the past, a first draft would lead to notes and discussions, and a second draft would offer the writer the chance to produce a synthesis that is acceptable to all sides. John August's perspective on one-steps, as an A-list writer, is that they tend to poison relationships between writers and producers because of the neurosis about delivering the perfect draft: "It essentially becomes a situation where you just never deliver. And you're pretty confident that the studio has actually kind of already seen it and they're really sort of getting extra work out of you."[42]

Another common studio practice is to pressure writers into producing expanded treatments or other (pre)script materials before a project is sold. As WGA West executive director David Young reported in 2010, "What some members are telling us is, 'I'm being asked to write a film before I've been hired to write a film.'"[43] The WGA attempted and failed to get a formal agreement on "producer's passes" in the 1990s after finding that more than two-thirds of its members had been asked to do free rewrites. An arbitration claim, filed in 1999, failed after the arbitrator ruled that "studios were not liable for the behavior of producers, who are usually a writer's point of contact yet aren't signatories" to the standard guild contract, unlike the studios.[44] The result has been that many professional screenwriters have felt obliged to undertake free drafts and prewrites in order to get hired and to stay on projects that they will likely share credit for with other writers.

The contractual class division between the A-list and less-established screenwriters manifests itself most clearly in the arena of unpaid drafts. A-list writers are far less likely to be signed to one-step deals or to be obliged to do prewrites. As we have noted, the recent studio practice has been to employ inexperienced (cheaper) writers for the first (one-step) draft of a project in development and then to bring in more experienced (expensive) writers for rewrites and polishes, as journalist Tatiana Siegel noted in *Variety* in 2010: "In recent years, the trend of tapping the industry's most expensive writers to polish studio pictures has become a high-end cottage industry as the majors increasingly bank on tentpoles and seek the extra bit of insurance that comes from getting the second (or third, or fourth) opinion of writers they trust.... The downside, of course, is that so many hands on a screenplay can leave the voice of a picture disjointed at best and schizophrenic at worst."[45] The use of rewrite specialists, many of whom are not given writing credits (Daniel Bernardi, for example, has been paid to do this type of work but is uncredited and had to sign a nondisclosure agreement), during the development of a movie is, of course, nothing new in Hollywood. What has changed is that the process has become further institutionalized as a codified industrial trend, as an agent explained to Siegel: "With the top-tier writers, the studios get one meeting with the guy.... The cheap writers often come from TV, where they are used to being super-collaborative and working in rooms with other people. These writers will give a studio exec 30 meetings on a project ... and they're super hungry."[46]

This trend is also designed to cut established writers out of higher first-draft fees, as a literary manager explained to Siegel: "You don't need to hire [the highest-paid writers] anymore for the original draft because you're going to hire them later anyway for the uncredited rewrite or polish. It's simple math. Now, you see a studio pay a new writer rather than a high-paid veteran and save $5 million right there. And then the studio gets [David] Koepp or [Lowell] Ganz and [Babaloo] Mandel on the rewrite."[47] Craig Mazin describes the current state of the screenwriting industry as an increasing split between the top and the bottom of the hierarchy, with the "elimination of the middle.... Now you just have A-list and new guys."[48]

It should be noted here that the credits writers receive on studio movies reflect both the working relationships involved in the screenplay's development and the level of involvement of the individuals, as negotiated and arbitrated by the WGA. In this way a credit in which writers are linked by an ampersand—Writer X & Writer Y—indicates they collaborated on a draft. This is distinct from a credit that lists Writer X and Writer Y, indicating that both contributed to the writing separately such as in a case where Writer Y took over after Writer X was fired from the project. Similarly, "story" or "character" credits are lesser in terms of involvement and (probably, but not necessarily) in terms of the pay and residuals the writer received.

Although a number of A-list screenwriters like Jim Uhls, writer of *Fight Club* (1999), based on the Chuck Palahniuk novel, now make most of their money from uncredited rewrites, it is typically the ones who are able to subsume their personal style under the tone of the project who get regular assignments. Studios in this way rarely use those writers who have a very individual or recognizable voice: "You don't see Diablo Cody doing polishes. Her voice is too original, and if she came in and punched up dialogue on someone else's script, it would probably sound out of place."[49] Indeed, the pressure on highly paid rewrite specialists to deliver in the short time they are working on a project can be intense as J. C. Spink, executive producer of *The Hangover* (2009), script by John Lucas and Scott More, notes: "You don't get many strikes for that kind of money." Some studio executives also acknowledge that rewrites can cause as many problems as they solve: "sometimes you have to spend more money to fix the problem created by the script doctor you just hired. It's a crapshoot."[50]

Another means by which studios try to secure A-list writing talent is by fostering relationships and making deals with selected groups of screenwriters or writers' collectives. This trend began in spectacular fashion in 1999, when Sony made an unprecedented deal with thirty-one A-list writers, offering them all 2 percent *gross* point profit participation on the movies made from their screenplays, "effectively putting those writers on par with a select number of directors, producers and movie stars—the chosen few who had hitherto been granted exclusive access to the gross participation club."[51] In the immediate term no other studio followed Sony's lead in offering gross point participation to writers—although Fox (among others) would countenance a similar arrangement in the next decade—and opinion in the industry has varied about the impact of the deal for A-list screenwriters. In December of 2003 *Variety* published a follow-up to its reporting of the Sony deal, in an attempt to assess its impact on the industry. The trade paper's conclusion was that while some writers, notably David Koepp, author of the 2002 *Spider Man* screenplay, had done well, the main beneficiary had been Sony because the deal had encouraged A-list writers to consider Columbia for their specs, and it "guaranteed the studio would stay in business with top writing talent; to date it's been used on more than 75 projects."[52]

The broader lesson, that there might be economic power in collective deal making below the Writers Guild level, was not lost on prominent writers. Collectives offered established screenwriters at least temporary power to push back against some of the more egregious abuses of their status. For the cost-conscious studios in the first decade of the new millennium, these deals were also attractive—despite potentially higher back-end payments—as they typically amounted to up-front cost savings against their depleted development budgets. The Writers Co-op was formed at Warner Bros. by

John Wells *(ER)* in 2007, and the independent 1.3.9. collective, organized by Chris McQuarrie *(The Usual Suspects)* and Erik Jendresen *(Aloft)*, was established later that same year. Another group, called Writing Partners and led by John August *(Big Fish)*, Michael Arndt *(Toy Story 3)*, and Simon Kinberg *(X Men: Days of Future Past)*, was set up at Fox.

The Fox deal paid each member of the group a $300,000 fee (well below their usual rate) to write a feature for the studio. In return for the low payment, the writer was to retain creative control of the project "and can make his or her own decisions about which studio notes he's willing to do and whether to allow another writer on board at the studio's or potential director's request.... The incentive for both parties is to move the script forward toward production, in which case the writer gets his full standard fee and 2.5% first-dollar gross points."[53] In comparison, the Sony/Columbia deal involved assignments rather than specs, and the up-front fees were to be higher. John August, in an article by Michael Fleming, outlined the agenda for Writing Partners in economic terms but also as a direct attempt to nudge the studio in the direction of producing more creative work:

> There is no organizational structure here, no *production company* or profit-sharing, just nine writers who've made the same deal at the same studio. If there is a frustration with how development works right now, it would be how hard it is for A-list writers to write original material. Development budgets are limited, and studios want to spend money on movies they think they're going to make, which tend to be adaptations and sequels. They hire writers like us for those jobs, rather than to write original scripts. Aside from bigger backend, there is a potential here to encourage better movies.[54]

The 1.3.9. group's plan was not to partner with a single studio but rather to generate scripts for A-list talent and to act as both writers and producers, taking low up-front payments while a project is in development but benefiting from gross point participation on the back end.

The group's strategy was to offer another route toward presenting creative alternatives to the kind of movies being produced by the majors. The writers would also have creative input as producers "and a guarantee [their stories] won't be rewritten unless they agree to it." Speaking to *Variety*, McQuarrie contrasted his group with the Writers Co-op in terms of the relationships they intended to develop with actors: "Wells' group is reducing the cost of developing commercial material for a studio, while we're developing more personal projects for actors who can't get them made themselves.... Every actor I ever met has a dream project. They're frustrated, because they have rich development deals at studios and the power to make what they want to make, so long as they never make the movies they really want to make."[55] At the time they were founded, the trades were skeptical that writers would commit long-term to the groups' strategies, turning down studio work and other opportunities if they came along. But groups like the Writers Co-op were not established as permanent entities; rather, they were the focus for temporary deals. The groups also had the good fortune—or good sense, depending on one's read—to be formed shortly before the industry was rocked by the 2007–8 industrial dispute, which pitted screenwriters against the studios and disrupted or destroyed many of the old "first look" agreements and working relationships between studios and writers. Perhaps understandably, the collectives have been the focus of considerable resentment from many rank-and-file WGA members who saw them merely as mechanisms to further entrench already wealthy and successful A-list writers within a shrinking marketplace. For example, one anonymous writer complained: "The Co-Op will give other studios leverage to threaten agents as to why they cannot afford to pay a writer's quote. They'll have more fuel to cry bottom-line poverty."[56]

There has been at least one attempt to develop a similar short-term relationship since the writers' strike. Imagine Entertainment partnered with the Indian corporation Reliance Big Entertainment in 2010 to establish a writers' lab, under the auspices of the director Ron Howard, whose employees were to be paid exclusively to develop scripts and consult for the group for one year. These new commercial arrangements need to be understood in a context in which the studios have otherwise been cutting costs by greatly reducing the number of first-look, "overall," or "housekeeping" deals they have with screenwriters. Typically, these deals ran for two or three years and gave studios first refusal on pitches and screenplays developed by writers or writing partners in return for some combination of an operating and development budget and office space and overheads (a "shingle" in *Variety*'s lexicon), often amounting to payments of mid–six figures per annum, providing some financial stability for the established writers.

In the model of the 1980s and 1990s the attraction of overall deals for the studios (which also covered many producers, actors, and directors) was to ensure they maintained "a deep bench of creative talent to draw from and . . . a defensive move to ensure that those creatives would not be able to deliver a big hit to a rival studio or network."[57] Pamela McClintock reported in *Variety* in 2010 that "first-look pacts have been on the decline in the past decade, and particularly the past two years."[58] They have been replaced in many cases by cheaper, shorter-term arrangements or, as Claudia Littleton notes, by simple "blind" script deals in which a studio agrees to buy one or two scripts from the writer sight unseen. The cost-cutting accelerated after the economic crisis, and the writers' strike of 2007–8 also gave the studios a *force majeure* excuse to cut more than seventy overall deals with writers at once. In short, the strike served as a wedge that the studios and networks used to limit the number of writers with development deals.

Since 2008, then, Hollywood institutions have used manufactured uncertainties in the economic model of moviemaking as a wedge to retool their relationship with the screenwriting craft. In the end, though, much of the change can be put down to the fact that the studios are simply less and less invested in developing big slates of movies. In today's Hollywood, like the Hollywood represented in *Barton Fink*, studios care less about the art and craft of motion pictures than they do about maintaining creative control and thus financial viability. They view maintaining their long-term relationships with a small pool of established screenwriters as a necessary step toward that end.

THE WIDGET

For conglomerate Hollywood, the value of cinematic action principally lies in the anticipation of a kind of phenomenological reciprocity for an audience, what we labeled manic aesthetics in chapter 1. Once again this reflects Michael Bay's positioning of the *Transformers* franchise in competition with Six Flags rather than other movies. Action in tentpole movies of this kind—*Total Recall* (1990) remade as a chase film (2012), for example—is consistently being deployed toward maximizing a particular kind of embodied, or better yet haptic, affect.

The screenwriters of tentpole movies certainly understand the imperatives of studio productions, often making explicit reference to the "theme park ride" potential of the action sequences within their scripts. This example is from Joss Whedon's late (second blue revisions) draft of *The Avengers* (2012):

```
Still being chased, Iron Man dive-bombs towards Grand
Central, leading the aliens into —

INT. HELMSLEY TUNNEL — CONTINUOUS

Where he's pursued by the remaining charioteers — who score
a couple of good hits — as we roller coaster through . . .[59]
```

Writers, in other words, are adjusting to industrial trends, working their scripts in a production culture mix that supports economic imperatives over all else. And what seems to sell most, or have the greatest chance of selling most widely, are the new iterations of cinematic thrill rides.

Since the 1980s, this cinematic impetus has been paralleled in screenwriting by an incremental process of paring down the standard master-scene screenplay style. Writers have been taught to whittle away at the bones of story under the rubric of what is often referred to as the "new spec format." Although the new spec format applies to all genres, it is a screenwriting style that exposes, more transparently than ever before, a kind of raw kinesis-on-the-page that promises reciprocation with future action on the screen. Of course, to state that affect has always to some extent been written into movies is a commonplace. But recent iterations of this writing-in have been part of a broader process of retooling how screenplays look on the page, commensurate with the changed realities of the conglomerate spec market. The format and writing style of the spec screenplay are directed as much toward its initial studio readers as toward a thrill-seeking cinema audience. Scripts are being written for studio execs and their assistants and script readers, which means less description on the page and more "roller coaster" metaphors.

The impetus toward a refinement in screenwriting style came as a direct, if deferred, consequence of the adoption of a freelance story development and script sales paradigm in Hollywood that began in the late 1940s. The paradigm shift from in-house to freelance surfaced after studios downsized in the wake of the Paramount Case, after which they were obliged to divest from cinema exhibition.[60] With the studios transitioning to unit production, their story departments culled, screenwriters no longer on long-term contracts, and production slates shrinking gradually over the decades, competition increased for spec and pitch sales and for in-house studio writing assignments. It was a professional environment in which, as Bridget Conor notes, screenwriters had to redefine the trappings of their own worth. For Conor, "forms of worker currency such as the collection of credits and residuals payments, used as tools for reputation building, are more firmly entrenched."[61]

At the same time, the lure of freelance—sold more forcefully, from the 1980s onward, by the burgeoning screenwriting paraindustry—encouraged more aspiring writers to try their luck in Hollywood. In short, the "changing dynamics of screenwriting as work and as myth" gave rise in part to the proliferation of spec scripts.[62] The rise of spec scripts increased the risk of lawsuits and thus the development or reinforcement of various mechanisms to mitigate risk to include, for example, requiring that agents submit scripts. The access that new writers have to studio executives has diminished greatly over the last several decades.

With more and more scripts to read, the industry deployed stringent gatekeeping mechanisms. As a result, freelance screenwriters learned over time to accommodate their writing styles to the working conditions of the gatekeepers as much as for the producers and development executives behind the gate. These gatekeepers are lowly script readers who write concise analytical "coverage" reports on piles of spec screenplays so their employers are spared the need to read most of them.

Over time the style of spec screenplays and the look of the script on the page became more important because these documents were now being written to be read before they became working development documents.[63] Increasingly, from the 1980s onward, screenwriting style came to speak not only through the literary merits or even the cinematic potential of a given writer's work but also through its expression as "an easy read." The gatekeeping of screenplays being placed in the hands of interns and assistants to decision-makers has long been a focus of frustration among well-established Hollywood screenwriters. Throughout the last three decades, writers have complained bitterly about gatekeeping and the state of the spec market. At the third annual Screenwriting Expo in 2004, for example, the director Ivan Reitman *(Ghostbusters)* warned that "you have to find a way to get your art out there, because it's not going to get read by people who have gatekeepers."[64] William Goldman *(Butch Cassidy and the Sundance Kid)* echoed this sentiment: "Executives don't read scripts anymore. They don't like us."[65] In 2005 Larry Gross *(We Don't Live Here Anymore)* offered an even bleaker, if by now familiar, perspective: "There's never been less interest in an original screenplay. . . . Now all movies are borrowed and ripped off. They want to stamp out all signs of a distinctive original voice."[66]

Pulitzer Prize–winning and Oscar-nominated writer David Mamet *(Glengarry Glen Ross; The Verdict; Wag the Dog)* expressed the feelings of many screenwriters in 2007 when he argued that the process of gatekeeping, of flanks of script readers working as assistants to studio executives, was itself institutionalizing mediocrity and an aversion to originality in the industry. He had especially harsh words for the script readers: "Now, like anyone newly enrolled in a totalitarian regime, these neophytes get the options pretty quickly—conform or die. The script reader adopts the notion that inspiration, idiosyncrasy, and depth are all very well in their place but that their place has yet to be discovered and that he would rather die than deviate from received wisdom."[67] When studios and agents do read original material in the tentpole era, material given the rare grade of "consider" or the even rarer grade of "recommend" in their assistant's coverage reports, it is unlikely to be with the intention of buying the script in question. Howard Rodman explained to the *Hollywood Reporter* that distinctive specs now typically serve as calling cards for aspiring writers rather than as potential sales: "You write something original that springs full blown from your forehead in order to launch or reinvigorate your career. The studios use them to figure out who's a good writer. But they don't get made. What the studios consider a studio movie has never been narrower than it is now."[68]

An increased awareness between both aspirant and established writers of the quotidian realities of the freelance screenwriting paradigm, and of the process of script readership in particular, alongside the contraction of acceptable forms and genres on the spec market, helped to initiate a gradual stylistic shift toward a "new spec format" for screenplays. Initially something of a loose yet contested category within professional screenwriting, this variant on the master scene format emerged through the 1980s and 1990s as writers were advised by agents, producers, and paraindustry teachers and journalists alike to write lean and to make their style easy for overworked gatekeepers to read. Importantly, this was also the period during which screenwriters adopted computers and dedicated screenwriting software for the first time, giving a significant boost to another paraindustrial market. As we noted in our introduction, paraindustry software programs like *Warren Script Application* and, later, *Final Draft* and *Movie Magic Screenwriter* helped to embed default developing orthodoxies of screenplay format for the new generations of writers at least. The visual rhetoric of screenwriting became more proscriptive with lessons about proper format often becoming of greater concern to aspiring writers than story and character development.

By 1999 the screenwriting paraindustry teacher Robert McKee's advice was to avoid writing in "a thick block of single spaced prose." The alternative was to use short lines, split with white space to imply shots or discrete moments as the scene developed.[69] In 1998 writers in *Creative Screenwriting* magazine were reporting on the emergence of a sparer screenplay style, with "a look and flow conducive to . . . a pared down read."[70]

Coincident with this unofficial, yet increasingly prevalent redrafting of spec style, the development of immersive digital special effects from the late 1990s also began to influence how (and when) action screenplays wrote spectacle. In the development of high-budget tentpole pictures at least, the previsualization process began to take on more direct creative responsibility for primary storytelling, complicating or shifting forward in development the moment of "handoff" from the screenplay. In other words, the responsibility for writing the cinematic into some action scripting was changing.

The status quo ante in the period of typewriters and analog effects—the period of miniatures and matte paintings—was for shooting scripts to describe practical action in detail and in blocks of text. The style is evident in this example from the opening sequence of Lawrence Kasdan's script for *Raiders of the Lost Ark* (1981).

> Indy swings his whip across the floor. Fifteen feet of
> it cuts open beneath the lash, falling away to reveal a
> black pit as wide as the hall. The illusory floor was made
> of dust-covered cobwebs. Satipo picks up a stone and drops
> it down the pit. No sound. The two men exchange glances.
> Indy looks up at the high roof of the hall. He swings the
> whip up around a support beam, tests its strength with a
> pull and swings over the pit on the whip. From the other
> side he swings the whip back to Satipo, who throws Indy the
> torch. Satipo swings across. When they are both standing on
> solid floor there is a moment of quiet in which they hear,
> from far, far below -- SPLASH! Indy wedges the whip handle
> into the wall and leaves it strung to the beam for quick
> retreat.[71]

When postproduction effects work was required, the tendency was to split action sequences into clearly defined shots in a shooting script as a specific guide to the effects houses as well as for budgeting and scheduling purposes.

In Leigh Brackett's and Lawrence Kasdan's shooting script for *Star Wars Episode V: The Empire Strikes Back* (1980), we can see how the screenplay is navigating the special effects technicians, the crafters of haptic thrills, through the sequence, splitting action up into achievable units with slug lines, and calling shots. The screenplay specifies the movement both of camera and miniatures: "Pan through foreground legs of walker as speeder banks and turns away." Or: "Moving across the top of the walker as Luke's speeder skims across it. Trucking [sic] with the speeder then it flys [sic] overhead."

> EXT. ICE PLAIN - BATTLEFIELD - HOTH
>
> FULL SHOT - Pan through foreground legs of walker as
> speeder banks and turns away. Two other speeders pass the
> first speeder going in the opposite direction.
>
> EXT. ICE PLAIN - BATTLEFIELD - HOTH
>
> MED FULL SHOT - Three walkers marching right to left firing
> all cannons . . .
>
> INT. WALKER NO. 3 COCKPIT
>
> Two pilots watch the distant gun emplacements as they
> maneuver their war machine forward . . .
>
> Luke's speeder banks in from the side and heads straight
> for the viewport, blasting away. A huge explosion hits the
> window and dissipates. The speeder roars over the window.
>
> EXT. ICE PLAIN - BATTLEFIELD - HOTH
>
> FULL SHOT—Moving across the top of the walker as Luke's
> speeder skims across it. Trucking with the speeder then it
> flys overhead.[72]

In Peter Hyams's shooting script for *Outland* (1981), camera direction is not called but the description of what will be achieved through special-effects miniatures and practical lighting, dust, and wind effects is both detailed and explicit:

EXT. SHUTTLE LOADING BAY

The outboard engine nacelles belch flame . . . as the ponderous shuttle fires its retro engines. There is a huge low growl. The ground shudders. A storm duct [*sic*—of dust?] is kicked up . . . flaring in the hard landing lights.

INT. SHUTTLE LOADING BAY

The giant hydraulic landing access arms fold back . . . waiting to receive the descending shuttle. The four orange gantries swing back to a horizontal position. The blast deflector plates slide up.

Compare these to the writing of a fully digital battle scene from *Star Wars Episode I: The Phantom Menace* (1999), script by George Lucas, the key transformational text in marking the shift toward fully digital production:

EXT. NABOO GRASS PLAINS - DAY

A DESTROYER DROID blasts one of the shield generators, causing it to EXPLODE. The protective shield begins to weaken and fall apart. OOM-9 sees the shield weaken and orders his tanks forward. The GUNGAN GENERAL signals a retreat as the tanks enter the battle.

The GUNGANS flee as fast as they can. JAR JAR is blown off his KAADU and lands on one of the tank guns. A GUNGAN WARRIOR signals JAR JAR to jump off. JAR JAR is afraid. The gun swings around trying to knock JAR JAR off. JAR JAR hangs from the tank barrel as it moves along. Finally, he jumps onto a KAADU behind a GUNGAN WARRIOR. EXPLOSIONS from the tank fire are everywhere. It is chaos.[73]

In this example the description of cinematic action is no longer bound to the preproduction requirements of analog effects technologies. Unlike the previous example from *Raiders of the Lost Ark*, which takes place over a sequence of shots but in a single location, this sequence flows fluidly between multiple implicit camera positions. Some of them are not even specified in the draft. The material is also to be realized entirely in postproduction through digital effects animation work. This sequence is further developed in the final film, but even from this draft it is clear that the old rules for scene and shot calling have been superseded. Depending on how one chooses to read it, the short text above calls for at least ten distinct effects shots. However, the simple master-scene style tells us that in the digital era complex special effects no longer have to be deferred to in the same way in the writing. Comparing this example to the scripted battle scene from *The Empire Strikes Back*, it is clear that the handoff to collaborators for further development is already being implied, not by labored specificity—by loading instruction and description onto individual shots—but by the instructional lacunae in the screenplay. "Do it like this" becomes "start from this." Digital effects workers flesh out the story in the practice of imaging what the short text describes.

The transition from analog to digital—*The Abyss* (1989), *Terminator 2: Judgment Day* (1991)—and, with *The Phantom Menace* (1999), immersive digital special effects rewrote storytelling in terms of the ability of filmmakers to show anything that could be drawn or animated. It also shifted the writing and development process on effects-heavy movies by changing the timing at which the active collaboration between screenwriters and visual effects teams occurs. Of course, the collaboration between writers and effects technicians does not begin with digital effects production; however, it has become increasingly institutionalized within the development process. As Kathryn Millard notes, collaboration "has only intensified with the proliferation of digital cinema, previously discrete stages of pre-production, production and post production can be happening simultaneously."[74] The cinematic scripting of Lucas's screenplay for *The Phantom Menace* is undertaken by other creatives as part of the ongoing "layered" process of design and previsualization, as the director outlined in an interview with *Wired* during preparation of the movie: "Instead of making film into a sequential assembly-line process where one person does one thing, takes it, and turns it over to the next person, I'm turning it more into the process of a painter or sculptor. You work on it for a bit, then you stand back and look at it and add some more onto it. . . . You basically end up layering the whole thing. Filmmaking by layering means you write, and direct, and edit all at once."[75] Lucas's working practice was certainly neither consistent nor universal, but the trend away from locking the cinematic (as distinct from the haptic) into tentpole screenplays continued. Partly as a consequence of the frequent concatenation of the studio production process and partly enabled by the capabilities of new technologies, previsualization often begins long before a script is complete. Moreover, the shooting script is completed after effects sequences are blocked in previs. In this way the role of the tentpole screenwriter can be to progress the story to the point at which this handover can be affected and then to reinscribe the fruits of that secondary narrative/technological development back into the shooting script. The writer is more than a hired dialogue hand; however, the responsibility for certain kinds of writing is certainly understood to be spread more broadly across creative departments than in previous iterations of the movie development process.

John McTiernan, the director of *Die Hard* (1988), *Predator* (1987), and *The Hunt for Red October* (1990), among other Hollywood films, acknowledged the impact of time pressure on the development process in conversation with Michael Bay and other action directors back in 1998: "A 'tent pole' movie ... is very often a large decision for the corporation involved. So they will not make a commitment early. They will make it at the last minute. [He nods at Bay.] We've both made movies in nine months door-to-door [from green light to premiere]."[76] More recently, in preparing to direct *Oz: The Great and Powerful* (2013), Sam Raimi developed much of the cinematic detail in the film during a parallel process of story development in both screenplay and previsualization: "Raimi employed previs not only to flesh out sequences in the still-evolving script—a typical use of previs—but also to explore specific gags and CG character performances.... Raimi also used the previs process to develop humorous gags for the film. 'Sam was looking for any opportunity to sneak amusing moments into the movie ... so he would have our artists previs his humorous ideas. Even if he didn't know where those gags might occur, he wanted to block them out and see if they worked.'"[77] Similarly, scripting and previsualization occurred in parallel and cross-fertilized during the development of *Iron Man 3* (2013), according to Jody Duncan's account in *Cinefex*: "Marvel initiated the enterprise with stylized animatics created by the lead in-house storyboard artist Federico D'Alessandro, which simultaneously illustrated and inspired [Shane] Black's evolving screenplay in the months leading up to the shoot."[78]

The previsualization supervisor for Halon Entertainment, Justin Denton, recalls working with director Peter Berg in a similar fashion during preparations for *Battleship* (2012): "The script was not complete when we started working with Pete.... He walked me through scenes. I took notes and then we started animating in Maya."[79] In its account of a public appearance by *The Avengers* writer-director Joss Whedon, Collider.com reports that, although Whedon claims to be a very detailed action writer when given the time, "he repeatedly praised the storyboard artists, Brian Andrews in particular, for *The Avengers* who filled in the blanks for his action scenes."[80]

This cinematic development process has a major impact on a film's budget, and embedding action and other effects beats into the final script through previsualization is frequently concerned as much with controlling costs as it is with visual storytelling. Arthur Windus, a visual effects producer on *Jack the Giant Slayer* (2013), with five writers sharing credit, recalls the approach taken to scripting effects sequences in that film: "We tried limiting the number of giant shots, while constantly striving to come up with scenes that [director] Bryan [Singer] felt he hadn't seen before in fantasy movies. From that brainstorm of ideas, our storyboard artist, Doug Lefler, created 'beat boards'—rough sketches scanned into the computer—to work out action beats." Windus concludes: "Then we created storyboards and started laying out shots."[81]

Spectacular sequences in some tentpole movies are written as sparely as possible. We can compare the transitional style of *The Phantom Menace* to the new spec format in its more recent form, the shooting script of a recent superhero movie: *Captain America* (2011), screenplay by Christopher Markus and Stephen McFeely. Even a quick glance shows that the two scripts are very different styles of document. Apart from the (over)use of capitalization, which can be put down to the writer's own stylistic intervention in writing a chase scene, the use of short discreet sentences separated by white space in *Captain America* accelerates both the read and the perception of action in the way of the new spec format. This sequence plays off characters' and bystanders' looks, and it uses capitalization to enhance the visual impact of the flow of action on the page. Perspective implies shot structures but never specifies them. The scene also hands off perspective through ellipsis, a common technique in action writing, and emphasizes character and vehicle movement in every line. Even the kids playing "LOOK" to the action.

```
EXT. BROOKLYN STREET - DAY

STEVE VAULTS OFF THE CAR'S ROOF AND LANDS ON THE TAXI.

INT./EXT. TAXICAB - DAY

KRUGER PULLS HIS GUN AND BLASTS AT STEVE. Steve ducks,
clinging to the side of the car.

They swerve through the streets.

A HORN BLARES. KRUGER LOOKS TO SEE A TRUCK ROARING AT HIM.
Steve sees the same thing. Kruger yanks the wheel.

THE TRUCK SIDESWIPES THE TAXI, THROWING IT INTO A ROLL.

KIDS LOOK OVER FROM THEIR BASEBALL GAME TO SEE . . .

STEVE ATOP THE TUMBLING CAB, RIDING IT LIKE A ROLLING LOG.

THE CAR CRASHES TO A STOP.[82]
```

The way *Captain America* is written assumes that cinematic specificity will also be addressed in that second order of what Maras frames as *scripting* in preproduction and previsualization to come.[83] Julian Hoxter elaborates: "This is less a 'screenplay as blueprint' waiting to be implemented, and more a 'screenplay as concept sketch' to be carried forward by further creative collaboration. In anticipation of a reciprocal encounter with its future audience, the writing style jettisons descriptive language to sustain the speed of the read and to generate a kind of visceral excitement in the reader. What is paramount in a screenplay of this kind is to establish and maintain kinesis-in-prose: the 'concept sketch' illustrates how fast the story moves."[84] This can be seen in, for example, the science fiction shooting scripts for *Green Lantern* (2011), and *Prometheus* (2012) among many others. This example from *Green Lantern* breaks sentences with white space, forcing us to leap ahead to obtain syntactical completion and thus accelerating the reading track while handing images on and off with hyphens. Words are at a minimum.

```
INT. CAVERN - CONTINUOUS ACTION

As he plummets into the abyss he shuts his eyes, braces for
impact --

-- but it doesn't come. Instead he finds himself suspended
in mid-air --

-- in an enormous CAVERN, illuminated by pulsing GREEN
LIGHT. At its center is a huge JAGGED ROCK. And at its
peak, bound like Prometheus by WEBS of GREEN ENERGY --

KRONA

An immortal with a brilliant mind, he studies the Commander
with a scientist's sense of wonder.[85]
```

The scene from *Prometheus* is somewhat denser stylistically, the action written more directly toward character motivation, but its use of acceleration techniques—including midsentence breaks, overcapitalization, underlining for emphasis, the isolation of operative words and decision moments, and ellipsis—is by now familiar.

```
Shaw and Vickers exchange a look. They both have exactly
the same instinct at exactly the same time.

RUN.

WITH AN EAR-SPLITTING SMASH, the JUGGERNAUT HITS THE
SURFACE ON ITS SIDE -- And because of its unique design, it
does not STOP THERE --

IT ROLLS. END OVER END LIKE A CRUSHING WHEEL OF DEATH—BIG
AS A MOUNTAIN.

Shaw and Vickers both RUN for their lives -- FULL SPEED
WITH EVERYTHING THEY'VE GOT -- BUT THE SHEER SPEED OF THE
JUGGERNAUT IS OVERTAKING THEM --

VICKERS is a machine. A MARATHONER. Tip-Top SHAPE. Running
in a FLAT OUT SPRINT. Shaw has no chance of keeping up, but
she TRIES and --
```

> TRIPS! Hits the SAND.
>
> Vickers STOPS for a moment. Just looks back at Shaw. Could help her . . .
>
> But doesn't.[86]

In each case the industry reader is pulled along by formatting and by a variety of stylistic techniques, in precise combinations individual to the writer but all designed to speed the read, to imitate and prefigure in text form the kinetic, muscular power of the imagined spectacle. Action is now being written to bring screenwriter, reader, director, and effects artists together in a way that transcends much of the blueprint era's periodized functionality. It's an excellent example of narrative economy on the page.

When directors develop their own scripts for in-house tentpole science fiction movies, they are not pitching concept and access through style in the way of a spec script—or at least much less so. Recent *shooting scripts* of this kind are often denser, reading more like directors' notes either for the previsualization to come or for inserting specific blocking after it is developed, but they also utilize frequent kinetic markers, as in this example from writer-director J. J. Abrams's shooting script for *Super 8* (2011):

> EXT. LILLIAN, OHIO -- MAIN STREET -- NIGHT
>
> The kids round a corner -- ON MAIN STREET, COUNTLESS METALLIC OBJECTS -- ANYTHING METAL AND LOOSE -- has been INVISIBLY DRAGGED -- FLOATING -- toward the WATER TOWER -- at different speeds and with different personalities, metal objects BULLET TO THE TOP OF THE TOWER AND STICK THERE.
>
> Suddenly THE DINER WINDOW SHATTERS as a STOVE RIPS THROUGH IT -- we PAN WITH IT as it TUMBLES TOWARD AND UP THE WATER TOWER! HUNDREDS OF OBJECTS move past them -- from bicycles to silverware and sinks! DISHWASHERS AND TVS SMASH THROUGH THE TOWN'S APPLIANCE STORE WINDOW -- A TV FLOATS UNPLUGGED, PAST THE KIDS -- AND IT IS ON -- AND SHOWS AN EPISODE FROM THE TWILIGHT ZONE -- all things eventually SLAMMING into the WATER TOWER, the objects BEGINNING TO CRUSH TOGETHER, FORMING ONE DENSE METALLIC MASS.
>
> BAM! BAMBAM! Sounds like GUN BLASTS -- the KIDS TURN: behind them are the RED CARGO CONTAINERS -- ONE BY ONE those cubes BURST THROUGH THE CONTAINERS: BAM! BAMBAMBAM! BAMBAM! AN ODD CRESCENT SHAPE ABOVE THE TOWER! Alice is cry-laughing at seeing it work --

Abrams is still selling the narrative push of the sequence by privileging the phrase over the sentence, through the dynamic and repeated use of onomatopoeia, and by pulling the eye from one image to the next by means of frequent hyphenation. In this second example of a director's own shooting script, from Joss Whedon's *The Avengers* again, the action has by now been fully blocked, with basic cinematic instructions embedded and more limited hyphenation to pull the read:

> ```
> ANGLE: FIRST FLOOR: where he lands amidst the people, who
> scurry out of the way just in time --
> 
> ANGLE: SECOND FLOOR: the third soldier grabs cap [sic] from
> behind, one hand over the top of his head, going for the
> eyes -- he peels off Cap's cowl in the ugly struggle.
> 
> The first soldier grabs a gun and spins to fire on Cap --
> who throws himself up, arcing backwards over the second
> soldier, who takes the hit in the chest, and comes down
> behind his lifeless body, using it for cover for one more
> blast --
> 
> ANGLE: THE GRENADE starts to whine as it is nearly at blast
> status.[87]
> ```

In all these scripts, kinesis-on-the-page now stands in place of narrative complexity—even other kinds of action. In contemporary science fiction cinema it suits the reduction of *wonder*—to borrow film scholar Vivian Sobchack's term—to a narrower conception of kinetic action that dominates the grid of attractions of the typical tentpole movie.[88] Early film theorist Siegfried Kracauer wrote of the physicality of the film experience in terms of the "lure" of "dimensions where sense impressions are all important."[89] At its most inventive this kinetic action can be character driven and visually imaginative, as seen in *The Avengers*; at its worst it replays well-known tropes with very minor variation as seen in *Man of Steel* (2013) wherein superheroes punch each other through walls over and over and over again.

The Avengers adopts many of the kinetic principles required of contemporary tentpole moviemaking, but it integrates spectacle with storytelling. The climactic action sequence in the film is integrated thematically and structurally to resolve the story as well as the plot of the movie in a way that integrates the special effects. The plot events chronicle the battle between the eponymous superhero group as it faces off against an invading alien army unleashed on the world by the villain Loki. In the story, however, the battle also resolves the movie's theme of putting together the hero group—"Avengers assemble"—by unifying its disparate, egotistical, mutually suspicious elements into a functioning team. Screenwriter/director Joss Whedon has acknowledged that the extended climax was written in "five acts." In practice the first two of these acts bring the group together, the third signals the unification of the team under the leadership of Captain America, and the fourth and fifth acts follow the now-assembled Avengers as they demonstrate the power of their newfound unity to defeat the enemy. The entire sequence binds on the fulcrum, in "act 4," of what Whedon calls a "tie-in shot" that pays narrative and cinematic homage both to the conventions of comic strip splash pages and to the new unity of the group:

> Iron Man dives towards the Park Avenue ramp, barreling through a mass of alien footies before joining Cap on the viaduct where he blasts his repulsors into Cap's Vibranium shield - the two working together to take out a horde - we circle around them and then follow Iron Man as he rockets towards a Chariot, smashing it and leaving us an angle on Hawkeye who fires an arrow that we chase as it takes out another Chariot, which flies into the Leviathan that Hulk has commandeered, where Foot Soldiers pop from their pods and Hulk smashes them as Thor joins him and the two relentlessly wrest the Leviathan into the side of a multi level mall's giant window -- ending the tie-in shot.

It is in the recent history of the screenwriting process, as much as in finished films, that we can trace an accelerating impulse toward an increasingly specific form of haptic encounter in tentpole films. The intersection of the perceived need for screenwriters to accommodate the new spec format, originally deployed to make freelance spec screenplays more appealing to script readers, with the development of immersive digital effects came at a time in which the studios were also retrenching toward tentpole production. In the sense that the new spec format was a writing style waiting for a production context, it found it in the kinetic excess of digital tentpole cinema. In the conglomerate period, however, the pool of screenwriters trusted by the studios to deliver this kind of screenplay also contracted. Paradoxically, the costs of development increasingly relegated these A-list writers to undertaking rewrites. New and cheaper writers found opportunities to work on big-budget productions but their contracts often shut them out of much of the creative development of the projects they had been hired to "complete."

CONCLUSION

In chapter 1 we assessed the impact of the corporate transformation of the studio system from the 1980s on the freelance screenwriting paradigm, as well as its cognate offshoot, the paraindustrial model of cinematic storytelling. We considered the impact of digital technologies on the labor relations of the movie industry and, to a lesser extent, on the style, the format, the practice, of Hollywood screenwriting—and the distribution and exhibition of its products—since the highpoint of the "spec boom" of the late 1980s and early 1990s. We also investigated the role of the WGA, the trade union that, we argued, zipped up the tent to protect already established writers heading into the era of convergence.

As screenwriting entered its digital era, the look and function of those screenplays changed from the once standard "master-scene format" to the pared down "new spec format." The importance of format shifts to professional writers who work with and master it, and the revelatory power of the new spec format in articulating the manic pace of tentpole genre narratives cannot be overstated. Similarly, the recalibration of the screenplay toward the literary in order to pass the gatekeepers of Hollywood altered the nature of written storytelling for screenwriters, if not the structure of the stories themselves. Mainstream screenwriters value narrative economy above all things. Feature films have to tell their stories within fairly strict temporal parameters, averaging out at between ninety minutes and two hours in length, and one of the key skills a successful movie screenwriter learns over time is how to fit as much story as possible into the fewest pages. Screenplays are still formatted to equate a single page with a minute of screen time, so changes to the way a script looks on that page have a significant impact on the writer's sense of her own craft priorities.

Although the mainstream spec market—servicing a studio sector that no longer makes many movies and thus requires less and less product—continues to be in crisis, new and old opportunities for aspiring and established writers do still surround the bare Hollywood tent. The studios are on the lookout for franchise opportunities and safe green-light decisions. As a consequence, they are still interested in acquiring and developing material from other media with a proven track record, and, over time, this has tilted the balance of Hollywood screenwriting firmly away from the spec and to the assignment. Spec scripts are now little more than calling cards for aspiring writers who hope they will open the door to the assignment marketplace. As we have argued, this shift from specs to assignments has further eroded the vestigial control most movie screenwriters have over their own creative product and has placed the control of movie stories more firmly than ever in the hands of studio development departments. The example of Marvel Studios and the consolidation of the control of story across the megafranchise of the MCU in the hands of Kevin Feige is only the most public—and most successful—instance of a far less spectacular tendency that for the most part plays out quietly through the quotidian bureaucratic processes of conglomerate studio development.

We will return to the new normal of movie development, with its bake-offs and one-step deals, in more depth when we discuss the state of independent drama in chapter 4. For now, we move our focus away from Hollywood movie production. As we have argued, the shadow of the tentpole and the consolidation of story beneath it have driven many established writers to relaunch or diversify their careers in the sunnier climes of expanded television and other new and convergent media. We will explore recent developments in television drama in the next chapter and other contexts in which screenwriting is escaping or bypassing the end of cinema in the chapters that follow, including the alternative or adjacent practices of independent and microbudget screenwriters, writers of video games, and creators of online content.

3. Running the Room
Showrunning in Expanded Television

> Truly creative people refuse to be constrained, when you try to put them in a box, they simply refuse to go into that box.
>
> FX president JOHN LANDGRAF[1]

> A showrunner (or show runner) is a person responsible for overall and day-to-day operation of a television series—a position more often credited as executive producer. A showrunner's duties often combine those traditionally assigned to the head writer, executive producer, and script editor. In some films, directors have creative control of a production—but in television, the showrunner always outranks the director.
>
> *Wikipedia*

In the sixth season of Shawn Ryan's series for the FX Network, *The Shield*, in an episode titled "Back to One," written by Adam Fierro under the direction of Ryan, police Strike Team detective Vic Mackey (Michael Chiklis) seizes the pregnant girlfriend of a notoriously violent Mexican gang leader. The detective wants to coax the gang leader, Guardo (Luis Antonio Ramos), out of hiding. In what television drama writers call the "A," or primary, story of an episode, Vic pursues Guardo because he believes the gang leader killed a fellow member of the Strike Team, Curtis "Lem" Lemansky (Kenny Johnson). After getting Guardo on the phone, Vic snarls: "Next word out of your mouth better be *when* or I will rape and kill that bitch while you're listening." Vic is no ordinary cop. Standing next to Vic is one of his Strike Team partners, Shane Vendrell (Walton Goggins). Here the narrative arc of the series puts the audience ahead of Vic: we already know that Shane killed Lem. He, too, is no ordinary cop.

Directed by Gwyneth Horder-Payton, the scene is shot with Vic in close-up, the handheld camera moving almost 180 degrees across his face, vacillating between low and eye-line angles. This allows the audience to see the character's facial expressions evolve from unrestrained vengeance to skilled manipulation. Jarring cuts to Shane in high angle, bent at the knees and looking up at Vic with trepidation, enable us to experience the detective's guilt over killing his former partner and fear of what Vic is about to do to

Guardo and, if the Strike Team boss discovers the truth, perhaps to him as well. *The Shield* offers us a complicated group of compromised cops.

The two detectives eventually capture Guardo. But Vic, an antihero in the tradition of HBO's New Jersey Mafia boss Tony Soprano (James Gandolfini), doesn't place him in police custody. Instead, he takes the gang leader to a secluded building, pulls out rope from a duffle bag, and suspends him by his handcuffed wrists from a pipe just below the ceiling. What makes Vic a particularly complicated antihero is that, unlike Tony Soprano, he represents law and order. Even as a dirty cop, he has a tremendous sense of loyalty to the other dirty cops that make up his team. Vic has been decorated for valor on more than one occasion. He operates by his own moral code, taking care of wayward prostitutes on the one hand and not hesitating to brutalize a pedophile on the other. Ryan and his above-the-line and below-the-line crew took great care to craft a character that attracted a passionate investment from the show's loyal viewers.

With Shane by his side, Vic pulls a heavy chain from his bag, wraps it slowly around his hand, and with methodical precision whips it into the prone gang leader's side. "I'm going to get to the truth," he tells the otherwise innocent man. "I didn't do it," the gang leader responds. In what is the epitome of a dark scene, Vic proceeds to thrash the chain across the man's shoulders, rib cage, chest, and back. As Guardo screams in agony, bones breaking with every thud, the camera cuts to Shane in the foreground turning away, unable to witness the torture of a man he knows to be innocent. Vic is written and shot to be as unmercifully cruel as he is rabidly loyal to his team. Shane, on the other hand, is written and shot to be both a survivor and a coward. In this scene and across the entire series the actors play their roles brilliantly—working alongside Ryan and his team to make *The Shield* a unique television show in a familiar genre at a time when antiheroes were popular with audiences.

By lingering briefly on one graphic and controversial scene in one episode of a long-running series like *The Shield*, we hope to point to a space in Hollywood where the writer is king. While we argued that the tentpole paradigm of the dream factory curtails the creativity of feature film screenwriters, there are both settled and emergent spaces in the broader Hollywood industry that allow writers an opportunity to craft original and compelling stories while also making a living. These stories must make profits for their networks, of course; however, most TV storytellers are not required to sustain or grow a range of ancillary markets as do their peers in the tentpole factory.[2] They are afforded a great deal of creative room, especially when working for newer entrants into the arena of expanded television whose SVOD delivery frees the creatives entirely from the need to placate advertisers and (typically) from the tyranny of overnight ratings.

Given the new conditions of employment imposed on many feature writers in the wake of the WGA strike of 2007–8, such as sweepstakes pitching and one-step deals, what are the institutional constraints placed on these television drama writers? In particular, what is the position of the showrunners who are charged with producing shows, writing episodes, managing the writers' room (and thus episodes written by other writers), overseeing directors and editors, and reporting to network executives? More pragmatically, how do showrunners and writers more generally marshal the structures of the television script and navigate network notes and directives from Standards and Practices departments to develop new storylines for established characters during the manic production schedule of series television, where there is always at least one episode in preproduction, one in production, and one or more in postproduction.

In addressing these questions, we focus on one of the more creative showrunners in Hollywood, Shawn Ryan, whose duties, as *Wikipedia* accurately defines, "often combine those traditionally assigned to the head writer, executive producer, and script editor." Through our extended case study of Ryan we consider how his writing and production team's uncompromising work on *The Shield* broke new ground for storytelling and representation on basic cable, setting a new standard for series production on the cusp of television's expansion online. This history speaks to a space of relative creative freedom for writers working inside the dream factory.

Although we focus on Ryan, and thus an above-the-line writer with an identifiable voice, we take pains not to create the illusion that the work of a television showrunner simply equates to that of an auteur. According to the auteur theory, the director's intent and much of the meaning of a film can be found in his (and it is mostly applied to male directors) thematic choices and stylistic signatures. Putting aside for the moment the "intentional fallacy" that the auteur theory perpetuates—that is, that the meaning of a text lies in its creation rather than, as critical theorist Roland Barthes reminds us, its destination with diverse audiences—the working world of the Hollywood screenwriter is always already collaborative, across all the crafts involved in the syncretistic process of filmmaking.[3] Nonetheless, it is important to understand the position of television showrunners, who have a kind of authority that is otherwise uncommon in Hollywood. Their duties, and thus their creative influence, stretch across every aspect of preproduction, production, and postproduction.

A SHOWRUNNER PRIMER

When *The Shield* episode "Back to One" returns from a commercial break, Guardo is covered in blood and spit. Vic, sweating profusely, continues to beat him in what is arguably one of the most violent scenes in US television history. The sound design exacerbates the graphic images as the bone-crushing thuds from Vic's chain smashing against Guardo's body are punctuated by agonizing shrieks and groans. Shards of light through a few grimy windows and a proverbial lightbulb convey a foreboding sense of doom. Chiklis's haunting acting style, what Ryan often refers to as "Vicilicious," punctuates the chilling intensity of the scene. Ryan didn't write this episode, but in his capacity as the series' showrunner, he directed both the writing *and* the edit. His granular notes to the director and editors of the episode read: "I think it's a mistake to focus solely on Shane right before the shot. Yes, it does add to the surprise, but I saw some dailies where Vic gives some amazing performances right before the shooting. Let's not be so married to Shane about to confess that we roll right past the Viciliciousness of this scene. . . . Make the end of this scene more about Vic."[4]

Following Ryan's charge to "make the end of the scene more about Vic," the final edit has the camera dwelling on the Strike Team boss as he throws down his chain, seethes, and contemplates his next move. To the surprise of all but perhaps the most loyal fans of the show, Vic pulls out his gun and shoots Guardo in the face—fitting the pattern of brutality established back in the pilot episode, written by Ryan on spec, when he shot an internal affairs detective in the face and then blamed his death on an African American drug dealer. As critic Dusty Saunders described the series shortly after it premiered: "In the 80's, *Hill Street Blues* broke new TV ground, creating police-show realism. The 90's produced *NYPD Blue* and *Homicide: Life on the Street*. Now we have *The Shield*, which, at times, makes these predecessors look like *Car 54, Where Are You?*" *The Shield* was no ordinary cop drama. Yet Ryan came to his show like many other successful showrunners. He moved up through the ranks of television writers to the level at which he could pitch a show on spec. His pitch landed, and he ran with it.

The television showrunner sets the narrative arc of the show, defines the characters and their relationships, plots out the story progression from episode to episode, and establishes its thematics, metaphors, and allegories. For Ryan and his team of writers, cinematographers, directors, and editors, for example, the violence in "Back to One" is in service of a story with a consistent political arc. Indeed, if Ryan does have something like an auteur's signature, it would be an emphasis on graphic violence, handheld shooting, and raw photography in pursuit of a political message. As the writer of the episode, Fierro, explains: "Vic is ostensibly this guy that will do bad to accomplish good and that's always the central question and the central argument about this guy—is it worth it? He's always pushing one way and coming back the other way. The war in Iraq is a model for Vic . . . and for the show."[5] Nominated by Human Rights First for an Excellence in Television award for this episode, Fierro went on to explain that the scene "illustrates what happens when you torture the wrong person." The point, he continues, is that "torture doesn't work—it doesn't work the way *24* illustrates it."[6]

Fierro is referring to the counterterrorism show on FOX, *24* (2001–10), created by Robert Cochran and Joel Surnow, and claims made by Human Rights First that the heroic and successful use of torture by the show's lead character, Jack Bauer (Kiefer Sutherland), promoted illegal and unethical interrogation techniques and adversely affected the training and performance of real US soldiers in Iraq, Afghanistan, and Guantanamo Bay, Cuba.[7] Contrary to *24*, in *The Shield* torture is presented as being tragically sadistic and ineffective, taking its contextual cue more from Abu Ghraib. It is a political arc established by Ryan in the pilot. As the showrunner, he crafted a series that spoke in subtle ways to America in the aftermath of 9/11. In other words, the Strike Team is offered as a metaphor for all that was torturously paranoid during the wars in Afghanistan and Iraq. They are police special forces, the tip of the spear for an occupying force in decidedly hostile territory in "The Farm," the invented Farmington police precinct in Los Angeles. At the heart of The Farm *The Shield*'s police operate out of "The Barn," a kind of FOB or Forward Operating Base. *The Shield*'s "terrorists" are people of color, gang leaders that may be guilty of something, but not of the crime that leads to their torture.

Ryan also based *The Shield* on the real-life corruption scandals afflicting the Los Angeles Police Department (LAPD) in the early 1990s, specifically Rampart Division's supposedly elite CRASH unit. Although CRASH was successful at reducing gang-related crime in some of Los Angeles's most notorious neighborhoods, its officers were accused of dealing drugs, engaging in shakedowns of gang members for money, and framing innocent people. Ryan used the notoriety generated by this story of corrupt LAPD cops as social fodder for the police drama he pitched to FX, a fledging network that, until that point, was best known for airing reruns of *The X-Files* (1993–2002) and *Buffy the Vampire Slayer* (1997–2003). The series went on to leverage hot-button issues like the war on terrorism, homophobia and conversion therapy, gender discrimination, and, of course, racism, drawing stars to its lineup as prominent as Glen Close (season 4) and Forest Whitaker (season 5). The show put FX on the map of producers of quality, cutting-edge television.

As Daniel Bernardi and Kevin Sandler argue, *The Shield* ushered in a new era of network television characterized by controversial themes.[8] Throughout the police drama's run, racial conflict, homophobia, misogyny, government corruption, and war were offered up to viewers through a documentary style, shot on 16 mm celluloid. The popular and critical success of *The Shield* shows us what most writers inside and outside Hollywood already know—indeed, what most scholars and television viewers already know: the craft of dramatic writing is alive and well in many parts of expanded television. When asked why she elected to join the series for an entire season, Academy Awarding–winning actress Glenn Close explained: "I'm a sucker for good writing and for people who are really passionate."[9]

Collaboration is also core to the work of the television showrunner, perhaps more so than to his or her feature film counterpart. Yet scholars have yet to fully grapple with the implications of this distinction. As John Thornton Caldwell, commenting on the state of television scholarship and research, reminds us: "Part of the problem is that media scholarship and commercial marketing research alike (strange bedfellows indeed) tend to use a binary model of media industry and culture. In it, industry's above-the-line producers interact with consumers to produce entertainment and economic value." Like the auteur theory, what is left out of these models is the complexity of the production process, including its divisions of labor. Caldwell concludes: "Unfortunately, this model simplistically conflates 'industry' with 'producers'—a thin stratum that comprises only industry's 'executive crust'—and completely ignores an important third leg of the industry-culture stool: production workers."[10]

Television showrunners draw on the craft labor and creative practice of a range of below-the-line production workers. Within a show's writers' room they work with teams of writers, generating plot ideas, polishing series and character arcs, and breaking episodes. Here, again, Caldwell provides an insightful metaphor that is worth quoting in full:

> A dozen writers, working sixteen-hour days, collectively generate, shoot down, and hybridize the culled ideas into working form. Executive producers then dredge this story idea pit for narrative and script elements from which episodes and series are produced. But the hiving and distribution doesn't end there at the production's "front end," since each script poached from the writers' room is then sent out and broken down by all of the area heads and distributed among their own production departments' "hives." This distribution/harvesting

continues until production's "back end" when the producing power structure artificially determines which executives will hijack "creative" credit for features or series actually created by hundreds of other lower-level workers.[11]

Simply put, television-writing functions much like a hive, with multiple voices making interventions at multiple points in the production process. This was certainly the case with the making of *The Shield*.

To tease out Caldwell's metaphor, the showrunner is the queen directing the hive's economy; her work plan includes staffing decisions that determine who moves up in the world of work and who doesn't, and her performance is a major determining factor in the survival of the show. The showrunner doesn't direct the meanings that audiences make from what they watch, as the auteur theory predicts, though she does facilitate it in collaboration with a host of other creative professionals, below and above the line, and studio executives. In a phrase, she directs the story that a large team of people assembles from episode to episode. There are very few individuals in the feature film division of Hollywood that are vested with this level of creative freedom and responsibility.

Our case study of Ryan and the making of *The Shield* will reveal the contours of prominent and successful showrunners' creative latitude in basic cable in the twenty-first century. When the shows they are running are picked up and show signs of ratings success, showrunners play a decisive role in virtually all aspects of production. They create series bibles, which are what guest writers and directors use to make their creative proposals and, as we have noted, lead the development of story arcs across each season. Showrunners also approve budget adjustments, decide on casting, review deal agreements with guest actors, revise scripts, direct revisions of scripts with notes, frame the goal of the series with directors, review cuts of each episode and further direct the director's choices, provide notes on how to best market an episode, and, most important, decide who writes and who directs an episode, when to bring in a guest writer or director, and how to respond to a network that pushes back on budget changes, scene descriptions, or cuts. Unlike their tentpole feature counterparts, today's showrunner is experiencing something of a golden age of creative management.

GOLDEN AGE OF THE TELEVISION DRAMA WRITER

Not all television shows are run equally. With the relative freedom and authority to create and run a show come the pitfalls of overreach and failure in the form of cancellation. HBO's series *The Newsroom* (2012–14) is a case in point. The series took as its core subject the state of politics and journalism in the era of cable news. The ensemble format of the show's narrative, a hallmark of HBO's style, binds it to a tradition of quality television drama that stretches at least as far back as 1981 with Steven Bochco's groundbreaking ensemble police show, *Hill St. Blues* (1981–87). *The Newsroom* was created and produced for HBO by one of the exemplar showrunners of the TV drama, Aaron Sorkin, who made his reputation writing another show about politics and journalism *(The West Wing)*. Despite this impressive pedigree, the principal critique of *The Newsroom*, both during and after its three-season run, centered on its writing.

Sorkin is criticized for preaching at his audience, for patronizing his female characters or turning them into hysterics, for hewing his story arcs too closely to the sequence of recent political events—for being too "on the nose," in screenwriting vernacular. Whereas in *The Shield* violence was a key aspect of its story, in *The Newsroom* the key theme of politics came under a much more explicit analysis. Ryan provides a sense of his more subtle approach to running *The Shield:* "I think one thing that we tried hard to do is not to have an end agenda when we write these episodes. It's not like we start at a place of let's attack Christianity or of attacking homosexuality or supporting homosexuality or supporting liberalism or attacking conservatives and vice versa we never take that position . . . . I'm not trying to sell a belief system at the end of it. I think the moment you do that, the audience is very sophisticated and can smell that out."[12] Unlike Ryan, Sorkin was seen by his critics as attempting to sell a belief system—and doing so poorly.

Sorkin took his series in an explicitly polemical direction. By entering the overt political sphere, the showrunner was also critiqued from both left and right for picking the wrong target for his views. Popular critics complained that *The Newsroom* strained credibility by assuming that cable news in the wake of the less than "fair and balanced" Fox could be reformed and in promulgating the notion that it could offer, as critic Richard Lawson wrote in *Vanity Fair*, a "last bastion or bulwark against the lazy mediocreism of the Internet." Lawson cited the writing, and the lead writer and showrunner in particular, as key evidence of the show's "troubles." At the end of the show's run the magazine's critic even apologized to his readers for having offered a positive review after the show's premiere.[13]

A show that critiqued the dumbing down of journalism on the Internet also became a target of trenchant online critiques for the way it handled complex and controversial stories, not least the investigation of a campus rape. In trying to dissuade a female victim from going public, one of *The*

Newsroom's fictional producers cautioned her: "The law can acquit; the Internet never will."[14] Ironically, the Internet did not acquit *The Newsroom*. Blogger Cory Barker's review of the final episode stands for many and follows the thread Lawson offered but with flaming prose:

1. *The Newsroom* was not a good show.
2. The final season of *The Newsroom* has been largely dull and pointless.
3. Aaron Sorkin is, by all accounts, a pompous, privileged, and out-of-touch idealist who would rather lecture than tell stories, and who presumes that everyone enjoys watching television shows about white men—Sorkin's proxies—doing that lecturing to young people, women, or ghosts.[15]

Sorkin stands in for all that this critic sees as wrong with a show produced by a network, HBO, known for pushing the boundaries with stories that often investigated and illuminated complex and fraught social and cultural conditions—with series like *OZ* (1997–2003), *The Sopranos* (1999–2007), *The Wire* (2002–8), and even the short-lived *Deadwood* (2004–6)—but not for preaching.

What is most interesting about these critiques of Sorkin is how they focus on the show's writing. *The Newsroom* is proof, albeit to some extent in the negative, that American television drama is now perceived to be located firmly in the age of the showrunner. The focus on Sorkin's writing style and overall biography in debates around the show brings with it the clear assumption that the readers of newspapers, magazines, and media websites are not coming into that discussion blind. In the era after *Hill Street Blues*, and especially after *The Sopranos* and *The Shield*, critic and audience expectations for consistently good writing are high. Indeed, the criticism assumes that the consumer of "quality" television drama has at least a working knowledge of what a showrunner is and does. In fact, it assumes that we are conversant with the body of work of a number of showrunners and that this knowledge likely inflects our decision-making in seeking out a particular show, in following it, and in framing our assessment of it. For better or, at least in the case of Sorkin's *Newsroom*, worse, the concept of the showrunner, if perhaps not always the word itself, already functions as a brand.

The debate between traditional and Internet journalism that plays out across the long arc of *The Newsroom* is also a sign of the broader shift in convergent television away from the technologies of broadcast and cable toward digital and multiplatform distribution. From the perspective of the current generation of television screenwriters, however, the importance of the more recent seismic shifts in the ownership and distribution models of television, begun after the era of fin-syn, the Financial Interest and Syndication rules set by the Federal Communications Commission, and latterly digital and online distribution, is linked directly to their entrepreneurial ability to pitch innovative projects and to control the narrative on their own shows. In short, the successes of models of network monetization that do not rely on advertising revenue have contributed to a radical shift in the representational boundaries of storytelling on small screens. The wedge created by the economic and creative success stories of HBO and its fellows has also opened doors for shows like *The Shield* in the older economic model of basic cable (and, more recently, for some broadly cognate series in network television, like *Hannibal* on NBC and *The Following* on Fox).

The rebalancing of creative control in the favor of small-screen screenwriters suggests two overarching principles. The first is that the further television moves away from its broadcast network roots, the less influence the risk-averse, censorious network Standards and Practices departments have on its product. This is the case with the Standards and Practices notes found in the archives of *The Shield* that we detail later and hint at in our analysis of "Back to One" above. The primary role of Standards and Practices departments in network television is to protect advertisers from potentially embarrassing or damaging associations with controversial material in the shows that their commercials or direct sponsorship are financing. Standards and Practices departments also work to ensure that the government does not step in and enforce community standards, though that is far less a concern to networks than is mollifying the advertisers that finance their productions.

The Shield provides an interesting case study here, in that it appeared on a basic cable network with looser constraints with respect to standards than the traditional broadcast networks. Nonetheless, FX Standards and Practices Department memos, most written by Darlene Lieblich Tipton, then vice president of the department for the entire Fox Cable Networks Group, shows its primary concern centered on nudity and language. For the most part, showing genitalia and female nipples was not acceptable to FX's Standards and Practices Department. Additionally, many vulgar words, like *pussy*, were okay; hard-core words such as *fuck* were not. Yet the department is not always consistent, as this example from a Lieblich Tipton memo regarding the episode "Postpartum," from season 5, illustrates: "Page 50, Scene 46—Please find a less graphic alternative for the underlined portion of Spank's speech: 'Every chick's got a hole in her heart. *And just like the ones in their pussies*, no two's alike [emphasis in original].'"[16] All of the Standards and

Practices memos written by Lieblich Tipton or a member of her staff end with the rather Orwellian line: "We appreciate your cooperation."

Another concern centers on legal risk, the job of Lieblich Tipton being to ensure that the network is not sued for copyright infringement or slander. This exchange is illustrative:

> Given the pending charges for Michael Jackson, and the fact that we don't know at what stage the proceedings will be when this airs, please note that we may want to edit or replace Danny's unscripted line from Scene 71 when she locates the laptop filled with kiddie porn, "[I found it] underneath directions and a parking pass for the Neverland ranch." Particularly if he is acquitted, Michael Jackson's legal advisors could easily construe this as slanderous. The original "Lolita" line would be a much more prudent choice. However, you may want to record both versions and be prepared for a last minute edit depending on the legal proceedings at time of air.[17]

The scene was changed in the second revision of the script:

```
71 INT. BARN—BRIEFING ROOM—NIGHT       71
Dutch walking through as Danny and Julian approach. Danny
holds a laptop computer.

                    DANNY
    Recognize this, you big perv?

                    DUTCH
    Where was it?

                    JULIEN
    Desk drawer back in the storage room.

                    DANNY
    Underneath a first edition copy of Lolita with your name
    on it.

                    DUTCH
    Funny later. Not funny now. Thanks.
Dutch rushes off with the computer.

                    JULIEN
    Happy deleting.
As Danny and Julien watch him go.[18]
```

A final concern of Standards and Practices centers on ratings. The network department also looks to ensure key demographics are not alienated by the show, although interventions from the department on this basis were extremely and necessarily rare for a series like *The Shield*. Similar to advertisers, the concern here is the economic interest of the network. "My only major concern with the shooting script for Slipknot," writes Darlene Lieblich Tipton, "is with the name of the character Charlie Chun. The Asian-American community has given us a clear and strong message that they find the 'Charlie Chan' character, and even references to the character, stereotypical and offensive in the extreme. Since this homophonic character name apparently serves only to give Vic on *[sic]* reaction line on Page 32, we would appreciate it if you could create another name for this character."[19] Ryan agreed, and the reference was changed.

The above examples notwithstanding, Standards and Practices has less sway in cable production today than in the broadcast past. Ryan cooperated when he believed the stakes were low; he did not cooperate when he thought the story would be undermined by his "cooperation." Standards and Practices has even less influence on newer models of television production. As the distribution paradigm of convergent television moves through Advertising-supported Video on Demand (AVOD) platforms such as Hulu and Crackle and toward Subscription-supported Video on Demand (SVOD) platforms such as Netflix and Amazon, advertising dollars have less and less direct influence on the business model of the distributor. Indeed, in SVOD the role of Standards and Practices is largely obviated, and showrunners typically have much more creative leeway in areas that were once taboo, such as the representation of sex and violence.

The second principle of the rebalancing of creative control in the favor of small-screen screenwriters is that television is undergoing a wholesale transformation in the way it targets, measures, and values the size of its audiences. In particular, the monetization paradigms of digital distribution bring with them new and much more precise targeting algorithms— powerful new demographic marketing codes for niche and more specific audience building that have contributed to a consequent increase in the quality and diversity of televisual product. Moreover, digital platforms such as Netflix and Amazon are using quality drama to boost subscription rates for their services (such as Amazon Prime), not to sell advertising. As a consequence they measure the value of their audiences very differently.

The same has been true of more traditional pay cable channels like HBO and Showtime. Showrunners working for cable typically report far less corporate pressure, and far fewer fear-driven notes from executives, about the development of their story lines, for example. In short, the unappealing vision of the Internet as the herald of a wave of click-driven pseudo-journalism that was sold by *The Newsroom* must be seen in parallel with another vision of the Internet as the enabler of television drama's new golden age. As Ryan notes: "their metrics are different. It's not just about how many people watch because they are not selling ads based on those ratings. Which shows are driving people to subscribe and to keep those subscriptions active? And which shows are generating press that's generating attention?" The runner of *The Shield* goes on to provide an example: "*Mad Men* is a great example of a show that's not necessarily a ratings behemoth but the attention and cachet that it's brought to AMC is invaluable."[20] *The Shield* lasted seven seasons (six if we put the seasons that sandwich the WGA strike together) without ever securing high overall ratings.

The traditional method of measuring television audiences, the Nielsen rating, has become increasingly obsolete in the era of time-shifting DVRs, digital distribution, same-day series releases, binge viewing, and niche-marketed shows. Increasingly, official marketing of new shows has also shifted to the Internet, and the influence of online taste arbiters and fan communities has challenged the old hypodermic models of audience creation. As screenwriter Neil Landau suggests, the relationship between producers and the new cultural influencers has been transformative: "It used to be that a hit show built an audience. In today's world, the online community—aka the audience—builds a hit show. In return, the brand pumps up the audience via special events, merchandizing, and bonus content. It's a 2-way street, a yin and yang of interconnectedness in which authenticity is the tie that binds."[21]

The notion of the television showrunner as brand has its roots in the career of Norman Lear with situation comedies like *All in the Family* (1971–79), *The Jeffersons* (1975–85), and *Maude* (1972–78), as well as James L. Brooks, from shows like *Mary Tyler Moore* (1970–77) and *Rhoda* (1974–78), stretching through *The Simpsons* (1989–). But our point here is that the rise of the showrunner in the late twentieth century, and the rise of writers like Ryan and Sorkin in the early twenty-first, aligns with this history but also with the broader transformation of the industry. Although not all prominent showrunners today are known for genre projects, the television showrunner began to reemerge into public visibility in the 1990s, at the intersection of an expansion of smart genre television on network and cable and the broadening of fan culture via the emergent Internet. In particular, the association or branding of particular showrunners like Joss Whedon *(Buffy the Vampire Slayer)* by genre and within fan culture since the 1990s has done much to increase public awareness of the role of the television screenwriter in general. Publics sharing the same "habitus," to use sociologist Pierre Bourdieu's term, have catalyzed a certain realignment of audience identification with writing and have also helped to raise the profile of the showrunner-as-asset within the industry.

The circuit of culture here begins with a team that has one person—a queen, to continue our play on Caldwell's hive metaphor, as its head. Ryan, like many showrunners, does not physically direct the shows or even write every episode. He operates as the head of a team of creatives, each of whom is dedicated to the particular aesthetic that makes *The Shield*, in the catchphrase of the show's crew, "Shieldy." Ryan explained what *Shieldy* means to him: "it means no compromises for TV. The actors and actresses shouldn't look prettier than they really should—I joke that this is the only show where actors go into the trailer and come out looking worse, which I like. *Shieldy* means being true to that moment." He doesn't claim he is the only showrunner on TV to go in that direction, pointing to David Mamet (*The Unit*, CBS 2006–9), but he concludes: "I don't think you'll find any more fervent believers in what we're doing in that regard. I'm committed to making the show feel unpolished, raw and real."[22]

This sense of the show's wider production culture supporting the writing in being Shieldy filters throughout the below-the-line crew. For example, one of the makeup artists, Jennifer Seata, described the term to media scholar Kevin Sandler this way: "Shieldy is very original when it comes to characters and their description. It really is what it is. We want to leave the blotchiness in their skin tone. We're not going to put bases on most everyone. We'll do a little bit of powder, but we want to see those flaws. We want to see those lines."[23] And Post Production Supervisor Craig Yahata described it this way: "something that I have to learn, and unlearn from all the processes from other shows and things, is that it is supposed to be a rough documentary feel that isn't over-produced isn't over-rehearsed; it's kind of just run and gun."[24]

Bernardi and Sandler argue that no other contemporary showrunner has had the same impact on television as Ryan did by branding FX as a cutting-edge risk-taking network with *The Shield*.[25] The loyalty of the audience to Ryan, and thus the modest but sustaining ratings of *The Shield*, encouraged FX to develop a diverse stable of innovative or boundary-pushing shows like *Nip/Tuck* (2003–10), *Rescue Me* (2004–11), and *Justified* (2010–15). Along with *The Shield* these shows established FX as a network of choice for viewers within the lucrative younger demographics and the advertisers that sought their buying power. FX is now widely considered one of the most provocative and risky producers of original drama of its era. In other words, it did not matter that *The Shield* failed to attract the ratings of shows on the traditional broadcast networks like *Law and Order* (1990–2010) or *CSI* (2000–2015); the series offered viewers interested in the police genre more intrigue, risk, and social insight in a way that not only branded Ryan but also FX, enabling yet another circuit in the working world of television culture, as well as helping to define the new golden age of television dramatic writing.

A SHIELDY NETWORK

The Shield premiered on FX, the seven-year-old basic cable network of Rupert Murdoch's News Corp conglomerate, in March 2002. The introduction of the series marked another reinvention of the channel's identity, one that had undergone several transformations since its inception. Launched in June 1994, FX was an early pioneer of interactive television, adopting the Internet as a method of feedback from viewers for several of its shows broadcast live every day from its "FX apartment" in Manhattan's Flatiron District. Hampered by budgetary issues and low-carriage rates on cable systems, FX relaunched itself in early 1997, targeting men eighteen to forty-nine years old mainly with sports programming (NASCAR, Major League Baseball, etc.), talk or variety shows *(Penn and Teller's Sin City Spectacular; The X Show; The New Movie Show with Chris Gore)*, the established film library of 20th Century Fox, and several off-network and off-demo, Fox-owned dramas *(Ally McBeal; The X-Files; Buffy the Vampire Slayer)*.[26] FX had one original comedy series, the Howard Stern–produced *Son of a Beach*, and a series of original films dealing with topical issues like the First Amendment *(Deliberate Intent; The Sight; A Glimpse of Hell)*, as well as controversial subjects relevant to the day, notably *Sins of the Father*, the "true" story of the complex relationship between a son and his ex–Ku Klux Klan father indicted for the Sixteenth Street Baptist Church bombing in Birmingham, Alabama, that killed four young girls in 1963.[27]

The success of dramas targeted at particular audience demographics on other basic cable networks convinced FX that an original series like *The Shield* could be viable. Lifetime, for example, had its female-skewing originals *Any Day Now* and *Strong Medicine*. Network management decided that FX could target an entirely different demographic with the kind of provocative, daring fare that characterized its original TV movies like *Sins of the Father*. At the same time, it could help the network distinguish itself from the commercial broadcast networks while linking itself in the public consciousness to the groundbreaking product of HBO. Peter Liguori, FX's president at the time, made his strategy clear: "There was HBO on one pole, on one side, that had almost this monopoly on great authentic or adult-like challenging programming, and then there were all the networks like TNT, TBS, and USA on the other pole and there was nothing in the middle. And it just didn't seem possible in the world of basic cable that there wasn't a channel which was a little more adult, a little more muscular, a little more authentic, a little more fearless."[28] Liguori selected *The Shield* as the network's first dramatic series.

From the beginning, FX viewed the pilot script—one, as we have noted, inspired by a real-life scandal involving the antigang squad in the LAPD Rampart Division—as a means for the network to establish a brand identity to distinguish it from the traditional broadcast networks. For Liguori and his partner, FX president of entertainment Kevin Reilly, the pilot had to have a level of authenticity, truth, and emotionality unlike any previous police drama. First-time showrunner Ryan, with the supervision of FX executives, assembled a team of industry veterans for the pilot to reimagine the genre, including director Clark Johnson, who directed additional episodes including the season finale, and series cinematographer Rohn Schmidt. The use of an actual abandoned church in downtown Los Angeles for the precinct house ("The Barn"), the inclusion of graphic violence and explicit language, and the murder of a cast member (Reed Diamond, familiar to many viewers as a star of *Homicide*) by the show's main character, Vic, immediately signaled *The Shield*'s departure from the conventions of broadcast television. As a result, *The Shield* filled a niche between subscription cable channels and commercial broadcasters, eventually cementing FX as the home of cutting-edge dramatic series that were character driven, graphically and emotionally direct, and reflective of a contemporary American reality.

Before the first day of shooting on June 6, 2001, several months prior to 9/11, the development of the series went through requisite fits and starts. For example, the network was uncomfortable with Ryan being the sole showrunner, as he lacked experience, so it brought in Scott Brazil as coshowrunner of the series. The relationship between Ryan and Brazil flourished from the start, with Brazil supporting Ryan's emphasis on engaging gritty social themes through the show's characters.

The character descriptions provided to casting agents before the first day of shooting are illustrative. For example, Danny Sofer (originally named Altamore) is described as follows:

[DANIELLE "DANNY" ALTAMORE] Late 20's. Caucasian ... A uniform police officer, Danny's a woman in a man's world and has learned to co-exist, if not completely fit in. Constantly curious to learn more and to be as good a cop as she can be, she'll always have some doubts about whether she passes muster on the job, but she hides it well from others. Recently partnered with a rookie cop, she's now, for the first time, in the position of teaching someone else, a challenge and a responsibility she relishes. A single gal, Danny finds herself extremely attracted to Vic, something the two of them have acted on once or twice in the past, but which Danny ended, yet can't seem to put completely behind her. She's still struggling to come to terms with her identity as a cop and a woman. She's completely believed as a uniformed policewoman, but when we see her out of uniform for the first time, she reveals a softness and accessible beauty that we hadn't seen before . . . SERIES REGULAR (1)[29]

Also telling is the description of David Aceveda (at that point, named David Hernandez):

[DAVID HERNANDEZ] Early-mid 30's. Hispanic . . . Highly intelligent, fiercely ambitious and politically savvy, David is the new "posterboy" for the L.A.P.D. It's only now, four months into his new job as Captain of the Farmington District Police Squad, that David realizes he's been installed, not to affect any real change, but merely to act as the public face of the police department and to maintain the status quo. Younger than many of the men he's commanding, David is looked upon as a "test taker" and a "quota baby," despite the hard work he's put in to advance quickly up the ranks. David's determined to win his squadhouse's respect and feels there's no better way to do it than to take down a corrupt cop like Vic Mackey. Happily married with a young daughter, David finds himself in the middle of a missing child case, torn between doing the right thing or the thing that will save time, but jeopardize his career . . . SERIES REGULAR (3)[30]

The writing here makes clear that the show is going to explore what it means to be a "beautiful" woman in a testosterone-dominated environment and to be a Latino charged with managing it all. Ryan set up the characters both to evoke and to challenge stereotypes. His vision, of course, changes for creative and pragmatic reasons throughout the development of the series. For example, the Wyms character was initially envisioned as a man:

[CHARLES BENNETT] Mid 40'S-early 50'S. African-American . . . A world weary detective with a disarming manner that gets witnesses and suspects alike to open up to him, Charles remains a cop now more out of habit than anything else. Death and tragedy are more likely to elicit a reaction of disappointment from Charles than one of outrage or shock. He's simply seen too much in his time to be affected by the latest atrocity. Divorced for a while now, Charles is very much alone in the world, many of his contemporaries retired or promoted past him.

Despite his situation, Charles isn't a sulker or a complainer. Instead he finds simple joys in life like walking his pet dog or the occasional practical joke at his partner's expense . . . SERIES REGULAR (1)

Deborah Aquila Casting initially recommended primarily male actors for the part:

Glynn Turman

Carl Weathers

James Avery

Brent Jennings

Obba Babatundé

Grand Bush

Mel Winkler

Ellis Williams[31]

The one woman recommended for the part was CCH Pounder, who was hired. Pounder's character became by many accounts the moral voice of the series, carrying many story lines, becoming a captain, and dealing with racism and misogyny, although Wyms was also involved with numerous situations that were unconnected to those issues.

In the days after 9/11, Fox executives wondered whether the series was inappropriate. After all, New York City's police officers were now seen as heroes. In that context, did audiences want to see Vic Mackey? Peter Liguori, chairman and chief executive of FX; David A. Grant, president of Fox Television Studios; and Ryan nervously proceeded but were uneasy about possible critical and audience fallout. So, too, were the actors. As Michael Chiklis recalled: "We were genuinely all so blown away and devastated by what had occurred that we had some very sober conversations about is this the time to do this show. With what law enforcement—police and fire—had gone through in this situation and the unity of the country right after—is this the time to explore this antihero? Now the question is not just what are you willing to accept from law enforcement to keep you safe, it's what are you willing to accept from your law enforcement post 9/11 to keep you safe?" The stakes were indeed high in the patriotic aftermath of 9/11. "It made us understand that we could now, as a result, face potentially being run out of town," Chiklis reflected. "This could evoke a horrible reaction."[32]

A turning point came on the weekend of October 5, 2001, when the Warner Bros. film *Training Day*, screenplay by David Ayer, about a corrupt Los Angeles policeman, opened to good reviews and unexpectedly powerful box-office revenues of $22.5 million. Denzel Washington, who played the bad cop, went on to win an Academy Award for his portrayal. "We saw there was an audience out there who wanted to see a fully dimensionalized representation of the police," Liguori reported.[33] In a later interview, he recalled: "There is a sense of the station house besieged, and of angry, cynical, paranoid cops hunkered down inside both their inner-city bunker and a fundamentalist freakview, like a Trotskyite or Hezbollah sect, lobbing jokes as if they were grenades. Which may be why the camera gets jumpier every season—and the nation, too, on the verge of [a] nervous breakdown."[34]

Before the episode actually began at the 10 o'clock hour, FX unveiled *The Shield*'s rating: TV-MA (Mature Audience: May be unsuitable for children under 17). The TV-MA rating is the most restrictive of the age-based Parental Guidelines System for broadcast and cable networks in effect since January 1, 1997. Despite being part of a voluntary system with no legal force and whose ratings the networks themselves determine, the TV-MA rating had been rarely used on commercial network and basic cable television up to this point. On basic cable, only Comedy Central's *South Park* and the short-lived *That's My Bush* had previously carried the tag. Pay channels like HBO and Showtime embraced the TV-MA rating on a regular basis, whereas the broadcast networks first used it in fall 1997 with CBS's *Brooklyn South*. The TV-MA rating not only signified that *The Shield* would contain explicit sexual content, graphic violence, and/or strong profanity but that it was clearly a conscious decision on the part of FX to push the envelope of ad-supported television. The network pursued programming, stated Kevin Reilly in an FX press release announcing his appointment as FX president of entertainment, "which embrace[d] a point of view not available on network TV, but of a quality not found on basic cable."[35] In short, *The Shield* was basic cable's first successful attempt to compete with HBO.

The first two minutes of the pilot of *The Shield* served as a harbinger for the grittiness that led to "Back to One." Originally titled "The Barn,"[36] an overtly racist epithet referring to the nickname of the fictional central Los Angeles precinct of Farmington, the first episode of *The Shield* opens with Captain David Aceveda (Benito Martinez), the self-assured, career-driven Latino precinct chief, flanked by his Asian public-relations officer (Tamlyn Tomita) addressing the media. "The Farmington District of Los Angeles," Aceveda proclaims, "has traditionally been one of the most dangerous and crime-ridden districts of the city. Some reporters have gone so far as to label Farmington a 'war zone.'" Intercut with the captain's remarks are other single one-second shots of uniformed officers Danielle "Danny" Sofer (Catherine Dent) and Julien Lowe (Michael Jace) patrolling Farmington and a fight between prisoners locked up in the "Cage" at the Barn. We are also introduced to the title cards for the lead actors of the series, unique in the sense that their font has a grimy, aged patina to it and is presented as if filmed by a handheld camera. The latent volatility of these images quickly gives way to a scene on the street: a black man named Booty, caught selling cocaine to teenagers, pursued at a frenetic pace by an all-white, antigang task force, the Strike Team, led by Chiklis's Vic Mackey. Shot strictly handheld or on Steadicam on location with natural lighting as Latino music blares on the soundtrack, the visual style and mise-en-scène of the show, scripted by Ryan and his team, immediately situated it alongside police dramas like *Homicide: Life on the Street* and *NYPD Blue* but far from procedurals like *Law and Order* and *Nash Bridges,* one of Shawn Ryan's previous writing gigs.

The irony of Aceveda's statement quickly sets in as *The Shield* starts to look more like the fictional counterpart to the long-running reality television show *Cops* than a genre disciple of *NYPD Blue*. A montage, crosscutting between the PR machine of the Barn and the quasi-legal tactics of the Strike Team, creates a dynamic dialectic that characterizes the political thrust of *The Shield,* shocking viewers into reconceptualizing the social discourses surrounding representations of race, sexuality, and authority on American television. Aceveda tells the press:

```
I am proud to announce that murders, rape, armed robberies,
and many other violent crimes have decreased dramatically
in this district in the last six months. . . . Under my
direction, law enforcement officers now participate in
neighborhood outreach programs. Already the effect is being
felt by local families. Mothers feel safer as they shop for
groceries. With the continued support of community leaders
and ordinary citizens, we can make the Farmington district
a safer home for all of us.
```

What instantaneously follows these last words is a scene that reads as anything but police protection of citizens. The Strike Team has cornered Booty down an alleyway behind a Mexican supermarket. With a "local family" looking on from a balcony of a tenement building, Vic, who has witnessed Booty swallowing the evidence, punches him directly in the gut. "Thanks for running, asshole," Vic tells Booty, now writhing in pain on the ground. Pulling him to his feet, Vic subsequently pulls Booty's shorts and underwear down, his backside now exposed directly at the camera. "Looks like you got some kind of third hand going down there," Vic tells him as he rips some extra contraband off his testicles, pocketing it himself rather than giving it to his partner, Lemansky, to place in an evidence bag. The drug dealer runs into an alley as Latinos watch the scene from their balconies. This is an African American drug dealer in a Latino neighborhood chased by an all-white strike team. Bars metaphorically surround them, an iron fence, providing a visual foreshadowing of what is to come. His team looks on, smiling, like we have seen in shots of southern audiences at lynchings.

The episode's B story line sets up the model of short procedural, crime-solving narratives that will run parallel to the longer season and series arcs of the Strike Team's corruption and the reform of Farmington police station. This plot strand focuses on a murder investigation by two of the show's uncorrupted detectives, Dutch and Claudette Wyms. It starts with a naked female body lying dead on the floor. A shot of her feet in close-up reveals her breasts in the middle ground just above a noticeable pool of blood. An oven mitt covers her vagina. This is not your father's television. Dutch makes a reference to the dead woman's breasts: "You do not see a pair like that every day." In an extreme low-angle of Wyms, establishing her prominence over Dutch and, in fact, the series, the African American detective retorts: "You want to give them a squeeze?" The sexual innuendoes do not end there, as Ryan and the network continue to push the boundaries past previous broadcast standards. A grieving sister falls to her knees in front of Dutch, her head at the height of his groin. We see uniform officers smiling—seeing an off-color joke on Dutch in the works.

The Shield pushed the boundaries of representation and broadcast standards starting with the writing. As the actor that plays Dutch, Jay Karns, commented: "I think it's awful Shieldy that often Dutch could make jokes on dead bodies. The pilot, the woman with the oven mitt over her vagina lying there naked and Dutch was making jokes about what a great rack she's got. That's very Shieldy. . . . It's in the writing and I do my best as an actor to inhabit [it]."[37] The network was supportive from the start. In the network notes for the July 5 cut of the premiere, FX and FTVS advised: "not sure if the cops' POV of the blowjob is clear. Please insert shot of Janet going down on Dutch before and after shot of cops laughing."[38] The network wants to make sure its audience will understand the visual joke as well as the culture of the uniform police officers and detectives. At the same time, FX was mindful of its language standards: "Did Shane say 'fuck you'? Please omit."[39]

The premiere of *The Shield* did exceptionally well, and FX capitalized on it with a boastful press release: "The critically acclaimed, first original drama series from FX, achieved ratings history for its premiere on Tuesday, March 12th (10 PM ET/PT). The debut episode recorded 4.1 household ratings, 3.1 million homes and 4.8 million viewers, making it the most-watched original series premiere in basic cable television history. In addition, it was the highest-rated, most watched program in cable on Tuesday March 12, and it was the highest-rated, most-watched entertain[ment] program in FX's seven-year history. FX was also the highest rated cable network in prime time on Tuesday, March 12, with a 3.2 household rating." These ratings would not be considered all that impressive on the traditional networks, but they were, as FX boasted, landmarks on basic cable.

Critics also praised the premiere, ensuring the series entered the penultimate industrial discourse. "FX breaks new ground in a big way with 'The Shield,' the most innovative, electric and foul-mouthed hour to hit the air since one of its obvious influences, 'The Sopranos,'" wrote Michael Speier for *Daily Variety;* "a tour de force of assorted emotions, layered relationships, and raw dialogue, quality plots and relevant leads are the key." James Poniewozik wrote the following for *Time:* "*The Shield* is a self-consciously different animal.... It's already the most riveting player in the tapped-out field of cop dramas." And Caryn James of the *New York Times* solidified the rave reviews: "It echoes reality closely enough to create a chilling resonance.... The smooth mix makes the series intriguing, and its energy is relentless."[40] Of course, FX included these and many other reviews in its press release.

The Shield put FX right in the bull's-eye for moral media reformers and conservative politicians, which is exactly what the then-fledgling network was hoping for: a battle of ideologies that extended the trade chatter about the series. For example, the Parents Television Council, a nonprofit organization, successfully persuaded several advertisers not to buy time during the series because of the show's graphic material, including nudity, depictions of sexual activity, and foul language. Ryan recalled his reaction:

> This show's been targeted from the beginning. We got a letter from the Parents' Television Council that referred to us as "*The Shield* immediately establishes itself as the single most vulgar piece of primetime basic cable piece of garbage ever produced by Hollywood," and you have to wear that as a badge of honor. These people tried to shut our show down, they tried to get advertisers to boycott us and then when you come out of the other side of that and win awards ... you know and win critical praise—they don't talk about it as much anymore, we're the ones that showed the clip to Jay Rockefeller because they're trying to curb cable TV now until there's nothing on TV that won't offend an eight year old.[41]

As the series continued, it remained faithful to its initial intent to engage socially contentious issues in a gritty, violent, and dramatic fashion: from the crime and drugs that plague Los Angeles barrios and the people of color that live there to an all-white strike team managed by an ambitious police captain. The negative press likely helped propel the series into the national spotlight. Even bad news for a fledgling network with a new, cutting-edge TV show can be good news for the marketing department.

"What is underestimated is the degree to which *The Shield* and to some extent *Nip/Tuck*," John Landgraf recalled, "was really a bridge between what the networks were doing and what HBO was doing."[42] It's no coincidence that he was formerly president of Brad Grey Television, the television production arm of Brillstein-Grey Entertainment, which produced *The Sopranos*. *The Shield*'s narrative complexity and stylistic originality also made it a significant contributor during its run to the rise in DVD rentals and sales for television series that facilitated a culture of binge viewing before the advent of SVOD and downloads. Although rough and gritty, its style has, as film scholar Jason Mittell notes, the "rewatchability" factor. If, like more traditional television, the narrative is straightforward and the characters always wholesome, consumers are less likely to purchase or rent the DVD—unless, of course, they're doing so for nostalgia, which is a much smaller market. If, however, as Mittell notes, "a show has a complex narrative construction and richly detailed content, viewers will be more inclined to want to rewatch episodes or segments to parse out complex moments."[43] DVD sales of *The Shield* also did exceptionally well, illustrating the point that its stories, characters, and visual style possess the rewatchability factor evident in contemporary quality television.

Considered visually dynamic and narratively complex by the Hollywood community, the series attracted A-list directors such as Frank Darabont and David Mamet to its production crew. In 2003 the police drama made history in its initial season by becoming the first basic cable drama to earn a Golden Globe for Best Television Series. Chiklis, a stocky actor previously known for his role as a "sensitive" police commissioner on ABC's *The Commish* (1991–96), also earned a Golden Globe and an Emmy that year for his work on the show. Building on his personal success with *The Shield*, Shawn Ryan subsequently became one of Hollywood's most prominent showrunners. The writer-producer teamed up with Mamet to create CBS's *The Unit* (2006–9), ran the second season of Fox's *Lie to Me* (2009), and went on to showrun *Terriers* (2010) and *Timeless* (2016, awaiting renewal decision).[44]

Critics and scholars typically argue that HBO's *The Sopranos* and not *The Shield* has had the greatest impact on television drama in the postnetwork era.[45] The *Chicago Tribune*'s Maureen Ryan calls it "the most influential television drama ever."⁴⁶ MIT professor David Thorburn identifies it as the "first great work of American art of the twenty-first century."⁴⁷ There is good reason for this high praise. Premiering three years before *The Shield*, *The Sopranos* offered viewers a complex antihero, Tony Soprano. Part ruthless killer, part family man, and part depressed godfather, Tony is, in fact, the prototypical antihero that led directly to Vic Mackey. Moreover, *The Sopranos* offered an ensemble cast that allowed its actors, writers, and directors to create a number of complex story arcs and characterizations. The show's influence extended to HBO's other series—from *The Wire* to *Deadwood* to *True Blood* (2008–14)—and into prime-time broadcast and basic cable television with shows like *Lost* (2004–10), *Battlestar Galactica* (2004–9), and, as the aforementioned critics noted, *The Shield*. And then there's *The Sopranos'* endless media coverage and high cable rating numbers, averaging eleven million total viewers at its peak during season 4, the equivalent of a top-ten to top-fifteen show in the broadcast universe.⁴⁸ During its seven seasons each episode of *The Shield* was watched by an average of slightly more than three million viewers.

Despite never reaching the popularity and popular cultural status of *The Sopranos*, *The Shield* promises to have a greater, more lasting impact on the institutional, commercial, and stylistic dimensions of US television. First, *The Sopranos*, as noted film scholar Dana Polan observed, was scripted for an actor-driven theatrical model drawn from European art cinema—what he called a "sobriety of style" in framing and composition.⁴⁹ *The Shield*, however, offered a stylized appropriation of documentary and reality form integrated with the evolving stylistic traditions familiar to its genre in broadcast and cable television that matched the unconventionality and complexity of its story lines and character. The team behind *The Shield* wasn't alone in experimenting with this kind of style. Joss Whedon was also using coverage plans and a shooting style influenced by documentary in his own influential, if short-lived, ensemble science fiction series *Firefly* (2002–3, Fox). Yet *The Shield*, which began broadcasting the same year, takes the style to an extreme. Its writers' use of language and their representation of violence and sexuality in these narratives were more graphic than anything on commercial television at the time, realigning the boundaries of permissibility on the small screen. Second, after the series' success, *The Shield* effectively reshaped the landscape of US commercial television. HBO continued to make hit shows for upscale subscribers as a result of *The Sopranos*, but FX solidified the business model for ad-supported cable networks that now dominate prime-time viewership. At the same time, *The Shield* offered budget-conscious networks a more cost-effective mode of production.

Each episode of Ryan's police drama was shot in seven days on 16 mm film, as opposed to eight or more days on 35 mm film as is typical with one-hour dramas like *The Sopranos*. This cost-effective strategy permitted FX executives to take greater risks with the show and to focus on its branding power.

Other scholars have identified *The Shield* as an important series. In her seminal book, *The Television Will Be Revolutionized*, Amanda D. Lotz argues that *The Shield* "was unlike any show created or financed during the network era" and proved that original series could bring profits to basic cable networks in the twenty-first century.[50] And John Thornton Caldwell, in *Production Culture: Industrial Reflexivity and Critical Practice in Film and Television*, uses examples from *The Shield* to illustrate his perspective on the culture of television production. Pointing to its hyperactive visual style, Caldwell makes the case for the series' "hit-and-run" method of shooting scenes uninterruptedly for sometimes five minutes or more. "Unlike traditional hour-long dramatic production in, say, the 1960s or 1970s," he says, "the camera never stops running and moving, and the actors create kinetic interactive scenes never knowing where the camera is actually framing."[51]

Yet neither Lotz nor Caldwell dive into *The Shield* in a comprehensive manner; their projects are focused on other dimensions of television studies. Additionally, only a handful of journal articles and anthology chapters engage with *The Shield* in a meaningful way, either from a film and media studies or other disciplinary perspective. These pieces explore representations of masculinity and race, police brutality and criminality, media effects and virtual reality.[52] An exception is Brenton J. Malin's insightful industry study that links *The Shield* and *The Sopranos* to the economics of masculinity on television: "Programs such as *The Sopranos* and *The Shield* demonstrate how contemporary versions of this hard-boiled masculinity can earn both profits and critical acclaim within the context of present-day television economics."[53] Nonetheless, most film and media scholars give short shrift to the show's importance, and almost all ignore the critical role played by its showrunner.

To better appreciate the contours of a showrunner's imprint on, or creative management of, a series, we consider in more detail the development of "Mum," one of the show's most creative yet socially critical episodes of *The Shield*, written by Ryan and Kurt Sutter. The Internet Movie Database (IMDb) provides a rather tame synopsis: "As Dutch and Claudette continue to pursue a rapist who is targeting elderly women, the arrest of a local gang member threatens to expose the Strike Team's involvement in the money train heist."[54] The episode, however, features a disturbing rape scene. Captain Aceveda, in pursuit of glory, is jumped and subsequently raped by a Byz Lat (Byzantine Latino) gang member while another Byz Lat records the act. Brandon Nowalk's synopsis for A.V. Club is more accurate: "And then one forces Aceveda to suck his dick at gunpoint."[55]

The shooting schedule for that scene in "Mum," a document that lists production locations with brief story content, only states: "INT Aramis' House: Revenge on David."[56] That is all that was needed by the time of production, as Ryan worked with the network, director Nick Gomez, director of photography Rohn Schmidt, and Benito Martinez, the actor who plays Aceveda, to align them with his creative vision. A violent and disturbing act for fans and critics of the show, Ryan and Sutter went so far as including a sketched storyboard, visually scripting how the scene should be shot affixed to each draft of the script:

It is in the script and notes that we see Ryan's creative management (figs. 2–6). With Sutter, they tease out the rape throughout the episode, crosscutting between scenes, calling for close-ups but making clear that the Latino captain is raped. We first read of the violence in act 2:

```
Juan SLAMS David in the face again. The Captain falls to his
knees. Juan grabs an electrical CLOCK off the counter, ripping
the plug out of the wall. Throws it to Ricky.

                    JUAN
    Tie him.

Ricky obeys. Ties David's hands behind his back. The clock
dangles from David's bound hands.

                    DAVID
    (Spits blood) Don't throw your life away.

                    JUAN
    I ain't afraid of prison (unbuckles his belt). But you should
    be (unzips). You ever suck a dick like a cell bitch, copman?

                    DAVID
    Don't do this.

                    JUAN
    Time for you to gag on something.

Ricky watches on horrified and enthralled as Juan puts David's
gun to his head.

                    JUAN
    Open up, sweetheart.
```

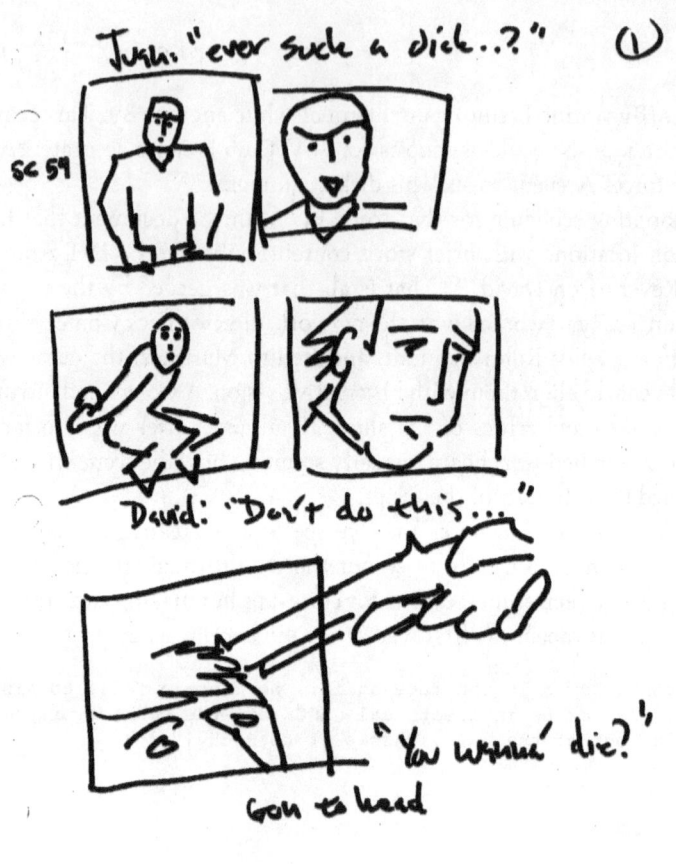

Running the Room   /   129

                    DAVID
          No.

Presses the gun against David's temple.

                    JUAN
          You gonna die instead?

                    DAVID
          No.

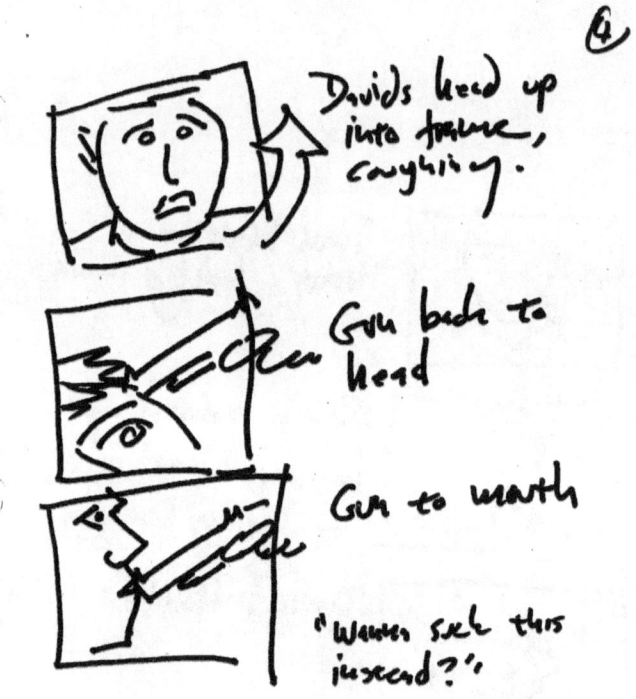

Ryan and Sutter create additional drama—and prurient anticipation—by having at that moment two uniform police officers knock at the back door. Of course, the economy of television script writing is not unlike the economy of feature script writing, at least with respect to dialogue. But in the scene descriptions it is more economical; fewer words are used to set and move the scene along. This is about dramatic conflict at the level of plot and character. Within seconds the uniformed officers leave. The captain, as we suspected, is not to be saved. "Let's see that mouth," Juan says as Sutter and Ryan's direction calls for a "SMASH TO BLACK" and the end of act 2.

In keeping with the show's established approach to dramatic build, act 3 does not start with the rape but with the A story line involving Vic. But it moves speedily to the rape:

```
INT. Aramis' HOUSE — KITCHEN — DAY

David and Juan in mid-oral rape. David on his knees, Juan
still with the gun to his head. Ricky looks on, increasingly
skittish.
```

Running the Room / 131

                    JUAN

    Don't make me do all the work, puta. Put some groove into
    it (beat). Suck it.

David gags, half-coughs.

                    JUAN

    Little bigger than you're used to? (to Ricky) Get your
    phone, man.

                    RICKY

    What?

                          JUAN

    Your phone. I want a Kodak of this. (to David) Keep on it.

Ricky reaches into his pocket, pulls out one of the newfangled
camera phones. David starts to pull away.

                          JUAN

    (re: the gun) You gonna suck this instead?

Juan pulls David's head back with one hand, drills the gun
into David's temple with the other.

                          JUAN

    I'm almost there, baby. (to Ricky) You ready?

                          RICKY

    (aiming camera) Yeah.

Juan poses, smiles for the camera. Ricky snaps a picture on
his phone.

                          RICKY

    (nervous) Got it.

Ryan and Sutter end there, David's humiliation cemented in digital form. Most interesting in this scene is the way the writers construct Ricky. He's tough, a true gangbanger. Yet he is written with some complexity, apprehensive, offended, and with a hint of disgust. In this way he represents the show's implied viewer, the fan of *The Shield*, interested in the edge but, with some whiplash, also disgusted by it. Ryan and Sutter push the story further, with David saved by the police after the rape but before they could see it. David, true to Ryan's original vision of a talented but political cop, says nothing save for: "I was able to fight 'em off."

Standards and Practices dug into the script. Of this scene, Craig Sunderland from the department wrote: "Please be careful how the male rape scene is portrayed both visually and audibly. Please make sure no genitalia is shown." And next: "Please remove or change Juan's 'puta.'"[57] Several days later, Sunderland retracts the request to remove "puta."[58] Yet days thereafter, the department's Neil Klasky repeated the request to take care with the scene: "Please be careful how the male rape scene is portrayed both visually and audibly. Please make sure no genitalia is shown."[59] Sunderland follows the request a day later, repeating it verbatim.[60] Clearly, Ryan was pushing back on the Standards and Practices team. And he continued to do so, as Standards and Practices, this time in the person of

Darlene Lieblich Tipton, requested changes to the next episode, "Posse Up," written by Kim Clements and Charles H. Eglee, which followed the rape arc. In response to her request to "In the opening recap, please lose the 'action' shot of Acevedo's rape—specifically, where he's down on his knees," Ryan responded: "How exactly are we supposed to let the audience know that he was raped then?"[61] Lieblich Tipton agreed but continued the request, nonetheless thanking Ryan for his "help and humor!"[62]

The work of Standards and Practices goes to a kind of self-censorship, yet we could find no record that someone from Standards and Practices, let alone the network more broadly, demanded that "Mum" not depict the male rape of one of its stars. What is interesting in this and other exchanges, at least for our purposes, is not how they expose the bureaucratic architecture of network censorship but, in fact, the remarkable freedom they reveal of the established showrunner to craft stories and story arcs that are relatively new to television, that are highly controversial. They also demonstrate the ability of the showrunner actively to push back, to resist in the language of cultural studies, when he thinks doing so is in support of the story he and his collaborators are telling. To some extent showrunners still need to pick their battles, of course, but the documentation of Shawn Ryan's interactions with Standards and Practices shows how far the relationship had shifted by the time of *The Shield*'s production and how much further a Shieldy showrunner who was, in turn, protected by an invested network could move the internal debate on scripting and representation.

"Mum" aired on April 6, 2004. The acting is unnervingly precise, as Benito Martinez, playing the alpha-male Latino cop, performs fear followed by self-loathing with palpability. The actor playing Juan, Kurt Caceres, is no less haunting in his performance. He screams with fierce jubilation at the end of his rape. Wilmer Calderon's performance of Ricky reveals what Ryan and Sutter wrote: excitement turned into fear and then disgust. Gomez's direction, coupled with Rohn Schmidt's shaky cinematography and, in postproduction, further scripting through the edit and sound design, makes for an unsettling scene of male rape that threatens the masculinity of the series with the same brutal masculinity represented in Vic—and without shots of genitalia or penetration. This is disturbing television, visceral in its ideological brutality—Shieldy in the extreme. It represents the creative authority of Ryan, a showrunner who has the relative independence to write drama without fear and then direct its production with clarity. He thus represents a different story arc for the working screenwriter. Ryan is less tentpole widget maker and more creative manager charged with the deployment of a wide range of convergent skills in the service of *his* show—from writing to directing to editing to producing.

A SHIELDY SHOWRUNNER

To borrow from the sociolect of the show's crew, *The Shield* is Shieldy because its showrunner remained committed to his original vision. Ryan pushed the political and social agendas of the series to remain consistent to its gritty realist pilot. He engaged the media to ensure, or help ensure, that the series was framed as such for critics and fans alike. The respect he commanded from other showrunners, writers, and stars, helped to turn him into an emergent brand, just as it did FX. Most important, perhaps, for the recent history of screenwriting in Hollywood, Ryan achieved a certain prominence in the industry at a moment when the new generation of showrunners would be obliged to have a leading role in the writers' strike. Given the reputation of an earlier generation of showrunners within the Writers Guild of America for undermining a previous dispute, Ryan and his colleagues were under intense scrutiny by the wider community of professional screenwriters as the dispute ramped up. As we have noted, their colleagues and the wider industry were well aware that the decisions they made about how to deploy the power of their screenwriting labor would have a major impact on the conduct, duration, and outcomes of the strike. In short, rank-and-file WGA members hoped their wealthy and successful showrunner colleagues would turn out to be the right kind of Shieldy when push came to shove. Ryan's attitude during the strike, which of course interrupted production of *The Shield*, is illustrative. At the start of the strike he released a statement outlining his personal reading of the hyphenate nature of his employment as an executive producer:

> Fellow Showrunners and Television writers: As you all know by now, we are on Strike. It's sad that we have arrived here and I don't know each and every one of your opinions, but I wanted to share my personal plans for what I intend to do until we have a fair contract.
>
> I am currently quoted in today's *Hollywood Reporter* as saying that I will do some producing work, but won't do any editing as I consider that to be writing. While I said something similar to that earlier last week (I've learned you can't trust a word of what these trades report), that was before I went to the Showrunners Meeting yesterday and became very crystalized in what I need to do.

It may be easy to read these first couple of paragraphs as Ryan "walking back" his earlier position to produce in an effort to maintain credibility with his fellow writers, but that would be a simplistic interpretation. Showrunners are "hyphenates"—producers as well as writers, as we have noted—and thus their professional position simultaneously within and outside the guild offers enough potentially contradictory complexity that makes Ryan's statement a bit more nuanced. He goes on to frame the issue as he sees it and, in so doing, also offers a revealing and expanded definition of screenwriting—or scripting—from the perspective of the writer-producer:

> Like many of you I have spent the last week contemplating what to do in case of a strike. What are my responsibilities to my writers, my cast, my crew, my network and my contract? How do I balance these various concerns?
> At the Showrunners Meeting it became very clear to me that the only thing I can do as a showrunner is to do nothing. I obviously will not write on my shows. But I also will not edit, I will not cast, I will not look at location photos, I will not get on the phone with the network and studio, I will not prep directors, I will not review mixes. These are all acts that are about the writing of the show or protecting the writing of the show, and as such, I will not participate in them. I will also not ask any of my writer/producers to do any of these things for me, so that they get done, but I can save face.
> I will not go into the office and I will not do any work at home. I will be on the picket line or I will be working with the Negotiating Committee. I will not have an avid sent to my house, or to a new office so that I can do work on my show and act as if it is all right because I'm not crossing any picket lines.

At this point, Ryan has made his position clear to his fellow writers, as well as to the network executives that fund his show and led him to the Shieldy brand. He continues:

> I truly believe that the best and fastest way to a good contract is to hit these companies early, to hit them hard and to deprive them of ALL the work we do on their behalf. How do we ask our staff writers to go out on strike as we continue collecting producer checks?
> How do we ask the Teamsters to respect our picket lines if we won't ourselves or if we're sneaking around to do the work off-site?
> Just so you all know what I am prepared to give up . . .
> Tomorrow, we begin to film the Series Finale of "The Shield." I think it's the best script our writing staff has ever written. This is the show that made me. This is the show that is my baby. If the strike goes on longer than two weeks, I won't be able to step on set for the final episode of the show. I won't have a writer on set, as I have had on every episode since the fourth episode. I won't be able to edit this final

culminating episode. I won't go to the wrap party that Fox TV and FX are paying for. You can't tell me that any episode of television is more important than this one is to me, and I am ready to forgo all those things in order to strengthen my union.

Ever the writer, Ryan is framing the arc of his own story with a nod to industrial spin. Yet his comments also accurately mark the role he has assumed as a showrunner: hands-on through all aspects of preproduction, production, and postproduction.

> Tomorrow, we begin filming a new pilot, *The Oaks*, that I am Executive Producing. It's an amazing script that David Schulner wrote and I signed up to help him make this show. Until we have a fair deal I cannot do that now and it kills me.
>
> We are currently filming Season 3 of *The Unit*, a show that does fairly well, but against *House* and *Dancing with the Stars*, usually finishes in 3rd place. We have no guarantee that we will [be] back for a 4th season. I just gave a director friend of mine his first TV directing gig. I'd like to see him succeed. He'll have to finish the show on his own now without a writer on set, or my help in the editing room.[63]

He further points to the complexity of his role as a showrunner: he is as concerned with mentoring talent as he is producing a creative show:

> Some people have made the argument that if they don't do this producing work or this editing, that someone else will do it, and this act won't hurt the companies. I respectfully disagree. If we ALL stop ALL work tomorrow, the impact of this strike will be felt much more quickly, much more acutely and it most likely will end sooner, putting our writers, our cast and our crews back to work sooner!
>
> I spent nearly 12 hours today in the Negotiation Room with the companies. I watched our side desperately try to make a deal. We gave up our request to increase revenue on DVDs, something that was very painful to give up, but something we felt we had to in order to get a deal made in new media, which is our future.
>
> I watched as the company's representatives treated us horrendously, disrespectfully, and then walked out on us at 9:30 and then lied to the trades, claiming we had broken off negotiations.
>
> I can't in good conscience fight these bastards with one hand, while operating an avid with the other. I am on strike and I am not working for them. PERIOD.

And here Ryan advocates for other showrunners to take the same position he has taken despite the cost, cementing his role as a leader of strikers (if only a little late to the part):

You will use your own instincts and consciences to decide your own actions. But if you would like to follow in my footsteps (and those of many, many others who made this pledge at the showrunners' meeting on Saturday), I encourage you to sign the trade ad that the WGA will be putting out on Tuesday by the dozens and dozens of showrunners who will simply not work at all beginning in the morning.

I'm only writing to those writers whom I have e-mail for. Feel free to pass this on to your fellow writers and to your showrunners if you feel inclined. I respect you all and look forward to discussing these issues more on the line. Feel free to write or e-mail and good luck!—Shawn Ryan

In these last paragraphs Ryan is not simply explaining his choices to his fellow writers, taking the lead among showrunners to do so, but also revealing the vast, often conflicting (at least in terms of the network and WGA), responsibilities he has as a showrunner—and, of course, the stakes in making this decision.

CONCLUSION

Shawn Ryan's work as showrunner on *The Shield* did much to recalibrate the representational and dramatic norms of cable drama series. Our extended account both of his work and his public statements also shows how many writer-producers understand the broader boundaries of television scripting both in terms of professional practice and, when these boundaries are foregrounded by industrial disputes, the complex and overlapping contractual responsibilities they owe to their fellow craftspersons and their employers. In addition, Ryan's work is so instructive because it sits right at the historical intersection between preconvergent and convergent, or expanded, television. In screenwriting terms, the specific arc of *The Shield* runs as a kind of B story in parallel to and intersecting with the broader A story of the development of television—and specifically television writing—into the online and digital era. Like any good movie B story it also has a direct influence on the resolution of the A story. In short, *The Shield* did not initiate that broader move, but it did much to reconstitute the codes of many of the dramas that now populate the expanded digital realm.

Of course, not all contemporary shows look anything like *The Shield* or share its political or representational concerns. Ryan's own later work on shows like *Timeless* clearly illustrates his own stylistic flexibility as a writer and producer. But the example of Ryan as a showrunner navigating and, in doing so, helping to chart the course of a changing institution is still instructive. FX typically brands its shows for a younger and predominantly, but by no means exclusively, male audience. However, the example it offers of the ability of convergent cable, and latterly online networks, to survive and even thrive by marketing their product to particular demographics illustrates how television can create expanded opportunities for writers to find an outlet for a much broader range of genres, stories, and themes than the Hollywood studios are currently invested in.

This chapter has focused on one relatively recent show that changed a very old genre. It is not intended to be the sum of our coverage of television but, rather, the at least half-familiar locus with which diverse examples can intersect throughout this book. Thus, it has already provided specific context for our ongoing discussion of the WGA and recent challenges to labor relations for screenwriters in Hollywood. Similarly, and looking forward, our interview in the next chapter with Pamela Gray, an established independent screenwriter searching for opportunities to tell female-led stories, develops the narrative of broadened themes and niche demographics in television set up by our case study of Ryan. Similarly, our discussion of the scripting of new shows and formats that are instances of online content creation in the final chapter can be better understood in the context of recent developments in the convergent cable sector. These new formats are at once beholden to some aspects of televisual tradition and dismissive, or at least independent, of others. In the end a key lesson to be drawn from the pioneering career of Shawn Ryan for the new generation of online content creators, like the animation writer Robert Moreland, also profiled in the next chapter, and even the Twitch streamer Will Frampton, covered in the conclusion, is about the entrepreneurial value of being, on their own terms, distinctly Shieldy.

4. New Markets and Microbudgets

"Independent" Storytellers

> I couldn't sleep one night and I was sitting in my office and I realized that I was an independent filmmaker.
>
> DARREN ARONOFSKY

> Indiewood is *the* alternate pathway to creating films other than the Hollywood Studio System. Many exceptional filmmakers have found creative freedom in their work by creating films outside the Hollywood Major Studio System.
>
> *Wikipedia*

The plot of *Garden State* (2004), written and directed by the actor Zach Braff *(Scrubs)*, bears all the hallmarks of the kind of quirky independent— "indie" in the Hollywood vernacular—romantic comedy drama that has been a staple of US independent production since the early 1990s. It is the story of a young television actor, Andrew Largeman (Zach Braff), who returns home to New Jersey after the death of his mother. Having been estranged from his psychiatrist father (Ian Holm) and larger family, Andrew reflects on the uncertain trajectory of his life, his need for antidepressant drugs, and his guilt about events from his childhood. He soon meets a girl—a manic-pixie-dream-girl as described by the *Guardian*'s critic Ben Beaumont-Thomas[1]—named Sam (Natalie Portman). Sam, also troubled, helps Andrew get perspective on his distress; in serving his needs, she serves hers. In Hollywood fashion the two sidestep their way toward love.

Garden State screened to positive reviews at Sundance in 2004. Film critics at the time joined in. Todd McCarthy's review in *Variety* compared it to a classic: "A sort of 'The Graduate' lite for a generation unacquainted with the original, 'Garden State' is an overly sedated comic romance with sweet little moments scattered here and there."[2] Financed independently of the studio system, the movie was purchased by Miramax and Fox Searchlight for $5 million. It performed well at the box office, earning $35,825,316 worldwide.[3] It also developed an enthusiastic fan following, with an 86 percent positive score on Rotten Tomatoes.[4] Roger Ebert's review also compared it to *The Graduate*. Importantly, in 2004 he wrote that *Garden State* was "smart and unconventional," noting also that the movie displayed "a good eye for the perfect detail."[5]

Garden State may have seemed "smart and unconventional" to some critics and moviegoers on its release in 2004, but its reputation has not fared so well over time. A film everyone now loves to hate, it is ranked at number 8 in *LA Weekly*'s list of the "20 Worst Hipster Movies of All Time."[6] In fact, the movie's title is often used as shorthand by movie fans and filmmakers to describe all that has gone wrong with American independent filmmaking during the mania of the new millennium—a reduction of independent storytelling to its most conventional tropes. Film fan Christian R. Allen's personal recollection of his journey with *Garden State* speaks for many. Allen remembers liking the movie on its release when he was fourteen, but, having seen it again, he found his opinion had changed dramatically: "As my first foray into the Indie scene, it felt relatively unique and interesting—especially in comparison to the tosh Hollywood was knocking out at the time—however, having explored the genre further, its script comes across as a series of ticked boxes, designed to identify 'things/moments that make an Indie movie.'"[7] Allen is suggesting that *Garden State* is an exemplar of "indie by the numbers."

Various arguments have been proffered to explain this remarkable reassessment of the movie. It has been suggested, for example, that writer-director Braff's extratextual reputation as a sitcom actor in *Scrubs* (2001–10) influenced an elitist dismissal of his pretention to be an indie auteur. Others argue that Natalie Portman's Sam is an offensively one-dimensional character serving only to magically cure the lithium-dulled ennui that afflicts the protagonist. And still others make the case that the movie speaks to the generation of self-involved shoppers during the war-torn Bush years.

Garden State's shifting discourse from meritorious to meretricious mirrors the decline of American independent filmmaking from creative movement to niche market in the era of conglomerate Hollywood. Whereas in the 1990s the indie boom was a prime topic of discussion in Hollywood, positioning its product and distribution squarely within Maras's "business" frame, or the art of deal-making inside the Hollywood system, its subsequent decline has relegated it to Maras's "discourse" frame, whereby critical discussion of the films in and outside Hollywood is all that remains meaningful in understanding its diminished impact. The movie was produced at the moment when the burgeoning US independent film sector of the 1990s was transforming into a much smaller specialist marketplace for prestige crossover movies that would attract corporate distribution. Yet the backlash against *Garden State* is a broader cultural acknowledgment of a transformation of the independent sector that has caused profound dislocation for a generation of established screenwriters and filmmakers. At the time of *Garden State*'s rise, the term *Indiewood* had grown into familiar usage: "Indiewood is *the* alternate pathway to creating films other than the Hollywood Studio System."[8] Irrespective of *Wikipedia*'s current and rather naive definition that serves as an epigraph to this chapter, *Indiewood* now describes a co-opted industrial remnant of the independent Hollywood cinema that *Garden State* uneasily represents.

While we find the shifting use of *Indiewood* alongside the shifting criticism of *Garden State* to be interesting in itself, what is most interesting to us is that both discourses speak to the unstable definition of "independent cinema" as it relates to the "independent screenwriter." At a basic level, independent filmmaking—in this case films made independent of Hollywood financing—is more complicated than Indiewood production as defined by the authors of the *Wikipedia* entry. It encompasses a very wide range of practices, from student films, documentaries, avant-garde, and experimental cinema to microbudget narratives distributed through online networks. It also encompasses the "outside" work of screenwriters and directors that once enjoyed success in Hollywood.

This broad definition of independent cinema in the wake of the millennium begs several interesting questions for the profession of screenwriting today: What has independent cinema become, and, associatively, what characterizes an independent screenwriter today? What does the shifting meaning of *independent* in the context of media convergence portend? How has the new screenwriter leveraged the shift amid the rise of the tentpole paradigm and corollary reduction of the ranks of the traditional screenwriter? Most fundamentally, does it still make sense straightforwardly to position "independence," whether in relation to films or screenwriters, against the definition of Hollywood cinema?

In addressing these questions, we argue that "independent" cinema is best understood as a discourse, or series of discourses, similar to Michel Foucault's definition of the author as a function of discourse. Foucault was concerned with a simple but radical question: does the understanding of a text, from a novel to a film, necessitate an understanding of the author of the text's intent, personality, or politics? Situating the emergence of the author in the context of legal history—i.e., texts constitute IPs attributed by the state to an individual or corporation—Foucault makes the case that the discourse of authorship, its varying meanings, is nonetheless critical to understanding how a text is read or received by readers (or, in the case of films, viewers).⁹ The author's intent is not important (and perhaps not recoverable), but the notion of the author as having intent, the filmmaker as auteur, is important insofar as it signals one way among many to read a text in relation to context. Similarly, irrespective of the definition of *independent*, the notion of independence, changing as it does over time and within given contexts, its various incarnations such as "indie" and "Indiewood," is critical to understanding the conditions that impact today's working screenwriter.

Although an admittedly abstract proposition, by understanding independent cinema as discourse(s), we can better understand the working conditions of screenwriters who either see themselves as independent at a given point in their career or cast themselves as independent—the Aronofskys of the world that wake up one morning to discover they are independent filmmakers. We can also better understand why some screenwriters elect to work—or can only work—in particular genres or modes that do not fit within the blockbuster or tentpole paradigms. And the notion of independent cinema as discourse can also help us understand how some storytellers succeed at weaving styles, narrative structures, and themes that are found only superficially, if at all, in mainstream cinema, while others, like Braff, arguably fail in the end.

In this chapter, then, we consider forms of the screenwriting craft that fall outside, or at least adjacent to, the conglomerate studio paradigm discussed in the previous chapters. We employ the method of industry studies mixed in with interviews of working screenwriters, offering case studies to show how the screenwriter, both the traditional and the new, is materially positioned by, through, and against the discourse of the "independent." The crux of our analysis rests on three case studies: drama screenwriter Pamela Gray, animation screenwriter and producer Robert Moreland, and microbudget filmmaker Travis Mathews. Their cases point to screenwriting paths other than the blockbuster or tentpole and to how the notion of the independent screenwriter both opens up and bottlenecks their work.

INDEPENDENT DISCOURSES

There is simply no settled answer to the question of where in the media industries a typical independent screenwriter now works. This is because it is surprisingly hard to define what independent cinema is outside discourse as Maras defines it and Foucault theorizes it. No one definition seems to fit the bill at any one moment. Scholarly and popular discussions used to center on whether, and to what extent, a given feature film was produced independent of Hollywood financing or, conversely, whether "independent cinema" was simply a euphemism for low-budget genre films. The question then shifted to whether *independent* signaled a distinct visual or narrative style or a set of distinct stylistic alternatives (e.g., Quentin Tarantino's *Pulp Fiction* [1994], which started with the end of the story).

Yet even mainstream filmmakers participate in keeping this definition a bit unstable, at least indirectly. Steven Spielberg, for example, acts largely independent of studio decision-making given that he has final cut on the films he writes, directs, and produces; in other words, he gets considerable freedom to decide the films he makes and how they end up on the screen. Final cut is an earned privilege very few Hollywood filmmakers have and one that signals a kind of independence from studio executives interested in shareholder bottom-lines.

It should be clear that the vast majority of Hollywood storytellers do not have final-cut privileges, and we know of no screenwriters who have anything close to final-draft approval of their script—not least because their scripts are made into films by directors and teams of below-the-line and above-the-line professionals. Even in the cases of films made independent of studio financing, once picked up for distribution, they are often recut to fit specific market conditions. In this way both the style and themes of the work depend to some extent on the choices distributors and their marketing departments make.

Media convergence and the emergence of expanded distribution channels via new and multiple screens is further broadening the definition of cinema and, thus, the premises of the "independent" debate. In the new millennium the new screenwriter is as likely to be working among the Hollywood studios and the video games industry as she is to be splitting her professional time between writing independent features, producing online comedy sketches, and publishing novels. Of course, traditional screenwriters might also move between mainstream and indie as defined by budget or style, as they did throughout the twentieth century. Indeed, some have found a way to float in and out of diverse writing opportunities across diverse media.

Writers have often worked across different media, further complicating our efforts to fix the independent screenwriter outside discourse. Hollywood's history is replete with novelists, playwrights, and journalists moonlighting as screenwriters in the style of *Barton Fink*, and this trend has become a kind of norm as the millennium matures. As media markets change and converge, so the career paths of the traditional and not-so-traditional writers who work inside and outside Hollywood have become more diverse and complicated. More professional writers are producing content for more screens and formats than ever before.

Film scholars have attempted to define and circumscribe the idea of independence by categorizing movie texts according to shifting sets of adjacent, alternative, or subaltern creative practices to Hollywood storytelling and by positing it as a broad ideological counterweight to the cultural product of classical and postclassical cinema. Hollywood has remained the subject, independence the shifting object. In this vein film scholar Yannis Tzioumakis suggests an approach that offers three key points of orientation for positioning independent cinema: "industrial location, aesthetics, and political and ideological disposition."[10] Here independent films are defined by the economic relationships their filmmakers have with the dominant institutions of blockbuster and tentpole cinema; by the creative choices of the filmmakers, made manifest through film style and storytelling practices; and by the perceived attitude of the film, conscious or otherwise, toward the themes dominating the industry and the culture more broadly. This, to us, is a useful way to think of independent cinema, yet it falls a bit short in that it fails to identify the discourse of independent cinema that, at least with *Garden State*, moves a film into and outside of the category with some ease.

Film scholar Annette Insdorf focused her own discussion more narrowly around filmmaking practice, suggesting that the independent films of the 1970s can be distinguished from their mainstream Hollywood counterparts by "casting, pace, cinematic style and social and moral vision."[11] This kind of distinction is also taken up, in different language, by a number of nonacademic paraindustrial texts that discuss independent films from a practitioner's perspective. In his book *Which Lie Did I Tell? More Adventures in the Screen Trade*, for example, William Goldman describes the difference between Hollywood and independent movies as between stories that provide comfort and those that deny it: "There are really two kinds of flicks ... generic Hollywood movies, and what we now call independent films. Hollywood films ... want to tell us truths we already know or a falsehood we want to believe. Hollywood films reinforce, reassure. Independent films ... want to tell us things we don't want to know. Independent films unsettle."[12] Style and subversive themes end up defining independent cinema as an unsettling counterpoint to Hollywood. Independent cinema thus becomes a kind of resistant cinema.

Building on Goldman's neat epigrammatic construction, one might suggest that the shifting relationship between Hollywood and its more or less independent correlatives and alternatives in the last decades can be understood in part as attempts by the studios to co-opt, cohere, and commercialize the unsettling. For Hollywood, if a film of any kind generates sufficient revenue, those like it are worthy of investment either at the production or distribution stages. Of course, there are also many individuals, interest groups, and other constituencies from within the worlds of so-labeled independent filmmaking with their own significant political, economic, or creative investment in such definitions. And, in the end, to be seen on a theatrical, cable, or broadcast screen, even a streaming screen, a film, however it comes to be produced, must be distributed, suggesting, to be a bit circular, that even the low-budget "resistant" films nonetheless must have had some level of investment before being seen by audiences.

There is, to be sure, an economic history to all these competing discourses. From the perspective of a Hollywood studio executive in the late 1950s, for instance, the category of independent films would certainly include most of the movies then distributed by the majors. Once the economic effects of the Paramount Consent Decree of 1948 became clear, for example, the Hollywood majors (led in this instance by the business model of United Artists, under the management regime of Arthur Krim and Robert Benjamin) aspired toward the production of more and more "independent" films. According to this rather reductive definition, by 1959 approximately 70 percent of the movies distributed by the major studios were independent. These movies may well have been produced entirely by semiautonomous producers, or other subsidiary entities, and often without the direct involvement of studio personnel. Nonetheless, most of them were commissioned, financed, and distributed by MPAA studios. There is only a narrow sense in which they could be claimed to be independent.

The history of film is also filled with low-budget independently produced and financed genre and exploitation movies, notably hyperbolized social-problem films, horror, and science fiction. Exploitation movies have experienced a sequence of economic peaks and troughs, often in response to shifts in the business model of "respectable" Hollywood. In the 1960s and into the early 1970s there was good money to be made from the expanded drive-in circuit (around six thousand screens at the time) and a burgeoning youth audience poorly served by the old-fashioned product still being released by the majors. In the late 1970s, during another economic downturn, the market for low-budget alternatives cooled into crisis. This market change was due in no small part to the major Hollywood studios' rediscovering exploitation genres in the late 1960s, with the new addition of blaxploitation films (most produced by white Hollywood insiders and distributed by studios), in an attempt to corner the youth market and later repackaging them as the new blockbusters in the wake of *Jaws* (1975) and *Star Wars* (1977).

Low-budget genre production was revived in the 1980s, fueled by the unprecedented transformation of the economic model of film finance offered by the newly lucrative ancillary market of home video. New companies such as Vestron and Full Moon produced straight-to-video horror, action, and science fiction movies. As the subsequent DVD market shrank through the first decade of the new millennium, exploitation has come under renewed pressure. In response, low-budget producers joined other sectors of the industry in moving toward new screens and delivery platforms such as Video on Demand (VOD). They have also maintained the tradition of capitalizing on new communication technologies, as online and social media have been recast as a site for the distribution of horror as well as a new locus for terror in the horror stories themselves. For example, the current success of the otherwise independent horror production company Blumhouse (*Paranormal Activity*, 2009; *Insidious*, 2011), with first-look deals at Universal (for cinema) and Lionsgate (for television), indicates that there are still significant big- and small-screen audiences for lower-budget genre storytellers—and thus still jobs for genre screenwriters seeking financing at some stage of the creative process, screenwriters who might also aspire to secure their own "first-look" deals.

Definitions of *independent* that single out stylistic and narrative influence can be drawn between the works of filmmakers in several distinct periods of drama production. This thread becomes evident at least from the late 1950s with the "New American Cinema" group that coalesced around the journal *Film Culture* and was inspired by trends in European cinema. In particular, the work of John Cassavetes (*Shadows*, 1959; *Faces*, 1968) provided inspiration to future generations of filmmakers, including contemporary microbudget writers and directors. Cassavetes's work still resonates because of his raw and immediate film style and his actor-centered working practices but also because he demonstrated that a different kind of low-budget, character-driven drama could successfully be produced entirely outside the auspices of Hollywood.[13]

A new generation of writers and directors, often working far from Hollywood, continued to transform the look, subject matter, and attitude of classical cinema. These included leading figures in the "New Hollywood" or "Hollywood Renaissance" period of the late 1960s such as the screenwriter Waldo Salt (*Midnight Cowboy*, 1969; *Serpico*, 1973) and the actor-director Dennis Hopper (*Easy Rider*, 1969), as well as emerging writer-directors like Francis Ford Coppola (*The Conversation*, 1974). The movies of the New Hollywood filmmakers (notably *Bonnie and Clyde* and *The Graduate*, both 1967) redefined the representation of sex, violence, and the counterculture from within the classical studio style. Their importance for the future of an independent cinema came not from their separation from the studios but rather from the way they were shot and how they told their stories.

The rise of the new American independent film as "indie," a marketable "crossover" genre in itself, is usually tracked from the success of *Sex, Lies, and Videotape* (1989), written and directed by Steven Soderbergh, at the Sundance Film Festival. Creatively marketed by Miramax, the film made $25 million domestically and set the scene both for increased investment in independent features and distribution in the 1990s and for the majors to take notice of the profit potential from this burgeoning sector. Studios bought out indie distributors (Disney purchased Miramax, for example) and launched or revived their own classics divisions (Paramount Vantage, Fox Searchlight) to capitalize, thereby incorporating the earlier independent work into their economy.

Since the mid-1990s, Hollywood has largely taken over "prestige" independent production, promoting for a time a particular crossover incarnation of independent drama through the kind of Indiewood production we discussed in reference to *Garden State*. Film scholar Geoff King describes Indiewood as "the area in which Hollywood and the indie sector seem to merge or overlap.... [The studios are] seen as having gained or exerted undue control over the sector as a whole, particularly through their ability to dominate access to theatres."[14] By the early 2000s, as the tentpole paradigm was fast becoming the New Abnormal in Hollywood, the majors had lost interest in the smaller profits to be obtained from distributing independent or Indiewood films. The production of dramas of all kinds contracted, in favor of big genre movies, as we saw in the previous chapter. Pamela Gray, screenwriter of *A Walk on the Moon* (1999) and *Conviction* (2010), describes the situation from the perspective of the character-driven and, in her case, female-driven drama writer: "We faced [the problem], even when we were looking for distributors for *Conviction*, where distributors—studios and even the independents and smaller studios, like CBS Films—would say: 'Well, we have our drama for the year.' I had a greenlit project at a studio when the economy started crashing and they said: 'Yours is the drama. It's now a red light. We're only going to do tentpole films because we're doing fewer films.'" Gray further notes that even when female-driven drama projects are developed, they are often the first to be shelved when circumstances change at the studio or distributor. Studio executives, she continued, would be "looking at what else was out there. They'd be looking at whether any female-driven projects made money and then they'd say, 'You did a good job; we're not making this movie.'"[15]

Tzioumakis notes that there has also been a decline in interest in the very notion of independence from movie fans in recent years, with the term being replaced by alternatives such as *original, complex,* and *intelligent* in online reviews and fan discourse. Pointing to "independent" as a discursive function, he argues that "the ideological basis of independence was not fixed, but time specific."[16] With a progressive shift in American politics, both the adoption of "indie aesthetics" by more mainstream Indiewood cinema from the 1990s and the commercialization of the term as a marketing tool, the value of independence-as-industrial-location diminished. He continues: "At some point in the long voyage from the 'European-style' independent films of the 1980s to the Indiewood blockbusters of the late 1990s and 2000s, from the quality films of the pre-Sundance-Miramax era to the infinitely more commercial films of the third wave of the studios' specialty divisions, the notion of 'independence' as a real alternative to Hollywood cinema lost both its appeal and its exegetic power."[17] In short, the independent movie of the 1970s and 1980s was transformed into the "specialty" movie of the 1990s and 2000s, thereby pointing to one consistent aspect of the definition of *independent:* that it is a shifting discourse with economic and ideological implications.

For established screenwriters in particular, definitions of independence are understood most keenly in terms of changes in the labor market and often in the explicit or implicit context of the WGA's attempts to navigate those changes contractually. Over time, new opportunities for employment emerge, and old ones contract or transform. The emergence of scripted content on SVOD platforms such as Netflix, Hulu, and Amazon and the collapse of the market for "quality" feature dramas are recent examples. Any discussion of contemporary screenwriting would need to take account of these new independent yet corporate high-end content providers, just as it would need to acknowledge the expansion of microbudget production, operating largely below the radar of the Writers Guild of America.

For microbudget screenwriters the challenge of independence means something else again. Compared to the distributor-led model of the Hollywood majors, "indie" used to be thought of as a director's medium. Given the development contexts of independent cinema, until recently we might have spoken as often of screenwriter-directors or even screenwriter-producers as we did of "pure" screenwriters. After the co-opting of post-Miramax indie and Indiewood, Geoff King argues that it is in lower-budget—and microbudget— filmmaking that "Indie 2.0" attempts to return to its creative roots.[18]

For the WGA, however, adjusting to the ongoing transformation of independent cinema is often about fighting jurisdictional, contractual, and legal battles. As we saw in chapter 1, changes from within independent cinema and new media, defined broadly, are forcing the guild to adapt its understanding of what screenwriters do and to broaden its basic definition of screenwriting to ensure that its members are being appropriately compensated for their labor. The battle over digital residuals that led to the 2007–8 strike is indicative of this ongoing process, but most of the independent screenwriters we have spoken to in researching this book feel that the WGA is still struggling to remain relevant in a changing industry. "The Guild is fighting a hard battle to modernize itself and catch up with a landscape that's changing so quickly," animation screenwriter-producer Robert Moreland noted. "The old industrial model that the guild was based on is dust. Like there's these shows on YouTube that are being monetized. It's content! The guild is not even close to being up to the reality of what's changing."[19]

Miranda Banks argues that there are three overarching issues of perennial concern to professional screenwriters throughout the industry: "the shifting definitions of ownership and authorship, the meaning of a writer's name on a screen credit, and the perception of writers being outsiders within their own professional communities."[20] Banks's account speaks convincingly to the world of the established professional screenwriter but less so to the experience and priorities of the large number of creative players working outside the guild's jurisdiction or below its radar. Our exploration of independent screenwriting as discourse builds up and extends Banks's recognition that, in the end, "independence" is in the eye of the beholder. The rest of this chapter offers case studies that tease out the ways in which writers, either by design or circumstance, are adapting to working "independently" in the tentpole era. Regardless of any one definition of *independent, indie,* or *Indiewood* that one might use to situate these writers, all three see themselves as "independent" in relation to the discourse of independence that surrounds their evolving careers.

AN "INDEPENDENT FEATURE" WRITER: PAMELA GRAY

"The good news," screenwriter Pamela Gray told the WGA's *Written By* in 2010 (before the release of her well-regarded script for *Conviction*, directed by Tony Goldwyn and starring Hilary Swank and Sam Rockwell), "is I have not stopped working since 1997. The painful news is I haven't had a movie in theaters since 1999. Production is the only reward for this career. . . . I want my movies made."[21] Since she enrolled as a student in UCLA's graduate screenwriting program in 1990, Gray's writing career has taken her from a brief encounter with genre television, through the independent spec feature development process, to many years writing on assignment for studios, independent features, and, latterly, television once again. In all instances she has seen herself as an independent screenwriter.

Gray's first professional experience came from writing an episode of *Star Trek: The Next Generation* ("Violations," season 5, episode 12). It was an opportunity she obtained after winning the TV Academy film writing internship in her first year as a UCLA graduate student. The following year she wrote a spec screenplay, *The Blouse Man*, which won the Samuel Goldwyn Writing Award. The script would eventually be made as the independent feature *A Walk on the Moon*. Set in a Catskill Mountains bungalow colony in 1969, *A Walk on the Moon* explores an affair between a vacationing Jewish housewife and a free-spirited itinerant salesman, the "Blouse Man" of the original title. Directed by Tony Goldwyn and starring Diane Lane and Viggo Mortensen, the film was produced by Dustin Hoffman's Punch 21 Productions.

Reflecting on the four-year struggle to develop *A Walk on the Moon*, one of the key lessons Gray takes is that it can be just as hard to set up a female-driven story as it was twenty years ago: "It is, however, much harder to find a studio or producers willing to *develop* female-driven screenplays now than it was twenty years ago." Even in the mid-1990s, however, getting the film made arose from a bit of serendipity. "If Dustin Hoffman's company had not just signed a deal with Village Roadshow to make six indie films, we wouldn't have found a financier."[22] And now the development culture for the kind of movies she writes is even more difficult. "That was a time when an indie film could get enough attention.... But, female driven today? Well is it a comedy, is it a genre piece?" She points to similar discursive conflicts—replete with ideological charges—that we see elsewhere in the contested definition of *independent*.

Gray's second feature credit came soon after *A Walk on the Moon*. She had an offer from Miramax (in its second incarnation, as an Indiewood subsidiary of Disney) to adapt the documentary *Small Wonders* (1995) into a fiction script. The story of a teacher who instructs a group of underprivileged children in East Harlem to play the violin, the resulting movie, *Music of the Heart* (1999), was directed by Wes Craven and starred Meryl Streep. Gray describes the process as the only time in her career that she was green-lit after a first draft.

> This is how you used to get a job. Someone has a conversation with you. You tell them how you're going to write the movie. I mean I would walk into these meetings having broken down the movie, but that's all it took.... The one major difference in my career from that time to now

was that people were willing to believe that a good writer could do a job. I did not have to prove beyond an initial conversation that I could write a screenplay. I had a career as a writer on assignment for years. [Those assignments were contracted after I delivered] maybe an outline, maybe two meetings, whereas today I practically write the movie to get the job.

Dipping into common Hollywood sociolect, Gray calls this kind of pitching a "bake-off," a form of sweepstakes pitching we discussed in the last chapter: a method the studio uses to control freelance screenwriters while reining in development budgets.

Gray's own experience with bake-offs has taught her that the feature development process exploits writers in proportion to the level of fear and job insecurity experienced by the producers and executives with and for whom they work. As we have noted, green-lighting drama is an increasingly risky career decision for executives in the tentpole era. On the other side of the table, the writer is now "developing to get hired." She continues: "I've been up for jobs [having already worked through] five months of meetings, sometimes six months of work. I have boxes of index cards because they want a scene by scene description of the movie." The common expectation is that the writer will break the entire story before being contracted to write a draft, while competing for the assignment with an unknown group of peers. "They are doing that sometimes with ten people at once," Gray notes, "maybe more. It's not being offered jobs; it's being offered the chance to be in these competitions. This was going on after *Conviction*—I had a movie out with big stars, and I still had to prove that I was capable of writing a movie."

If the screenwriter is successful in the bake-off, she is ushered through a series of additional pitch meetings in an effort by the studio to whittle down the competition while putting the movie through a kind of "free" development. This new iteration of the process places key stages of story development, stages that used to take place after a writer was contracted, ahead of formal employment. As Gray notes: "You get notes if you have given them anything they like. And the more they like it, the more work there is. You get notes on your pitch and you come back and you re-pitch. And you get notes on that. The positive spin on this is you are getting notes from producers who really really want the studio to feel like they are being brought the right two or three writers to choose from." The studio, or the producer, obtains the benefit of significant professional work—the creative ideas of a number of writers—before dollar one has been spent on development. Moreover, it is not clear to any screenwriter in the bake-off who the other screenwriters might be—let alone how many competitors there may be or, for that matter, what "the motives are of the buyer." The bake-off ends either when only one writer remains or at the point at which the producer can offer the studio or distributor a final choice between two or three writers. In the process a group of professional writers have made a significant investment of their time and creativity without remuneration, providing the producer with the development insights he or she needs to lead the assigned writer(s).

Sweepstakes pitching like this breaks WGA rules. Historically, the WGA has attempted to arbitrate instances of what amounts to free rewrites more than it has abuses in the hiring process, however.[23] The guild has raised the issue with the AMPTP but has been able to do very little to prevent it. One reason for this is the understandable unwillingness of many writers to offer specific evidence of contractual malfeasance. Gray, for example, was conflicted for practical reasons: "There was another guild survey last year where you had to talk about practices that were against guild policy in work you had done. And you had to name the studio and name the executive. And I couldn't do it." According to other screenwriters we interviewed, several requesting anonymity, the amount of unpaid work that is now being expected has increased significantly as writers wish not to alienate buyers and thus future employers. "But you know it wouldn't be that big a deal for them to pay you," Gray concludes, "even if it was a small amount for the 'producers draft.' I don't know why the guild can't crack that."

The fear-based working culture that Gray identifies in contemporary studio development also translates into an increased tendency to replace writers that are eventually signed to the kind of "one-step" deals we discussed in chapter2. Screenwriter.io provides a succinct definition: "A one-step deal is a deal in which a studio hires a screenwriter to write a single draft of a screenplay, and all future work after the delivery of that draft is optional, at the discretion of the studio." Indeed, a common wisdom among screenwriters is that sweepstakes bake-offs do not merely lead to one-step deals; they actively encourage the firing of the writer who was finally signed or contracted.

Even when the producer or distributor entity has clear goals for the project, unlike with the notorious cases of Warner Bros. and DC Entertainment's development of new tentpole franchises for *Wonder Woman* and *Aquaman*, the result of one-step deals is usually a loss of continuity and voice. This is because the next writer will not simply rewrite the scenes or elements that are deemed to be problematic. They will, upon encouragement, rewrite the entire script. Hence, whatever inspiration or character the original writer was hired to bring will be diffused, or lost, as the script passes from hand to hand. The movie will lose its "Barton Fink feeling." Steven Knight (*Dirty Pretty Things*, 2002) agrees: "They look at what's worked before and think, '. . . we'll do that again because that worked.' Therefore, they will take a script they like—and then change it so it resembles something else because they think that's engineering it towards success, which isn't the case."[24]

This observation may be less applicable to the writing of some tentpole genre movies, where specialist writers are more likely to be brought in for particular purposes late in development, to punch up action or to polish dialogue once the plotting has been locked through the previsualization process, for example. Nevertheless, the current tendency throughout the industry is also to push the boundaries of what constitutes a deliverable step by getting as many "free passes" as possible from the selected writer. As Craig Mazin (*The Hangover Part III*, 2013) notes: "When the producer demands additional drafts, sometimes stretching that single step to multiple steps written over the course of a year or longer, the effective salary for [the] screenwriters is far below what the market value ought to be."[25] And as Gray summarizes: "The one-step deal is done to save money and to expedite getting another writer in for the additional step."

Another practice that Gray feels has become more challenging since she began working in the industry arises from the tendency for development executives and producers to pigeonhole independent writers by style or genre. In the same way that actors can be typecast and directors are often identified with certain genres or filmmaking styles, screenwriters have always had to deal with a certain amount of pigeonholing. Sometimes it can play to their advantage, of course, by being the first name on a list of likely candidates for assignment within their assumed specialty. Now, however, unless a writer has a sample script that fits a given assignment perfectly, Gray says they are not deemed an appropriate choice: "That has changed in my experience for the worse because two of the projects I got after *A Walk on the Moon* were comedies. I wrote a sequel to *First Wives Club* that was green-lit and [then] un-green-lit. Again, someone saw a little bit of humor in *A Walk on the Moon* and that was enough."

Gray feels that the state of the movie industry is now so inimical to drama writers that there is little opportunity to do good work. According to the accomplished screenwriter, the two key problems are the general lack of assignments in her field and an industry-wide double standard, an often unconscious yet, at the very least, functionally misogynist ideology that applies when assessing the viability of female-driven projects. She notes, "If a female-driven movie doesn't make money, it's a big mark against us, but no one ever says: 'Well we're not going to have any movies about men anymore.'

The numbers are worse in terms of female-driven screenplays being developed. They are worse than when I got started." A case, at least in Gray's situation, can be made that women writers writing scripts about women are inherently independent in ways that are inherently discriminatory.

Melissa Silverstein, writing an op-ed piece in the *Washington Post* in 2012, seems to substantiate the crux of the matter. Part of the problem, she argues, is the reduction of female-driven stories to the "girl ghetto" of "chick flicks," Hollywood's patronizing concession to female audiences in the principal form of the traditional romantic comedy: "a terrible movie about men does not mean the same thing in Hollywood as a terrible movie about women. In this box-office-centric world, where fewer movies about women get made in the first place, such films are held to a higher standard. Chick flicks taint all movies about women, even ones that are not regressive and demeaning."[26]

In industry parlance the "chick flick" is any movie deemed to appeal to a primarily female audience. All such films, no matter how generic and mainstream, are also tracked according to different assumptions about how female-driven audiences behave. For example, *Deadline Hollywood* reported that the early box-office returns from the release of the 2015 *Magic Mike XXL*, written by Reid Carolin and directed by Gregory Jacobs, both men, were positive, but then offered this caveat: "despite all these glorious stats, it appears *Magic Mike XXL* is front-loaded, which is a typical B.O. trend for chick pics where they all show up on opening day, and then slip away day by day. The first *Magic Mike* fell 41% its first Friday-to-Saturday."[27] The assumption is that films aimed at women, even those made by men, don't have the same box-office legs, to use a pun, as those aimed at men, including those made by women.

For all these reasons Gray has been attempting to move between feature screenwriting and writing for episodic television. "It used to be a step down," she admits, reflecting on the perceived status of such a move among writers, "and now I truly believe the best writing in the industry is on television." Knight agrees, making the case that "writers are left alone and directors shoot what's on the page."[28] Recently, Gray wrote an episode of *The Divide* ("And the Little One Gets Caught," season 1, episode 6) and made clear that she found the experience of series production "invigorating."

Gray's motivations align with those of many other talented dramatic writers in the movie industry who are being lured away from the big screen to the small screen. A recent WGA poll indicated that 90 percent of respondents intended to seek guild-covered work in television in the near future. The guild's statement in 2013 noted: "Members view television as a more writer-driven medium than feature film, and a growing slate of compelling, creatively satisfying shows is being produced for the small screen."[29] (We suggest that the guild's use of the term "creatively satisfying" is subtly gendered.)

The increased likelihood that writing for television will actually make it to the screen is also a major incentive. "With television," Gray explains, "you write it. It's prepped. It's produced. It's on the air. It's thrilling. It's complete.... I had two weeks to write the first draft. I had seventy-two hours to write the second draft. The head writer made some changes and there it was—it was on the air. I loved it. I was very proud of it." She also believes there is more openness and less fear in television development, because writers have much greater power in the medium. As we have shown, because trusted writer-producers run shows, they typically have a great deal more creative license from the networks than feature producers have from the studios and distributors. Television showrunners have risen through the writing ranks, and they have greater control over story development for the benefit of their series.

Another creative benefit for an independent-minded screenwriter working in television is the opportunity to work within extended series arcs. Exploring character over multiple episodes is a creative luxury that movie writers are denied in their medium unless, ironically, they write for franchises like the Marvel tentpoles. Of course, character development on television is constrained, to some extent, by the show's "bible" (the document that governs how writers are to craft stories for established characters). Not all shows put as much emphasis on a long series arc for their characters, although it is becoming much more common to do so. Nevertheless, on television characters are typically allowed to develop at a slower pace, and most series formats allow for a level of nuance, contradiction, and complexity that, Gray asserts, is missing from most contemporary features, where producers or executives are often pressing the writer to "firm up audience identification with the protagonist as early as possible in the script."

Another positive change that she has encountered as she moves between features and television is the increased creative collaboration that comes from working as part of a television show's writing team, even if only for a short period. The overall experience of writing for television is a less solitary process, even when the show is gearing up and hasn't yet established a proper writers' room. On *The Divide* the first episodes of the season were contracted out in advance, but during Gray's brief time in the room, she valued the collaborative process and the camaraderie. A screenwriter independent of a studio or network series contract may sometimes enter the writers' room, work for the studio or network on a short-term basis, and gain much from the experience of working with other writers, including those signed to long-term contracts.

Gray has followed a career path that has taken her away from working exclusively in what can be called independent feature filmmaking as a response both to changing working conditions within the industry and to the realignment of quality drama on television. Regardless of the definition of independent cinema one might prefer, Gray's career flips previous assumptions about the professional status of the Hollywood writer on their head. Many nonstudio screenwriters have made, or are attempting to make, the same move that Gray is now attempting to make. Indeed, in other arenas that used to be almost completely in the control of the major and minor Hollywood studios, new opportunities for screenwriters are being created by entrepreneurial writers, further eroding while leveraging the moniker of *independent*. We next turn to such a case in the convergent world of animation.

AN "INDEPENDENT" ANIMATION WRITER: ROBERT MORELAND

In one sense the media industries have been converging since the technology of Kinetoscopes for individual viewing gave way to that of projectors that served larger audiences. Of course, we primarily understand the term *convergence* as the result of such waves of technological change. Yet convergence also marks broader industrial and cultural developments. As Banks argues, "convergence has never been just about technological change. It is about the definitions of labor shifting, the lines between production and consumption compressing, and divisions between producer, product, and audience breaking down."[30] In the cinema of the late twentieth and early twenty-first centuries this expanded notion of convergence can clearly be seen in the case of animation.

The coincident development of new production technologies, new markets, and new distribution pathways caused the small independent animation sector to expand rapidly after 1990. This expansion took place in features and television, both well-established exhibition sites for animated content, but it also began to develop online, through the emerging Internet. In fact, independent animation expanded rapidly across all media at the turn of the millennium, offering new opportunities for traditional animation screenwriters and, as more content was required, for live-action screenwriters new to the animated form. The subsequent pressure placed on those new markets by increased media consolidation, and the consequent contraction of the traditional animation sector, helped to rewrite the formula for professional survival for many animation screenwriters. In this context independence required them to learn new promotional techniques and to become creatively flexible in producing content for different delivery platforms years before many of their live-action counterparts were obliged to do so.

Much like the career of Pamela Gray in the world of live-action drama, the career of Robert Moreland, an established screenwriter and producer of independent animation, illustrates these shifts in the definition of independent screenwriting labor. Although not an animator himself, Moreland's experience of animation development exemplifies how the roles both of the writer and of the screenplay in contemporary animation production differ significantly from those in live-action production and even in major studio animation. The changing marketplace for independent animation has positioned him, initially by necessity rather than design, as a creative entrepreneur working in the roles of both screenwriter and producer: "The problem is that you're not going to get in a room with somebody to pitch unless you're really well-known," he notes. "And, even when you do," he concludes, "you have to give a presentation that is unique, and the further you can develop something, the better off you're going to be."[31]

Moreland began his career writing independent science fiction and action features such as *Space Marines* (1996) and *Ground Control* (1998), both for Green Productions. He has written independent animated features including *Happily N'Ever After* (2006) for Lionsgate and *Space Chimps* (2008) for Vanguard; he also worked in TV animation, cowriting the award-winning Nickelodeon pilot for *Thunder Pig* (2002)[32] with his long-time collaborator, the artist and children's book writer Keith Graves *(Chicken Big; Frank Was A Monster Who Wanted to Dance)*. He has sold other projects to television and, like many of his peers, has worked on assignment "doctoring" scripts. In an attempt to respond to changes in the animation marketplace, he and Graves recently established the independent studio Graverobber Productions. In 2015 Graverobber's first project, *The Beef Sumo Show,* was successfully funded via a Kickstarter campaign for an initial run of online episodes.

Despite these successes and much like Gray, Moreland has experienced the problematic ratio of projects that get optioned versus those that survive development: "Keith sold two of his books to Nickelodeon. I was hired by Nickelodeon to adapt two other books [including] a Tony DiTerlizzi book. Keith and I optioned a project together for Sony, a really funny animated series. We've done a lot of stuff, and either it didn't get made or it got changed. But we were able to make a living doing that." They write mainstream animation as independent agents looking to shift to the new media that can sustain their livelihood: "there's actually loads of opportunities," he claims, " if you count getting your show produced and making a living as success. If it's making a million dollars off a spec script, then no."

By way of context, the emergence of commercial independent animation is a direct consequence of the revival of the once-moribund Hollywood feature animation sector. This revival began in the late 1980s and took place in two principal stages. The first stage followed the reinvigoration of Disney's traditional cel-animated features with *The Little Mermaid* in 1989, followed by *Beauty and the Beast* in 1991. The latter movie also pioneered the use of computer animation for select sequences. The second stage came with the further development of computer animation for feature production initiated by Pixar in the 1990s with the *Toy Story* franchise.

A boom in animation hiring followed. There was also a richer spec screenplay market for animation screenwriters and, as a result, more opportunities for animation writers to get their projects set up. As Moreland notes: "You could get [spec] sales then. You could get your script developed, or if you were good, you could also get a deal to adapt some novel or whatever. But now there's a spec market for shows [as opposed to features]. There's a market for you showing that you can write and produce and handle a show."

The first animation boom ended by 2000, partly as a consequence of, as the *Hollywood Reporter* noted, "the catastrophic effect on independent studios [of] the wave of consolidation," the corporate mergers and divisional cutbacks that flowed through the conglomerate studios from the mid-1990s.[33] Disney itself laid off four thousand staff in 2001.[34] The animation market also suffered from a glut of rushed projects attempting to capitalize on the rebound in popularity of animated feature films. Reflecting on these trends, Charles Solomon, a historian of animation, critiqued the formulaic scripts of studio films like *Dinosaurs* (1991), *Anastasia* (1997), and *The Road to El Dorado* (2000): "they were created by committees trying to second-guess the audience. What's missing is a sense of vision, the feeling that filmmakers had a passion for this story."[35] Solomon was not alone in this complaint, one more commonly directed at live-action genre films than at animation as we showed in the previous chapter, where the common assumption has been that longer development leads to better storytelling.

The second stage of the animation revival required the further development of computer technologies and the new visual style seen in Pixar's *Toy Story*. Prior to the release of this film, computer animation had only been used for experimental and short-form animation. The success of *Toy Story* (the franchise is now worth in excess of $10 billion) started a trend that drove the entire industry rapidly away from traditional cel animation and toward computer-generated images and then 3-D.[36] Pixar continued to produce a string of successful computer-animated movies, initially distributed through a joint venture deal with Disney. Disney purchased the company in 2006, allowing it to operate as a "silo" entity within the conglomerate, with creative control over its own product.

Other studios moved into the computer-animation marketplace in the years following the success of *Toy Story*. Fox and DreamWorks were the earliest adopters, Fox committing to computer animation and purchasing Blue Sky Studios to jump-start its animation arm in 1998. The studio found a franchise with the success of *Ice Age*, with numerous writing credits, in 2002. After making *Antz*, screenplay by Todd Alcott, Chris Weitz, and Paul Weitz, its own first computer-animated feature in 1998, DreamWorks founded its own animation division, DreamWorks Animation, under the new corporation's cofounder Jeffrey Katzenberg. The division achieved great commercial success with the *Shrek* franchise. Moreland was "part of the small team that set-up *Shrek* at DreamWorks."[37] Despite this success, the division foundered, accumulating significant losses. DreamWorks was sold to Viacom in 2006. After this purchase Paramount released DreamWorks Animation's feature products as a component of its conglomerate enterprise.

At the same time that computer technologies were transforming the style of high-end feature animation—and consequently putting many traditional animators out of work—they were also providing new opportunities for lower-budget independent production. Ron Diamond, copublisher of the online trade magazine *Animation World Network*, summed up this new window: "Technology has liberated independent animation and given them an opportunity to break into the motion picture realm. It's a huge shift."[38] Andy Heyward, CEO of DIC Entertainment, noted in 2001 that the main challenge for independents coming into the feature market was "to keep budgets down. As a result, we are seeing a shift to computer technologies, even in 2-D productions, and a search for different countries to outsource animation to."[39]

As far back as 2000, the principal site for these new opportunities was deemed by many in animation to be the Internet. As Chris Lucas, vice president and executive producer at Showtime New Media noted, "What we've seen is the technologies have advanced to the point where we can start exploiting the Internet as a separate distribution platform."[40] Yet the realities of insufficient bandwidth and limited processing speeds on domestic computers led to this early promise proving to be something of a false dawn. Despite the release of simple animation programs designed for online production, led by Flash, several online animation startups, including Pseudo.com and POP.com, failed. "The gold rush that sent so many people flocking to online animation has given way to a Klondike meltdown," a *Variety* reporter wrote in 2000, "where the late and less hearty are forced to come down off the mountain and sell their pickaxes."[41]

Despite these false starts, the Internet did begin to open up a new market for independent animation. Echoing Moreland's view, in 2000 CalArts character animation professor Frank Terry offered an insightful glimpse at the potential of online distribution and the kind of creatives who would be best placed to exploit it in the future: "If anything, the Internet is broadening the availability of the marketplace to the audience. Instead of a fixed distribution system, animators can be their own entrepreneurs and distribute their material to a global audience. That's the phenomenal aspect of this Internet explosion."[42]

The development of affordable off-the-shelf hardware and software for computer animation production also allowed independent studios and producers to reduce their animation budgets at a time of economic contraction. The potential advantages to independent producers working at lower budgets and controlling their own intellectual properties were clear. As David Bloom notes: "A hit developed inhouse [sic] means a company can reap nearly endless revenues from DVD and video, merchandising and TV spinoffs.... Production costs, especially for computer-based animation projects, are dropping. And thanks to the DVD boom and multiplying cable outlets, backend opportunities are bigger than ever, and not just for kid-oriented fare."[43]

By 2006 *Variety* was reporting the rise of a "different model" of animation production, in which screenwriters and animators were no longer part of what is called in the industry a "pipeline" of ongoing production. Rather they were "hired on a contract basis to work on a single project while using off-the-shelf technology."[44] Independent animation studios learned to be flexible. In some cases this involved following tax breaks for movie production around the globe. Moreland wrote *Space Chimps* and its sequel, *Space Chimps 2: Zartog Strikes Back* (2010), for Vanguard Animation. The company followed this pipeline-free production model by "establishing a team from scratch to execute each new feature."[45] Thus, Vanguard's feature *Valiant* (2005) was produced in the United Kingdom to take advantage of government incentives. When those became less favorable, they moved Moreland's *Space Chimps* to Vancouver.

At around the same time, the independents began focusing on selling their product to international markets. "Eighteen years ago," Heyward said in 2002, "licensing revenue was 25% international; today it's 75%."⁴⁶ But that was before the global economic crash of 2008. Since then, foreign finance has been much harder to obtain for independent animation projects, and producers are finding it harder to set up features, as Moreland notes: "The days of *Space Chimps* that I did with [director] Kirk De Micco, who went on to do *The Croods* (2013) with DreamWorks [are over]. That was a $44 million budget, and that's not workable right now. Now you can't get the foreign sales numbers that you need to get the equity component. It's too big of a financial risk, and part of the catalyst for that was the crazy financial crash of the stock market." The future of independent low-to-mid-budget animated features may be uncertain, but independent animation production for television and the Internet continues to be healthy.

Screenwriters coming to studio or independent animation from live-action often report that they find the collaborative environment a pleasant change from the way they are usually treated by the industry. For example, John Fusco (*Young Guns II*, 1990; *Thunderheart*, 1992; *Hidalgo*, 2004), a writer who specializes in western themes, was brought in by DreamWorks to write the script for *Spirit: Stallion of the Cimarron* (2002). After initial hesitation at working in animation he found the experience creatively fruitful. "Once I got going, the thing started to take the shape of prose and ended up more of a novella than a script. Then it evolved into a screenplay and then the storyboards. I was always welcome to come in and out of the process and look at what the animators were doing and adjust certain ideas." And not unlike Gray's experience in television, he notes, "Everything stayed true to the soul of the original script, which was a little surprising and very satisfying. I was told by a studio once that animation isn't for serious writers, (but) I found that it's a great place for serious writers."⁴⁷

The uniqueness of this development process also explains why most animators and animation writers have historically been represented by IATSE and not by the WGA. As the guild's Patric Verrone noted in 2005, "it goes back to the days when animated features were storyboarded, and instead of a script, the studios brought in a few gag men."⁴⁸ As a consequence, few animation screenwriters get residuals payments from the movies they write, other than small payments from individual territories, such as Germany and France, where rights of authorship are enshrined in law. Moreland notes that "the business plans for those companies and those movies do not forecast giving any passive payments to writers ever. There's no right of authorship. If you don't like it, fine, go do something else." In

Moreland's experience even the most successful animation writers on movies that obtain a theatrical release only receive a one-time box-office bonus, tiered according to the commercial success of the film.[49]

In contemporary animation the screenplay sits even less securely than it does in live-action as the authorial or blueprint governing production. Different animation studios operate their own minor variations on the story development process; however, they all arrive at a screenplay as either a first or second stage in the writing process. The script often emerges from a longer process of story development, working from story concept and theme up through visual development and storyboarding.

Alternatively—and this is more typical of the independent model experienced by Moreland and others—the writer's spec or assignment screenplay is the starting point from which the hired director develops the project. Either way, the screenplay as text is designed to be transcended even more quickly than in a live-action context. Moreland readily acknowledges this when talking about a current feature he has in development. "Now the film is going into production and now a director who I really respect and admire has come on. He's totally changing everything around, which is fine. It's animation; that's the way it goes."

Animation screenwriters understand and accept how this process works. They expect to share the long process of story development in a profound collaboration with directors and other members of the expanded movie development team. The adaptation of the screenplay to the boards inevitably exposes material that doesn't translate visually, and the script also often hides the importance of material that will perform better than it reads. The writing process of animation requires both stages of development, and both forms of scripting, in order for the director to prepare successfully for production. Moreland makes it clear:

> There are things that work in a script that are not going to work on the boards. And there are things that in a script are *well* [he gives the word an uncertain intonation] . . . but that really come to life on the boards. And there are changes you are going to need to make. I don't care who you are and how experienced you are, you are going to be surprised by what you see in those boards. And as you add the voices, as you add animation, things in layout—even pretty late in the pipeline—there start to be changes. Your script is not going to be exactly what shows up onscreen.

Animation scripting is, in short, an accepted negotiation between the screenplay and its transcended iteration as storyboard.

The team developing a typical animated feature script—whether at a major studio or an independent—is typically made up of creatives from all departments within the studio, not just the development executives common to live-action. At Pixar, the famous "Brain Trust" of roughly a dozen senior creative staff has been involved in creative critiques of all projects from an early stage. Rough cuts are also screened for the entire staff, and feedback is actively sought from all employees. This practice is by no means universal in animation. By some accounts it is even under pressure at Pixar.[50] Even so, the animation director is always employed to be, at the very least, a professional second-order screenwriter in a way that most live-action directors for hire are not. The director understands that his job is to be integral to the creative development of story, not merely its execution or interpretation.

Writing through drawing is also an important skill. When he was interviewed by the WGA's *Written By*, the animation writer-director of *The Incredibles* (2004) and *Ratatouille* (2007), Brad Bird, talked about how even simple drawing is an essential part of his own story development work: "I don't produce sketches until they've taken their first shot [at the story]. Then I'll do thumbnails and say, 'More from this angle,' or, 'Try it like this.' Even with Pixar [where the preplanning has to be particularly detailed], I'm known for doing elaborate boards, even simulating effects and camera moves."[51]

Typically, the development and production process for an animated feature takes much longer than for its live-action equivalent. High-end animated features produced by studio divisions usually have an especially long gestation period. At Pixar the writing and story development process takes even longer, with most of its features produced over a five-year period. Pixar is unique among the major Hollywood animation producers in allowing its features to gestate at this slow pace. The production schedule of an independent animated feature is typically much reduced—along with its budget. That puts pressure on the writer/s and director to get the script right without the almost endless iterations available to the major studio divisions. As *Variety* put it in 2008, "With brisk production windows of just 18–24 months for each project, indie toon producers don't have the luxury of finding story as they go along."[52]

When asked to identify the principal differences between major studio and independent story development in contemporary animation, Moreland answered without hesitation: "The difference is time. The studio has bigger pockets, and they are able to allow more time. It's how many passes can you do on the boards." Making script changes in independent animation writing is often complicated by the curtailed development schedules: "Once you start making changes, it's really complicated in independent animation because you are already in production, so you can only touch certain things.

You have to make lateral changes. You can't make upstream changes that affect the downstream and vice versa. You can't start screwing with stuff that's already been done. It becomes a really complicated jigsaw puzzle." By "lateral changes" Moreland means that scenes can only be changed in ways that will not affect story development or completed animation work elsewhere in the script. "You can't let it ripple—the ripple effect is huge."

To add to the challenge, most independent animated features are produced under a completion guarantee, or "completion bond," providing insurance to the investors that the movie will be finished. If a film's development falls too far behind schedule, the insurers will intervene: "they are just going to come in and take over the movie. And you lose face, and the movie is not going to be as good, usually. So the pressure in independent is very different than in a studio situation, where they can be more flexible." Moreland points to his experience working on *Shrek:* "On *Shrek* I was part of a small team that optioned William Steig's kid's book and set it up at DreamWorks. I was helping John H. Williams, the producer, doing development for him. That was like a seven-year process. That movie stopped a few times, when it kind of hit the wall.... It needed to pause, breathe, and reset its course. There were big story questions being explored, and different versions of the script. That's a very different experience working on a movie where you have the luxury of fixing things that need to be fixed." Moreland essentially invokes Maras's practitioner frame to line the "how" of writing in this context to the business frame climate operating in independent and studio development.

The launch of online streaming services like Sony's *Crackle* and Walmart's *Vudu* promise new outlets for independent content. Yet in Moreland's experience, most streaming services don't have adequate budgets for creative development. "Everyone's becoming a contractor and content creators are having to be much more resourceful and aggressive and inventive, with the only difference being that you can actually create your show whereas you never could have done it in the past." As a response, Moreland is developing three series through his studio, Graverobber, to include the aforementioned *Beef Sumo,* an adult animation comedy series brought to him by voice talent Tara Strong (*Ice Age; My Little Pony: Friendship Is Magic,* 2010–15), as well as a kids' series based on his partner Keith Graves's best-selling children's book *Chicken Big.*

Moreland's experiences as a screenwriter and, latterly, as a producer charting a path through the rapid expansion, subsequent contraction, and fundamental transformation of the distribution models and marketplaces for independent animation over the last two decades is indicative of the kind of professional flexibility many "independent" writers are now required to show. To remain independent in this way, perhaps the only way to write in animation given the few studio jobs in that aspect of the industry, Moreland became an entrepreneur and, with his partner, started his own studio. He looks to all distribution outlets, from traditional to online, and opened up his skills to incorporate production and now studio management. Independent by most definitions, Moreland is also a studio executive in charge of developing the work of other writers in animation.

AN "INDEPENDENT" MICROBUDGET WRITER:
TRAVIS MATHEWS

The fruits of Indiewood screenwriting, promoted by studios, and often by name and niche recognition, are certainly more visible in culture and popular discourse than much of the product of the independent fringe. And yet in Indie 2.0, to borrow Geoff King's term once more, recent generations of writers and directors who define their practice further from the studio tent are flourishing, at least in terms of their access to the affordable means of production with which they can express their visions. The availability of cheap digital technology for production and postproduction, including DSLR cameras and editing programs like Final Cut Pro and Adobe Premiere, has made feature film production accessible to more filmmakers than ever before.

The scale of *microbudget* production covers a wide range, from movies made for effectively nothing (friends making a film entirely with the resources they have on hand, for example), through independently financed and crowd-funded projects at very different levels of professionalism and ranging from the low three figures to professional features that still come under the WGA Low Budget Agreement set at $1.2 million. As we have already seen in the context of independent animation, the emergence of the Internet as a platform for distribution has also enabled microbudget filmmakers to find new audiences for their work. The expanded film festival network also offers the possibility of exposure and recognition for films made at this budgetary level. It is now possible to submit your film to hundreds of film festivals, as well as to push screenings online via social media marketing.

The additional advantages of working in microbudget cinema include maintaining a level of creative freedom that is almost impossible in other sectors and at higher budgetary levels. The technical and budgetary viability of microbudget production has also enabled filmmakers with unconventional stylistic approaches or niche, radical, and/or minority political and cultural agendas to produce more work than at any other time in the history of filmmaking. Microbudget filmmakers do not have to follow the Hollywood style, nor do screenwriters working at that scale have to conform to the industry norms of spec-screenplay format and three-act structure, even if many still choose to. In this way many microbudget writers and filmmakers have greater allegiance to the broad field of experimental filmmaking (though here there is a worthy distinction to be sure).

Production activity might be vibrant in the microbudget arena, yet not unlike the screenwriters featured in *Dreams on Spec* discussed in our introduction, it is far less secure in terms of its ability to sustain the careers of screenwriters and directors in economic terms. Microbudget filmmakers often have day jobs. Of course, this has always been the key trade-off for the kind of filmmakers who separate their creative work as far as possible from what they see as the meretricious conglomerate mainstream. Nevertheless, producing content through microbudget filmmaking does still provide its old ancillary function of apprenticeship for those who aspire to work in Hollywood or at least at higher-budget levels. It is nonetheless hard to generalize about the career paths of the filmmakers who are working in microbudget production, other than to say that it remains more solidly the domain of the independent writer-director than any other area of North American moviemaking.

The microbudget sector has launched one significant movement, of sorts: mumblecore. Branded by canny programmers, notably by SXSW (South by Southwest), mumblecore is an otherwise disparate collection of filmmakers.[53] Never officially a movement, the work of the individual mumblecore filmmakers, spread over the last decade and more, shares certain broad preoccupations and stylistic tendencies. Most of their work is shot on digital equipment, with the notable exception of Andrew Bujalski's *Funny Ha Ha* (2002), which was shot on 16 mm celluloid. Influenced in part by the tradition of semi-improvised, character-driven filmmaking that emerged from the work of Cassavetes and others, most mumblecore films also use nonprofessional actors and, as Hoxter has noted elsewhere, "an approach to story that was about professional and emotional stasis and drift amongst the current post-college twenty-something generation."[54]

Among the most prominent filmmakers who have risen from mumblecore production toward Hollywood is Lena Dunham. Her microbudget film *Tiny Furniture* (2010) received critical attention, and Dunham went on to make *Girls* for HBO. Other mumblecore filmmakers to move up the professional and budgetary ladder in this way include Joe Swanberg (*Hannah Takes the Stairs*, 2007), who went on to write and direct *Happy*

Christmas (2014); Lynn Shelton (*Humpday,* 2009), who went on to write and direct *Your Sister's Sister* (2011); and, the brothers Jay and Mark Duplass (*Humpday,* 2009). Mark is now a successful actor (*The League,* 2009–15; *Safety Not Guaranteed,* 2012) and Jay a director who made *Togetherness* (2015) for HBO. The Duplass brothers recently signed with Netflix to produce four movies for theatrical release, followed by exclusive streaming transmission via the website. Indeed, feature production in the sector is remarkably diverse. Innovative filmmakers like the science fiction writer-director Shane Carruth have produced influential work across many genres and at very low budget levels. Carrruth's first, prizewinning feature *Primer* (2004) was made for $7,000. His next science fiction film, *Upstream Color* (2013), won a prize at Sundance and cost a reported $50,000.

The independent writer-director Travis Mathews has managed to forge a career and become an influential figure in the microbudget community of storytellers. Speaking in 2014 about the state of microbudget movie production, he echoed Moreland's assertion of the need for entrepreneurship in contemporary independent animation production: "I see everyone, including myself, searching for case studies and models for how to get a movie together in 2014," he noted. "Because so much has changed and continues to change—driven by technology and a collapse of more traditional models from production to distribution—it seems like anything is possible." He goes on to complement Moreland's larger point: "But to harness that energy, and to sustain yourself, I think you have to imagine yourself as an entrepreneur as much as an artist. Even at the micro Indie level, making a film is like starting a small business."[55]

Mathews, a San Francisco–based independent filmmaker who writes his own material in an often collaborative fashion, has been linked by critics to Andrew Haigh (*Greek Pete,* 2009; *Weekend,* 2011) and John Cameron Mitchell (*Hedwig and the Angry Inch,* 2001; *Short Bus,* 2006) as one of the leading figures in the newest wave of independent gay cinema.[56] Mathews's first narrative feature, *I Want Your Love* (2012), emerged from a body of work in independent documentary (*Do I Look Fat?* 2005) that has always been engaged with the importance of sex to gay identity. He made his mark with fans of microbudget filmmaking with *In Their Room* (2009–present), a series of intimate, sometimes explicit documentary-style interviews about gay men in their spaces.

In Their Room was originally hosted online as a web series by the independent publication for "alt" gays, *BUTT Magazine,* which describes itself as "THE place where gays can speak candidly about their ideas, work and sex lives."[57] In 2009 the first iteration of *In Their Room* won Mathews the

Best Film award at the Good Vibrations Indie Erotic Film Festival. He produced more *In Their Room* material in Berlin and later released a third episode, shot in England.

The frank approach to sexuality and identity he fostered for *In Their Room* led directly to his working practices for *I Want Your Love*, which premiered at the Frameline festival in San Francisco and played in numerous festivals around the world. The film's wide exposure, and the ongoing discussion it generated about the use of real sex acts in cinema, encouraged the actor and director James Franco to collaborate with Mathews on an experimental hybrid narrative-documentary feature, *Interior. Leather Bar*. That film explored the representation of gay identity by reimagining the lost scenes from William Friedkin's feature *Cruising* (1980), starring Al Pacino, screenplay by William Friedkin, and creating a hybrid documentary narrative that follows a straight actor taking the original Al Pacino role as he, in turn, navigates the pressures of "playing gay." *Interior. Leather Bar* played both the Sundance Film Festival and the Berlinale, as well as seventy-five other festivals internationally, and was distributed theatrically by Strand Releasing. The film was made for around $80,000.

An account of the preparation and production of Mathews's *I Want Your Love* offers alternative and provocative ways to think about what constitutes writing for the screen. The film uses real sex acts as integral cues for drama and character development. The way these acts were written and rewritten through script and performance stretches the boundary of negotiated scripting into challenging arenas. The film tells the story of Jesse, a young gay man whose performance art career has not taken off. He is about to leave San Francisco to return home to the Midwest, and his group of friends throws him a going away party. The movie follows Jesse and his friends before, during, and after the party as he comes to terms with this new and unwelcome chapter in his life. In the course of events he reflects on past relationships and flirts with new ones.

Through it all, Jesse and his friends are seen engaging in explicit sex acts that speak more to the status of the relationships and friendships from which they emerge than they do simply to the notion of sexual gratification or, for that matter, to the familiar cinematic conventions of erotic display. Far from a conventional pornographic film, but nonetheless inevitably positioned discursively as one, the explicit sex acts also function as tropes that speak to both the history of gay filmmaking and the role of sex in the gay community and beyond.

Sex is a persistent trope in Mathews's microbudget films. As a writer and director, he uses sex as a revelatory narrative device that articulates character and feelings just as other kinds of social interactions do. He offers a very different model of sexual representation from the typically exploitative, adolescent, and often prurient deployment found in Hollywood features, as well as many independent genre movies. In other words, Mathews's films use sex-as-storytelling, and, as such, it needs to be written-in in a particular way, alongside dialogue and other kinds of action. In this example from his screenplay for *I Want Your Love* the characters may be unsure about love, but they are certainly having sex:

> INT. AARON'S BEDROOM. CONTINUOUS
>
> Pete is standing up. Aaron is eating Pete's ass as Chris sucks Pete's dick. This goes on for a bit, then Aaron and Chris meet between Pete's legs and start making out. Chris pauses momentarily.
>
> CHRIS
> Now I can taste his ass on your lips.[58]

Leaving its explicit content aside for a moment, we can see with a quick glance at the form of the screenplay extract above that screenwriters and filmmakers working outside the orthodoxies of the Hollywood paradigm are often less beholden to the "tyranny of format" than their mainstream counterparts.

At the microbudget level there is often no requirement to navigate industry gatekeepers or to produce a document that will conform both with "professional" expectations and industry standard screenwriting software. As a result, the writer is freed to present story material however he or she wants. In this case Mathews writes in Arial font rather than the Courier variant required of industry screenplays. His slug-line format (the material in capitals above the scene description) is also somewhat unconventional, and he formats character names and dialogue justified left. None of these matters in terms of readability, but it would certainly have been considered heretical to any industry professional coming across it.

Of course, Mathews is still observing an approximation of standard screenplay form. He divides his material into scenes, introduced with standard information noting whether the scene will be shot interior or exterior, the location, and the time in reference to the previous action of the screenplay. The format of his script also makes clear distinctions between scene description and spoken dialogue, introducing a character's speech with his capitalized name. This is by no means an experimental script in terms of its format, then, merely an eccentric one. As the examples in film scholar Scott MacDonald's excellent collection *Screen Writing: Texts and Scripts from Independent Films* demonstrate, truly experimental screenplay—or text, or outline—form is necessarily as diverse as the filmmakers and the films they produce.[59]

Mathews varies the format of his own writing to suit the project at hand. He did not use a conventional screenplay for his second feature, *Interior. Leather Bar*, yet his screenplays for an unproduced narrative feature, *Brontes and Rick*, and for his current project, *Oscillate Wildly*, are entirely conventional in their format. This formal orthodoxy is deemed by Mathews as a necessity for a microbudget feature that needs to persuade different development and funding constituencies such as grant committees on the page.

Yet it is the writing of explicit sex that really stands out from this screenplay extract. Not only does Mathews's screenplay anticipate the deployment of real sex acts on screen in *I Want Your Love*, as we will discuss below, but, in seriously engaging with cinematic sex at all, it stakes out a position very far from a Hollywood mainstream that has almost entirely stopped doing so. There are several reasons for this recent institutional reticence, which can, perhaps unsurprisingly, be reduced (under one grid) to issues of economics. For example, sexual content tends to play against attracting the "four-quadrant" domestic audience that studios are now almost exclusively courting. It also causes problems for films in some international territories and in ancillary markets such as airplane licensing. Moreover, major DVD retailers such as Walmart and Sam's Club have made a policy of locating mainstream movies with sexual content adjacent to directly pornographic material, in separate or curtained off sections of the retail environment.[60]

From the progressive fringe of independent film, *I Want Your Love* offers an eloquent alternative discourse to the Indiewood narratives and the studio tentpole screenplays. It is instructive in terms of its screenplay style but also in terms of its dramatic content and the unique processes of scripting and development that brought this screenplay to the screen. And, although the movie's genesis was hardly typical of independent microbudget movies, its very uniqueness speaks to the fragmentation of development strategies after the retrenchment of the independent sector since the period of the so-called Sundance–Miramax boom of the early 1990s. Given this diversity, *I Want Your Love* serves less as an exemplar of microbudget screenwriting, if there is such a thing, than as a wedge to prompt discussion of a range of issues, opportunities, and challenges with which screenwriters on the fringes of American narrative cinema have been grappling.

I Want Your Love was financed and produced by San Francisco–based NakedSword, a gay porn company. Matthews was certainly surprised that a porn company would want to finance an independent narrative feature.

He had met Jack Shamama, one of the NakedSword producers, through a friend: "The whole thing felt very old-fashioned in that it was so much based on gentlemen's agreements and trust, without a lot of interference from them," he recalled. Pointing to the role of NakedSword in the development process, he revealed a key element of the microbudget discourse: "When I showed them the first incarnation of the script, they were interested. They also hear from people all the time [who tell them] that they can film real sex—that was one of the complaints they always get: these people seem like robots, they seem like they are 'playing porn stars'—they wanted proof that I could avoid that."[61]

NakedSword had Mathews observe their shoots—as an exercise in instruction-in-the-negative—and asked him to make a narrative short based on the themes of *I Want Your Love* to prove that he was able to direct sex in the very different way the story required. Thus, the idea of a potential tension between the script as written and the sex acts to be depicted was established up front by the porn professionals. The short won an immediate audience online. "We had a tremendous response, both in terms of number of viewers and critical response," Mathews recalls. "I think almost four million people have watched it on [NakedSword's] site now. . . . After that, they were comfortable with green-lighting the feature film."

By all accounts, NakedSword gave Mathews his space throughout development and production, respecting the creative process required to make a character-driven feature film. They never gave him specific instructions regarding the sexual content. Nor did they give him a "minute count" or otherwise indicate how much explicit material should be in the film: "They never gave me minutes, or number of scenes, or number of cum shots, or anything like that. There was actually a point where I remember Jack [Shamama] saying: 'If anything, make it less porny.'" Of course, given the funding, the discourse of gay sex as pornography remains an element of the film's own discourse.

Matthews's work, which he sometimes refers to as "mumbleporn," has always attempted to portray the emotional truth of sexual relationships as he sees it. This has earned him a devoted fan base within the gay community. Based on word of mouth and views of the short, the release of the feature version of *I Want Your Love* was highly anticipated by an alternative or "hipster" gay demographic that looks to Mathews to deliver portrayals of gay men expressing their sexuality with refreshing honesty and unusual vulnerability. Unlike with the one-off experiments of Michael Winterbottom and other directors, for Mathews's fans the explicit is already the expected. The decisions he made about how to approach sex in *I Want*

Your Love speak in part to his desire to fulfill those expectations of a positive and honest portrayal.

Although he went into production with a full screenplay, Mathews acknowledges that he saw his script more as a rigorous starting point than as a locked blueprint for his storytelling. Specifically, he expected his rehearsal and shooting process would transfer some of the responsibility for scripting to his performers. "I knew that it was going to get totally ripped to shreds, but the core of the story elements were necessary to continue with.... At least, I wasn't married to what I had as long as it felt realistic." When Mathews first recalled his approach to writing sex scenes in interview, he did so in terms of attempting to express a move from the physical action to the emotional situation. This is certainly reflected in the structure of some of these scenes on the page. Initially, he recalled a process that led from notes in the script toward full choreography only on set:

> At certain times I was specific about sexual things.... More often than not it was more like "they're going to mess around, it's going to get heated in this way and then [a character] is going to be brought out of the moment because he sees [something] that's going to change the mood and then there's going to be a break."... I mean there was sex stuff in there, but it was very bullet pointed. It was never so choreographed. Often [it was] when we got on set and we saw the limitations of the space we were in, the lighting, the time, that we then choreographed things.

Having referred back to drafts of his original screenplay, Mathews was surprised to find how specific he had been in writing sex into his script during its development: "What I'm struck by, and apparently had considerable amnesia around, was how much I had actually written into these early drafts."

It is certainly instructive, in reading these drafts of the sex scenes, to observe a gradual "writing down" of the sex. It is clear that Mathews's process had been to write the sex in detail as he was laying out the scenes in his early drafts. He then pared the action descriptions down in subsequent drafts. The later drafts were more focused on foregrounding the catalytic role of sex in advancing beats in the emotional story, although the final draft is still explicit, in a matter-of-fact sort of way: X does Y to Z. Importantly, Matthews's scripted sex scenes feel much more like director's notes than attempts to engage the viewer's libido.

We can follow this writing process through screenplay drafts in the sequence that plays during the climactic party in which a couple, Wayne and Ferrin, experiment with a threesome. Previously, there has been some tension between them around the negotiation of moving in together and sharing space, and we are not certain how strong their bond really is. The threesome sequence serves to confirm their deep affection and the potential of their relationship as the other partner in the threesome, Jorge, realizes he is very much the third wheel and leaves them to it. Their sex is passionate, their connection obvious, and Wayne and Ferrin end up laughing and happy together. The laughter was a moment found on the set, not in the screenplay, but it emerged directly out of the goals of the scene, as scripted and as enacted through the sex itself.

In an earlier draft of the scene Mathews writes the sex as a series of specific instructions, both for the sex acts themselves and for the emotional meanings surrounding them. This is clearly a "working it out" draft, which incidentally breaks with standard screenwriting conventions by specifying character intentionality in a way that we cannot *see* for the sake of communicating emotional clarity. The second extract reads like a cross between conventional screenwriting and the more explicit interventions of director's notes—in Mathews's term it is "bullet pointed":

> Jorge reaches over and touches Ferrin's leg, rubs his hand up it. Ferrin just watches with an emerging grin as Jorge's hand moves very slowly up his leg, to his underwear. Ferrin rubs his hand over Jorge's crotch, leans over and starts kissing him.
>
> Wayne watches, turned on, feeling at his crotch, outside his underwear.
>
> Ferrin reaches his hand into Jorge's hair and starts messing it up.

And again:

> Ferrin/Wayne reconnect, focusing mostly on each other. Wayne is looking lovingly in Ferrin's eyes, a non-verbal appreciation for Ferrin willingly moving out of his comfort zone and experiencing something less controlled. Wayne is reconfirmed in his love for Ferrin and vice versa. Jorge notices their moment. He remains engaged, involved, but pulls back some, allowing for space.[62]

In a later draft the sequence of the sexual activity is still specified, but the description is shorter. The scene also *reads wide* in that, although we are told who is doing what and to whom, the writing does not attempt to lock us into imagined coverage. In other words our focus is implied, but we are not directed specifically to a sequence of shots, more to a sequence of actions.

The inclusiveness is reinforced by how the focus of the action continually plays outward from the bodies of the individuals to their relationships. The writing sketches the emotional implications of character interactions and is now less concerned with giving explicit motivational instructions to the actors:

> Wayne is lying on his back on the bed. He stares up at the Christmas lights, conflicted, as he gets blown. Ferrin pulls away from Jorge's cock, rises, watches Wayne and Jorge. Jorge slowly kisses his way up Wayne's body. As he moves upward he notices Wayne's unease ...

And later:

> Ferrin stands while Jorge blows him, licks his balls. Wayne is rimming Ferrin all the while. Ferrin is only partially enjoying this.
>
> Jorge and Wayne start making out between Ferrin's legs. Ferrin notices—again—a slight unease with Wayne; he pulls back.[63]

One gets the sense, in comparing these drafts, of Mathews gradually shifting the focus away from the choreography of sex in isolation and onto the dynamic of the ensemble. The writing is also becoming *less* overtly erotic as the drafts progress. The sex is still central to revealing the dramatic function of the scene, but the emotional drama feels better-integrated into the activity. It signals direction without completely breaking the screenwriting convention of not introducing internal dialogue or literal motivation within scene description. We can sense "conflict" and "unease" in a character through the externalities of performance, without being directed toward a specific internal thought process, for example.

The writing of sex in the screenplay of *I Want Your Love* is very different to the approaches taken by the writers of well-known simulated sexual encounters in movies. The sex scene in Milo Addica and Will Rokos's screenplay for *Monster's Ball* (2001), for example, plays directly to displaying the physical attraction of its female participant, and Joe Eszterhas's script for *Basic Instinct* (1992) reads as simple onanistic titillation—in other words: exactly as intended. Of course, both of these scenes required a level of selling to the reader that the promise of improvised, but real, sex in *I Want Your Love* would seem to obviate. Compare Mathews's emerging style above with an extract from a sex scene from the opening of *Basic Instinct*:

```
She leans close over his face, her tongue in his mouth ...
she kisses him ... she moves her hands up, holds both of
his arms above his head.

She moves higher atop him ... she reaches to the side of
the bed ... a white silk scarf is in her hand ... her hips
have his face now, moving ... slightly, oh-so-slightly ...
his face strains towards her.

The scarf in her hand ... she ties his hands with it ...
gently ... to the brass bed ... his eyes are closed ...
```

```
tighter ... lowering hips into his face ... lower ... over
his chest ... his navel.64
```

Unlike Mathews's increasing matter-of-factness in anticipating the real sex that will speak for itself onscreen, Eszterhas is writing to sell a conventional notion of cinematic eroticism. He pitches the opening of his screenplay to the presumed arousal of his reader, just as the first scene will eventually play to the presumed arousal of the viewer, both clearly assumed to be straight and male. Of course, the genres are very different, but note the way Eszterhas's writing attempts to inscribe the reader's voyeurism into the sex act through a sequence of specific images. We are locked into a fractured continuity by the repeated use of ellipsis, which also draws the read forward. This works in much the same way that we discussed in terms of the writing of spectacular action—another kind of attraction—in tentpole films in chapter 2. In this way both the individual shot and its place in the sequence speak loudly. The writing even implies an editing rhythm. The writing style is all about teasing, and that sells the tone and address of the whole movie: it will *look* and *feel* exactly like *this*.

Of course, sex in cinema is always an attraction. In *Basic Instinct* that attraction is written with heterosexual arousal as its leading haptic special effect.[65] In the emerging screenplay of *I Want Your Love*, spectacle is incrementally written out of the sex, its spectacular nature finally becoming an almost incidental given. This anticipation of control in simulated sex scenes is also clearly present in the screenplay for the award-winning, character-driven drama *Monster's Ball*. When Hank and Leticia have sex, the tone and style also reflect the complex emotional knot in which the two unlikely interracial lovers are bound. The screenwriters turn the sexual performance toward character, emotion, and *the moment*:

```
Leticia takes off her blouse. Undoes bra. Her breasts fall.
Hank puts his mouth to her nipple. Leticia leans back. Hank
stops and leans back. Puts his arm around her.

Leticia's head falls to his lap. She undoes his belt.

Hank manages to get her skirt off. Leticia gets on the
floor and pulls his pants down.

Hank slides off the couch. She takes off her panties.
Starts to cry. Hank freezes. Leticia pulls him to her.

                    LETICIA
Please ... please

                     HANK
I can stop ... I don't want to hurt you ...
```

>   LETICIA
>   ... I know ...
>
> Hank puts Leticia against the couch. He takes her from the
> rear and starts pumping her. Leticia turns, eyes meet.
>
>   HANK
>   I'm sorry ...
>
> Leticia changes position. Crawls around and rides him gently.
>
>   HANK
>   (cont'd): ... Dear lord ...
>
> Hank, using his pelvic muscles, lifts her into the air.
> Leticia maintains her mount.[66]

This is another scene of heterosexual sex, but it is abundantly clear which character's body the writing—and, thus, the film to come—is paying most attention to. The sexual gymnastics, disguised as emotional need, speak to the display of Leticia as "rider." There is no doubt but that she is the key attraction. The writing in *I Want Your Love* is much more democratic in terms of its assignment both of activity and audience attention, until the sequence takes its emotional turn and Jorge backs out. Explicitness in that scene is also written more toward the goal of collective rather than individual sexual display.

Mathews moved away from screenplay-as-blueprint on *I Want Your Love*, but not away from his story. This process began in workshopping the nonsexual elements of the story with his actors. Rehearsals for the sex scenes were all undertaken with clothes on. In comparison, Michael Winterbottom went into production on *9 Songs* with no script whatsoever. His plan was for story, of a kind, to emerge organically and necessarily from the intimacy generated through sex. "The idea was to try and capture—whilst they were together, intimate in bed—some sense of what that's like and what it's like to remember that—because this is all told through Matt's [Kieran O'Brien] memories," he told us. "We hoped that if we filmed it intimately enough, and they were honest enough, the smallest little changes in mood and atmosphere would come through in the film. There was no script at all at any point."[67]

The problem for many press critics was that Winterbottom was asking too much of his sex. Roger Ebert wrote that "*9 Songs* is more interesting to write about than see. It's minimalism is admirable as an experiment, but monotonous as an experience."[68] Philip French, in the United Kingdom, agreed: "*9 Songs* resembles not so much conventional hardcore porn as a rather solemn sex-education film."[69] Under this grid Winterbottom's experiment ceded control of the film to a sequence of spectacular displays that were unable not only to speak for themselves but to fill in interstitial spaces, usually the province of other forms of storytelling. Film scholar Linda Williams argues that asking this of the film misses the point: "To appreciate *Nine Songs* one must abandon the expectation that the sex scenes will illustrate and thus become part of a larger plot and character development. Winterbottom's gamble—which only partly pays off—is that the sensual substance of a love affair can just as well be captured through sensual and musical lyricism as through dramatic event or extended dialogue."[70] For his part, Mathews, in *I Want Your Love,* integrates sex into a narrative rather than a lyrical trajectory. His sex scenes speak to the specific story moment in which they occur and work to develop or resolve relationship arcs. This is readily apparent in the sequence in which Wayne and Ferrin try a threesome and end up happily excluding Jorge.

It was around the shooting of sex that the challenges of loss of story control and the transformative potential of filmed sex also emerged in Mathews's film. Although the filmmakers were working from a fully realized script, every film—made, as the old saying goes, three times: in writing, in production, and in postproduction—has something of the palimpsest about it, and this sense of "writing over" would be amplified by the sex in *I Want Your Love.*

Both in physical and in story terms, the most important sex scene in the movie, between the protagonist, Jesse, and his friend, mentor, and fellow performance artist, Keith, broke down on the set. The scene was intended to be the loving and supportive culmination to a sequence in which Keith reassures Jesse that he'll be okay in the end. Owing to a combination of emotional stress from the intense performance work of the previous days, and to a particular physical incompatibility, the actors were not capable of playing the scene as written. The sex did not take place.

Scheduling pressures, and Matthews's uncertainty that the performers would be physically able to do what was required, meant no reshoots of this material were possible. Although he wasn't overly precious about repeating a "live" experience for the purposes of storytelling, he was keen to minimize this kind of work: "When their sex was just kind of breaking down and wasn't working, really there was nothing else I could do other than go with it." This decision also speaks to a particular collaborative relationship he developed with his performers in order to gain their trust: "I'm asking a tremendous amount of people. They're not actors, and they're not porn people.... I was always coming back to, Does this feel natural? Does this feel honest? I was looking for a particular performance out of people while I was asking them to go to places of extreme vulnerability.... So I had to go where things were going energetically because, if I didn't, I was going to lose them or I was going to create something that I felt would be super false." Given these commitments, and the fact that the physical incompatibility of the actors was not going to change, the film had to be significantly rewritten, with reshoots planned around the dysfunctional version of the sex as shot. This darkened the tone of the story, and Matthews was worried that he would have difficulty reworking the film to offer the positive message of gay sexual identity he had scripted. He feared that he had been hoisted by his own petard of authenticity. After all, in a film that foregrounds the actuality of sex, faking it clearly was not a good option.

Mathews's film was reworked successfully to accommodate this new reality, but in its deployment of real sex acts in a search for a kind of emotional authenticity, it also exposed the perils of integrating narrative modes (fiction and documentation, if not exactly documentary) that lies at the heart of the current "microbudget conversation." In practical filmmaking terms, then, the challenge of writing the explicit in *I Want Your Love* was manifested in the need to bend narrative around the sexual event and not the other way round. Sexual performance, or in this case its absence, rewrote the script on the set and forced another order of rewriting after the event. In so doing, it also collapsed any residual sense of the strict periodization of the screenwriting—or scripting—process in terms of that project at the very least.

If the intention was to explore the emotional reality of relationships through sex, the production of *I Want Your Love* exposed an ironic story about the unpredictability of sexual compatibility that can transcend or trump emotional attraction. The filmmakers were left with the challenge of picking up the pieces left by that uncomfortable situation. The rewriting and reorganization of the narrative buried, at least in part, an inconvenient truth about relationships and the scripting process simultaneously. After all, how often does sexual incompatibility become an issue in either mainstream or indie storytelling? The sex in movies always seems to work, or, when it doesn't, the failure plays for simple comic effect. It's the getting to it and beyond it where the drama usually lies.

Although there may be caveats along the way, the principle of perilous exploration evidenced in the production of *I Want Your Love*, at the microbudget end, is a potential spur for the rejuvenation-by-avoidance of a largely moribund and increasingly corporate independent filmmaking movement. It speaks to the work of a new generation of independent filmmakers finding their own ways to articulate truths about life and love as they see them. In doing so, they are also offering new creative formulae through combinations of script, performance, and story to blur modal and authorial boundaries and to push once again beyond the inherited, reified security of the screenplay-as-blueprint.

CONCLUSION

Although in the introduction to this chapter we took issue with *Wikipedia*'s definition of *Indiewood* for its naivety, the crowd-written online encyclopedia is correct in highlighting Indiewood's "alternate pathway" to the Hollywood studio system.[71] We would also identify it, as well as "independent cinema," as first and foremost a discursive category that functions to position the reader and the filmmaker. Of course, we are academics looking to complicate the collective understanding of the "independent" screenwriter today, so we're also saying that the definition of *independent* should depend a bit on the way the screenwriter sees him- or herself.

The challenge of independence has been about negotiating the terms of its difference, negotiating that separation, within a nonmovement movement (or, perhaps more accurately, a series of nonmovement movements) whose diverse practitioners variously aspire to use the opportunities provided by independence, of financing, genre, or state of mind, to bridge the gap with the mainstream and struggle to maintain that divide. In this contradiction there is a sense in which the recent history of American independent cinema mirrors that contradictory notion of an auteur in a film and business practice that requires multiple voices and competing financial interests at each stage of preproduction, production, and distribution. If the meaning of a film lies in destination rather than origination, as Roland Barthes has theorized, the meaning of *independent* lies as much in the work of the screenwriter and others as it does in the multitude of industrial definitions of *independent* from Hollywood, to academia, to other paraindustries.

The sense of *independent* as discourse sheds light on a distinct (but, in historical terms, repeatable) moment of filmmaking in which a new burst of creativity from the margins of the industry is first recognized for its transformative, and sometimes transgressive, political and aesthetic power or potential. Alternative mechanisms, such as independent production companies, quickly emerge to facilitate and encourage such work. This sparks the rapid development of the form or movement in and outside Hollywood.

It also prompts an almost equally rapid process of economic exploitation by the mainstream, the hegemony of dominant cinema, which uses its resources and market power to co-opt the revenue streams from the once alternative and resistant forms and cultural practices.

The corporate mainstream then generates its own, typically safer and paler, versions of the original creative work to maintain those streams. Eventually, the media industry redefines its economic priorities, retools for the next thing, and moves on. Meanwhile, new generations of creative players strive to redefine the margins of the form on their own terms and to produce work that explores the edges in very different ways once more—including writers like Gray, who writes female-led drama against the grain of the industry; Moreland, who is developing an adjacent model for commercial production; and those "like" Mathews, whose practice is much further from the shadow of the tentpole.

In the crowded world of microbudget filmmaking it can often be difficult to get one's voice heard, as Travis Mathews's writing and producing partner Keith Wilson suggests, but individual and authentic voices are still audible in the babble:

> While I continue to struggle to find funding, exhibition opportunities, viable distribution outlets and appreciative eyeballs, my biggest challenge now cuts deeper. With so many filmmakers and content creators, platforms and apps, C300 cameras and iPhone filters, I often feel drowned out, lost, behind. I spend a significant amount of time trying to hear my artistic voice amidst and above the clutter and the Kickstarters. I most definitely don't think that filmmaking is a precious art form belonging in the talented hands of a few chosen people. No way. I wouldn't have made any films without digital technology and a DIY attitude. But I am often unsure how to go about creating work that is personal, honest and singular in this bizarre, busy, fragmented world we now live in.[72]

Microbudget filmmaking is perhaps the most diverse and, thus, comprehensive example of independent film, its writers and directors the most diverse and, thus, comprehensive examples of independent storytellers. Yet, as we have shown, some of them do also go on to get "picture deals" from the studios. Some of their voices do enter the mainstream. Many, in fact, aspire to do so, such as the mumblecore "graduates" like Lena Dunham, whom we noted above. Of course, they slip in and out of independence depending on what they are doing, how they're financing it, how it is distributed, and how they articulate their position in relation to Hollywood.

One of the more obvious lessons we draw from our account of the state of independent screenwriting is that many experienced professional screenwriters who once felt they had a career path that could be wholly contained in and by the independent sector no longer feel that way. In other words, the life of an independent screenwriter, while never comfortable or easy when viewed through the prism of Maras's business frame, at least seemed more settled when viewed through the practitioner and story and structure frames. In the early twenty-first century, however, many writers no longer have the luxury of working in one sector or one medium—or even between established media such as features and television, like Pamela Gray. For many writers the migration from one medium to another is a wrench. Not only do they have to acquire and develop new skills and sustained professional networks, but they have to go through a significant personal redefinition; they are no longer the kind of writer they once assumed that they were and aspired to become.

For many younger screenwriters the idea of commitment to a single medium has never had the same resonance. Many screenwriters from Generation X and beyond have embraced the chance of working in and between new media like video games that were influential in their own childhoods and were always an accepted part of a broader world of mediated storytelling in a way that wasn't the case for their forebears. In the next chapter we examine the recent history and practice of writing for video games and consider the way the screenwriting craft and its union attempted to adapt to this emerging industry and, by extension, to convergent media in general.

5. Screenwriter 2.0

The Legitimation of Writing for Video Games

> Video games are a waste of time for men with nothing else to do. Real brains don't do that.
>
> RAY BRADBURY

> The video game writer is part of the design team, during pre-production, and creates the main plot of a video game but can also focus on the dialogue, the character creation and development or the world-building. During the game development process, the design may change and a video game writer can also be asked to fix the eventual narrative issues.
>
> *Wikipedia*

The "Leeroy Jenkins" digital playing card from Blizzard Entertainment's *Hearthstone: Heroes of Warcraft*, an online collectible card game (CCG), possesses the powerful "charge" ability. "Charge" allows Leeroy to immediately injure an opponent in the game. As a balancing mechanism, when one player plays Leeroy Jenkins, two "Whelp" minions (immature dragons) appear automatically to fight for the other side. Because of the card's abilities, in some iterations of the *Hearthstone* gameplay meta, Leeroy Jenkins has been played as a powerful "finisher." He is used to ensure what is referred to as a "lethal"—to kill the enemy hero and thus win the game.[1]

The *Hearthstone* Leeroy Jenkins card stemmed from Blizzard's genre-defining Massively Multiplayer Online Role Playing Game (MMORPG) *World of Warcraft* (WOW). The digital cards are based on characters, monsters, magic spells, and other items that were originally created for WOW's fantasy universe. As any keen *Hearthstone* player knows, the Leeroy Jenkins card is special because it is based on a second-order creation. Leeroy was not part of Blizzard's original world design. The card represents the in-game character of a *World of Warcraft* real-world gamer, Ben Schulz. Schulz came to the attention of Blizzard and the broader WOW player base in 2005 when a gameplay video titled *A Rough Go* was posted on the Internet. In this video—arguably the most famous player-created video made for the *World of Warcraft* community—Ben-as-Leeroy causes his in-game community of play (the guild PalsForLife) to be massacred by a flock of Whelps—hence the card's special power.[2] Schulz has Leeroy Jenkins, his in-game avatar, charge into battle shouting his character's name, completely ignoring the battle tactics the other members of his group had carefully worked out while he was "afk" (away from keyboard) getting some food. His friends curse Ben-as-Leeroy out ("Leeroy you are just as stupid as hell"), to which he famously replies: "At least I have chicken."[3]

It is quite possible that the events in the original video were set up as a staged entertainment for other fans and players. Indeed, in interviews Ben Schulz has been coy about the authenticity of his character's gameplay.[4] What is beyond dispute, however, is that Leeroy Jenkins became hugely popular among players of *World of Warcraft*. The character's antics quickly attained the status of a meme, spreading virally both within the game and in the wider mediascape. Leeroy is now a metaphor of sorts, as players commonly refer to Leeroy Jenkins when someone does something reckless or stupid. In the wider gaming community and beyond, "his" name is often used as an alternative to "YOLO" (You Only Live Once). Similar to the Latin phrase, "carpe diem" (seize the day), YOLO reminds gamers that their characters—and by proxy, the player—should go all out to win, to game with abandon, despite the risks. It is also a statement made before doing something otherwise considered "stupid" or against carefully crafted tactics.

Leeroy Jenkins has also become a meme that stretches well beyond its origins in *World of Warcraft*. He makes an appearance as a character in other companies' games, such as the *Arcadia Quest* board game (Cool Mini or Not).[5] Indeed, *Wikipedia* has an entry for Leeroy Jenkins that currently cites twenty-four examples of intertextual reference across TV shows, novels, comic books, and movies, from *Phineas and Ferb* to *The Daily Show with Jon Stewart*.[6] As the release of the *Hearthstone* card demonstrates, this fan-scripted metacharacter has since been commodified, reincorporated into official Blizzard products, and otherwise sold back to members of the company's broader community of play through official and unofficial channels. Official Leeroy Jenkins merchandise, or "merch" as fans call it and the company markets it, includes pint glasses and other ancillary commodities. The fans engage in extending an unofficial market, selling T-shirts through their own websites. This is YOLO economics.

The screenwriter Gary Whitta, who wrote an early draft of the *Warcraft* movie (2016), even included a version of the character in his screenplay.[7] The scene with Jenkins did not make it into the final film, but in 2015 numerous WOW sites celebrated the tenth anniversary of Leeroy's "birth" into fan culture in the original video. Finally, the Leeroy Jenkins meme was reintegrated into the official *World of Warcraft* game, first through the award of his surname as a character achievement and subsequently as a nonplayer character in the expansion *Warlords of Draenor*. In that expansion, Upper Blackrock Spire, the original dungeon in which Leeroy Jenkins's reckless charge brought "him" to fame, was retooled: an event was introduced through which Leeroy can be gained as a follower for the player. Despite not making it to the big-screen movie, Leeroy Jenkins has nonetheless made the video game big-time.

We have in Leeroy a character generated by a fan, *scripted* both through the game's official character creation process and through the vagaries of subsequent play by that fan that crossed into a range of ancillary markets, the result being that its creator-producer and the company that leveraged it earned the opportunity for additional marketing. In this way Leeroy Jenkins as both meme and commodity exemplifies the phenomenon of *emergence* in the ludisphere of video games.[8] Emergence is a term adopted by ludology (the study of games) to express a form of complex systems analysis. It describes the development of complex social and interactive instances that emerge from relatively straightforward game mechanics. Steven Johnson describes emergence in relation to systems as distinct as ant colonies and software design, noting that such systems

> solve problems by drawing on masses of relatively (simple) elements, rather than a single, intelligent "executive branch." They are bottom-up systems, not top-down. They get their smarts from below. In more technical language, they are complex adaptive systems that display emergent behavior. In these systems, agents residing on one scale start producing behavior that lies one scale above them: ants create colonies; urbanites create neighborhoods; simple pattern-recognition software learns how to recommend new books. The movement from low-level rules to higher-level sophistication is what we call emergence.[9]

This idea of emergence and emergent play fits within the history of an active and creative fandom, producing liminal texts from fanzines to slash. Looked at as the intersection of complex systems, the emergence of Leeroy Jenkins is a hybrid product of WOW's instance design, of player guilds, of the expansion of community-based play through the Internet and of the growth of video-sharing websites like YouTube. This context alone, however, does not fully explain its appeal, as emergence is not confined to in-game interactions. Unplanned emergence takes different forms in different games. In *World of Warcraft* it can be seen in everything from the development of restrictive forms of play, such as "Iron Man leveling," to the use of in-game animations to create independent cinematic narratives or machinima.[10]

Emergent gameplay is, in short, a phenomenon that places an unusual amount of creative control and, importantly for our purposes, of a kind of scripting in the hands of players.

Scholars who study video games and virtual worlds often distinguish between ludic and paidiaic modes of play: the former is rule-driven and structured (e.g., *Hearthstone*); the latter is unstructured and open-ended (e.g., *Second Life*). The virtual worlds and communities of play that are sustained by these designed modes enable somewhat different forms of social emergence. However, common examples of emergence still include the formation of social guilds, in-game marriages, forms of in-game resistance to perceived inequities in gameplay, and the development of informal marketplaces for in-game items.[11] Under this grid, as a game *World of Warcraft* sits firmly within the ludic mode of play, as the phenomenon of Leeroy Jenkins illustrates, serving as a kind of creativity that transcends the rules and restrictions of its source in ways that are both intended and unforeseen but also leveraged and extended for market success. Equally important, it reminds us of the slippage between design (including planning and coding) and writing in the development of narrative-driven video games.

Leeroy's emergence from and subsequent reintegration into the canon of Blizzard's product line is an example of the kind of creative loop between designers and players that helps to differentiate the ongoing, postrelease iterations of video game scripting from the still-periodized writing processes of movies and TV discussed in previous chapters. More broadly, emergence and postrelease scripting are both indicative of the new creative environment faced by screenwriters (and, indeed, by the WGA) adapting to a converging media industry that relies on the fluidity of employment conditions and working practices. As such, the boundary around what the media industries define as "screenwriting" shifts periodically to reflect the establishment of new media forms, changes in creative practice, and the emergence of new markets.

The release of the Leeroy *Hearthstone* card is an important step in a complex intertextual journey that reveals much about the unique nature of scripting in contemporary video games. What does it mean to the profession and culture of writing to have a media-world that requires writers to also be designers of a world that allows their creations to be recreated by fans acting as second-order designers that can and often do upend the diegesis? How does a writer design an open-ended world that potentially allows millions of people to rewrite, even doctor, her craft? On the one hand, is Ray Bradbury, as quoted at the opening of this chapter, right—"Video games are a waste of time . . ."—or has he fundamentally misunderstood the scripting process of fan writers and the writer-designers that set them up for play? On the other hand, are the authors of the Video Game Writer entry in *Wikipedia* right when, after defining the term as outlined in the other epigraph to this chapter, state: "Also as video games are more recent than other media, video game writing is still a field to be conquered."

In addressing these questions, we make the case that one direction in which the definition of screenwriting is expanding is toward forms of fan practice within specific communities of play and the broader ludisphere. Moreover, screenwriter 2.0, as we think of the screenwriter in the age of convergence, is less easy to pigeonhole than were her peers from previous generations. Now survival for many professional screenwriters often necessitates having at least a working knowledge of video games from the perspectives both of the player and the official writer-designer.

FRAMING VIDEO GAME WRITING

Convergence between the motion picture and video games industries has accelerated since the replacement of the short-lived CD-ROM with DVD technology, beginning in 1997. This new standard format for mastering both movies and video games facilitated the development, marketing, and release strategies in primary and ancillary markets for both industries. Convergence has been sustained by the subsequent move toward digital downloads for movies and games. At the corporate level, both industries have also been experiencing an ongoing process of corporate consolidation. Major games companies have merged (Vivendi Games merged with Activision to form Activision Blizzard in 2008) or bought up smaller entities (Electronic Arts purchased BioWare in 2008) to take control of valuable properties and increase market share. The conglomerate media's ongoing search for synergies has linked the production of major tentpole movies with video game adaptations as central components in the strategy of cross-platform and cross-media exploitation. This strategy of releasing games on the back of motion picture properties has followed the exploitation of major genre franchises, including superhero movies, *The Lord of the Rings*, *Harry Potter*, and *Transformers*. Since the 1990s, video games have also been sources of content for movie adaptations, albeit with mixed critical and bottom-line results. Notable examples include *Super Mario Brothers* (1993), *Street Fighter* (1994), *Lara Croft: Tomb Raider* (2001), *Resident Evil* (2002), *Prince of Persia: The Sands of Time* (2010), and *Warcraft* (2016).[12]

It is much too simplistic to suggest, as Robert Alan Brookey does, that "screenwriters have become game writers and therefore the production of a cinematic narrative and a game narrative have become similar practices."[13] While it is true that more writers are now working between the two media, there are significant creative challenges screenwriters have to overcome to adapt their craft and labor to the unique culture and protocols of the games industry. It is incorrect to assume that the traffic in screenwriters between movies and the games industry flows in one direction only. For example, the screenwriter Gary Whitta (*The Book of Eli*, 2010; *After Earth*, 2013; *Rogue One: A Star Wars Story*, 2016) came to feature films from a career in games journalism, comics (*Death Jr.*, Image Comics, 2005) and video games (*Prey*, Human Head Studios, 2006).

From within the WGA in 2009 Deborah Todd made an argument for the legitimation of the games writers who had made this "reverse move" into screenwriting. In *Written By: The Magazine of the Writers Guild of America, West*, Todd highlights some of the many differences between writing screenplays and writing games scripts. These include script length and the production of a range of ancillary materials: "In the mid-'90s game writers started joining the WGA based on their game scripts—typically 500-plus pages with branching storylines, separate dialog scripts, asset lists that spelled out all of the props, or clickables or hotspots in a game. Game writers were justifiably recognized as talented screenwriters, capable of developing great story and characters and award-winning entertainment."[14] Referring to what amounts to a short history (in that she published the piece in 2009 about the 1990s), Todd makes clear that writing between Hollywood and video games is a two-way street.

The WGA has done much to bring games writing under its auspices in craft-cultural terms, if not in terms of formal jurisdiction. And, of course, screenwriters, including established WGA members, work on all kinds of video games, not only on movie adaptations. Thus, when Brookey suggests that the convergence between the two industries manifests itself primarily in terms of games adapted from movies and movies adapted from games, he is missing the point when it comes to craft and creative labor. If the definition of *screenwriting* is to be expanded to cover writing for video games, then that definition transcends cross-media adaptation. For established screenwriters, convergence is about major changes to the entire labor market to accommodate new media forms. As media scholar Jonathan Gray has argued, the failure of many video game adaptations of major studio movies can directly be ascribed to a lack of effectively managed creative convergence between development teams across both media. Frequently games developers are given limited licenses as subcontractors. They are, as Gray summarizes, "rarely given full access to the creative team behind the licensed entity and are usually restricted from doing certain things with characters or locations."[15]

Another mitigating factor is that genre is defined differently in video games than it is in movies, at least with respect to how films are marketed as genres. Rather than speaking simply to familiar movie story types—westerns, science fiction, horror, musicals, etc.—video games genres are also defined, and marketed, according to the gameplay experience offered by a particular playing interface. A first-person shooter (FPS) presents a distinctly different ludic experience from a real-time strategy (RTS) game, for example, and their respective conventions require writers to think differently—and write differently—about characterization, plotting, arcs, and endings. FPS and RTS titles may, of course, offer science fictional, fantastic, or historical worlds in which to play, but all of these familiar generic distinctions are of secondary importance to the interface between gamer and game. A player who does not enjoy the RTS experience is unlikely to be persuaded by other generic categories if she has to experience them in an RTS context, and so forth. Writers for games understand these as higher-level generic conventions.

Narrative-driven video games, such as role-playing games (RPG), may also be categorized according to the particular experience of storytelling within their fictional worlds. Specifically, there is the ludic-paidiaic distinction we have already referenced between more linear/"closed" and nonlinear/"open world" narratives. The former restricts interactivity and player choice or foregrounds and rewards the completion of highly plotted quests in the service of tighter progression or story control and a specified ending or reboot. The latter relaxes story structure to allow for a more complex and free-form experience in which the player explores the world of the game and may sideline, bypass, or temporarily suspend the central narrative of the game in order to do so. As Michael Wellenreiter notes, the writing of open world games subordinates narrative flow and plot progression to the broader interactive system. "RPG screenwriters must learn to function more like designers," he notes, "communicating their ideas through the building of 'models' or 'systems' for players to make narrative meaning within, rather than risking their own, narrow, enforced dramatic messages that may or may not be able to be narratively supported."[16] Fiction films have always played with the identification of the audience with a character, of course, most obviously through the point-of-view shot. Yet in games the player is more directly persuaded that she is, in fact, the star.

The technological and experiential paradigms that articulate the ludic or paidiaic experiences of the medium also require their writers to set aside conventional notions of a linear story that may have served them in movies or television. Ian Bogost has argued that games are designed according to a procedural rhetoric that is the core of their persuasive power. "Procedural rhetoric," he writes, "is a general name for the practice of authoring arguments through processes.... Arguments are made not through the construction of words or images, but through the authorship of rules of behavior, the construction of dynamic models."[17] This is a reminder that the scripting of video games is about coding at least as much as it is about storytelling, as the rules and parameters of the game as well as the plot are preprogrammed. Typical screenwriters are only engaged in the latter aspect, storytelling. The most effective and successful screenwriters understand the complexity of filmmaking, of using every aspect of the language of cinema to tell a story, and the same holds true to some extent for the tech-literate game writer. But while both forms of writing serve to embed and enhance the procedural rhetoric of the player's experience, in the medium of video games it is usually coding that leads and story that follows.

A key challenge for writers who work in video games has been to share the design process with programmers. The in-game stories that writers help to tell may now be integral to the success of a project, but unlike in movies and television, their work is still secondary to the needs of gameplay. For these reasons and more, screenwriters in the games industry have to integrate their creative labor in general and storytelling in particular with the specific needs and working practices of the new industry. They often follow story development as much as they lead or open it up.

The WGA has adjusted relatively slowly if, in the end, pragmatically to important developments in the media industries. Unsurprisingly, the guild has been more responsive when many of its existing members are already seeking work in new platforms than it has been when expanding its jurisdiction into media where the internal pressure from the membership is less strong. The guild does not always succeed in achieving such expansions, but we can at least follow its intent as instructive. Indeed, the internal debates around inclusion and accommodation are usually solid indicators of where established screenwriters see their current or future interests at a given historical moment. The strike of 2007–8 was a pertinent example. The WGA fought for a formula for building digital residuals into the Minimum Basic Agreement, and it won. But it was also seeking to expand its jurisdiction over animation writers and writers in reality television, and those battles were lost.

As we have noted, the WGA abandoned its attempt to cover reality television partly because of the strength of opposition to the expansion from within its own rank-and-file membership. Many established screenwriters were unconvinced that reality television writing was worthy of inclusion (and thus deserving of a kind of de facto *legitimation*) under the WGA's definition of professional screenwriting. In so doing, and neglecting the history of their craft during the emergence of television, they embraced a common "high" art (television drama writing) and "low" art (reality television) dichotomy. The distinction was not lost on critics. Susan Christopherson assails the WGA (along with all of the other craft guilds) for operating as a block to progress for creative labor rights in the era of convergence. She argues that the power of their members' vested interests means that the unions are "perceived more than ever as gatekeepers for a labor aristocracy whose goals and working style are not relevant to the younger generation of multi-skilled independent contractors."[18]

Miranda Banks agrees that the guild suffered from being passive as convergence overtook the industry. With the benefit of hindsight, the brief period of union activism under the leadership of Young and Verrone looks to have been more an anomaly than a trend. Banks argues, in contrast to Christopherson, that the WGA began to reform its outlook and has attempted to be more inclusive in recent years: "In the process of reassessing the parameters of professional writing, the Guild was transformed from an 'inbox' union that waited for new writers and signatories to approach it to one that reached out to professional writers working in new genres, forms, and platforms within American media industries."[19] Banks is correct in acknowledging the survival efforts of the guild, yet it is clear that self-interest remained, of course, a primary—if not the primary—factor.

Central to the challenges of staying relevant and of broadening the jurisdiction of the WGA during convergence has been the validation for its own members of the practice of screenwriting in new media and for new platforms. The internal argument may not have convinced members when it came to reality television writing, but the WGA has had more success persuading its membership of the need to cover the emerging industry of video games. Indeed, the WGA has undertaken what amounts to a process of cultural legitimation in the way it dealt with the video games industry in its own publications. Over time, the WGA also instituted internal changes that sought to validate the labor of those guild members who were now working in video games. It also participated in outreach activities to the games industry, encouraging employers to view the Writers Guild favorably, and to improve terms and conditions for its members. In so doing the

WGA successfully legitimated a once "illegitimate" medium, at least for its own membership constituency.

During a 2015 panel at Comic Con in San Diego, the actor Ben Foster praised the talents of his *Warcraft* (2016) director Duncan Jones. For Foster, Jones is "a man who has a specific vision. He brought that vision to a beloved game and he elevated that game to a film."[20] The compliment may well have been heartfelt, but it is also exactly the kind of pablum that creatives always use when talking about their peers in public fora. This is also another instance of John Thornton Caldwell's notion of "industrial spin" outlined in our introduction. What makes it particularly revealing in this case is how the actor explicitly evoked a hierarchy of media forms. Foster used the word *elevated* to suggest that movies are a more worthy form of popular culture than video games, replicating the old high-art-vs.-low-art distinction. Under Foster's grid it was Jones's talent that legitimated content from the lesser form of a game (Activision Blizzard's *Warcraft* franchise) by transforming it into the more respectable form of a feature film.[21]

In this way Foster is delegitimizing video games by association. His statement implies that, on its own merits, *World of Warcraft* is "beloved" yet only through its transformation into cinema can it be "elevated" into a work truly worthy of praise. We are picking on Foster only because he states publically what many in the Hollywood-side of the entertainment industry say privately and because establishing the principle is important for what follows. The reverse claim, in other words, would almost certainly not be offered in public discourse, outside the specialist discussion threads of gaming websites.[22] Indeed, genre films are often criticized for being too much like video games. That association carries with it the assumed baggage of formula, exploitation, and shallowness. The cultural status of video games has been consistently debased. Games have been blamed for any number of supposed social ills and for the decline of youth culture, not unlike how the comic book, television, and cable "original programming" (at least in its early days) were all decried in decades before.

Michael Z. Newman and Elana Levine call this *cinematization*, noting that while it is seldom flattering to compare a movie to a television show, the latter are often praised by association with the former. This kind of legitimation works by associating television with a medium that has already achieved a degree of cultural legitimacy.[23] They argue that the process of television's cultural legitimation, begun in the 1940s but accelerating since the 1970s, involved the critical elevation of newly respectable television forms led by "quality drama" series like *Hill St. Blues, St. Elsewhere, The Sopranos, The Wire, Mad Men, The West Wing, Breaking Bad, House of*

Cards, and *Orange Is the New Black* on networks, pay cable, and now through the new streaming services. At the same time, older and supposedly lesser forms and genres of television, such as game shows, soap operas, and reality television, as well as their audiences, are denigrated by comparison (often also in gendered ways, as was the case with television being positioned as a "woman's medium" and cinema as a "man's"). Newman and Levine find this bifurcation troubling because they see in it a reproduction of "unequal structures of social position more generally—certainly those of class and gender": "Television's convergence is aesthetic and social as much as it is technological, and cinema is as important for television's convergence as computers. In the context of convergence, movies and television (and to an extent video games) become less distinct and more interchangeable.... The historical modes of television textuality and experience rooted in the U.S. network era are revealed in their manifold limitations, as the present of media is valorized at the expense of the past. In this way, television is a problem that convergence solves."[24] Or, in Foster's terms, games are the problem that movies solve.

In creating a legitimate space for video games within both their jurisdictional and craft-cultural remit, and not doing so for reality television, the WGA is, de facto, investing in hierarchies and making exactly this kind of cinematized comparison. But it is precisely the issue of distinction that has exercised the guild in addressing new forms of screenwriting. Convergence has served to foreground the video games industry as an important marketplace in which the union's members can now find work, their dues continuing to serve the guild's mission and leadership. The remuneration levels, while still below those for movie and television writing, do not overly concern a membership with one eye on its retirement benefits. Television screenwriter Suzanne Oshry outlined the attraction of the games industry for screenwriters in an article for *Written By* in 2004: "As any game enthusiast can tell you, the worlds of film, television, and interactive entertainment are merging. Facing increased competition, developers and publishers need authentic dialogue, riveting plots, and compelling characters. Content matters and that's good news for writers."[25] That realization has pressured the WGA both to accommodate an expanded definition of screenwriting and to rethink the limits of its own jurisdiction once again. As screenwriter Michael Utvich noted optimistically during a groundbreaking "Roundtable in Cyberspace" on interactive writing hosted by and transcribed into the *Journal of the Writers Guild of America, West* (as it was then titled), in 1996, "the Guild has been through this before about fifty years ago. Television was a big shift in writing styles and approaches, and the Guild pulled it off very nicely."[26]

Utvich glosses over the tumultuous period in the history of American screenwriting labor that gave birth to the WGA in its current form. As discussed in our introduction and chapter 1, the integration of television occurred only a few years after the hard-fought battle for the establishment of a union contract between the writers and the Hollywood studios had finally been won. The first Minimum Basic Agreement for cinema was signed in 1941, but the idea that writers in the new medium of television would join the Screen Writers' Guild (SWG) rather than establish an organization of their own was by no means a sure thing. Indeed, in 1952 a rival Television Writers Association (TWA) was established, claiming sole jurisdiction over the representation of writers in the new medium. The TWA operated out of New York, in association with the Authors League of America, and applied to the National Labor Relations Board (NLRB) for certification and for the right to represent. In 1956, after two years of rancorous dispute mediated by the NLRB, the organizations merged to form the Writers Guild of America.[27]

Television writing was duly accommodated under the WGA's jurisdictional umbrella. For a long time after, however, members reported the existence of an implicit internal class system between film and television writers. Banks quotes television writer David Harmon: "We were the kid brother, as it were.... The screenwriters would list credits that went back to the early '30s. They were noble writers. We would list credits of things that were already off the air."[28] The obvious technical similarities between movies and television, the use of recognizable story types and genres, and the precedent of the SWG's existing contract for feature screenwriting made at least the principle of representation for television writers by the craft guild relatively clear. The reality of bringing video game writers under the auspices of the WGA has proved to be a much tougher proposition, however. The unconventional structure of the video games industry, the established terms and culture of employment therein, and the less formalized and more fluid position of writing within the creative process of game development made the assumption that the WGA should have jurisdiction over it at the very least questionable from the perspective of employers.

Back in 1996, when the participants in the "Roundtable in Cyberspace" were asked what the WGA should do in response to the growth of the games industry, the panel's responses went straight to core concerns and complaints that screenwriters have carried throughout the union's history. Most important, the participants wanted the union to ensure that the "great error" of employee status that many writers see as underpinning their history of bad deals with the movie studios would not be repeated with video games. As Utvich bitterly noted in the roundtable: "'Employee' in interactive is the same as 'janitor.'"[29] In short, the position was that the WGA should negotiate artist status for its members working in video games so that they could retain intellectual property rights to their creative work.

The fraught issue of employee status goes to the ability of the Hollywood employer to categorize a writer as an independent contractor, producing material to order and thus assigning away the creative rights (copyright) on the product of their labor to the producer or studio. Screenwriters are, in effect, work-for-hire employees that negotiate, via the guild, for back-end royalties. Writers in other media are not treated as employees in this way. Playwrights hold the copyright to their plays, for example, but movie screenwriters typically do not hold the copyright to their screenplays. Accepting employee status was a compromise deemed necessary for the writers to win a first union contract from the studios, but it has been a source of great regret to professional screenwriters ever since. Writing in response to a piece by the novelist Raymond Chandler, published in the *Atlantic Monthly* in 1945, the screenwriter Philip Dunne (*Last of the Mohicans*, 1936; *How Green Was My Valley*, 1941) wrote in the SWG's journal, the *Screen Writer*: "as long as the writer accepts a salary, as long as he does not share the producer's financial risk, just so long, thinks Mr. Chandler, will he be a lackey, a creator constrained from creating, a second-class citizen in the Hollywood community."[30]

If the importance of authorial rights was clear to the roundtable's participants from the get-go, the question of what writing for video games actually involved for professional screenwriters was much less so. In retrospect, the WGA *Journal*'s early attempts to make sense of what it called "interactive writing" often read as quaint. Although it may be assumed to have been offered in a faux naive spirit, the first question asked by the moderator in the "Roundtable in Cyberspace" was revealing: "What constitutes interactive writing? Is it writing?"[31] Utvich's response argues against Brookey' notion of easy convergence. It also sets up a key principle of classification that has persisted in the way screenwriters speak about the challenge of working in games as opposed to cinema or television. "Interactive writing is not writing in the sense of movies, TV or novels," he notes, "because the structure of interactive is entirely different.... The audience is key in interactive, and involving the audience is the key! Any design depends on involving the audience so they push buttons. This is one reason, I think, why many linear stories don't work very well in interactive form."[32]

Another participant reflected that the introduction of story was already transforming the video games industry. "Being involved in action, and being involved in a person's life are two very different things."[33] As video games became more complex, and moved from arcade machines and early television consoles to PCs and more advanced generations of networked consoles, game developers began to employ writers more regularly. Like early cinema at the end of the cinema of attractions and, thus, at the beginning of narrative integration, they needed professional writers as story became a marketable element across a wide range of emerging game genres, and they asked different things of their talents, but by the mid-1990s the games industry was rapidly becoming a verifiable market for screenwriters. Its growing economic power in comparison to the established media industries was also undeniable.[34] Indeed, the importance of the video games marketplace has not been lost on leading publishers in the screenwriting paraindustry either. For example, Michael Wiese Productions released a new how-to manual, *Slay the Dragon: Writing Great Stories for Video Games*, in 2015. The book's page on the publisher's website even prominently features a legitimating blurb of its own: "Practical and original advice on narrative writing for video games that treats the world of gaming for what it is: an emerging art form."[35]

The WGA took important steps in its internal process of legitimation-through-cinematization by establishing the Videogame Writers Caucus (VWC), having first created a Northern California Interactive Writers Caucus, based in San Francisco, in 1996.[36] According to the guild's mission statement, the VWC's purpose is to "promote the professional and artistic interests of interactive writers in the multibillion dollar videogame industry. The VWC seeks to raise writers' status and influence within this industry, build a community of professional videogame writers within the WGAW, and expand the coverage of videogame writing under WGA contracts."[37] The WGA also reached out to prominent creative players in the games industry and made its mark by promoting and validating writing in video games at industry conventions, as Deborah Todd wrote in 2009: "The WGA became involved in the games industry in a way that was, in hindsight, a visionary move. It nurtured relationships among game developers, publishers, and writers. It set out to create visibility for writers in the games industry. In the early days, the WGA was instrumental in getting writing sessions at conferences like Digital World, the IMA Expo in New York, and the Computer Game Developers Conference ... which is now the most esteemed game conference in the world."[38] Despite the attitude of some of its members, the WGA was prescient in recognizing the potential that this market brought if its writers could be professionalized within the guild hierarchy.

Another important step in the process of legitimating video games for screenwriting was the establishment of a Videogame Writing Award in 2008, presented during the annual WGA awards ceremonies.[39] In an industry that thrives on its annual round of self-congratulation, awards are a visible and important marker of value and legitimacy in the wider Hollywood creative community. The rubric for the Videogame Writing Award reads as follows: "The WGA Videogame Writing Award was established by the Guild's Videogame Writers Caucus to encourage storytelling excellence in videogames, *improve the status* of videogame writers, and promote uniform standards within the videogame industry. It recognizes the creative contributions videogame writers have made to a host of globally popular videogame titles and to the burgeoning videogame industry as a whole."[40]

In a subsequent interview with *Written By* on the occasion of his winning the WGA Videogame Writing Award in 2014 and 2015 for *The Last of Us* (a postapocalyptic game produced by Naughty Dog), video game writer/programmer Neil Druckmann expressed the hope that video games would achieve cultural legitimation: "It's important to me that games be recognized as a legitimate narrative art form that is just as strong as film or comics or TV. Hopefully being recognized by the WGA and being talked about, we can get out there more and more that videogames are more than just shooting people and killing them. It's more than just Pac-Man gobbling. It's more than just an adrenaline rush. It can be about something meaningful and interesting that can actually move and affect people."[41] Interestingly, he included comics with movies and television under the grid of already legitimate media.

Druckmann's formulation is probably not one that a previous generation of screenwriters would have offered. Yet Druckmann is from a generation of screenwriters who are also comic book fans. His is also the generation of the comic book movie, and the ubiquity and economic power of the new genre has raised the cultural profile of its source material among many Hollywood screenwriters.[42] Somewhat reminiscent of Foster's statement about *Warcraft*, Druckmann's argument is that story raises all boats. Games without stories, he implies, are reduced to being mere haptic thrills. A medium worthy of legitimation must be about more than this. He is speaking both to the hopes of his fellow writers for increased validation and to an industry that has been reluctant to grant them the benefits accruing from union status. We argue that the VWC and the Videogame Writing Award were used both internally and externally as public-relations wedges, promoting member acceptance as well as jurisdictional expansion. The appropriateness of the WGA's claim for jurisdiction in the video games industry was being sold, in part, through public demonstrations of existing internal legitimation by the guild.

The Videogame Writing Award has been the target of significant criticism from entertainment journalists and unaffiliated writers in the video games industry. Many have expressed surprise at some of the award's recipients over the years and believe the results are not always reflective of the best writing in the industry. By contrast, the WGA has acted too often like the ignorant outsider, trying to ingratiate itself with a community that it doesn't fully understand. Writing for *Forbes* in 2012, critic Paul Tassi congratulated the WGA for raising the profile of games writing through the award; however, he strongly criticized the nominations as unrepresentative. "The WGA is doing the industry no favors by doling out awards to games that don't deserve them," he wrote, "and nominated titles that just flat out don't make any sense. It's nice games are getting recognized for having scripts, but let's try to make this a far less random affair."[43] Similarly, in a 2011 interview Mary De Marle, lead writer for Eidos Montreal, also criticized the WGA's award. In doing so, she repeated an inaccurate assertion that was commonly held at the time, namely that only members of the union were eligible for the award.[44] Micah Wright (*Sopranos: Road to Respect*, 7 Studios, 2006), the chair of the VWC, responded by asserting that membership of the VWC was required for award eligibility, but full membership of the WGA was not. As part of his defense, however, Wright elaborated on the reasons why the WGA set up the award, viewing it as a strategic wedge to develop contacts in the industry as much as to acknowledge excellence in games writing: "The reasons we created [it] are threefold: (1) we wanted to honor the craft of the game writer/narrative designer, (2) we wanted the game companies to begin to fairly credit the writers on their games, and (3) we want to know who all the best game writers are so we can sit down with them and find out what their concerns and ideas about improving work conditions in the games industry are . . . and then to implement those ideas."[45] Wright also noted that eligibility for the award is limited to those games for which writers were actually credited and for which a script was made available to be evaluated, in the same way the WGA evaluates screenplays—another instance of craft legitimation through cinematization.

As another integral part of its outreach to the games industry, the WGA drafted a simplified Interactive Program Contract (IPC) that guarantees games writers employer-paid Pension and Health Fund contributions and the right to dispute resolution through arbitration.[46] Signing this contract has never been a requirement for WGA members to work on games industry projects, however. The IPC has been taken up only haphazardly by entertainment companies, many of which see it as the thin end of a wedge toward unionization. Screenwriters coming to the games industry from features and television often reflect on the very different expectations many games companies have of their employees, where, as Christy Marx *(Lord of the Rings; The Matrix Online)* notes, "They're used to abusing people. It's common for managers to work people 80 hours a week and run them into the ground. It's sort of taken for granted in the game world."[47] Interestingly, both Marx and Bruce Feirstein *(James Bond* franchise writer for Electronic Arts and cowriter of the features *The World Is Not Enough, Tomorrow Never Dies,* and *Goldeneye)* expressed confidence that it was the process of media consolidation that would eventually resolve the issue of union representation for games writers in the WGA's favor. "It's an evolving business," Feirstein reflected in 2004; "as media consolidation continues, this is going to be a wedge. The rest of their businesses are unionized."[48] It should be noted that more than a decade after Feirstein's optimistic statement, the WGA has still not been able to bring the games industry under its formal jurisdiction.

The reluctance of the games industry to accept union contracts for its writers notwithstanding, it is the integration of story into video gaming that drives the convergence of the film and games industries from the perspective of the screenwriting craft. Despite the relative lack of progress in outreach, the parallel move to legitimize the creative labor of games writing for the WGA's own membership continued through the 1990s and into the new millennium. In 1996 the WGA gave the VWC's members a regular column in *Written By* to reflect on the state of their industry. It came in the form of Terry Borst and Deborah Todd's "alt.screenwriters," which ran for five years (1996–2000).

Borst and Todd's column took the form of a lighthearted dialogue. Arguably, the humorous tone spoke of an attempt to make the new world of what was then often referred to as interactive writing both accessible and unthreatening to the established membership. Certainly no column in *Written By* covering movie screenwriting took quite this tone, or adopted the dialogic, explanatory form of alt.screenwriters. The column began to address the wide range of issues that would be expected in the coverage of a legitimate industry. From 1997 through 1999, for example, alt.screenwriters addressed topics including advice on back-end protections for interactive writers, finding an agent, industry jargon, formats for interactive scripts, interactive genres, writing for the children's interactive market, screenwriters websites, contracts for interactive writers, entrepreneurism for interactive writers, entertainment convergence, technological developments and the failure of CD-ROM, corporate mergers in multimedia, media consolidation, the advent of HDTV, Y2K issues, Disney's multimedia strategy, advice on working in corporate new media, TV series websites enhancing content and building audiences, and women's issues online.

There is an arc to the tone of these entries, moving gradually from explanation to commentary. At the beginning of its run alt.screenwriters focused on establishing for its professional readership what this new industry was and how it might be relevant for screenwriters. A shift comes around the beginning of 1998 with a lighthearted column in the December/January issue of *Written By* in which the authors offer jokey predictions of what the future might hold for the games and tech industries: "Microsoft completes its acquisition of every major movie studio and decides to merge them all—putting out one movie a year which movie 'end-users' will have no choice but to see (because there are no other studio movies)."[49] This column assumed its readers would understand the tech industry and the world of interactive entertainment well enough to get the jokes. After this date the alt.screenwriters columns tend to assume more knowledge on the part of the reader and a solid level of acceptance of the premise of screenwriting for games.

Written By also interviewed WGA members and members of the VWC who were prominent in the games industry. It reported on the experiences of established feature screenwriters who took assignments in games writing. The coverage of games writing in *Written By* offers a unique perspective on how screenwriters legitimate the terms of their own creative labor in a new medium. Also, by following these reports and interviews, the WGA's broader membership was able to learn a great deal about the creative differences between writing for movies and television and writing for video games.

The short history of negotiation over video games labor suggests that a larger negotiation over the definition of *writer* is at stake—a definition that has significant implications for the convergent writer. Yet it also suggests a kind of ignorance on the part of the WGA to fully understand the nature of the video game writer as scripter, leaving writers in this new industry in much the same position as the animation writer historically—trapped between old models of labor relations and new work culture trends. Indeed, in many ways this is the industrial context for the work of screenwriter 2.0 in all new media.

SCRIPTING VIDEO GAMES

In the early years of convergence, screenwriters often found that writing tasks in game development had previously been assigned without much regard for their importance. John Zuur Platten, a WGA member and writer on *Transformers: The Game,* recalled: "When I started writing games, the girl answering the phones at the front desk, who took a creative writing class in junior college, wrote the game's dialogue and didn't get any extra pay for that."[50] To recap, even though some screenwriters have been at the heart of story development in video games almost from the beginning, the definition of writing in the industry changed significantly. As Tim Langdell, CEO of Edge Games, recalls: "In the '80s *game writer* meant *coder, programmer.*"[51] It should also be noted that some of the earliest computer video games, including multiuser dungeons (MUD), were text based (e.g., *Zork I,* 1980) instead of being built around bitmap or vector graphics. Indeed, the development of graphics initially took the industry away from story before returning to it later. "The issue back in the early days was storage space," Dave Ellis remembers. "There was no room for story."[52]

Central to the culture shift required of screenwriters coming into the games industry has always been an acceptance of a more collaborative notion of story authorship yet also an effacement of that authorship within the game text to create and sustain the illusion of agency and control in the person of the player. As we have shown, in Hollywood features—and television—even scripts with one credited writer go through a process of development and end up with the imprints of many uncredited hands on their pages. The equivalent process in games design is typically much more diffuse, and the writer's labor is also likely to be deployed for more discreet and specialist tasks. This is partly a consequence of great variation in the use of story across different video game genres and in different periods in game design, but it applies in story-driven games as well. For example, writers may be employed to write dialogue for characters, or notes for sprite or prop usage, without any broader input into story or world creation. Other groups or departments in the game design team often handle these aspects of story development exclusively in-house.

Here, for example, is the opening text from a character creation document written by the games designer (and comic book writer) Chris Avellone for the RPG *Planescape Torment* (Interplay Entertainment, 1999). It illustrates the kind of specialist-development documents games designers and writers work with that will feed into other script forms as they are further integrated into the game. Note the references to other supporting documents that contribute to the scripting of the character, like preliminary artwork, suggestions for the integration of the character into cinematics, proposed character and combat statistics for programming into the game, and potential requirements for casting voice acting talent to play the character in the future.

Chris Avellone 1
Ravel Puzzlewell Version 1.0 Interplay
RAVEL PUZZLEWELL
Location: Black-Barbed Maze, Chapter of the Mad
NPC Type: "Enemy."
Portrait: See Eric Campanella's concept sketches.

Morality Play: A night hag who was foreshadowed as some great, evil witch, but is really nothing more than a puttering old crone who has been in prison for the past few centuries. Prison has made her more than a little loopy, and it manifests itself in her bent speech and her occasional lecherous advances to the player character.

Design Note: Movie where Ravel is walking through her garden, tending the black-barbs, when suddenly she pauses and turns to look out across the blasted landscape and starts to cackle. "He comes. He comes soon, my pretties." The mad cackling. Ravel's mad sister may want the secrets that her sister/mother possesses . . . or one of Ravel's mean-spirited children want the powers that she has at her disposal.

Design Note: The player has to find a children's story that features Ravel in order to get access to her prison.

Design Note: Ravel occasionally refers to the player as the "greatest of my puzzles."

Design Note: "I beat death," she cackled. "But it was more like a bribe than a thorough thrashing. Cracking open the Cage was going to be my ultimate challenge."

Design Note: Once upon a time, Ravel could have rode [sic] the dreams of others, now she may only be able to visit for a short while.

Design Note: Ravel needs to shed a tear in order to be able to escape the maze that she is in. It was a fitting punishment for one such as her, considering how many tears she caused others to shed.

Voice Actors: A classic wicked witch voice, like from *The Wizard of Oz*. The female gargoyle in *The Hunchback of Notre Dame*, perhaps?

Statistics: Sex: Female, Race: Night Hag, Class: N/A, Level: N/A, Hit Dice: 8, INT: 21, Faction: None,

Alignment: Neutral, AC 0, MV 12, hp 47, THACO 13, XP 12,000, Form of Attack: Poisonous Bite or Spell, Damage: 2–12 Poison Damage.[53]

Writing for video games is typically a much more anonymous endeavor than writing for other media. Even when credited—and games writers are not always given official credit for their work, to the frustration of the WGA—writers are not well known to the player/fan community. Aphra Kerr argues, with some justice, that the collaborative nature of the game design process makes authorship especially hard to assign.[54] But players often invest the authorship of a game in the producing company, at the level of design quality and of gameplay-genre. It is, in other words, the design and interface that become or form the "author's" signature, and that is ascribed to the companies that produce and brand the game. Blizzard is known principally for developing RTS games and MMOs like the *Warcraft* and *StarCraft* franchises, for example; BioWare made its reputation on RPGs like *Baldur's Gate* and *Star Wars: Knights of the Old Republic*, whereas Eidos is known for its third-person shooter (TPS) games such as the *Tomb Raider* franchise.

When members of a game design team are recognized by name, it is usually the leading designers and prominent company executives. These figures are variously lionized or excoriated in online fan discourse. This is often a function of their web-chat "personalities" and perceived attitudes to fans and players as much as it is of their design or scripting skills however. The notorious reputation of the irascible Sergey Burkatovskiy (known to players as SerB), Wargaming Public Co Ltd.'s lead designer on the armored combat MMO *World of Tanks (WoT)*, is a case in point. SerB is an iconic figure that fans and players of that game love to hate, even if they have never had any form of personal interaction with him. Images of his face are used by players as emoji in online chat. In-game chat on *World of Tanks* is full of ironic prayers to SerB for players' shots to hit and, more often, curses directed at him when shells miss their targets, when they bemoan the failings of their avatar vehicles, or when they use expensive premium consumable ammunition to "pay to win" (or have it used against them). As the popular Twitch TV *WoT* streamer Will Frampton (a.k.a. Quickybaby) often says, "When you fire prem, SerB wins."[55]

Blizzard's former senior vice president of story and franchise development, Chris Metzen, would be a relatively rare example of the reverse condition. Metzen is highly regarded by most fans of the *Warcraft* franchise as a writer and designer (as well as for his distinctive voice acting across the range of Blizzard titles). There are threads on discussion boards full of appreciative humor and so forth.[56] When Metzen retired in 2016, the fan community was genuinely saddened, and most of the popular *World of Warcraft* streamers and YouTube broadcasters (including *FatBoss TV, Trade Chat, Preach Gaming*, and *Asmongold*, inter alia) dedicated lengthy sections of their shows to emotional discussions of his legacy and impact on their gaming lives. Of course, these examples are merely illustrative, as the scripting of these very different texts makes a direct comparison unhelpful.

Game authorship is doubly effaced for screenwriters. Not only are their efforts an often-anonymous element within the broader scripting process of games design, but their writing is also always in the service of the interface. That reorients the impression of authority away from the writer and onto the player. The critical literature on the nature of agency in games play broadly splits between those, like Jenkins, who argue for an active, constructive role for the player whose choices drive story in a particular direction and those, like Brookey, who see such choices as more indicative of a process of incorporation and conformity.[57] Terry Borst (cowriter of *Wing Commander III,* Origin Systems, 1994) articulates the narrative of player agency from a writer's perspective: "Characters are going to change or stagnate based on your actions; they are going to live or die. You're Rick in *Casablanca:* you have to decide who gets to use the letters of transit, or whether to let the woman win at the roulette table. If the world created is rich enough and textured enough, interacting with this world is going to emotionally engage you."[58] Mise-en-scène, to use another term from cinema theory, is also critical to the sense of authorship, but here, like cinema and television, credit usually falls to someone other than the writer that described it in words.

The experience of video games is sold using variations of the mantra "You are the hero," and games writers are employed to improve interactive delivery so that players can be heroic. But Mark J. P. Wolf argues that interactivity in video games is directed toward winning, and that requires conformity to rules.[59] Brookey agrees, noting that "video games require compliance."[60] Although the phenomenon of emergent play complicates this binary, a full discussion of player agency is outside the scope of this book. For screenwriters, however, whether player agency is actual, illusory, or somewhere in between, the *scripting* of a game is designed primarily to efface writing and invest playing, as Brookey writes: "Just as the film industry uses the construct of the auteur to stroke directors' egos and to market films, the video games industry provides a similar sense of creative agency to engage the game player. In both cases, this sense of agency is conferred by the media producers and is constrained by their interests."[61] The writer is at best accounted second to another author. In the case of video games she is also usually absent from consideration.

Banks notes that in the early years of video gaming, movie writers were more likely to be employed to backfill story elements into developed games, to link levels and provide scripting for cut scenes and so forth, than they were to help develop properties from scratch.[62] Screenwriters were usually employed on a freelance basis, asked to perform particular or specialist writing tasks that the in-house development team either felt unable to do or did not have the time to accomplish. In *Written By* several interviewees reported that they were often asked to perform what were, for feature screenwriters, very unusual tasks. "My favorite job was where I got paid $6,000 for writing 200 things you could say while you're killing terrorists," Wright recalls. "'Say hello to your 72 virgins!' ... They were literally in the studio recording when they called for me."[63] F.X. Feeney reported that Jay Lender had a similar experience working on *Looney Tunes: Back in Action*: "We had to write 7,000 lines—a little over a hundred lines for sixty Warner's cartoon characters in all, including Al Jolson, who was in a Looneytoon in 1938. Each of the lines had to be funny, and they each had to be in character." What's more, the pair were directed to work from Excel spreadsheets. "*Bugs Bunny runs into a wall,*" recalls Wright. "*Bugs Bunny hits someone on head*, and on and on for 80 lines. You'd turn the page and there would be 80 identical prompts for Porky Pig."[64]

The use of Excel spreadsheets for some aspects of games writing is still commonplace in the industry. Games companies often use two generic forms of script material in the development process. Raphael Chandler, a writer/designer at Red Storm Entertainment with credits that include titles in the *Ghost Recon* series, identifies them as "active" and "passive" formats by reference to the kind of experience that the player is having at the time. Thus "passive" scripts resemble, or even duplicate, conventional screenplay format and are used for noninteractive sequences (NIS) such as cut scenes, cinematics, and other moments when the player's experience is passive—when she is watching a scene rather than mashing buttons. Chandler describes the style of passive format he personally uses as a condensed version of screenplay format, "removing all of the marginal formatting, and ... using a more efficient font (like 10-point Times New Roman)."[65] The example he offers is instructive but is not excerpted from a real game script (format as original):

> INT. FIRST CITY BANK – NIGHT
>
> SENSEI grips his katana and squints with steely-eyed equanimity. ICE QUEEN and BULLETPOINT are standing near the vault. Two GUARDS have their pistols aimed at the door. Everyone is waiting for OVERCHARGE to attack. The PLAYER is in the middle of the room, facing the doors.
>
> GUARD: Who – who are these guys? The ones who are going to be attacking.
>
> SENSEI: They're called the Corporation. Their leader, Overcharge, was once the CEO of a major credit card company.

```
        Sensei sighs with world-weary sadness. His character model
        executes a clumsy shrug.
        BULLETPOINT: And he gave it up to be a supervillain? Why?
        The guy was rich, powerful — I mean, seriously Queenie,
        does that make sense to you?
        ICE QUEEN: Don't call me Queenie. Hell, don't talk to me,
        period.⁶⁶
```

Note the instructions to the animators embedded in the action description and the explicit positioning of the player's character within the world of the story. Chandler's example uses a number of recognizable tropes from conventional master-scene format such as the slug line at the top of the scene and capitalization for character names. But the overall format is more efficient, and the font is smaller and not a Courier variant, because there is no need to maintain the Hollywood convention of one page to a minute of screen time.

Unlike the above example, Chandler's own variant on "active" script format is generated using Microsoft Excel spreadsheets (see table 1). It relates to dialogue taking place in-game, during active play. As the writer is unlikely to be present at voice recording sessions, the active format spreadsheet often includes a range of information to help in the direction and performance of the lines. This information is collected under spreadsheet headings such as "Context" and "Inflection," the entries directing line readings as "Serious," "Sarcastic," or "Incredulous," and so forth. The pragmatic guidance about the inflection and performance of lines of dialogue overrides the typical movie screenwriter's practice of not including reductive direction in a screenplay but is clearly essential when the lines will be provided for voice actors without the context of a full script. Other spreadsheet headings provide filing and organizational information that locates the dialogue in the context of the overall game structure—positioning it within the arc of active story. Here Chandler reworks his own passive format example into active scene format.

Not all active scripts are presented as spreadsheets, as the following script example by Wendy Despain from a game based on the Bratz line of fashion dolls, *Bratz: Forever Diamondz*, shows. Note how the instructional writing specifies the playing context in which the dialogue will be spoken and how it will appear onscreen during gameplay. Some of the dialogue barks are to be programmed as responses to correct in-game player action, uttered when the player's avatar poses in the right way during the fashion modeling task that this sequence covers. Once again the format is distinct from that of the conventional screenplay but does not reflect any kind of official games script model other than that adopted by the developing company for this project.

TABLE 1 Example of Active Scene Format

Actor	Cue	Context	Inflection	Location	Area	Effect	Filename
Guard	So who's going to be coming through that door?	The guard is waiting for the supervillains to bust through the door and attack.	Nervous	Bank Lobby	3		m3_a1_01
Sensei	They're called the Corporation. Their leader, Overcharge, was once the CEO of a major credit card company.	Sensei is answering the guard's question.	Serious	Bank Lobby	3		m3_a1_02
Bulletpoint	And he gave it up to be a supervillain? Why? The guy was rich, powerful – I mean, seriously, Queenie, does that make sense to you?	Sensei has just explained the origin of Overcharge.	Incredulous	Bank Lobby	3		m3_a1_03
Ice Queen	Don't call me Queenie. Hell, don't talk to me, period.	Bulletpoint annoys her, and she's trying to shut him up.	Irritated	Bank Lobby	3	Echo	m3_a1_04
Bulletpoint	Ooh, someone get me a blanket, I'm getting the cold shoulder here --	Ice Queen just blew off his attempt at making conversation.	Sarcastic	Bank Lobby	3		m3_a1_05
Sensei	Quiet! I can sense them. They're outside!	The team is bickering, but the enemy is approaching and Sensei wants them to focus.	Serious, tense	Bank Lobby	3		m3_a1_06
Caribou	This is Caribou. I've got a visual on Overcharge.	He's on the roof of the building, and has just spotted the enemy.	Serious	Bank Lobby (off-camera)	3	Radio	m3_a1_07

Bratz: Forever Diamondz Game Script Excerpt — Wendy Despain

SF3–5: Special Feature 3–5 — Fashion Show Gameplay

Task Detail:

Player will need to enter the fashion show from the now open backstage door. Player will then complete the fashion show gameplay mix of posing and photography.

Dialogue:

(The task dialog for the fashion show will play over the actual gameplay, in the style of a show commentator. Byron Powell will not be visible for the duration of the task.)

Model 1 approaches pose point#1

BYRON POWELL

Alright, let's show these people the hottest fashion in Manhattan.

Model 1 approaches pose point#2

BYRON POWELL

They need to see all the angles—hit it.

Model 1 approaches pose point#3

BYRON POWELL

Own the stage, girl. You look great.

Model 2 approaches pose point#1

BYRON POWELL

Okay, time for you to show us what you've got.

Model 2 approaches pose point#2

BYRON POWELL

Spotlight's on you!

Model 2 approaches pose point#3

BYRON POWELL

This is it—make it a good one!

[Successful pose dialogue will be randomly selected from the following selection every time the player succeeds in performing a pose move from the current pose list]

Successful pose#1

BYRON POWELL

Nice!

Successful pose#2

BYRON POWELL

Woo!

Successful pose#3

BYRON POWELL

Gorgeous!

Some of the differences in common script formats are determined in part by the interface or gameplay genre of the title under development. Stephen E. Dinehart IV, a 2.0 game writer and proponent of transmedia and interactive storytelling with game credits including entries in the *Company of Heroes* series, expresses the distinction between scripting different types of communication in RTS titles. His two-format model is similar to Chandler's, only inflected with the accreted sociolect of the RTS development world (here he uses the transmedia acronym *VUP* to refer to the viewer/user/player role): "Writing for RTS tends to be divided into system responses (MP) and storyline (SP). MP speech consists of non-linear lines of speech which is associated with structures and units. It is meant primarily for tactical communication with the VUP, but also as a means of creating narrative flavor. SP speech consists of all campaign related speech, that is, linear scripted moments of dialog for tutorial or story purposes."[67] Here the distinction between otherwise common script formats is determined by the interface or gameplay genre of the title.

In Dinehart's experience, MP and SP interactions in RTS require differently formatted scripts. SP format is treated in a similar manner to Chandler's "passive" scripts, using minor variants on standard screenplay format. Given that general similarity, as Dinehart notes, "the writing format chosen is as diverse as there are RTS games and RTS writers."[68] Unlike SP interactions, MP instances of so-called barks—nonlinear interactive multiplayer dialogue—are handled via spreadsheets. "The MP scripts are long lists of lines that refer to the state of the NPC, vehicle, or unit on the battlefield." He continues: "For each unit there is a separate script. Depending on the expected use of that unit during gameplay, it receives its line count. The speech here is a multidimensional array navigated buy [sic] the user based on actions and unit states."[69]

According to Dinehart, the final deliverable scripted package of the RTS writer comprises the campaign screenplay, individual single-player mission scripts, and system speech scripts. It is, thus, a hybrid collection of documents using a variety of formats efficiently to express different kinds of in-game communication. Whereas the feature screenwriter uses established master-scene, or new spec, format both to conform to expected deliverable norms within the movie industry and to adhere to inherited templates and models of writerly efficiency, the game writer often breaks from these norms for exactly the same reasons.

As a result of having to work with variants of active or MP format, some screenwriters working in games have applied techniques and practices learned in other media to help the performers and to bring a semblance of professional control to these kinds of assignments. Deborah Todd writes character bibles for actors, for example. "On *101 Dalmatians*," she recalls, "I invented a backstory for Cruella De Vil: what she looked like when little and how she got to be so twisted. That said, I didn't add anything that wasn't true to the material—I never made her nice."[70]

Once games developers understood that they needed story to cohere and drive the more sophisticated gaming experiences that their coding and graphics were enabling, writers became an important piece in the development puzzle. As Micah Wright asserted in 2009, "it used to be enough to shoot zombies, but now it's, *Why am I shooting zombies?* Story is the next platform."[71] Even so, in some companies, notably independents like Naughty Dog Games (*Uncharted* franchise), the writing of video games stories has continued to be spread between specialist and nonspecialist personnel. Amy Hennig outlined this approach in detail in an interview in 2010. The way she described her role sounded like something akin to that of a showrunner in television, only working with an ad hoc pro-am writers' room spread through the company:

> We don't have the luxury of a group of writers like in TV, so the effort is spread across the entire team. Anyone who's interested can make suggestions. I guess my job is to be a head writer, in a way, to shepherd the whole thing. I do most of the writing, just by necessity because we're all so busy, but that doesn't mean someone else might not take a stab at a scene or suggest revisions on anything I've written. . . . With movies it's kind of a known quantity. It's very schedulable. For us it's not. We're writing new software and writing new engines every single time we make a game. There are a lot of unknowns. You have to be willing to go on faith and deviate as you go.[72]

She explains that the writing of games stories has to be flexible as the game goes through multiple iterations during its development. In this method of working we can see similarities to the way an animated film is developed, only with the coding of levels and sequences replacing passes on the boards. "The narrative has got to be flexible," Hennig argues, "because maybe I had an important story event in a level and now it's gone.... If you write ... the screenplay in a rigid, traditional way and you think you're just going to record it, you end up deviating from the game play experience."[73] Under this version of the development grid, writing—conventionally defined—is always the junior partner behind design and coding.

Writers may also be asked to review development documents and to consult on all elements of narrative as a project progresses. Screenwriters are sometimes brought in to consult on game design from a writer's perspective and to oversee story development, even if they are not writing the actual game script themselves. Gary Whitta has consulted for Microsoft, EA, Activision, and Midway Games, for example. Nevertheless, for many of the screenwriters who commented to *Written By* over the last twenty years, the ideal situation was to come into the development phase of a game early on or even at the beginning, as Feirstein recalls: "My second experience was the dream date: 'We know we need this number of levels, we know we need this to happen. Here's the money, go create.' Not, 'Now go create a story around this.' The first game I did, I got that phone call. I came into it late, and it was as John described: They were in territory they had never been in before. They were bolting things into the game afterwards, shifting points of exposition. It would be like endless reshoots in a movie because they hadn't gotten the story right the first time."[74]

In 2004 Lee Sheldon *(Wild Wild West)* noted that being brought into development early could result in similar problems to coming in late. "It's just as bad, though, when they hire you at the beginning, then say, 'Thank you for your work. Goodbye.' ... What comes out the other end can be just as much a mish-mash as when you're brought in too late in a project. You want to build the story as you build the game, period."[75] Anne Toole, WGA-nominated writer on *The Witcher* (Atari 2007), was involved with the development of that game from the start. Perceptively, she describes the particular form of screenwriting labor she brings to game design as that of a "narrative designer." Toole points to the primary task of the writer being less to write story and more to craft the narrative experience of the interactive product: "I wouldn't necessarily be writing a script, I would be exploring ways to put the story in particular locations and hint at the story. That's the difficulty with coming in as a Hollywood writer. Your instinct is to write scenes, write characters, write dialogue. But this might not be that kind of game.... Ultimately the question we always ask is, 'How do you want the player to feel? What kind of fun do you want your player to have?' So it depends on the developers and their strengths."[76]

Narrative design, in the sense that Toole evokes, requires not only a high level of flexibility and collaboration on the part of the screenwriter but also a good working understanding of the structure of the medium of video games. Although games writers do not need the ability to code, they do need to share a discreet knowledge base with the designers. Once again, this emphasizes how for many screenwriters the transition from working in movies to working in games is by no means simple or straightforward. "You have to think like a game designer," Flint Dille *(Chronicles of Riddick: Escape from Butcher Bay)* argues. "[Writers must] understand what their issues are.... For technology you look at what the engine can do and you say, 'Okay, this is what we can accomplish and this is what we can't accomplish.'"[77]

Movie and television screenwriters learned to prepare themselves for future employment in the new field by playing games and learning about the unique genres that make up the industry. The importance of undertaking this kind of preparation is cited as conventional advice throughout the paraindustrial literature of screenwriting. In their interviews for *Written By*, members of the VWC and others working in the games industry consistently offered similar advice to their fellow writers. Knowing the form and understanding the state of the market was as important to gaining employment in games as it was to selling a pitch or a spec screenplay in Hollywood. For example, in 2009 Dave Ellis recommended that his fellow WGA members research the product line of BioWare and learn to play the RPG franchise *Neverwinter Nights* (2002–6), because the company was a major employer at the time: "You have to know games. Game companies can smell a non-gamer a mile away.... You are not in control of your work. You work with a team. Games are still isolated from other branches of the entertainment industry—an entity unto itself that does not welcome outsiders. Verse yourself in the technical aspects: in game dialogues, prompts, mission objectives; even in clothes, accessories for characters. Game writers write that too."[78]

The same peer-to-peer advice applied to the specifics of interface- or game-play-genres, as John Zuur Platten noted in 2004: "If you're writing a story around a first-person shooter you'd better know how first-person shooters work.... You've got to understand how those games work, what's important to them, how they draw people through the levels, how a person is going to respond to a cinematic."[79] The specific needs of the medium notwithstanding, the common expectation expressed among professional screenwriters coming to games writing through the 1990s was that it would be similar to writing for established media but with important conceptual differences. Characters still change in video games, and the player's experience of those changes or development is central to his or her enjoyment of the game narrative. Typically, in the process of playing through the game, something significant has been accomplished, or learned, by the player's avatar. It has also developed new abilities, acquired new equipment, and increased in power in doing so. "The essential task is the same," Feeney suggested in 2009. "A character, or set of characters, aims for a goal and either achieves it or fails, struggling against steeply ascending odds and obstacles but armed with unpredictable skills and strengths."[80] Nevertheless, some aspiring games writers reported to *Written By* that they felt the need to prepare for their career shift by undertaking other forms of professional development, including educating themselves in new techniques. Anne Toole noted that animators and animation writers have a "leg up" in games design because they already understand what can be drawn and what can't. For this reason Toole enrolled in a storyboarding class, a kind of story-design process, as preparation for her extended involvement in game story development. "You can't just hand off what you've written and say, 'Bye.' It's an ongoing conversation. You say. 'Do this.' They say, 'No, we can't.' You insist, 'Yes, you can.' Then they ask, 'Can we try this instead?' And you say, 'Genius.'" She continues: "People in film and television know this from experience—you have the original idea, but by the time it actually gets done, it's gone through so many iterations, you almost wonder, 'Is that my idea?'"[81]

As we have suggested above, the structure of story in video games is not identical to the structure of movie narratives. Strictly linear narratives do not usually "play" well as interactive experiences, for example. An exception would be Druckmann's award-winning storytelling in *The Last of Us*. Although games writers still speak of character arcs, scenes, and sequences, just like movie screenwriters do, games designers and writers conceptualize the experiential structure of their interactive stories using a different vocabulary. This applies more to open world games than more linear stories, but there are always differences with cinema in the way story unfolds for the player. The linearity of movie and television storytelling is always replaced by a variety of branching structures. The player is regularly presented with options, and the game story will change to a greater or lesser extent to accommodate her choices. Terry Borst described a simple version of a branching story structure—a simple "system," in Wellenreiter's terms—that he used in the *Wing Commander* titles in the 1990s. "In a sense, the *Wing Commanders* are long hallways with lots of doors that ultimately keep leading you back to the hallway and a final destination. The doors are often of 'The Lady or the Tiger' variety—one's a good choice; the other isn't. There are two or three possible conclusions—the crisis is averted, you've saved the galaxy, and now it's Miller Time."[82]

Screenwriters also note that an important element of the interactive experience is its relaxed temporality. Often a player is able to explore a space or consider in-game material or strategies for progress in ways that are impossible in other time-based platforms. Again this relaxed temporality is a clearer function of open world games than it is of "button mashers" like fighting games, but it applies more broadly. The writer Marc Guggenheim *(Green Lantern)* notes that "if a player wants to stop and go look at this web diary or watch this little film strip, they have that opportunity, so you're going vertically as well as horizontally."[83] He aligns this experience of time in-game with the expansion of writing character and world backstories. In movies backstory informs character behavior and motivation, but it is often largely unspoken or dealt with efficiently. In games the level of world creation can be explored in greater depth. "In movies," Guggenheim's colleague Lindsey Allen reflects, "you create a backstory and don't talk about it. In video games, players are interested in that. They're constantly seeking information about the worlds they're in, so you're constantly creating these little stories."[84]

The craft of the video game writer, either as a programmer moving into it or asked to do it or a screenwriter seeking an additional career path, is in many ways distinct from the craft of screenplay and television writing. Of course, the impetus remains writerly in the sense that stories are crafted, characters outlined, plots plotted, and worlds created and inhabited. The writing process and delivery formats are distinct because the scripting labor involved is collaborative with other kinds of design and programming and because the intended ludic experience of the game is typically privileged over the narrative aspect and is also leveraged to draw on the technical and narrational specificity of video game genres.

CONCLUSION

The main consequence of this interactive engagement that makes the context in which screenwriters in the video games industry work and create truly unique is that fans and players have the potential power to influence storytelling decisions outside of gameplay. This is the phenomenon of emergence that we illustrated through the intertextual journey of Leeroy Jenkins. Although this is by no means common, the updateable nature of the video game product makes it possible for corrections to be made at a level beyond fixing the technical bug or the ongoing issue of tweaking game balance. Movies may be released with alternative, explicit, or "director's cuts" for fans on DVD, but this is very different from cases in which the internal structure of the product's narrative is actively negotiated by player input or complaint. There have even been instances in which player discontent at logical gaps in open world storytelling and at the inability of players and their avatars to avoid bleak endings in narrative-driven games has led developers to make major changes in the structure and resolution of video games stories. This famously occurred when Bethesda Game Studios released the *Broken Steel* downloadable content (DLC) to appease players' dissatisfaction at the resolution options of *Fallout III*. As Wellenreiter notes, "Screenwriters who introduce—and then, in a way, violate—the principle of co-authorship in the RPG genre by attempting to make a forced ending 'statement' may find their work met with disappointment, anger and rebuttals, counter to their dramatic intentions."[85]

Even from this brief illustration of the specific challenges of writing narratives for games, it is clear that there needs to be considerable creative flexibility in the labor of screenwriter 2.0 when working across platforms. The particular challenges of designing and storytelling through interactivity and the centrality of the experience of play in the medium of video games ask new questions of screenwriters accustomed to working in the more linear storytelling of legacy media. It is not enough to suggest that screenwriting for movies and television and for games is "similar." The complex and varied lessons of emergence within communities of play and the unique development of games media through multiple iteration cycles postrelease, where actual rather than anticipated player responses often become integral to the scripting process, set the medium apart and require screenwriters to adapt or rethink the principles of their craft in significant ways. It is evident that the lessons screenwriters are learning when they work in video games writing, or read about the experiences of their colleagues who do so, are indicative once again of the changing nature of craft labor during convergence.

And yet writers employed in video games are still working on contract; they are still participating in the production culture of an established media industry. Over its short history the games industry has developed and defined its own working practices and has positioned the labor of established media production crafts, including screenwriting, to fit the remit of its distinct project development processes. Writers learn the ropes of the new media in order to be bound by them. Despite the collaborative nature of those processes, the typical writer in video games is no more creatively independent than the tentpole writer in Hollywood. The mere fact of convergence does not always imply increased creative license. But many more opportunities for entrepreneurship and creative independence for writers and writer-producers are embedded closer to the heart of the convergent media, in the Internet itself.

Conclusion
Scripting Boundaries

> The '80s convergence of comics' new adult sensibility with the movies' advancing technology was bound to catch the attention of even slow-on-the-uptake Hollywood, and this particularly was true when "Watchmen" and "The Dark Knight Returns" became phenomena.
>
> STEVE ERICKSON, novelist and avant-pop critic

> Content creation is the contribution of information to any media and most especially to digital media for an end-user/audience in specific contexts. Content is "something that is to be expressed through some medium, as speech, writing or any of various arts" for self-expression, distribution, marketing and/or publication. Typical forms of content creation include maintaining and updating web sites, blogging, photography, videography, online commentary, the maintenance of social media accounts, and editing and distribution of digital media.
>
> Wikipedia

During each of his thrice-weekly, five-hour Twitch streams Quickybaby (QB), a.k.a. Will Frampton, plays the MMO game *World of Tanks* live to audiences of thousands of fans. He also streams on an ad hoc basis outside of these scheduled times, typically once or twice a week. Quickybaby sometimes uses these ad hoc streams to react promptly to the release of new WoT DLC and to play other games such as *Hearthstone, Alien Isolation,* and *Total War: Arena*. During his streams he offers a running commentary on his gaming, which is full of expert player analysis and trenchant self-critique. His stated priority is to help his fans improve their own gameplay by learning from his example. As he plays he also interacts with comments on his live text-chat stream, talking about both personal and game-related matters and also responding to questions and observations from followers who tip him—that is, who pay small amounts of money to put their issues to him directly.[1]

The real-time interactive narratives of his streams are constantly inflected by this kind of participation in the form of live contributions from his fellow players and teammates, the wider community of subscribing fans, and those who are so invested that they pay to get his direct attention.

Fan interactions contribute to the scripting of the streams in that they often lead or guide discussion. Online polls also allow his fans to direct some of the choices QB makes during his streams. As a consequence, a Quickybaby livestream generates its own fluid interactive community that offers an immediate intimacy that even reality television cannot match, albeit with a minor (and optional) pay-to-play component.

Quickybaby also releases a range of crafted YouTube videos to accompany the more improvisatory nature of every scheduled stream. Some of these videos are simple "Let's Plays" (LPs) of interesting *WoT* games he has played, or recordings of games that contributors have submitted with his own post facto commentary added. But Quickybaby also creates a wide range of other minimovies, repurposing proprietary source material from Wargaming with the IP owner's approval. He also benefits from his popularity as a *WoT* community contributor in being given official early access to incoming game features and other content about which he broadcasts to his gamer-followers. This is part of a relatively recent tendency on the part of entertainment media corporations to embrace the poacher and outsource a lot of their marketing to fans and contributors within the community of play of a given IP. Of the many examples in play, *Minecraft*, an Electronic Arts online game, has a list of hundreds and hundreds of videos by fans illustrating how to play the game, often with great humor, with some reaching star status as they sell the game to children and adults alike.

Quickybaby sometimes also streams *Minecraft*, but in his *World of Tanks* YouTube videos, the content creator is most visible as a *scripter*, pushing at the definitional boundaries of screenwriter 2.0. He reviews new or updated tanks and other incoming DLC, offers tactical advice about particular game maps or about competitive play modes, produces guides to aspects of the game such as how to maximize earning in-game currency from play and which skills to choose for different kinds of tank crews, and offers amusing or informative clip collections that illustrate or poke fun at some aspect of *WoT* gameplay. For example, his most recent YouTube video, as of this writing, was a sixteen-minute preview of a new tank, the AC 1 Sentinel, to which he was given official early access for the purposes of in-game testing and review.[2]

This short introduction to Frampton's Quickybaby incarnation, a case study we return to later in this conclusion, begs an obvious question: is any of this actually screenwriting? If the craft of screenwriting is defined simply as the writing of formal screenplays or scripts, then Quickybaby does not fit into that category. Much of the content of this book has focused on the labor of writers that, despite the pressures of conglomeration, convergence, and innovation, still falls relatively easily within that well-established definition, with the writer of video games pushing the boundary but not breaking it. If we blow up the definition, however, radically expanding our understanding of the creative processes of media production to encompass new kinds of scripting represented by content creators like Quickybaby among others, then we have a worthwhile topic to critically challenge conventional assumptions about the boundaries of the craft of screenwriting today.

The key issue is that entrepreneurial streamers like Frampton are developing new formats of narrative content produced for a public that is less invested in the institutions of traditional and even conventionally convergent media. As befits their already liminal status as professional fans, they are exploring the internal structure of their streams and program series using a variety of techniques borrowed and adapted from the histories both of drama and of emergent media-making fandom and stardom, including improvisation and the poaching of raw materials from corporate media. They are also crafting narratives that combine forms of interactive storytelling, journalism, and commentary within the context of their own consistent programming formats. Moreover, many of them are making a sizable living from their scripting work.

In this conclusion we focus on a topic that has emerged in different contexts throughout the book: scripting. Although, as we acknowledged previously, the term originates in Maras's work, here we extend his definition to include the practice of online content creators like Frampton. These scripters point to an ongoing transformation in the industrial content, work culture, and craft of writing for and working with digital media. In short we argue that the term *scripting* better encompasses the complex interface between the conventionally circumscribed labor associated with the traditional screenwriting craft in movies, television, and legacy media and the emergent, adjacent, and otherwise cognate labor of media writing in the era of convergence. In teasing this out, we summarize some of the arguments we have made in the preceding chapters.

Shifting our focus more formally from screenwriting to scripting also allows us to return to the screenwriting paraindustry, specifically to film schools, with a critical and somewhat polemical intention. We do this to show that, while radical change confronts today's aspiring screenwriter, academia, despite its charge to mix research with teaching, is functioning much like the Writers Guild of America: maintaining siloes of old craft practice, keeping the circle of the screenwriter small, and thus falling woefully behind the curve of conversion that has gripped not simply the technology of storytelling or its industrial benefactors but the labor of content creation, its diverse skill sets, and the experience of audiences, with fans like Frampton at the helm, that are crafting stories off old and new media alike.

OFF THE PAGE

From the perspectives of writers in different sectors of today's entertainment industry, the craft of screenwriting would seem to be in a manic state: both thriving and in decline. Old markets for media writing, notably in theatrical features, are shrinking. New and renewed markets—notably in expanded television and video games—are burgeoning. All of these markets, old and new, are also being redefined as new media develops, converges, and transforms how stories are experienced by an increasingly diverse audience. The recent contraction in the types of studio movies—the kinds of stories—that make it to the big screen, and the expansion of quality drama series delivered via cable television, like *The Shield*—as well as the various iterations of online and digital on demand—have overturned some long-held assumptions about career paths for traditional screenwriters. Against historical expectation, in its convergent forms television has become the writer's medium, and its showrunners now have the opportunity to win greater creative control over their projects than their colleagues in motion pictures ever had.

The upheaval has forced unprecedented migrations of screenwriting talent to new media. Experienced movie writers like Pamela Gray are now moving fast and hard toward TV because there is a healthier market for character-driven drama on smaller screens and a greater capacity for stable income. Opportunities for independent visions to find a home in cinema boomed in the early 1990s before sliding into their Indiewood decline. At least one iteration of indie has seen something of a resurgence in recent years thanks to the digital and mobile production technologies and distribution economics that enabled microbudget production.

This microbudget arena is at least beginning to sustain some important voices from outside the mainstream like Travis Mathews. But many writer-filmmakers of the mumblecore generation see the restrictions of microbudget as little more than a necessary famine before the anticipated feast, a first step toward larger budgets and the career progression they promise. Indeed, some independent writers even argue that digital filmmaking "destroyed screenwriting" by creating a new generation of ignorant microbudget producers who do not value script and by placing the writing budget once again at the very bottom of funding priorities.³ Nonetheless, the potential of crowd-funding and online distribution has also provided new opportunities for established professional animation screenwriters like Robert Moreland to set themselves up as writer-producers in a way that was not open to their peers in previous generations.

The creative crafts have always bent before the winds of change in the media industries. Indeed, we should not think that the road to today's traffic snarls is all that new to the screenwriting profession. Novelists jumped to screenwriting during the cinema of narrative integration, characterized by the work of D.W. Griffith and others, between 1908 and 1915. With radio came radio dramas, and writers moved between these worlds as well (Orson Welles comes immediately to mind). Previous generations of movie screenwriters accommodated themselves successfully to radical creative innovations like the development of the feature film and then the coming of sound. Not too soon thereafter came television, followed by original programming on cable, then programming on expanded cable networks. And while that was happening, the Internet shifted from being a kind of library of information to a platform for streaming content. And during this latter period came mobile devices, led by iPads and iPhones, simultaneously launching yet another "new" in media's always-already history of new technologies. And at no point that we are aware of have readers stopped reading short stories and novels, on e-book readers or traditional paper. The history of American media tells us that such creative and technological birth pangs are sometimes painful but that they tend quickly to subside, at least until the next pregnancy.

What is a bit different now is the pace of change brought about by media convergence.⁴ If convergence could be argued to be a more or less settled matter on the side of media consumption, it is still very much ongoing from the perspective of the traditional production crafts. The professional screenwriters we know as friends and colleagues, as well as those with whom we have actively explored the current state of the craft in this book, now renegotiate and redeploy their labor in anticipation of, or in response to, a still-shifting dream factory that requires swift reactions on the part of those who wish to navigate it. It is not so much that screenwriting has reached a crossroads, in other words, but rather that the craft has entered a major traffic circle with multiple exits, not all of which are signposted or even paved and some of which, like a badly written genre movie, change direction or destination without a good setup.

The definition of craft—of what it is that screenwriters actually do to receive a paycheck—is thus changing and expanding. One writer's professional labor in a given medium may now involve a different set of activities from another's. In some ways every Hollywood screenwriter's experience of the underlying processes of feature-film development is likely to be broadly consistent, with minor variations in terms of status and the studio for which she or he is working. Yet the same is not necessarily the case when working in new(ish) media, where the expectations placed on writers' labors are much more fluid and the default three-act structure of features and four-act structure of dramatic television far less accepted by convergent writers and fans alike. For one writer, adapting skills she has developed in Hollywood feature screenwriting for her work in video games may require little more than to come to terms with a new structural grid and more open-ended plotting within which to tell a story. For another it might require developing whole new fluencies across a wide range of creative development activities—from storyboarding to programming (to scripting instead of screenwriting)—that are distinct in significant ways from those that were learned in film school, in paraindustry peripherals, and on the Hollywood job. Hollywood, as Steve Erickson points out in the opening to this chapter, is aware yet, we would add, playing catch-up.

To succeed, screenwriter 2.0, or convergent screenwriters and scripters, must not only be capable of working between conventional definitions of craft, like their peers in the previous generation (the screenwriter-producer), but also of embracing real-time shifts in media (the screenwriter-games designer, the movie-TV-online writer, and so forth). As we have argued throughout this book, the convergent screenwriter is required to be even more entrepreneurial and flexible in her approach to craft and career than was the traditional, or better yet analog, screenwriter.

Even the video games industry is no longer developing product for an especially new medium. Its rise to prominence was more recent than television's, but domestic video game consoles were already into their fourth generation by the late 1980s. Narrative-driven video games—games that depend on the talents of screenwriters for their scripting as much as on computer programmer coders—are a more recent phenomenon, but they still predate the Internet explosion by a measure. Video games are often categorized in the muddle of new media because the industry produces for the PC as well as the console and because now our games consoles are networked and Wi-Fi enabled. In addition, as our short case study in chapter 5 of the Leeroy Jenkins meme demonstrates, creative emergence and the ludisphere are both vested in the Internet. And the Internet morphed at light speed into the World Wide Web, which went from a mosaic of pages to viral videos faster, or in less time, than cinema went to television and back again.

The professional craft has had ample time to adjust both professionally and institutionally to the message of the medium. Even though we tend to view video games as a key partner in the cross-media dance of convergence, other kinds of online content are throwing the hippest shapes. The latest opportunities for online scripting are stretching the craft of screenwriting far beyond its traditional boundaries.

In the Internet era a new kind of creative entrepreneur colonizes, exploits, and redefines the intersections of convergent media, scripting new iterations of narrative in an expanded delineation. This kind of online content piggybacks on or fits somewhere between cinema, animation, television, comic books, journalism, and all kinds of games and game-like articulations as a new refracted circuit of culture. It is, to bring back some of the theory that underpins the book, sometimes counterhegemonic despite much of it also being usurped by conglomerates at digital speed. Many of the new content creators, the radicals and individualists looking to either upend or ignore the entertainment industry's IP economy, are emerging from the specific communities of play of video games or from the ludisphere and from fan culture more broadly. They also include all kinds of vloggers, comedy and digital movie producers, reporters and commentators, owners of grumpy cats and corgis in costumes, narcissistic self-promoters like Sister Hibiscus (or any number of political candidates that leverage social media to craft their stories of worthy leadership), and other generators of the diverse materials that now sustain and develop the online media world.[5]

In the balance of this conclusion we focus primarily on those creating new forms of emergent entertainment at the online interstices of the legacy media in and for which screenwriters have previously dedicated their labor. In this way we can draw some pathways between the craft in old and newer media, between professional or emergent fan-generated scripting and corporate production in its convergent iterations, and within film schools that remain fixated on tradition despite the high stakes of the profession and culture they represent.

SCRIPTING ONLINE CONTENT

Considerable diversity of career options for aspiring screenwriters remains under the umbrella of convergent storytelling. For example, the in-studio guests on *Tabletop*, the actor-producer Will Wheaton's *(Star Trek: The Next Generation)* board-game review show that is broadcast online by Geek and Sundry, are typically online content creators themselves.[6] The convergent status of screenwriters 2.0 is evident from the way they introduce themselves during the opening segment of the show. To offer a small sample, recent *Tabletop* guests have included Allie Brosh *(Hyperbole and a Half)*, an artist-writer of web comics; Brea Grant *(Suicide Girls,* based on the alt-pinup website), an actress-comic book writer; Paul Scheer *(The League)*, an actor-podcaster; Joseph Scrimshaw *(Obsessed)*, a writer-comedian-podcaster; and Satine Phoenix, whose *Wikipedia* entry describes her as a "comic book illustrator, painter, cosplayer, model, actress, and former pornographic actress, and bondage/fetish model." Satine also developed the gaming web series *I Hit It with My Axe*.[7]

Within the media located between those new career-hyphens, some content creators still produce the kind of material that professional screenwriters of an older generation would recognize as being broadly cognate with their own labor. Narrative web series and Internet shorts require scripts, for example, even if their episode lengths are often shorter than established television formats (such as the sitcom) and their internal microstructure is sometimes more open-ended. The same is true, within the established conventions of their respective media, of digital comic books and some online games. To be sure, this kind of online production is already conventional enough in screenwriting terms for the craft's paraindustry to have begun to colonize and exploit it. For example, there is a class for aspiring online content creators offered by "Screenwriters University" (a division of *The Writers Store*) titled, "Creating the Viral Web Series." Despite claiming that the format of web series is "entirely new," the website's aspirational blurb clearly lays out entirely predictable connections to legacy media and established craft techniques and principles and makes assumptions about its prospective students' future mainstream media career aspirations. After all, this is how the paraindustry understands and markets all of its products, no matter their medium of distribution:

> In recent years, the Internet has created the space for an entirely new storytelling format: the web series. Cheap to make and easily accessible for viewers, a web series can be the perfect way for you to get started as a filmmaker and be noticed for your talent. All you need is the right set of tools and skills. Although unique in format and distribution, the web series at its core contains the same basic elements that we look for in every type of visual entertainment: memorable characters, satisfying stories, and intriguing conflict. If you can demonstrate your writing talent in a web series, you'll also be proving your ability to handle larger-scale formats like feature screenplays and television scripts.[8]

With some irony, therefore, the aspiring screenwriter is being sold hybridity, the end-state of conversion, in order to devolve into a classical screenwriter.

Diversity is persistent. Entrepreneurial and emergent online content creators are engaging in a much wider range of creative practices than writing webisodes. They are producing new styles and formats of programming, along with microdistribution solutions to the challenge of getting their work to a public, that certainly owe debts to the history of television but do not fit as easily into the conventional and even convergent grids of craft labor as apparently taught by Screenwriters University.

Viewed from the perspective of the professional media crafts, many of these content creators are hobbyists or, as Henry Jenkins might say, textual poachers.[9] They exist within a liminal, semipro gap that is fluid and hard to encompass.[10] Some of them produce material for their own satisfaction and for their immediate communities of fans and followers but have little expectation of receiving significant remuneration for their efforts. Even more than Jenkins's generation of semipros who write fanzines and slash, a growing number of content creators distributing their work online are becoming professionals. Some of these new creator-celebrities, YouTube stars, and Twitch streamers, like Frampton, can make a very good living from this kind of activity. The website *Business Insider*, for instance, recently attempted to quantify the earnings of the twenty most popular YouTube stars (ranked by the size of their online fan bases), concluding that they could all be making over a million dollars a year from advertising revenue alone.[11] In 2016, therefore, the international community of online consumers who support content in all its diversity spent a significant amount of money and often used other online services, like PayPal, to do so. Some of that financial support comes in the form of microtransactions, small-dollar subscriptions that are paid to individual creators, and as the article at *Business Insider* implies, a significant proportion of that market is being channeled away from corporate media.

More and more online content is being incorporated within larger commercial entities. The incentive for corporate investment in this kind of online product currently hinges on the perceived and actual benefits of linking with fan cultural taste arbiters as much as on direct profit generation. For instance, Legendary Pictures in 2014 acquired the actress-writer-producer Felicia Day's *(The Guild)* popular Geek and Sundry network to support the development of the media company's in-house digital division. Commenting on the deal for the trades, Bruce Rosenblum, president of Legendary Television and Digital Media, foregrounded the importance of the fan culture association: "Geek and Sundry has a passionate fan base with one of the most recognizable brands in the community."[12] The acquisition of Geek and Sundry fits a pattern for Legendary, which also owns a similar entity in Nerdist Industries started by Chris Hardwick *(The Nerdist)*, another celebrity in the online fan community who also presents shows on Comedy Central (owned by Viacom). Geek and Sundry is also the online publishing/broadcast hub for shows from smaller content creators, such as Wheaton's *Tabletop*, the third season of which was financed through crowd-funding on Indiegogo to the tune of $1,414,159. Today's fans still write for their peers to read and watch, but now they can make real money from that transaction. And divisions of entertainment conglomerates are taking notice, irrespective of the traditional legal and guild boundaries of IP attribution and ownership.

Smaller-scale independent content creators, the creative descendants of yesterday's textual poachers among them, work on the margins of official sanction from corporate media institutions, in either meaning of that term. The efforts of many independent creators are directly supported by some combination of online advertising, the now ubiquitous crowd-funding, and by subscriptions. Many are also international stars, again like Frampton, breaking the boundaries of conventional media territories to appeal to fans around the world. Just as Maras argues that the notion of scripting in feature films encompasses a range of activities from storyboarding to digital previsualization that take place externally or in parallel to the screenplay, so online fan culture has generated a wide range of new professional activities that do not necessarily originate with or manifest themselves exclusively in the written word.

As the online content creator/s who wrote the *Wikipedia* definition with which we opened this chapter correctly assert, online content creation is an amalgam of "speech, writing or any of various arts." It is not bound into a single medium or craft. As a consequence, much of this content does not fit within conventional definitions of screenwriting. At the same time, it is representative of the kind of scripted product that many people are now watching in parallel with their consumption either of legacy media (such as watching movies in theaters) or of more conventionally convergent media (such as binge-watching original Netflix series via SVOD).

Tracking this doubly emergent online production sector is increasingly important because nontraditional online content is especially popular among millennials and members of Generation Z, the generational diversity notwithstanding, whose patterns of media consumption are very different from those of previous generations. The growing popularity of Internet content is part of a broader move away from traditional delivery systems by consumers, and it also has a strong generational inflection. By way of context, statistics from the recent tenth annual "Digital Democracy

Survey" by Deloitte Consulting suggest that the move away from traditional television viewing is accelerating. The popularity of conventionally convergent VOD and similar streaming services among digital consumers has risen from 12 percent in 2012 to 61 percent, placing digital in a strong third place behind the Internet (95 percent) and Pay TV (79 percent), for example.[13] Indeed, it now eclipses Pay TV in popularity for those twenty-five years old and younger, in homes with streaming access. In short, "the proliferation of online content shows no signs of slowing down and the consumer appetite to consume content is equally voracious. . . . The survey data indicates that consumers are more willing than ever to invest in services to watch whenever, wherever and on whatever device they choose." Moreover, "about a third of all viewers—as well as about half of Millennials, those born between 1983 and 2001—watch TV shows and movies on a smartphone, tablet, or computer."[14]

Online media in all varieties is both key and core to the consumption patterns of the cut-cord and post-cord generations. They are also doing much to define the future shape of online media via production as well as consumption—hence, in part, the current scramble for corporate media to buy into that potential when and where it can. As Viktor Kislyi, the founder of Wargaming Public Co Ltd., noted in a recent interview, the most important developments in online content creation are happening independently of the big corporations: "The biggest thing happening now in media is video bloggers. Kids and teenagers with no professional education in TV just sit in their flats and talk and play games." Getting to the point, he concludes: "They have hundreds of thousands or millions of followers, and those followers follow what they say. You have to figure out what to do with that."[15]

The games industry has already responded to the surge in popularity of sharing and streaming gameplay. Cheap devices such as the Elgato Game Capture HD60 Pro facilitate downloading and sharing gameplay from computers for under $100, and newer game consoles such as the PS4 now come with built-in share play functionality. A 2014 episode of the animated comedy show *South Park*, titled "#REHASH," parodied this generational split in game playing versus watching streams of games being played, and in entertainment consumption more generally.[16] In one scene Gerald Broflovski invites his son, Kyle, to go bowling. Kyle responds that he has just purchased the new *Call of Duty* video game and wants to go play it with his younger brother Ike, as a bonding experience. Gerald demurs, but when Kyle invites Ike to play, he finds his brother is much more interested in watching the livestream of real-life controversial Swedish YouTube star PewDiePie (a.k.a. Felix Kjellberg) playing *Call of Duty*. Kyle does not get it, complaining to his friends: "That's not even entertainment. It's just rehashing things and shit." Conversely, for Ike "the living room is for old people." The media have moved on, and even his older brother, the gamer, is now behind the times.

QUICKYBABY

Will Frampton's Twitch and YouTube production is an example of the complexity and variety of the creative sphere of the entrepreneurial content creator (and of the nature of ludisphere celebrity).[17] Quickybaby is based in England, but the reach of his brand is international—and he is an exemplar of the postregional nature of much online content creation. As we have noted, his primary professional activity is similar to that of the more famous gamer, PewDiePie, the object of Ike Broflovski's fandom: Quickybaby plays the hugely successful MMO *World of Tanks* for his online fans, facilitated by the San Francisco–based streaming video platform, Twitch.tv.[18]

Frampton's Quickybaby is an exemplary convergent media producer. As we suggested earlier, within his own community of play Quickybaby operates in part as a legitimate virtual journalist. This legitimacy is bestowed on him by his fans—fans that expect corporate independence and creative rigor in the way he approaches the assessment of official content and policy. Quickybaby's approach to the respective fan-cultural and corporate hands that feed him (in different senses) is also consistent with the way most of the popular games streamers and broadcasters operate. YouTubers, deemed to be too close to game developers, come in for criticism and find it hard to sustain audiences. Those who are especially enthusiastic fans of the games about which they create online content (like *Trade Chat*'s "Panser," a.k.a. Danielle Mackey) even have to keep trying to persuade their viewers of the legitimacy of their own positive and constructive fandom when they are praising sponsored product.

Quickybaby vlogs about special events and trips he has made. These videos have included a vacation to Belarus to visit his (then) girlfriend, visits to a charity his stream supports, and public appearances at official Wargaming or sponsored military-historical events such as the annual "Tankfest" at The Tank Museum in the United Kingdom. Every year many of Quickybaby's fans make the trip to Tankfest as much to meet him as to see the military hardware on display, because he is selling more than just his expertise as a *WoT* gamer. His brand, and the loyalty it generates, is of course a projection of his performer's personality and biography, as well as his gameplay. Quickybaby is a genuine celebrity in his own online sphere and in the broader *WoT* community of play. His meet-and-greet sessions at Tankfest in 2015 ran for more than five hours a day because of the number of people waiting to meet him. He has used his celebrity to initiate a formal online community of players, known as a "clan" in *WoT* and equivalent to the guilds that are designed into *World of Warcraft* and from which the Leeroy Jenkins meme emerged. The clan, named QSF for "Quickybaby's Special Forces," has active branches in the European and North American server regions of *World of Tanks*. Quickybaby streams weekly matches in which he leads teams from a rotation of QSF gaming groups in competition against teams from other clans.

The personal connection is central to the attraction of Quickybaby's community of play. It is also common among other popular streamers and content creators, many of whom interact with their fans and viewers during streams and live shows.[19] Quickybaby maintains an attractive and articulate personality, offering a friendly, generally polite and welcoming (for which read: family friendly) atmosphere. With reference to the familiar grid of movie classification, he calls the tone of his streams "PG13," largely eschewing the profanity-rich style of many of his fellow streamers. Although there are parts of his private life that Will Frampton wisely keeps private, to follow his channels and public social media is to be given the kind of long-term biographical access to a celebrity in real time that is still unheard of in other media. For example, fans have followed Frampton's PhD studies—he was recently awarded his doctorate in geography from Southampton University (UK). They have discussed (at length) the value of higher education in general and the turn of his career away from academia to online content creation in particular.[20] They have helped to celebrate his marriage to his partner Tanya Frampton (a.k.a. PeppyPepper), whom he met through his online gaming. They have followed the pair's struggles to get her a visa from Belarus to live with him in the United Kingdom. They have also helped make a number of Quickybaby's real-life friends, relatives, fellow gamers and streamers, contacts at Wargaming EU, and prominent members of his online community of play minor online celebrities in their own right.[21] Finally, they have seen him integrated further into Wargaming's official eSports events as a panelist and official online broadcast commentator. Like the fictional Leeroy Jenkins before him, as a real-life emergent celebrity Quickybaby attains value for the original IP from which he emerged.

Like many other streamers, Frampton is an emergent media entrepreneur. He runs an online broadcast network from his home. With his Twitch streams, his YouTube content, and his personal appearances, his Quickybaby avatar has become a significant brand—and meme—within the *WoT* community of play. His career has been built on his performance and scripting skills as a gamer, as an on-camera performer, and as an analyst. His emergence as a content creator is both enabled and sustained by streaming technologies and by his ability to create, maintain, and be sustained by an audience from his own microcommunity of play within the broader concentric circles of the *WoT* community and the wider ludisphere.

Frampton is primarily an improvisational narrative and media-journalistic scripter. Despite the improvisatory nature of some of his commentary, however, his weekly Quickybaby streams—the broadcast schedule of his network-of-one—are carefully planned around different kinds of narrative scripting. Each stream focuses on one of the key social experiences of MMO games in solo, full-team, and small-group play. Each also emphasizes one of three important principles required for success in MMO play: competitiveness, cooperation, and leadership. Given that the avowed primary purpose of Quickybaby's content is to help his fellow players to improve their own play, this split also offers an endlessly repeatable educational experience for aspirant players, couched within the welcoming social realm of his community of play.

Quickybaby tells the story of each game he plays in LP mode either in real time or with retrospective reflection. The sequence of in-game events provides their own long-take plot over which he threads the personal interpretive arc of story. In his solo streams he integrates an entertaining expression of his interiority via audio—articulating his in-game process of planning, choosing, reacting, and reflecting—over the visual exteriority of digital tanks battling digital tanks. The commentary adds humanity, and specifically expressions of intellect and emotion, to invest his audience more deeply in the gameplay. In short Quickybaby's scripting serves to characterize events that are otherwise largely without character. The volatility of in-game plot events (the actions of other players) provides additional narrative excitement, and the interactive interventions from his stream shift the tone and content in unpredictable and often entertaining ways.

When Quickybaby streams 10-vs.-10 team games with the QSF clan or streams games played in a small group of friends, a "platoon" in the terms of *WoT*, the terms of the LP narrative change accordingly. As a team leader, outlining strategy and tactics and giving commands in response to in-game events, Quickybaby directs the mission and imposes a more rigorous—one might even say generic—story structure onto the gameplay. Here he is literally telling a war story to his teammates, opening with an introductory mission briefing during pregame prep that spells out what the team must do, where it must go, how the various groups of specialist tanks (potentially including a mix of heavy, medium, and light tanks, tank destroyers, and artillery) should cooperate, and how the team should prepare to react to the enemy's anticipated countertactics. Albeit tempered to some extent by his usual relaxed sense of humor, the team games highlight a more disciplinarian, even autocratic, side to Quickybaby's online personality. He plays into an "officer" more than a "fellow soldier" persona. Not even Quickybaby's plans survive contact with the enemy, however, and the narrative drive of the team games revolves around the speed and skill with which he adapts to circumstances as a commander. All of this is played out with the transparency of real-time audio, so the audience can assess Quickybaby's command judgment as the QSF team succeeds or fails according to its individual and collective skill.

Quickybaby's small-group LP streams replicate some of this generic war storytelling in a more relaxed setting. He and his friends do think about in-game tactics, and they adapt to in-game events. These streams, however, are often more about giving the audience an insight into Quickybaby's social personality as he interacts with his friends than they are about promoting intense competition. The small-group games are the indie character drama to the team games' mission-based war movie. They are, to extend this analogy, character-driven in comparison to the team games, which are distinctly plot-driven. In the small-group platoon streams Quickybaby and his friends will also engage in a kind of emergent play, deliberately restricting themselves by focusing on less competitive, or more specialist, vehicles to expose their inherent unpredictability or "silliness."

The stream's audience also enters into the terms and the spirit of this emergent play. There are fan-favorite tanks, such as the slow, cumbersome TOG 2 or the lumbering KV2, with its unreliable but overpowered "derp" gun, that make for unlikely team choices and which have developed their own "personalities" and micronarratives when played by Quickybaby and his friends over the course of his three years of streaming. For example, when the platoon plays the Soviet KV5 heavy tank, their game is often accompanied by its own ironic soundtrack: "You Gotta Be Dumb If You're Gonna Be Tough," by Roger Alan Wade. The fans also have come to associate some of these tanks with particular combinations of players ("The Mighty Jingles" with the TOG 2, or "Ikzor" with the T14, for example), and they also delight in requesting a player's known least favorite tank when they are on-stream, scripting the improv for comedy to emerge out of the resultant resentment and banter from the on-stream "cast." All of this establishes a different set of convergent narrative priorities for the improvisational scripting of the small-group streams in comparison to the other scheduled broadcasts on the channel.

Like many other YouTubers, Quickybaby has also created or adapted specific programming formats that channel his presentations through standardized structures. He is not alone in doing so. Many talented online content creators develop their own broadcast series that focus on one aspect of their service or reflect on broader issues in gaming. The following examples all emerge from the community of play of *World of Warcraft* and are only indicative of much wider production relating to this single game. FatBoss TV is known for broadcasting detailed and well-informed strategy guides to defeating World of Warcraft "bosses," but it also broadcasts a regular discussion show, *Laps around Dalaran,* covering and critiquing issues of the moment in the game world.[22] The YouTuber Tuskeh has recently supplemented his issue-specific game guides with a daily YouTube magazine show, *Teatime with Tuskeh,* which covers news of the day for the *World of Warcraft* community along with regular lighthearted segments offering advice and sharing user-generated content from his fans.[23] The influential WOW database site Wowhead broadcasts its own *Wowhead Weekly* discussion show (currently on episode 95), cohosted by the website's own staffer, Perculia, alongside *Trade Chat*'s host, Panser.[24] Finally, among its many popular YouTube series, *Preach Gaming* offers a strand of thoughtful, irreverently funny, visually sophisticated, and well-researched historical documentaries on the "Legacy" of the development of aspects of that game.[25]

In his own more journalistic "Quick Tank Review" YouTube videos, Quickybaby follows an episode format that opens with a discussion of various forms of metagame theory-crafting, using both in-game materials and fan-built Internet databases and other sites that allow him to illustrate key statistics such as an avatar tank's effective armor values graphically. Each episode then proceeds to show one or more expert level LPs to put this theory-crafting to the test in-game, with Quickybaby's to-camera commentary added. In the process he reverts consistently to stock statements that introduce, conclude, and otherwise punctuate his improvised script at operative moments. In screenwriting terms he plays to scripted beats.

Although Quickybaby does not write formal scripts as a traditional screenwriter might do, he does often work from notes, and his process clearly involves rigorous scripting that continues through the stages of research, production, and editing.[26] He spends considerable effort in streamlining his own commentary in postproduction, for example. This rigor can be discerned from watching the cut pattern on the talking-head insert shots that accompany many of his videos. Quickybaby's face appears in an insert on the left of the screen as he narrates/improvises the script of each show, all while his fans provide their own onscreen scrolling textual commentary rather in the style of an especially cantankerous Greek chorus. The audience's primary attention is focused on the main content, but even occasional glances show the video insert of the presenter's face frequently jump-cutting to keep the flow of the audio track clean.

Frampton, a professional who earns his living from his online content, has developed an appropriately professional lexicon through which to play the beats of his programs, following a de facto "series bible" that guides and governs the structure of each episode. Most of Quickybaby's YouTube programs, other than the simplest LPs, display a relatively sophisticated internal microstructure. His weekly Twitch streaming strategy is also designed to produce three distinct broadcasts with different generic leads. Over time, therefore, his emergent network-of-one has developed a number of distinct, and distinctly scripted, show formats.

The improvisational interactive community scripting practiced between Quickybaby and his audience represents just one commercial trajectory for independent online content creation. For our purposes, it also advances a discussion of writing craft in the convergent media by helping to define an emerging sector adjacent to the production mainstream. Even so, the potential for producing other forms of interactive narrative on streaming services like Twitch and Kamcord is also already part of a broader cultural conversation about the future of online storytelling. In addition to facilitating the careers of independent broadcasters like Frampton/Quickybaby, the streaming service has hosted more formal experiments in "crowd-led storytelling."[27] There have been public presentations on the subject at the service's annual Twitch Con event; concurrently, "Twitch Fiction" has been categorized by invested bloggers and participants as "a framework for interactive, participatory storytelling on live streaming video platforms." It leverages "Twitch features, such as the chat bar and customizable bots" and is "inspired by the *Twitch Plays Pokémon* phenomenon and *Choose Your Own Adventure* novels."[28] Although this kind of emergent experiment is by no means widespread, and most online scripting is of a more pragmatic order, the potential for interactive storytelling via livestreaming channels is exercising diverse creatives.

Frampton does not refer to himself as a screenwriter, but then as a professional gamer he does not fit conventional models of a media professional in many other respects. He doesn't refer to himself, for example, as an actor or a programmer or a producer or a director. Strictly speaking, in fact, he's also not even a professional gamer, even though he pays his rent by playing games. His craft skills are at least partially self-taught. His program formats were developed instinctively and then organically over time yet also informed by conscious decisions coming out of reading, research, and experimentation. His academic background is in geography, and he had no need to undertake the conventional film school apprenticeship common to many of those aspiring to media production careers. The forms of online production from which he makes his living involve the integrated labor of directing, sound recording, producing, editing, and performing, among other tasks. Moreover, his intent is to stream and discuss video games, not to write scripts. Yet scripting is arguably the most important of these craft and creative functions. It is where he develops the episodes and performances that constitute his series of fictionalized gaming. All of the integrated preconvergent media tasks that go into producing the Quickybaby product and brand are deployed in the service of the interactive ludic storytelling which keeps his rent paid and his audience coming back for more.

Unlike the more traditional screenwriters who are still driving on the traffic circle, trying to accommodate their careers to a changing road map, scripters like Frampton might more profitably be considered part of a postcraft, or converged-craft, era and generation. In 2016 the worlds of the professional movie crafts and entrepreneurial online postcraft production were still relatively distinct and were certainly perceived to be so by many professionals. Writing from the perspective of digital cinema as art, the Hollywood cinematographer and film school professor Harry Mathias claims with some justice that people "will never pay a filmmaker so that they can see a clever YouTube film."[29] But assessing the veracity of such a statement already depends on one's definition both of *film* and of *filmmaker*. Many people are already paying good money to support the distillation of all the classical Hollywood crafts into a new kind of YouTube product, one that entirely bypasses and obviates the need for their professional judgment.

Quickybaby and his ilk postdate the crafts in two key senses, the first in terms of convergence and the second in that developments in technology have transcended the need for a professional and technical training for many online media workers. And these media workers have demanding and knowledgeable audiences that force them to remain competitive by scripting, directing, and performing in ways that keep viewers coming back. They have found their own exit routes off the jammed traffic circle. In the end, what is demonstrably clear is that many of the programs Quickybaby produces tell a kind of story, and they all have structure. They are also indicative of what many of the kids (and adults) are now dedicating an increasing amount of their time and money to watch.

FILM SCHOOL FOLLIES

Our case study of Quickybaby also begs another important question: To what extent is the concept of distinct media crafts still relevant for many cut-cord and post-cord online producers and consumers? Even if convergence is not a settled matter, and we think in some respects it very much is, there is no doubt that the practice of a new generation of online content creators, online scripters by another word, already transcends the conventional boundaries of craft. For many online creatives, if not for established movie and television writers, screenwriting in its conventional delineation is already a legacy profession. If so, then, under the same grid so are the other traditional media crafts (at least in their own legacy iterations).

In the near future the pattern of screenwriting labor is going to look much more diverse and diffuse while the professional class system we have already discussed in this book is likely to be foregrounded even further, its trade union in greater crisis with fewer members on the inside track, only more clearly iterated between media. For if, as appears certain, online represents a key future strand for the media arts and professional crafts alike, then symptomatic of that future is the likelihood that much of the labor of online scripting will fall outside the formal imprimatur of unionization.

Despite the Writers Guild's ongoing attempts to legitimate and penetrate newer media, WGA members might well hesitate to accept independent online content creation as screenwriting in the first place. To many of them, like old Hollywood, or even the Hollywood of five or so years ago, the Internet is still primarily a marketing platform. But the guild's history suggests that if independent new-media workers keep making good money from their online content creation, and the new-hyphenate emergence continues to devour, digest, and reconfigure legacy media, then the guild will see the need to rethink its definition of craft once again—if only to maintain or expand its membership dues. Bringing the comparatively conventional video games industry under the WGA's MBA has already proved to be a step too far. From the perspective of early 2016, incorporating the labor of the diverse and independent entrepreneurs who are active in online content creation under a traditional union contract from the WGA (or any of the craft guilds for that matter) is likely to be even further beyond reach—even if the guild undertakes another process of internal cultural legitimation. After all, the WGA was an institution designed for the protection of the preconvergent screenwriter (screenwriter 1.0). As a consequence, the fact that it now finds it hard to remain relevant to the experience of the convergent screenwriter, to say nothing of a putative *scripter 1.0*, is hardly surprising. For the craft guilds as a group, the emergence of postcraft careers also inflects the thorny question of jurisdiction in new and deeply challenging ways.

Although in 2015 Will Wheaton's guests on *Tabletop* still found it necessary to announce their cross-media specialties, the time will come when that kind of new-conversion is taken for granted (and is, in fact, already taken that way by those who grew up post-cord). All we will need to know is a worker's credits to understand much of his or her craft. Going forward, therefore, accounting for the current status and potential future development of screenwriting will involve tracking changes both to the established professional craft in the legacy and convergent conglomerate media and to the postcraft synthesis of online content production.

The emergence of diverse new forms of online scripting begs two more linked questions. First, how is the professional craft of screenwriting being served by educational institutions that claim to be training the next generation for life on the convergent traffic circle and beyond? Second, given that many successful online content creators like Quickybaby have had no need of a film school or formal media education, how might the emergence of a generation of such entrepreneurial creatives affect the future direction of the screenwriting craft and education? The short answer to the first question is: incoherently and only very partially. The answer to the second is, at least as we full-time professors and part-time screenwriters see it: curriculum convergence.

Because of its essentially commercial and reactive nature, the screenwriting paraindustry has been able to pivot to feed off online and convergent production more rapidly than has American higher education, burdened as it is with historical accretions of pedagogical precedent and the vested interests of some tenured faculty. Most university film schools and departments are still fundamentally vested in teaching the legacy media of film and television—think of all those that still use titles like "broadcast" let alone "film." Most masters of fine arts (MFA) in screenwriting programs, or the professional film school degree offering, such as those offered by Chapman and Pepperdine in the Los Angeles area, currently frame their curricula around traditional screenwriting, focusing unapologetically on the craft of film and television writing.[30] They are the "high art" iterations of the paraindustry's labyrinth of low-art books, software, and websites.

For a range of historical inter- and intradisciplinary reasons, institutions of higher education in and outside the United States have siloed their film and television curricula, sometimes separating film from television in different departments, which tends to make collaboration between programs that focus on creative writing, journalism, design, and computer programming, among other disciplines, something of a structural and political challenge. There are, of course, some that seek intimate connections with these other areas, often through the auspices of digital humanities and arts and engineering, both in the United States and across the Pacific and Atlantic ponds, but these are the exceptions. One exceptional case is Loyola Marymount University, where the undergraduate screenwriting curriculum has been revised in the light of convergence. As of this writing, the university's screenwriting department is finalizing plans to relocate to premises in the emerging tech hub of Playa Vista to facilitate new media connections for its programs and students.

Many European schools, especially those with a vestment in the scholarly traditions of media and cultural studies and in more collaborative principles of production training, are often better positioned to respond both critically and pragmatically to convergence than are US schools. Their institutional structures already attend to a range of media and engage productively with related fields of enquiry, in the last decades featuring broad topics such as postmodernity and consumption. Frequently the production components of their programs, particularly those that attempt to link art and computer programming, are similarly vested in the breadth of digital media. In Europe this is in part a reflection of the historical weighting of the media industries toward television rather than cinema.[31]

In China, television at the university-level was structured within the propaganda wing of communist interests as opposed to film as art (and still censored, of course). The teaching of film is ironically more akin to the US model than it is to the European model, where the separation of now-convergent media resulted in the actual dimensions of convergence going untaught and underresearched.

Almost all film school screenwriting classes and curricula still reify the long-established formulae and formats of professional industry practice, notably the feature screenplay, the one-hour television episode, and the sitcom, to the exclusion of cross-media, much less transmedia, production. (Few offer writing for animation, though many universities have animation programs.) Of course, many of the faculty that staff typical film schools are professional practitioners and scholars that are—or were—equally vested in the crafts and practices of those legacy media. Some film schools might even hire well-known filmmakers toward the end of their production careers as departmental "show ponies" to, in effect, double down on legacy media while implicitly undervaluing the unique skills involved in teaching and research (not all that can make media can teach media, just like not all that teach media can make media). All are vested in what Thomas Kuhn called paradigms—the status quo of a method that fits the past more than it thinks anew of the future.[32] Some, of course, are excellent and forward-thinking educators, but this tends to reinforce the esteem lent to conventional screenwriting relative to newer scripting modes. A paradigm shift does not appear to us to be in the works at most university film and/or media schools.

Offering courses that teach traditional screenwriting skills is still academically appropriate. Many screenwriters are still contracted by an industry that may be experiencing a degree of creative and technological flux but which is still producing conventional narratives in traditional formats. This is particularly the case in television, as the tentpole era and the expansion of small-screen drama production has given television writers a great shot at creative and financial success. And there are a lot of valuable skills and even rules to learn by writing in traditional formats—if only better to understand them in a creative effort to master, alter, and even break them. And, of course, many students still aspire to work in these professional contexts, and despite our account of Quickybaby and his online community of play, in most cases story is still story and structure is still structure.

This suggests that the challenge for the future of film schools is a both/and, not an either/or, proposition—at least not yet. The schools do not have to stop teaching the screenplay and the sitcom. Rather they also need to respond expansively to the challenge of new and convergent forms and practices.

We are nonetheless experiencing a period of higher educational window dressing, where universities, like the larger paraindustry, are learning to speak the language of convergence in their marketing but have not yet truly embraced it in their programs. For example, the word *film* in some department titles has been replaced recently by *cinema* or even *screen*, as in "screen culture" or "screen arts," with an eye toward convergence but without the transformative curriculum to back it up. For example, the titles of USC's Writing for Screen and Television Bachelor of Fine Arts (BFA) and MFA programs have both moved past "film" in favor of "screen," even though their content remains largely conventional. Both degrees focus on teaching to the screenplay, and the one-hour television and half-hour comedy and drama writing formulae, supported by additional classes on the "profession of screenwriting." Despite the largely traditional structure of its actual curriculum, the website of the university's Writing Division tries to market itself with the language of expanded screenwriting: "It all begins with a script. Before any film, television show, web series, or video game can become a phenomenon, you need words on a page. The Writing for Screen & Television Division teaches students how to create the kinds of scripts that excite creative collaborators, agents, managers, and investors and become real projects. . . . You will learn to write short scripts, feature-length screenplays, television episodes in comedy and drama, web series, and scripts for games and other immersive media."[33]

This disjunction between marketing and reality at some schools is already evident to their current students. For example, California State University Fullerton, the first CSU campus to offer a screenwriting MFA, includes "interactive media" in its program description.[34] From the perspective of Sarah Mahan, a current MFA student at Fullerton, the department is still focused largely on teaching to the traditional media. Her assessment of the state of faculty-student discussion there is instructive, indicative of a situation that is currently playing out in similar ways in many schools:

> I've noticed that non-traditional media is starting to become more of [a] student to faculty conversation. . . . But for now it's this give and take of professors trying to [put] non-traditional careers in our minds and the students bringing their experience with it to light. For example, one guy in my cohort directs viral videos for several companies, HBO among them. He brought this experience up in class and the professor wanted to know more about it, so he scheduled a whole class where David (viral video guy) would just show his "oeuvre" and talk about that kind of career. So in short, I'd say Fullerton is getting there with group effort.[35]

Lest the reader think we are relying on one student account—and a student from a competing institution to ours—Mahan's comment speaks also to our experience as faculty in the School of Cinema at San Francisco State University: our students are teaching us about convergent opportunities, scripting included, as much as we are teaching them about story, plot, character, and structure.

At the intersection of the craft paraindustry and traditional higher education, newer online or hybrid low-residency commercial degree programs should be in a position to change, update, or introduce courses faster than established university departments and schools; however, their own marketing sometimes provides evidence that these institutions do not fully understand the nature of convergent media either. For example, National University's master of fine arts in professional screenwriting offers one of its three tracks in "transmedia" writing, although the institution seems to define transmedia in terms of conventional choices within new(er) media rather than as a distinct creative practice: "Course work covers screenwriting, television writing, transmedia writing (graphic novels, comics, web narratives, etc.), script analysis, script development, pitching and marketing as well as business aspects of entertainment programming."[36]

Compounding the challenge in academe is the unspoken norm that a range of faculty can easily teach screenwriting, whatever their area of expertise within the legacy media. In film schools it is the creative craft most often serviced without recourse to specialist faculty. Filmmakers frequently teach screenwriting, and that of course is not necessarily problematic in the era of convergence. But many still teach traditional formats, even the short film that now dominates online content as much as it does student's portfolio matter,[37] in support of an obsolescent vision of narrative film that will still be seen on a big screen. Theorists and historians often evolve into screenwriting teachers, sometimes on the presumption that textual analysis easily equates to understanding story or simply because they may be looking for a greater diversity in their course offerings. And then there are faculty that have written a script, perhaps with commercial success, in the distant past. Yet, much like painting or electrical engineering, we would argue that the craft requires constant practice and testing, research and exploration, to be taught with consistent success.

Our point here is that an aspect of the challenges faced by film schools looking to engage convergent media, scripting—and thus to engage students aspiring to work in the arena of screenwriter 2.0—is the implicit devaluing of the screenwriting craft and research through the academic hiring and committee process that allows almost anybody to teach screenwriting: from filmmakers who do not work in the world of today's screenwriting to "star" screenwriters from Hollywood's heyday who either don't conduct research or have not developed the pedagogical skills necessary to inspire students to think and write differently while mastering the norms of the past. To be sure, this is not easy for the two of us to write since some of this criticism can (and perhaps should) be leveled against us as well.[38]

Most film schools reflect and respect the traditions of the media professions by teaching screenwriting as a distinct craft, often within its own concentration or emphasis along with others in (typically) editing, directing, and cinematography. Within traditional screenwriting curricula, however, the best film schools have also striven to develop individual classes that more effectively interface with or at least moot professional practice as they understand it. For example, as part of its MFA the University of Texas at Austin has offered a TV "Writer's Room" workshop run by a working showrunner.[39] Innovative teachers have even begun to make formal connections with convergent corporate institutions, such as UCLA lecturer Neil Landau's recent "Writing the 1-Hour Drama" pilot workshop, in association with Crackle. Landau adds that the online distributor purchased three of the ten original pilot scripts developed in his 2014 class (although the sustainability of such a conversion rate is distinctly unlikely).[40] Other schools have developed individual classes that seek to expand the creative horizons of their students and facilitate cross-media and transmedia thinking and writing.

Classes like these are still very much the exception. Film schools will need to seriously rethink their curricula from the ground up to engage with the online and convergent future. What seems certain is that we will begin to judge the screenwriting programs they offer by the way their curricula engage with the twin tracks of traditional and emergent scripting we have identified. This suggests the need for a new kind of screenwriting curriculum, itself convergent as it interfaces much more organically and creatively with the work of the other crafts and looks to online, entrepreneurial practices as much as to the tentpole and the sitcom. Such a curriculum would maintain core teaching of the feature screenplay (in the short term at least) and its derivatives while expanding the kind of preparation its students need to work across platforms, across media, and to develop their own careers in a complex mediascape.

In the era of convergence the professors of screenwriting have joined their professional and entrepreneurial writer and scripter colleagues on the great traffic circle of convergence. The forward-looking among them are searching diligently for new exits, both for themselves and for their students. Many, however, are now looking increasingly like Robert Maitland, the modern Robinson Crusoe of J.G. Ballard's novel *Concrete Island*, stuck in the middle with only the resources they brought with them to survive.

EPILOGUE

Screenwriting off the page, circumscribed as it is by the homogenizing influence of tentpole franchises at one extreme and the diversity of micro-budget movies and online content on the other, is simultaneously vested in established skills and production disciplines and also increasingly "post-craft." The labor that defines the careers of A-list Hollywood rewrite specialists still requires them to be able to navigate the latest iterations of dramatic and institutional paradigms that were first established decades before they began their careers, when screen stories were told a little more slowly and the Hollywood studios were very different institutions than they are today. A new generation of writers and scripters, many of whom have had no formal screenwriting or filmmaking education and who may not even consider themselves writers or filmmakers, are carving out career paths that did not exist ten years ago. They are all standing on the shoulders of giants, as the saying goes. Yet unlike their movie and television contemporaries, online scripters like Frampton are standing on the shoulders of the giants of digital technology rather than of screenwriting. They are, however, creating the stories, formats, and networks that speak to many of their generational peers.

Out with the traditional screenwriter; in with the convergent scripter. The imperatives of a global and conglomerate iteration of Hollywood, we have argued throughout this book, limit the creative paths for aspiring writers while cementing the destinations of the few traditional writers adept at the tentpole formula. The WGA can do little to change the tentpole economy, obliged as it is to follow the interests of its current membership and unable to extend its remit through the convergent media. As a result, the default employment formulae presented by the studios and producers are resisted in detail but never truly threatened. But, as we have also shown, both the traditional screenwriters and the convergent content creators are bulldozing through previously charted and uncharted mediascapes. In so doing they are challenging the definition of the craft of screenwriting held by the industry, the Writers Guild of America, the paraindustry, and academia.

Screenwriter 2.0 is showing signs of thriving in today's expanding yet converging media industry. To make this case, we have attempted to engage critically and creatively with various methods of scholarly analysis. We have relied primarily on industry studies, production culture studies, and close textual analysis of scripts and related production documents. We have also employed theory, where necessary—from Gramsci's notion of "coercion and consent" and Foucault's notion of discourse to Maras's four frames and Caldwell's notion of hive production—in an effort to help explain what we have seen and read in the industries' production documents and paraindustrial discourses. In this way, another argument we have made throughout the book, albeit in subtle ways, centers on an approach to media analysis that sidesteps methodological and theoretical hierarchies, and hierarchies of evidence, in favor of a more democratic approach to critical analysis. As we noted in our introduction, it does not appear to us to be worthwhile, let alone rigorous, to judge one source of evidence, from the "lowbrow" paraindustry to the "highbrow" academic industry, as more or less valuable than another. It's best, we think, to look at all—and employ all—critically and creatively, at least when the research question focuses on the changing circuit of culture and its immediate history.

At turns by necessity and at turns by design, professional screenwriters are redefining the position of scripting across media, in some cases radically changing the culture of their labor and the creative possibilities of their craft. As this tension between craft and postcraft screenwriting implies, writers and educators are, to return one final time to our occasional motif of road networks, at an intersection. At first glance it would appear that the roads to tentpoles and Twitch lead off in very different directions, yet it is principally in the flexibility of writers' own definitions of their craft, their industrial spin and discourses, and its convergent potential that the map might draw those divergent paths toward one another again. We hope that our study has established a road map that is clear enough for future scholarly writers and creatives to chart the journey onward from this junction.

Notes

INTRODUCTION

1. Hortense Powdermaker, *Hollywood, the Dream Factory: An Anthropologist Looks at the Movie-Makers* (London: Secker and Warburg, 1951), 53.
2. Dennis Palumbo, quoted in *Dreams on Spec*, dir. Daniel Snyder (Mercury Productions, 2007).
3. Steven Maras, *Screenwriting: History, Theory and Practice* (London: Wallflower, 2009), 10–11.
4. Billy Ray, "A Warning for Our Next Great Screenwriters," Medium.com, Aug. 5, 2015, https://medium.com/art-science/a-warning-for-our-next-great-screenwriters-4af58oc2eob7#.p4dfld7dx.
5. See Henry Jenkins, *Convergence Culture: Where Old and New Media Collide* (New York: NYU Press, 2008).
6. On transmedia marketing campaigns like "Why So Serious" see, for example, Frank Rose, *The Art of Immersion: How the Digital Generation Is Remaking Hollywood, Madison Avenue, and the Way We Tell Stories* (New York: Norton, 2011), 8–15.
7. Gramsci offered an ideological account of dominance, or hegemony, one that sought the "consent" of the oppressed (in our case many screenwriters) through the "coercive" forces of ideology, producing a kind of "common sense." See Antonio Gramsci, *Selections from the Prison Notebooks* (New York: International Publishers, 1971). For a concise secondary source on Gramsci and the notions of coercion and consent, common sense, and hegemony see Tom Bottomore, ed., *A Dictionary of Marxist Thought* (Oxford: Blackwell, 1998). For a critical analysis of Gramsci's work see Dante L. Germino, *Antonio Gramsci: Architect of a New Politics* (Baton Rouge: Louisiana State University Press, 1990).
8. There is a great deal of work on narrative and film. With respect to cognitive-based film studies see David Bordwell, *Narration in the Fiction Film* (Madison: University of Wisconsin Press, 1985); and Edward Branigan,

Narrative Comprehension and Film (New York: Routledge, 1992). Much of the structural and poststructural work in film theory is based on the narrative theories of Vladimir Propp, Tzvetan Todorov, Roland Barthes, and Claude Lévi-Strauss.

9. Stephen Prince, *A New Pot of Gold: Hollywood under the Electronic Rainbow, 1980–1989* (Berkeley: University of California Press, 2000).

10. Alexander Boon, *Script Culture and the American Screenplay* (Detroit, MI: Wayne State University Press, 2008); Maras, *Screenwriting;* Steven Price, *The Screenplay: Authorship, Theory and Criticism* (London: Palgrave Macmillan, 2010); Jill Nelmes, ed., *Analyzing the Screenplay* (London: Routledge, 2010); Bridget Conor, *Screenwriting: Creative Labor and Professional Practice* (London: Routledge, 2014).

11. Miranda Banks, *The Writers: A History of American Screenwriters and Their Guild* (New Brunswick, NJ: Rutgers University Press, 2014).

12. See Andrew Horton and Julian Hoxter, eds., *Screenwriting* (New Brunswick, NJ: Rutgers University Press, 2014), 2.

13. See Steven Price, *A History of the Screenplay* (Basingstoke: Palgrave Macmillan, 2013).

14. John Thornton Caldwell, *Production Culture: Industrial Reflexivity and Critical Practice in Film and Television* (Durham, NC: Duke University Press, 2008), esp. 35.

15. See David Bordwell, *The Way Hollywood Tells It: Story and Style in Modern Movies* (Berkeley: University of California Press, 2006).

16. See Joseph Campbell, *The Hero with a Thousand Faces* (Novato, CA: New World Library, 2008); and Christopher Vogler, *The Writer's Journey: Mythic Structure for Writers* (Studio City, CA: Michael Wiese Productions, 2007). Julian Hoxter has also published two screenwriting textbooks: *Write What You Don't Know: An Accessible Manual for Screenwriters* (New York: Continuum, 2011); and *The Pleasures of Structure: Learning Screenwriting through Case Studies* (New York: Bloomsbury Academic, 2015).

17. It is hard to obtain accurate statistics for the number of screenplays registered by the WGA each year. The WGA West Registry acknowledges approximately seventy thousand registrations, but it does not differentiate among types of document. So within this overall number is material including, as the guild acknowledges, scripts, treatments, synopses, outlines, and written ideas specifically intended for radio, television and film, videocassettes/discs, or interactive media. The WGA West Registry also accepts stage plays, novels and other books, short stories, poems, commercials, lyrics, drawings, music, and other media work.

18. Terry Murphy's study of the screenplay in the light of Vladimir Propp's functional approach in *Morphology of the Folktale* (ed. Svatava Pirkova-Jakobson, trans. Laurence Scott [Bloomington: Research Center, Indiana University, 1958]) offers another useful addition to the limited paraindustrial theoretical lexicon. See Terence Patrick Murphy, *From Fairy Tale to Film Screenplay: Working with Plot Genotypes* (Basingstoke: Palgrave Macmillan, 2015).

19. Ken Dancyger and Jeff Rush, *Alternative Screenwriting: Beyond the Hollywood Formula*, 4th ed. (Burlington, MA: Focal Press, 2007), 37.

20. See Jenkins, *Convergence Culture;* and Lev Manovich, *The Language of New Media* (Cambridge, MA: MIT Press, 2001).

21. See John Fiske, *Television Culture* (London: Methuen, 1987).

22. Gregory Curry, "Cognitivism," in *A Companion to Film Theory*, ed. Toby Miller and Robert Stam (Malden, MA: Blackwell, 2008), 112.

23. Douglas Kellner, "Media Industries, Political Economy, and Media/Cultural Studies: An Articulation," in *Media Industries: History, Theory, and Method*, ed. Jennifer Holt and Alisa Perrin (Malden, MA: Blackwell, 2009), 95–107.

24. Ibid., 101–2.

25. Ibid., 97.

26. Richard Johnson, "What Is Cultural Studies Anyway?" *Social Text* 16 (Winter 1986–87): 38–80, 54 (emphasis in original).

27. Jennifer Holt and Alisa Perren, "Does the World Really Need One More Field of Study?" in *Media Industries: History, Theory, and Method*, ed. Jennifer Holt and Alisa Perren (Malden, MA: Blackwell, 2009), 5.

28. Ibid., 8–9. See also Stuart Hall, "Encoding/Decoding," in *Culture, Media, Language: Working Papers in Cultural Studies, 1972–79*, ed. Stuart Hall, Dorothy Hobson, Andrew Lowe, and Paul Willis (New York: Routledge, 1980), 128–38.

29. John Thornton Caldwell, *Televisuality: Style, Crisis, and Authority in American Television* (New Brunswick, NJ: Rutgers University Press, 1995).

30. Caldwell, *Production Culture*, 81.

31. Timothy Havens, Amanda D. Lotz, and Serra Tinic, "Critical Media Industry Studies: A Research Approach," *Communication, Culture and Critique* 2 (2009): 234–53.

32. Vicki Mayer, Miranda J. Banks, and John Thornton Caldwell, *Production Studies: Cultural Studies of Media Industries* (New York: Routledge, 2009), 4.

33. See, e.g., Timothy Havens, "Universal Childhood: The Global Trade in Children's Television and Changing Ideals of Childhood," *Global Media Journal* 6, no. 10 (2007); and Timothy Havens and Amanda D. Lotz, *Understanding Media Industries* (Oxford: Oxford University Press, 2012), 137–38.

34. Caldwell, *Production Culture*, 1.

35. Ibid., 425.

36. Sam Hamm, public statement during a master class in genre screenwriting, San Francisco State University, April 2014.

37. Julian Hoxter, introduction to *Screenwriting*, ed. Andrew Horton and Julian Hoxter (New Brunswick, NJ: Rutgers University Press, 2014), 1–10, 1.

CHAPTER 1. MILLENNIAL MANIC

1. Bridget Conor, *Screenwriting: Creative Labor and Professional Practice* (London: Routledge, 2014), 2.

2. Andrew Hart, "Film Industry Has Worst Summer Since 1997," *Huffington Post*, Aug. 29, 2014.

3. Motion Picture Association of America, *Theatrical Market Statistics, 2013*, www.mpaa.org/wp-content/uploads/2014/03/MPAA-Theatrical-Market-Statistics-2013_032514-v2.pdf.

4. See Chuck Tryon, *Reinventing Cinema: Movies in the Age of Media Convergence* (New Brunswick, NJ: Rutgers University Press, 2009), 110.

5. It is widely reported that in the 1950s Hollywood saw television as competition that drained box-office revenue. Douglas Gomery resists what is known as the "blame TV" argument, noting that theater attendance was slipping in the late 1940s, "long before most American families even had a set." Nonetheless, in an effort to increase attendance in theaters, Hollywood did introduce features like CinemaScope and 3-D in an effort to increase attendance and thus revenue. See Douglas Gomery, "Hollywood's Business Today," in *Media in America: The Wilson Quarterly Reader*, ed. Douglas Gomery, rev. ed. (Washington: Woodrow Wilson Center Press, 1998), 149.

6. Motion Picture Association of America, *Theatrical Market Statistics, 2013*, 2.

7. "'Transformers' Hauls in More at Box Office in China Than in U.S.," *Los Angeles Times*, July 15, 2014.

8. Clarence Tsui, "Why More Movie Theaters in China Could Be Bad News for Hollywood," *Hollywood Reporter*, Dec. 7, 2012.

9. Box-office statistics from Box Office Mojo, www.boxofficemojo.com/movies/?id=transformers4.htm.

10. Lynda Obst, *Sleepless in Hollywood: Tales from the New Abnormal in the Movie Business* (New York: Simon and Schuster, 2013), 4–5.

11. Walter reported this phenomenon during a talk, ironically titled "Training Hacks and Whores for Hollywood," given to students at San Francisco State University in 2010.

12. Scott Mendelson, "'Pacific Rim 2' May Be a Box Office Game-Changer," *Forbes*, June 30, 2014.

13. Pamela McClintock, "Box Office: Where Are All the $100 Million-Plus Summer Openings?" *Hollywood Reporter*, June 30, 2014.

14. Obst, *Sleepless in Hollywood*, 5.

15. Terrence Rafferty, "Indiana Jones and the Savior of a Lost Art," *New York Times*, May 4, 2008.

16. Annabelle Villanueva, "Action Dissatisfaction," *Cinescape* (March/April 1998): 46.

17. At least in terms of its affective intent, this kind of film works as the big-budget, mainstream Hollywood equivalent to the spectacular "electrocardiogram" paradigm of European exploitation cinema outlined by Christopher Wagstaff. Often subordinating narrative to the attraction, driven by unthreatening thrills and suspense—and, to a lesser extent, by tempering laughter—tentpole electrocardiogram storytelling offers its audiences two of Wagstaff's three "'physiological responses'" to the experience of watching a movie. For a number

of reasons, however, not least among them the need for international marketability, Hollywood generally dispenses with his third catalyst for a physiological response: sex. See Christopher Wagstaff, "A Forkful of Westerns: Industry, Audiences and the Italian Western," in *Popular European Cinema*, ed. Richard Dyer and Ginette Vincendeau (London: Routledge, 1992). See also our discussion of screenwriting sex in the case study of Travis Mathews in chapter 4.

18. Michael Grais, email to Julian Hoxter, Feb. 1, 2014.

19. Anne Thompson, "Original Screenplays Falling by the Wayside," *Hollywood Reporter*, Feb. 11, 2005.

20. David Denby, *Do the Movies Have a Future?* (New York: Simon and Schuster, 2012), 4.

21. Roger Ebert, *A Horrible Experience of Unbearable Length: More Movies That Suck* (Kansas City, MO: Andrews McMeel, 2012), 338.

22. Denby, *Do the Movies Have a Future?* 34.

23. Russ Fischer, "'Transformers: Age of Extinction' Writer Ehren Kruger: 'Logical Sense Doesn't Have to Be the Be-All, End-All,'" Slashfilm.com, June 27, 2014, www.slashfilm.com/transformers-logical-sense/. Incidentally, Kruger is an experienced writer *(Arlington Road, The Ring, The Skeleton Key)* and past winner of the prestigious Academy Nicholl Fellowship for screenwriting.

24. Julia Kristeva, *Intimate Revolt: The Powers and Limits of Psychoanalysis*, trans. Jeanine Herman (New York: Columbia University, 2002), 77. In an email exchange with John Lechte, Kristeva's former student, Lechte notes that he would translate "plus c'est bête, c'est mieux" as "'the sillier the better.' However, a case could be made for the fact that 'stupider' is a more direct opposite of 'intelligent,' which is the basis of the contrast Kristeva is trying to make."

25. Stephanie Argy, "Leaping Lizards: A Visual Effects Primer for Writers," *Written By: The Magazine of the Writers Guild of America, West*, June 1998, 19.

26. Sam Hamm, interview by Julian Hoxter, Feb. 18, 2014.

27. Domestic revenue reached $623,357,910; foreign revenue reached $895,455,078. Box Office Mojo, www.boxofficemojo.com/movies/?id=avengers11.htm.

28. Brian Truitt, "The New 'Secret War' Is Marvel Comics' Major Event of 2015," *USA Today*, Oct. 9, 2014.

29. Conor, *Screenwriting*, 27.

30. Hortense Powdermaker, *Hollywood, the Dream Factory: An Anthropologist Looks at the Movie-Makers* (London: Secker and Warburg, 1951).

31. All demographic statistics are from Darnell M. Hunt, "The 2014 Hollywood Writers Report: 'Turning Missed Opportunities into Realized Ones,'" *Writers Guild of America, West*, July 2014.

32. Quoted in Gregg Mitchell, "WGAW Releases Latest Findings of 2014 Hollywood Writers Report," *Writers Guild of America, West*, April 14, 2014, www.writersguildtheater.org/content/default.aspx?id=5491.

33. Anne Thompson, *The $11 Billion Year: From Sundance to the Oscars, an Inside Look at the Changing Hollywood System* (New York: Newmarket Books, 2014), 158.

34. Ibid.

35. J. Madison Davis, "Machine to Screen: The Evolution toward Story, 1895–1928," in *Screenwriting*, ed. Andrew Horton and Julian Hoxter (New Brunswick, NJ: Rutgers University Press, 2014), 32.

36. Marsha McCreadie, *Women Screenwriters Today: Their Lives and Words* (Westport, CT: Praeger, 2006), 71-72.

37. Quoted in ibid., 148.

38. All statistics from Writers Guild of America West Inc., *Annual Financial Report*, June 29, 2014.

39. In 2009, for example, the WGA assigned writing credits on 237 films, down from 299 in 2008.

40. Miranda J. Banks, "Spoilers at the Digital Utopia Party: The WGA and Students Now," *Flow*, Dec. 7, 2007, www.flowjournal.org/2007/12/spoilers-at-the-digital-utopia-party-the-wga-and-students-now.

41. Sales of DVDs have declined by more than 30 percent from a peak in 2004 through 2013. In 2012 digital downloads outpaced DVD sales for the first time.

42. The two branches of the WGA represent writers east and west of the Mississippi River respectively.

43. Nikki Finke, "WGA Strike One Year Later: Rodman," *Deadline Hollywood*, Feb. 28, 2009, http://deadline.com/2009/02/wga-strike-one-year-later-howard-rodman-8654/.

44. Cynthia Littleton, *TV on Strike: Why Hollywood Went to War over the Internet* (Syracuse, NY: Syracuse University Press, 2013), 67.

45. Verrone was reelected by 90.2 percent of voting members in 2007, per a WGA press release dated Sept. 18, 2007.

46. Andrew Gumbel, "Hollywood Cliffhanger: Will Militant Writers Leave Tinseltown in the Dark?" *Independent*, Nov. 11, 2007.

47. Cited in Nikki Finke, "Showrunner Explains Why He's on Strike," *Deadline Hollywood*, Nov. 5, 2007. (Originally posted in *Deadline Hollywood Daily*, currently accessed through archived posts at Deadline.com.)

48. This is despite the fact that the age group most likely to avail itself of the products of movie piracy are also the most frequent moviegoers.

49. Dina Smith, "Movies and the Art of Living Dangerously," in *American Cinema of the 2000s: Themes and Variations*, ed. Timothy Corrigan (New Brunswick, NJ: Rutgers University Press, 2012), 174.

50. Finke, "WGA Strike One Year Later." Rodman was elected president of the WGA West in 2015.

51. Littleton, *TV on Strike*, 70.

52. Distrust between labor and management was also inflected by the Hollywood industry's already notorious accounting practices, which saw very few movies ever officially reaching a state of net profitability. These were famously revealed in *Buchwald v. Paramount* (1990) Cal. App. LEXIS 634.

53. Cynthia Littleton, "Poll: WGA Wins Hearts; Studios Retain Muscle," *Variety*, Nov. 25, 2007, http://variety.com/2007/film/news/poll-wga-wins-hearts-studios-retain-muscle-1117976497/.

54. Obst, *Sleepless in Hollywood*, 163.

55. Littleton, *TV on Strike*, 94.

56. In full, the blog described itself as follows: "*United Hollywood* advocates for working people in the entertainment industry facing the digital revolution. We are not an official site of any guild or union, so our opinions are our own. Founded by a group of WGA strike captains, our contributors are both writers and non-writers." *United Hollywood*, http://unitedhollywood.blogspot.com.

57. Littleton, *TV on Strike*, 94.

58. David Latt, "The Devil's in the Details," *United Hollywood*, Jan. 20, 2008, http://unitedhollywood.blogspot.com/2008/01/devils-in-details.html.

59. Obst, *Sleepless in Hollywood*, 170.

60. Joss Whedon, "Do Not Adjust Your Mindset," *United Hollywood*, Feb. 6, 2008, http://unitedhollywood.blogspot.com/2008/02/from-joss-whedon-do-not-adjust-your.html.

61. Littleton, *TV on Strike*, 169.

62. Susan Murray and Laurie Ouellette, *Reality TV: Remaking Television Culture* (New York: New York University Press, 2008), 129.

63. Obst, *Sleepless in Hollywood*, 165.

64. Littleton, *TV on Strike*, 20.

65. Statement from IATSE president Thomas Short, Dec. 7, 2007. Quoted in Rebecca Winters Keegan, "Writer's Strike: The Directors' Cut?" *Time*, Dec. 13, 2007, http://content.time.com/time/arts/article/0,8599,1694286,00.html.

66. "DGA and AMPTP Reach Tentative Agreement on Terms of New Contract," press release, Jan. 17, 2008, www.dga.org/News/PressReleases/2008/0117-DGA-and-AMPTP-Reach-Tentative-Agreement-on-Terms-of-New-Contract.aspx.

67. Littleton, *TV on Strike*, 192.

68. Quoted in Michael Cieply, "Hollywood Wants Numbers on the Digital Box Office," *New York Times*, Sept. 15, 2013.

69. Littleton, *TV on Strike*, 195.

70. John Hazelton, "Tough Times in Hollywood," *Screen Daily*, March 16, 2011, www.screendaily.com/reports/features/tough-times-in-hollywood/5024539.article.

71. Mike Fleming Jr., "WHERE'S MY SCRIPT? Warner Bros Cracks Down on Screenwriter's Late Delivery Dates," *Deadline Hollywood*, June 18, 2010.

72. See Henry Jenkins, *Convergence Culture: Where Old and New Media Collide* (New York: NYU Press, 2008).

73. "Summary of the Proposed 2014 WGA MBA," www.wga.org/uploadedfiles/writers_resources/contracts/2014_MBA_summary.pdf. The WGA also sought to shorten the initial streaming window for TV shows.

74. Jillian N. Morphis, "Negotiations between the WGA and AMPTP: How to Avoid Strikes and Still Promote Members' Needs," *Pepperdine Dispute Resolution Law Journal* 12, no. 3 (2012): 529.

75. Littleton, *TV on Strike*, 185.

76. Jeremy Kay, "Int. Writers Meeting Room. Day," *Screen International*, March 16, 2011, archived at Screen Daily, www.screendaily.com/reports/features/int-writers-meeting-room-day/5024546.article (subscription required).

77. Nikki Finke, "Tentative WGA-AMPTP Contract: Writers Guild Negotiators Cave to Studios and Networks after Only 2 Weeks; Critics Say 'They Accepted Producers' First Draft,'" *Deadline Hollywood*, March 20, 2011, http://deadline.com/2011/03/wga-amptp-come-to-congract-agreement-115641/.

78. Dave McNary, "WGA Members Ratify New 3-Year Deal," *Variety*, April 30, 2014.

79. Dominic Patten, "WGA Members Approve New Contract: Less Than 15% of Eligible Voters Cast Ballots," *Deadline Hollywood*, April 30, 2014, http://deadline.com/2014/04/wga-contract-union-approve-vote-722065/.

80. Obst, *Sleepless in Hollywood*, 195.

CHAPTER 2. ATOP THE TENTPOLE

1. *Barton Fink*, dir. Joel and Ethan Coen, Internet Movie Database, www.imdb.com/title/tt0101410/.

2. Robert Iger, quoted in Lisa Richwine "Disney Projects up to $190 Million 'Lone Ranger' Loss," *Technology News*, August 6, 2013.

3. Motion Picture Association of America, *Theatrical Market Statistics, 2014*, www.mpaa.org/wp-content/uploads/2015/03/MPAA-Theatrical-Market-Statistics-2014.pdf.

4. For numerous specific examples see chapter 1 of Tino Balio, *Hollywood in the New Millennium* (London: BFI/Palgrave Macmillan, 2013).

5. Ibid., 151.

6. Motion Picture Association of America, *Theatrical Market Statistics, 2013*, www.mpaa.org/wp-content/uploads/2014/03/MPAA-Theatrical-Market-Statistics-2013_032514-v2.pdf. Note that in this period the number of movies released by non-MPAA members (mini-majors and smaller independents) rose 76 percent, from 310 to 545.

7. Richard Verrier, "Studios Cut Back Work for Writers," *Los Angeles Times*, July 3, 2010.

8. Andy Greenberg, "*Star Wars*' Galactic Dollars," *Forbes*, May 24, 2007, www.forbes.com/2007/05/24/star-wars-revenues-tech-cx_ag_0524money.html.

9. Entertainment Software Association, "2015 Sales, Demographic and Usage Data: Essential Facts about the Computer and Video Games Industry," *Entertainment Software Association*, www.theesa.com/wp-content/uploads/2015/04/ESA-Essential-Facts-2015.pdf.

10. Audience demographic figures for *The Hunger Games: Mockingjay, Part 1* are from Brent Lang, "Box Office: 'Hunger Games: Mockingjay—Part 1' Scores Year's Biggest Opening with $123 Million," *Variety*, Nov. 23, 2014.

11. John Hazelton, "Tough Times in Hollywood," *Screen Daily*, March 2011, www.screendaily.com/reports/features/tough-times-in-hollywood/5024539.article.

12. Patrick Goldstein, "Happiest Medium for Writers? TV," *Los Angeles Times*, Oct. 23, 2001.

13. Jason Scoggins, Cindy Kaplan, and Landon Rohwedder, "2013 Year-End Spec Market Scorecard," *Scoggins Report*, Jan. 24, 2014. The site reports an additional 106 pitch sales in the same period.

14. Todd McCarthy, "'The Hunger Games: Mockingjay—Part 1': Film Review," *Hollywood Reporter*, Nov. 10, 2014.

15. Film historian Tom Gunning makes the case that the earliest views exhibited were designed to appeal to the curiosity of looking rather than narrative. See "The Cinema of Attractions: Early Film, Its Spectator, and the Avant-Garde," in *Film and Theory: An Anthology*, ed. Robert Stam and Toby Miller (New York: Blackwell, 2000), 229–35.

16. Anne Thompson, *The $11 Billion Year: From Sundance to the Oscars, an Inside Look at the Changing Hollywood System* (New York: Harper Collins, 2014), 53.

17. Ben Friz, "Disney Warns of 'Lone Ranger' Loss," *Wall Street Journal*, August 6, 2013, www.wsj.com/articles/SB10001424127887323968704578652333260864280.

18. Quoted in Scott Mendelson, "For Universal Pictures, Zero Blockbusters Equals Record Profits," *Forbes*, Dec. 9, 2014, www.forbes.com/sites/scottmendelson/2014/12/09/for-universal-pictures-zero-blockbusters-equals-record-profits/#7c58d5b525fc.

19. John August and Craig Mazin, "Scriptnotes, Ep 167: The Tentpoles of 2019—Transcript," *Scriptnotes* (blog), Nov. 4, 2014, https://johnaugust.com/2014/scriptnotes-ep-167-the-tentpoles-of-2019-transcript.

20. The wizarding world of the Harry Potter IP is itself in the process of being reinvested for movies by the Newt Scamander prequels beginning with *Fantastic Beasts and Where to Find Them* (2016), written for the screen by the print franchise's author J.K. Rowling.

21. Devin Faraci, "The Marvel Creative Committee Is Over," *Birth. Movies. Death.*, Sept. 2, 2015, http://birthmoviesdeath.com/2015/09/02/the-marvel-creative-committee-is-over. Faraci's comment about "save the cat" formulas appears to be both a general dismissal of screenplay manual story strategies and an explicit reference to the series of books by Blake Snyder, beginning with *Save the Cat! The Last Book on Screenwriting You'll Ever Need* (Studio City, CA: Michael Wiese Productions, 2005).

22. Marvel's corporate master, Disney, is also well known in Hollywood for paying at the low end of the scale. Indeed, working conditions at the studio have caused it to be dubbed "Mousewitz" by many current and former employees.

23. Evan Campbell, "Why Edgar Wright Left Ant Man," IGN.com, May 28, 2014.

24. Chris Cabin, "Marvel's Creative Committee Is No More," *Collider*, Sept. 2, 2015, http://collider.com/marvel-studios-creative-committee-is-no-more-kevin-feige/.

25. Joanna Robinson, "Why It Matters That Marvel Studios Just Escaped Its Eccentric Billionaire C.E.O.," *Vanity Fair*, Sept. 1, 2015, www.vanityfair.com/hollywood/2015/09/marvel-studios-ike-perlmutter-kevin-feige.

26. Kim Masters, "Superman vs. Batman? DC's Real Battle Is How to Create Its Superhero Universe," *Hollywood Reporter*, Nov. 4, 2015, www.hollywoodreporter.com/news/superman-batman-dcs-real-battle-792190.

27. Subreddit: DC's process for *Wonder Woman* "felt like they were throwing shit against the wall to see what stuck." (Marvel Insider on the *Hollywood Reporter*), Reddit.com, www.reddit.com/r/marvelstudios/duplicates/34a5mz/dcs_process_for_wonder_woman_felt_like_they_were/

28. Mike Fleming Jr., "'Barbie' Movie: Sony Trying Three Poses with Three Scripts," *Deadline Hollywood*, Dec. 15, 2015, http://deadline.com/2015/12/barbie-movie-writers-three-scripts-lindsey-beer-bert-royal-hilary-winston-1201667609/.

29. See Chris Anderson, *The Long Tail: How Endless Choice Is Creating Unlimited Demand* (London: Random House, 2006).

30. Susan Christopherson, "Labor: The Effects of Media Concentration on the Film and Television Workforce," in *The Contemporary Hollywood Film Industry*, ed. Paul McDonald and Janet Wasko (Oxford: Blackwell, 2008), 155.

31. Sweepstakes or "cattle call" pitching can involve groups of writers being summoned to watch a movie and then being asked to come up with ideas for a sequel. As one writer complained: "We knew only one of us would get the job, but we all had to sit through this together." Stephen Galloway, "The Club," *Hollywood Reporter*, Feb. 1, 2000.

32. Dave McNary and Paul F. Duke, "Fight Draft Notices: Writers Guild Challenges Producers, Studios over Unpaid Rewrites," *Variety*, April 24, 2000.

33. Ibid.

34. Quoted in Hazelton, "Tough Times in Hollywood," www.screendaily.com/reports/features/tough-times-in-hollywood/5024539.article.

35. Jeremy Kay, "Int. Writers Meeting Room. Day," *Screen International*, March 16, 2011, archived at Screen Daily, www.screendaily.com/reports/features/int-writers-meeting-room-day/5024546.article (subscription required).

36. Ibid.

37. McNary and Duke, "Scribes Fight Draft Notices."

38. Dave McNary, ". . . But Rank and File Must Go the Extra Mile," *Variety*, April 26, 2010.

39. McNary and Duke, "Scribes Fight Draft Notices."

40. McNary, ". . . But Rank and File."

41. John August and Craig Mazin, "Scriptnotes, Ep 66: One-Step Deals and How to Read a Script—Transcript," *Scriptnotes* (blog), Dec. 7, 2012, http://

johnaugust.com/2012/scriptnotes-ep-66-one-step-deals-and-how-to-read-a-script-transcript.

42. Ibid.

43. Richard Verrier, "Studios Cut Back Work for Writers," *Los Angeles Times*, July 3, 2010.

44. McNary, "... But Rank and File"

45. Tatiana Siegel, "To Have and Have Not: Top Scribes Reap Rewrite Riches," *Variety*, April 26, 2010, http://variety.com/2010/film/features/top-scribes-reap-pic-rewrite-riches-1118018205/.

46. Tatiana Siegel, "Fast, Cheap and in Control: Franchises Rely on Newbies," *Variety*, March 29, 2010, http://variety.com/2010/film/features/talent-that-s-fast-cheap-and-in-control-1118016975/.

47. Ibid.

48. John August and Craig Mazin, "Scriptnotes, Ep 95: Notes on the Death of the Film Industry—Transcript," *Scriptnotes* (blog), June 28, 2013, http://johnaugust.com/2013/scriptnotes-ep-95-notes-on-the-death-of-the-film-industry-transcript.

49. Siegel, "To Have and Have Not." Cody was brought in to do rewrites on *Barbie*, however, as noted above.

50. Ibid.

51. Galloway, "The Club."

52. Dave McNary, "Sony Scribe Deal One of a Kind," *Variety*, Dec. 8, 2003.

53. Jay A. Fernandez, "Signing on to a Writing Co-Op: As Writers Take a Collective Turn, Heavy Hitters Accept Less Cash Upfront in Hopes of Bigger Returns Later On," *Los Angeles Times*, August 15, 2007.

54. Michael Fleming, "Fox Gives Top Writers Gross Points," *Variety*, August 14, 2007, http://variety.com/2007/film/markets-festivals/fox-gives-top-writers-gross-points-1117970235/.

55. Michael Fleming, "McQuarrie Starts Up Writing Venture," *Variety*, March 22, 2007, http://variety.com/2007/film/markets-festivals/mcquarrie-starts-up-writing-venture-1117965626/.

56. Ann Marsh, "The Reel Deal: Alan Wertheimer, Attorney," *Stanford Magazine*, https://alumni.stanford.edu/get/page/magazine/article/?article_id=32516.

57. Cynthia Littleton, *TV on Strike: Why Hollywood Went to War over the Internet* (Syracuse, NY: Syracuse University Press, 2013), 199.

58. Pamela McClintock, "Fox High on Hyphenate Kinberg," *Variety*, April 15, 2010, http://variety.com/2010/film/news/fox-high-on-hyphenate-kinberg-1118017789/.

59. Joss Whedon, "The Avengers," 2nd blue revisions, August 3, 2011, 114 (italics added). Scripts Collection (Unpublished), Margaret Herrick Library, Academy of Motion Picture Arts and Sciences (hereafter Herrick Library).

60. See William O. Douglas, *United States v. Paramount Pictures Inc.*, 334 U.S. 141, 167.

61. Bridget Conor, *Screenwriting: Creative Labor and Professional Practice* (London: Routledge, 2014), 28.
62. Ibid.
63. For a fuller exegesis see Julian Hoxter, "The New Hollywood: 1980–1999," in *Screenwriting*, ed. Andrew Horton and Julian Hoxter (New Brunswick, NJ: Rutgers University Press, 2014), 101–26.
64. Quoted in Davis S. Cohen, "Scribes Tell Tales of Biz Woe," *Variety*, Nov. 8, 2004, http://variety.com/2004/film/markets-festivals/scribes-tell-tales-of-biz-woe-1117913212/.
65. Ibid.
66. Anne Thompson, "Original Screenplays Falling by the Wayside," *Hollywood Reporter*, Feb. 11, 2005.
67. David Mamet, "How Scripts Got So Bad," *Variety*, March 5, 2007.
68. Thompson, "Original Screenplays Falling by the Wayside."
69. Robert McKee, *Story: Substance, Structure, Style, and the Principles of Screenwriting* (London: Methuen, 1999), 399.
70. Michael Lent, "Beyond Syd Field: A New Spec Format," *Creative Screenwriting*, March/April, 1998, 5. Lent noted common format changes in recent screenplays, including the loss of "cluttering distractions," such as CUT TO:s, CONTINUEDs and MOREs, and a general paring down of description to the "barest essentials."
71. Lawrence Kasdan, "Raiders of the Lost Ark," 6. Scripts Collection (Unpublished), Herrick Library.
72. Leigh Brackett and Larry Kasdan, "Star Wars Episode Five: The Empire Strikes Back," fifth draft, Feb. 20, 1980, 39. Scripts Collection (Unpublished), Herrick Library. Spelling as original.
73. George Lucas, "Star Wars Episode One: The Phantom Menace," fourth draft, June 13, 1997, salmon revisions through August 10, 1998. Scripts Collection (Unpublished), Herrick Library, 113.
74. Kathryn Millard, "After the Typewriter: The Screenplay in a Digital Era," *Journal of Screenwriting* 1, no. 1 (2010): 11–25, 15.
75. Kevin Kelly and Paula Parisi, "Beyond *Star Wars*: What's Next for George Lucas," *Wired*, Feb. 1997, www.wired.com/wired/archive/5.02/fflucas_pr.html.
76. Quoted in Amy Wallace "How Much Bigger Can the Bang Get?" *Los Angeles Times Online*, August 9, 1998, http://articles.latimes.com/1998/aug/09/entertainment/ca-11361.
77. Jody Duncan, "Tempests and Teapots," *Cinefex* 133, April 2013, 92. Citing Barry Howell, supervisor with digital previs house The Third Floor.
78. Jody Duncan, "Rough around the Edges," *Cinefex* 134, July 2013, 14.
79. Joe Fordham, "War Games," *Cinefex* 130, July 2012, 96.
80. David Trumbore, "20 Things to Know from the AVENGERS Screening and Q&A with Joss Whedon, Who Teases Another Hero and a Second Villain Who Almost Appeared in the Film," Collider.com, Dec. 19, 2012.
81. Joe Fordham, "Giant Steps," *Cinefex* 133, April 2013, 60.

82. Christopher Markus and Stephen McFeely, "Captain America: The First Avenger," revisions by Joss Whedon, final shooting draft, 2010, 39. Scripts Collection (Unpublished), Herrick Library.

83. Steven Maras, *Screenwriting: History, Theory and Practice* (London: Wallflower, 2009).

84. Hoxter, "The New Hollywood," 116–17.

85. Greg Berlanti, Michael Green, Mark Guggenheim, and Michael Goldenberg, *Green Lantern*, yellow revisions, June 1, 2011, 1. Scripts Collection (Unpublished), Herrick Library.

86. Damon Lindelof and John Spaihts, *Prometheus*, shooting draft, second pink revisions, Jan. 6, 2012. Scripts Collection (Unpublished), Herrick Library.

87. Whedon, "The Avengers."

88. See her illuminating discussion in Vivian Sobchack, *Screening Space: The American Science Fiction Film* (New Brunswick, NJ: Rutgers University Press, 1997).

89. Siegfried Kracauer, *Theory of Film: The Redemption of Physical Reality* (Princeton, NJ: Princeton University Press, 1997), 159.

CHAPTER 3. RUNNING THE ROOM

1. Quoted in Linda Moss, "FX Plans Takes [sic] Branding Campaign Out of the Box," *Multichannel News*, Dec. 11, 2007. Landgraf is pointing to his network's new "out of the box" branding campaign, yet his point about creative people working in television is no less insightful.

2. Ryan's *The Shield* produced a comic book, an online game, dolls, shirts, etc., but this was not a network requirement, an expectation of Ryan, but a business opportunity seized on for both.

3. Roland Barthes, "The Death of the Author," *Image/Music/Text*, trans. Stephen Heath (New York: Hill and Wang, 1977).

4. Shawn Ryan, Editing Notes, no. 514, May 29, 2006. All of the production documents referenced in this chapter are courtesy of Shawn Ryan.

5. Adam Fierro, interview by Daniel Bernardi and Kevin Sandler, Sept. 14, 2007. Much of the interview material in this chapter, and indeed some of the ideas relating to the branding of FX, is drawn from a series of unpublished interviews Bernardi and Sandler conducted on *The Shield*. We thank Kevin Sandler for his insightful work on this important series.

6. Fierro interview.

7. For the most detailed account of this controversy see Jane Mayer, "Whatever It Takes: The Politics of the Man behind *24*," *New Yorker*, Feb. 19, 2007.

8. Daniel Bernardi and Kevin Sandler, "Tonage: Redefining Basic Cable Standards," unpublished manuscript.

9. Glenn Close, quoted in Dan Snierson, "What Glenn Close Is Doing in 'The Shield,'" *Entertainment Weekly*, March 11, 2005, www.ew.com/article/2005/03/11/what-glenn-close-doing-shield.

10. John T[hornton] Caldwell, "Hive-Sourcing Is the New Out-Sourcing: Studying Old (Industrial) Labor Habits in New (Consumer) Labor Clothes," *Cinema Journal* 49, no. 1 (2009): 160–67, 167.

11. Ibid., 164.

12. Shawn Ryan, interview by Daniel Bernardi and Kevin Sandler, Sept. 14, 2007.

13. Richard Lawson, "What Went Wrong on *The Newsroom*," *Vanity Fair*, Dec. 15, 2014, www.vanityfair.com/hollywood/2014/12/the-newsroom-series-finale.

14. Quoted in Alessandra Stanley, "The Final Story for a Paean to Journalism: 'The Newsroom' Ends Its Final Season on HBO," *NYTimes.com*, Dec. 14, 2014.

15. Cory Barker, "*The Newsroom* Series Finale Review: A Wake for Don Quixote," TV.com, Dec. 15, 2014.

16. Darlene Lieblich Tipton, Standards and Practices email to the producers of *The Shield*, Feb. 4, 2006.

17. Darlene Lieblich Tipton, Standards and Practices email to the producers of *The Shield*, December 7, 2003.

18. Shawn Ryan and Adam Fierro, "Safe," second revision (pink), *The Shield*, Nov. 12, 2003.

19. Darlene Lieblich Tipton, Standards and Practices email to the producers of *The Shield*, Dec. 4, 2003, re: "Slipknot," written by Kurt Sutter, aired May 4, 2004.

20. Neil Landau, *TV Outside the Box: Trailblazing in the Digital Television Revolution* (New York: Focal Press, 2016), 313.

21. Ibid., 92.

22. Ryan interview.

23. Jennifer Seata, interview by Kevin Sandler, Oct. 23, 2008.

24. Craig Yahata, interview by Daniel Bernardi and Kevin Sandler, Oct. 25, 2007.

25. Bernardi and Sandler, "Tonage."

26. Ironically, 20th Century Fox, the producer of *The X-Files*, was sued by the show's star David Duchovny in August 1999 for allegedly selling the rights to the show for below-market prices to the Fox Broadcasting Company, FX, and the Fox-owned-and-operated station group. By not seeking the highest bid in a competitive auction, Duchovny claimed that the studio cheated him out of millions of dollars. The lawsuit was settled out of court in Duchovny's favor in 2001.

27. Spike Lee made a documentary on this very incident in 1997 entitled *Four Little Girls*.

28. Peter Liguori, interview by Kevin Sandler, March 19, 2008.

29. Shawn Ryan and Scott Brazil, "Character Description," May 31, 2001.

30. Ibid.

31. Deborah Aquila and Tricia Wood, memorandum to All Concerned, May 15, 2001.

32. Michael Chiklis, interview by Daniel Bernardi and Kevin Sandler, Oct. 23, 2007.

33. Peter Liguori, quoted in Bernard Weinraub, "Police Show Has Humans, Not Heroes; in FX's Hit 'The Shield,' Means Justify Ends," *New York Times*, April 3, 2002.

34. Peter Liguori, quoted in John Leonard, "Bad Cop, Worse Cop: Glenn Close Joins *The Shield*, Giving the Treacherous Vic Mackey His Own Lady Macbeth," *New York Magazine*, March 7, 2007, http://nymag.com/nymetro/arts/tv/reviews/11458/.

35. "Liguori Names Kevin Reilly President of Entertainment, FX," Market Wire, June 24, 2010.

36. "The Barn" was, according to FX memos, Ryan's preferred title. The network resisted the title, however, coming up with many alternatives. Some were on the nose, such as "At What Price Justice?" and "Gang of Bands?" Others were ironic, such as "LA's Finest" and "Badge of Honor." They eventually settled for "The Shield" as both a genre indicator as well as a subtle metaphor (who was the shield protecting?). Found in Edin Zane to Kevin Reilly and Gerard Bocaccio, interoffice memo, Sept. 25, 2001.

37. Jay Karnes, interview by Daniel Bernardi and Kevin Sandler, May 20, 2008.

38. FX and FTVS to Shawn Ryan, Scott Brazil, and Clark Johnson, correspondence, July 9, 2001.

39. Ibid. An interoffice memo from FX's Standards and Practices Department dated June 5, 2001, also requested the omission of the word *fuck* found in the May 31, 2001, draft of the script. It also advised: "when filming the naked woman lying on her back, do not actually show her breasts." This was repeated in a March 18, 2001, memo. Her breasts were shown, albeit a bit out of focus.

40. Michael Speier, "Review: 'The Shield,'" *Variety*, March 10, 2002, http://variety.com/2002/tv/reviews/the-shield-6-1200550906/"; James Poniewozik, "New Cops on the Beat," *Time*, June 10, 2002, http://content.time.com/time/subscriber/article/0,33009,1002616,00.html"; Caryn James, "Television Review; An Undercover Cop Crosses the Moral Line," *New York Times*, March 12, 2002, www.nytimes.com/2002/03/12/arts/television-review-an-undercover-cop-crosses-the-moral-line.html.

41. Ryan interview.

42. John Landgraf, interview by Daniel Bernardi and Kevin Sandler, Oct. 23, 2007.

43. Jason Mittell, "Narrative Complexity in Contemporary American Television," *Velvet Light Trap* 58, no. 1 (2006): 29–40, 31.

44. Prior to *The Shield* Ryan served as an executive producer and writer on *Angel* (1999–2004) and a writer for *Nash Bridges* (1996–2001).

45. Scholars generally use the term *postnetwork era* to differentiate US television from the era of the three dominant networks from the 1950s to mid-1980s. *Postnetwork* suggests a multichannel universe driven by technological, social, and economic shifts in which narrowcasting, DVRs, high-speed Internet,

generated content, time-shifting, and repurposing have replaced the traditional, linear, model of broadcasting. Amanda D. Lotz further differentiates this period, identifying the mid-1980s to circa 2005 as the "multi-channel transition" and after 2005 as the "post-network era." See Amanda D. Lotz, *The Television Will Be Revolutionized* (New York: New York University Press, 2007), 7–19.

46. Maureen Ryan, "Why *The Sopranos* Is the Most Influential TV Drama Ever," *Chicago Tribune*, April 1, 2007.

47. David Thorburn, "*The Sopranos*," in *The Essential HBO Reader*, ed. Gary R. Edgerton and Jeffrey P. Jones (Lexington: University Press of Kentucky, 2008), 68. In addition to numerous trade publications on *The Sopranos*, other academic books include Dana Polan, *The Sopranos* (Durham, NC: Duke University Press, 2009); Richard Greene and Peter Vernezze, eds., *"The Sopranos" and Philosophy: I Kill Therefore I Am* (Chicago: Open Court, 2004); David Lavery, ed., *Reading "The Sopranos": Hit TV from HBO* (London: I.B. Tauris, 2006); David Lavery, ed., *This Thing of Ours: Investigating "The Sopranos"* (New York: Columbia University Press, 2002); Maurice Yacower, *"The Sopranos" on the Couch: Analyzing Television's Greatest Series* (New York: Continuum, 2002). The number of books on the series does point to a critical and popular consensus on its cultural importance.

48. See Gary R. Edgerton, "Introduction: A Brief History of HBO," in *The Essential HBO Reader*, ed. Gary R. Edgerton and Jeffrey P. Jones (Lexington: University Press of Kentucky, 2008), 12.

49. Polan, *The Sopranos*, 91–95.

50. Lotz, *The Television Will Be Revolutionized*, 225, 230.

51. John Thornton Caldwell, *Production Culture: Industrial Reflexivity and Critical Practice in Film and Television* (Durham, NC: Duke University Press, 2008), 174.

52. Journal articles include Mike Chopra-Gant, "The Law of the Father, the Law of the Land: Power, Gender, and Race in *The Shield*," *Journal of American Studies* 41 (2007): 659–73; Karyn Riddle, "Always on My Mind: Exploring How Frequent, Recent, and Vivid Television Portrayals Are Used in the Formation of Social Reality Judgments," *Media Psychology* 13 (2010): 155–79; Brenton J. Malin, "Viral Manhood: Niche Marketing, Hard-Boiled Detectives and the Economics of Masculinity," *Media, Culture & Society* 32, no. 3 (2010): 373–89; and Jim Craine, "Virtualizing Los Angeles: Pierre Levy, *The Shield*, and http://theshieldrap.proboards45.com/," *GeoJournal* 74 (2009): 235–43. Essay chapters include Cecil Greek, "The Big City Rogue Cop as Monster: Images of NYPD and LAPD," in *Monsters in and among Us: Toward a Gothic Criminality*, ed. Caroline Joan (Kay) Picart and Cecil Greek (Madison, WI: Fairleigh Dickinson University Press, 2007), 164–98; and Robin R. Means Coleman and Jasmine Nicole Cobb, "*Training Day* and *The Shield*: Evil Cops and the Taint of Blackness," in *The Changing Face of Evil in Film and Television*, ed. Martin F. Norden (Amsterdam: Rodopi, 2007), 101–23. Pamela Hill Nettleton has an unpublished dissertation entitled "Rescuing Men: The New Television Masculinity in *Rescue Me, Nip/Tuck, The Shield, Boston Legal,* and *Dexter*" (University of Minnesota, 2009); and

Amanda D. Lotz presented a paper at the International Communication Association annual conference in 2007 entitled "Neither Hero nor Antihero: The Contest of Hegemonic Masculinity in U.S. Cable Dramas."

53. Malin, "Viral Manhood," 377.

54. Internet Movie Database, www.imdb.com/title/tt0699518/.

55. Brandon Nowalk, *The Shield (Classic):* "Mum"/"Posse Up," A.V. Club, July 16, 2013, www.avclub.com/tvclub/the-shield-classic-mumposse-up-99813.

56. Shooting schedule for "Mum," Oct. 24, 2003.

57. Craig Sunderland, Standards and Practices, to the producers of *The Shield*, email re: "Mum" shooting script white draft, Oct. 12, 2003.

58. Craig Sunderland, Standards and Practices, to the producers of *The Shield*, email re: "Mum" 1st revision script blue draft, Oct. 20, 2003.

59. Neil Klasky, Standards and Practices, to the producers of *The Shield*, email re: "Mum" 2nd revision pink pages, Oct. 22, 2003.

60. Craig Sunderland, Standards and Practices, to the producers of *The Shield*, email re: "Mum" 3rd revision yellow draft, Oct. 23, 2003.

61. Shawn Ryan to Darlene Lieblich Tipton, email re: "Posse Up"—Network/Studio cassette dated 12/8/03, Dec. 9, 2003.

62. Darlene Lieblich Tipton to Shawn Ryan, email re: "Posse Up"—Network/Studio cassette dated 12/8/03, Dec. 9, 2003. The email was sent four minutes after Ryan's initial response.

63. *The Unit* was, in fact, picked up for a fourth season. *The Oaks*, however, was unsuccessful.

CHAPTER 4. NEW MARKETS AND MICROBUDGETS

1. Ben Beaumont-Thomas, "Why the Manic Pixie Dream Girl Must Never Return," *Guardian*, July 16, 2014, www.theguardian.com/film/filmblog/2014/jul/16/why-the-manic-pixie-dream-girl-must-never-return.

2. Todd McCarthy, "Garden State," *Daily Variety*, Jan. 18, 2004.

3. "Garden State," Box Office Mojo, www.boxofficemojo.com/movies/?id=gardenstate.htm.

4. "Garden State," Rotten Tomatoes, www.rottentomatoes.com/m/garden_state/.

5. Roger Ebert, "Garden State," RogerEbert.com, August 6, 2004, www.rogerebert.com/reviews/garden-state-2004.

6. Michael Nordine, "20 Worst Hipster Movies of All Time," *LA Weekly*, July 17, 2014, www.laweekly.com/arts/20-worst-hipster-movies-of-all-time-4835099.

7. Christian R. Allen, Facebook discussion with Julian Hoxter, April 29, 2016 (quoted by permission).

8. "Indiewood," *Wikipedia*, https://en.wikipedia.org/wiki/Indiewood (emphasis added).

9. Michel Foucault, "What Is an Author?" in *Language, Counter-Memory, Practice*, ed. Donald F. Bouchard, trans. Donald F. Bouchard and Sherry Simon (Ithaca, NY: Cornell University Press, 1977), 124–27.

10. Yannis Tzioumakis, *American Independent Cinema* (London: I.B. Tauris, 2005), 2.

11. Annette Insdorf, "Ordinary People, European Style: How to Spot an Independent Feature," *American Film* 6, no. 10 (1981): 57–60.

12. William Goldman, *Which Lie Did I Tell? More Adventures in the Screen Trade* (New York: Vintage, 2001).

13. In this light a case can be made that the academic discourse surrounding "independent cinema" functions to support the auteur theory of film studies that was fast falling out of academic style by the 1970s and 1980s.

14. Geoff King, *Indie 2.0: Change and Continuity in Contemporary American Indie Film* (New York: Columbia University Press, 2014), 7.

15. Pamela Gray, interview by Julian Hoxter, June 15, 2015.

16. Tzioumakis, *American Independent Cinema*, 13.

17. Yannis Tzioumakis, *Hollywood's Indies: Classics Divisions, Specialty Labels and the American Film Market* (Edinburgh: Edinburgh University Press, 2012), 12.

18. King, *Indie 2.0*, 3.

19. Robert Moreland, interview by Julian Hoxter, June 19, 2015.

20. Miranda Banks, *The Writers: A History of American Screenwriters and Their Guild* (New Brunswick, NJ: Rutgers University Press, 2015), 12.

21. Quoted in Lisa Rosen, "Getting It Made: Pamela Gray's Career of Conviction," *Written By*, Nov./Dec. 2010, 39–41.

22. Pamela Gray, interview by Julian Hoxter, June 19, 2015. Unless otherwise indicated, all subsequent quotations attributed to Gray in this section are from this interview.

23. For a fuller discussion of the matter from the WGA perspective see the following (redacted) arbitration decision: https://my.wgaw.org/uploadedfiles/legal/arbitration.pdf.

24. Quoted in Dalya Alberge, "Film Bosses Accused of Mutilating Scripts and Pushing Out Writing Talent," *Guardian*, Jan. 10, 2015.

25. "WGA Screenwriters: In Meetings with Studio Chiefs and Executives, the Guild Presents Data from the 2011 Screenwriter Survey to Take Aim at Prewrites, Rewrites, Late Pay and Other Flagrant Practices," *Writers Guild of America West*, press release, June 6, 2013.

26. Melissa Silverstein, "Roll the Credits on Chick Flicks," *Washington Post*, April 19, 2012.

27. Anthony D'Alessandro, "'Inside Out' Takes the Lead over 'Terminator Genisys,' 'Magic Mike XXL,' on Thursday," *Deadline Hollywood*, July 3, 2015.

28. Alberge, "Film Bosses Accused."

29. Richard Verrier, "WGA Survey: Screenwriters Are Gravitating to the Small Screen," *Los Angeles Times*, Sept. 25, 2015.

30. Banks, *The Writers*, 231.

31. Moreland interview, June 19, 2015. Unless otherwise indicated, all subsequent quotations attributed to Moreland in this section are from this interview.

32. Winner of the "Best TV Pilot" award from the World Animation Celebration 2001.

33. Harvey Deneroff, "Tooning In," *Hollywood Reporter Animation Special Issue*, Jan. 22, 2001.

34. Dylan Callaghan, "Fine-Tooning: The Cyclical Business of Small-Screen Animation Is Slowly Making a Turn toward the Independents," *Hollywood Reporter Animation Special Issue*, Jan. 22, 2002.

35. Charles Solomon, "For Good Animation, It's Always a Question of Character," *Los Angeles Times*, May 31, 2000.

36. The figures on *Toy Story* are from Tino Balio, *Hollywood in the New Millennium* (London: BFI, 2013), 30. By 2009, as Balio notes, "technical standards for digital projection and a method of financing to cover the conversion had been found. The tipping point occurred in 2009, when the number of screens with digital projection reached 16,000 nationwide. Of that number 3,500 screens were equipped to show 3-D" (32).

37. Mercedes Milligan, "Star Voicers Join Graverobber's 'Beef Sumo' Project," *Animation Magazine*, May 5, 2015, www.animationmagazine.net/tv/star-voicers-join-graverobbers-beef-sumo-project/.

38. Richard Verrier, "The Little Guy Gets a Piece of the Animation Action," *Los Angeles Times*, June 19, 2005.

39. Quoted in Deneroff, "Tooning In."

40. Quoted in Paula Parisi, "Toon Time," *Hollywood Reporter Animation Special Issue*, Jan. 25, 2000, S24–26.

41. Wendy Jackson Hall, "Content Providers Question Next Big Move," *Variety*, Nov. 10, 2000, A4.

42. Andrew Blankstein, "As Studios Shift Focus, Animator Prospects Dim," *Los Angeles Times*, May 24, 2000, http://articles.latimes.com/2000/may/24/business/fi-33339.

43. David Bloom, "Indie Animators Try to Go the Feature Route," *Variety*, June 9, 2003.

44. Ben Fritz, "Budget Toons Prove Biggest Winners," *Variety*, Dec. 14, 2006.

45. Peter Debruge, "Cutting Corners: Indie-Style Producers Do without Pipelines," *Variety*, June 2, 2008.

46. Quoted in Callaghan, "Fine Tooning."

47. Robert Hofler, "Playing by the Book: Scribe Trio Keep Copyrights to Toon Tuners," *Variety*, June 22, 2005.

48. Quoted in ibid.

49. Moreland cites this example: "Joshua Sternin (*Rio*, 2011), is a TV show writer, a successful guy, and with his writing partner he's also done studio and independent features. People like him, at the top, they're just getting a box-office bonus. They are not getting residual payments on those franchises that are evergreen money sources, because there's always a new crop of six year olds [to refresh the audience]. It's just not a way for writers to get rich."

50. Writing in *Variety* in 2012, David S. Cohen noted that despite Disney's silo approach, the studio pressured Pixar to produce sequels, something it had

never done before becoming a Disney subsidiary. In addition, he suggested that the brain trust approach "works well when there are two or three movies in production but is much harder to implement when there are eight or nine movies in the pipeline." David S. Cohen, "Lucasfilm Could Face the Pixar Problem," *Variety*, Nov. 8, 2012.

51. F.X. Feeney, "Brad the Bard," *Written By: The Magazine of the Writers Guild of America, West*, Summer 2008, 56.

52. Debruge, "Cutting Corners."

53. See King, *Indie 2.0*, esp. chap. 3.

54. Julian Hoxter, *The Pleasures of Structure: Learning Screenwriting through Case Studies* (New York: Bloomsbury Academic, 2015), 59.

55. "In Focus: Travis Mathews and Keith Wilson on *Oscillate Wildly*," *SF Film Society Blog*, July 9, 2014.

56. Julian Hoxter worked as a story consultant on *I Want Your Love*, *Interior. Leather Bar*, and *Oscillate Wildly* and has collaborated with Mathews on other writing projects.

57. *BUTT Magazine*, www.buttmagazine.com/information/. The magazine's core readership was described by one blogger as "scruffy, impoverished, underexercised gay intellectuals." Joe Clark, "Quasi-Amateur Art Porn of Scruffy, Impoverished, Underexercised Readers of 'Butt' Magazine," Metafilter.com, April 25, 2010.

58. Travis Mathews, "I Want Your Love," unpublished screenplay, 2011.

59. Scott MacDonald, ed., *Screen Writing: Texts and Scripts from Independent Films* (Berkeley: University of California Press, 1995).

60. For more on the economics of sex in cinema see, for example, Edward Jay Epstein, *The Hollywood Economist 2.0: The Hidden Financial Reality behind the Movies* (New York: Melville House, 2012).

61. Travis Mathews, interview by Julian Hoxter, Nov. 6, 2011. Unless otherwise indicated, all subsequent quotations attributed to Mathews in this section are from this interview.

62. Mathews, "I Want Your Love." Characters' names in these and the following examples from the unpublished screenplay have been changed to their final names in the released movie.

63. Ibid.

64. Joe Eszterhas, "Basic Instinct," shooting script, 1992. Scripts Collection (Unpublished), Margaret Herrick Library, Academy of Motion Picture Arts and Sciences (hereafter Herrick Library). The repeated use of ellipsis is in the original.

65. This is not to suggest that nonheteronormative pleasures are unavailable to a potential viewer but rather that a straight male perspective is implied.

66. Milo Addica and Will Rokos, "Monster's Ball," shooting script, 2001. Scripts Collection (Unpublished), Herrick Library.

67. Adrian Hennigan, "Interview with Michael Winterbottom," www.bbc.co.uk/films/2005/03/03/michael_winterbottom_9_songs_interview.shtml.

68. Roger Ebert, "9 Songs," RogerEbert.com, August 25, 2005, www.rogerebert.com/reviews/9-songs-2005.

69. Philip French, "Where's the Soap?" *Guardian,* March 13, 2005, www.theguardian.com/film/2005/mar/13/philipfrench.

70. Linda Williams, *Screening Sex* (Durham, NC: Duke University Press, 2008), 261.

71. We would also take issue with *Wikipedia*'s assumption that all independent movies are feature-length films.

72. Keith Wilson, quoted in "In Focus" (see note 55 above).

CHAPTER 5. SCREENWRITER 2.0

1. In the video games community the term *meta* refers to the trends and tactics that successful players are adopting to win at a given time in a game's development. In *Hearthstone,* for example, as new digital cards are released and as players are seen to have success in tournaments with particular combinations of cards and strategies in using them, the way the game is usually played changes. In another online game, *World of Tanks,* the evolving meta is more about changes in how players are using the abilities of their avatar vehicles and in how they are exploiting the terrain of the digital maps on which the game is played.

2. In *World of Warcraft* a "guild" refers to a group of online friends and fellow players who team up to defeat the game's boss encounters and undertake other in-game tasks that require multiple characters to complete.

3. "Leeroy Jenkins—A Rough Go," www.youtube.com/watch?v=on_6AVyMwXI.

4. See, e.g., Joel Warner, "The Legend of Leeroy Jenkins," Westword, March 8, 2007, www.westword.com/news/the-legend-of-leeroy-jenkins-5091880.

5. The product blurb for the "Leeroy" character expansion for *Arcadia Quest* describes him thus: "Leeroy is known for his startling, epic charges. Monsters are often so stunned that they simply drop their defenses. Leeroy never quite understood the need for advanced tactics and battle strategies."

6. *Wikipedia,* wikipedia.org/wiki/Leeroy_Jenkins.

7. Will Fulton, "Leeroy Jenkins Might Make an Appearance in the Warcraft Movie," *Digital Trends,* May 20, 2015, www.digitaltrends.com/movies/leeroy-jenkins-warcraft-movie/.

8. Celia Pearce defines the ludisphere as "the larger framework of all networked play spaces on the Internet, as well as within the larger context of the 'real world.'" Celia Pearce, *Communities of Play: Emergent Cultures in Multiplayer Games and Virtual Worlds* (Cambridge, MA: MIT Press, 2011), 137.

9. Stephen Johnson, *Emergence: The Connected Lives of Ants, Brains, Cities and Software* (New York: Scribner, 2001), 18.

10. "Iron Man leveling" involves advancing a character through the game while imposing strict regimes of activity that make the process harder. One version involves never using advantageous weapons and equipment while leveling. The hardest version requires a character to rise to maximum level without dying (the game resurrects a character when it dies).

11. For a more detailed exegesis see Pearce, *Communities of Play*.

12. For a full discussion of movie and video game convergence at the level of the institution see Robert Alan Brookey, *Hollywood Gamers: Digital Convergence in the Film and Video Game Industries* (Bloomington: Indiana University Press, 2010).

13. Ibid., 77–78.

14. Deborah Todd, "For the Love of Fun: Hollywood Is Merging with the Game Industry. Are You Ready?" *Written By*, Jan. 2009, 44.

15. Jonathan Gray, "In the Game: The Creative and Textual Constraints of Licensed Video Games," in *Wired TV: Laboring over an Interactive Future*, ed. Denise Mann and Derek Johnson (New Brunswick, NJ: Rutgers University Press, 2014), 56.

16. Michael Wellenreiter, "Screenwriting and Authorial Control in Narrative Video Games," *Journal of Screenwriting* 6, no. 3 (2015): 343–61, doi: 10.1386/josc.6.3.343_1. 347.

17. Ian Bogost, *Persuasive Games: The Expressive Power of Videogames* (Cambridge, MA: MIT Press, 2007), 28–29.

18. Susan Christopherson, "Labor: The Effects of Media Concentration on the Film and Television Workforce," in *The Contemporary Hollywood Film Industry*, ed. Paul McDonald and Janet Wasko (New York: Wiley-Blackwell, 2008), 162.

19. Miranda Banks, *The Writers: A History of American Screenwriters and Their Guild* (New Brunswick, NJ: Rutgers University Press, 2015), 198.

20. Quoted in Amanda N'Duka, "Legendary Serves Up 'Warcraft,' 'Crimson Peak,' 'Krampus'—Comic Con," *Deadline Hollywood*, July 11, 2015, http://deadline.com/2015/07/warcraft-crimson-peak-krampas-legendary-pictures-comic-con-1201474492/.

21. We note, in passing, the obvious—and all too common—omission of the other *Warcraft* writers from Foster's compliment. This omission includes the credited contribution of Chris Metzen, who, as senior vice president of story and franchise development at Blizzard, has also been responsible for much of the creative world and story development on the *Warcraft* gaming franchise for more than a decade and is well known to fans and players of the games.

22. Gamers do often critique games for trying to be too much like movies. However, this is a relatively marginal debate in comparison with the broader assumption of cultural value.

23. Michael Z. Newman and Elana Levine, *Legitimating Television: Media Convergence and Cultural Status* (New York: Routledge, 2012), 5.

24. Ibid., 3, 5.

25. Suzanne Oshry, "Getting in the Game," *Written By*, Oct. 2004, 52.

26. "Interactive Writing: A Roundtable in Cyberspace," *Journal of the Writers Guild of America, West* (Feb. 1996): 28–29.

27. For a full discussion see Banks, *The Writers*, 117–54.

28. Ibid., 137.

29. "Interactive Writing," 29.

30. Philip Dunne, "An Essay on Dignity," *Screen Writer*, Dec. 1945, 37. Dunne was responding to Raymond Chandler, "Writers in Hollywood," *Atlantic Monthly*, Nov. 1945, 50–54.

31. "Interactive Writing," 22. Note also that the publication began using the term *new media* alongside *interactive* from 1998.

32. Ibid.

33. Ibid.

34. The market for video games grew from $7 billion in 2003 to a reported $22.41 billion in 2014. See *Essential Facts about the Computer and Video Game Industry* (Washington: Entertainment Software Association, 2015), 12–13, www.theesa.com/wp-content/uploads/2015/04/ESA-Essential-Facts-2015.pdf.

35. Robert Denton Bryant and Keith Giglio, *Slay the Dragon: Writing Great Stories for Video Games* (Studio City, CA: Michael Wiese Productions, 2015).

36. Todd, "For the Love of Fun," 48.

37. "Videogame Writers Caucus," (mission statement), *Writers Guild of America, West*, www.wga.org/the-guild/going-guild/caucuses/videogame-writers-caucus.

38. Todd, "For the Love of Fun," 46.

39. The first WGA Videogame Writing Award was presented to Dave Ellis and Adam Cogan for *Dead Head Fred* (Vicious Cycle Software, 2007).

40. "Videogame Writers Caucus," www.wga.org/the-guild/going-guild/caucuses/videogame-writers-caucus (emphasis added).

41. Quoted in Kevin Ott, "The Best of Us," *Written By*, Jan. 2015, 6.

42. Here we are in accord with Liam Burke's persuasive account of the substantiated status of comic book adaptations (and movies with similar heightened aesthetics) as a discrete genre. See Liam Burke, *The Comic Book Film Adaptation* (Jackson: University Press of Mississippi, 2015).

43. Paul Tassi, "The WGA's Baffling Video Game Writing Award," *Forbes*, Feb. 21, 2012, www.forbes.com/sites/insertcoin/2012/02/21/the-wgas-baffling-video-game-writing-award/#4c2042427c6f.

44. See Alec Meer, "Deus Ex: Franchise Evolution," interview of Mary De Marle, *Gamesindustry.biz*, Feb. 3, 2011.

45. Alec Meer, "The WGA's Micah Wright Defends Its Game Writing Award, *Gamesindustry.biz*, Feb. 4, 2011.

46. WGAW publicity material, *Take Your Game to the Next Level: Videogames Guide*, www.wga.org/uploadedfiles/writers_resources/vwc_guide.pdf.

47. Oshry, "Getting in the Game," 55.

48. Ibid.

49. Terry Borst and Deborah Todd, "Strange Days: A Forecast for the Millennium," *Written By*, Dec./Jan. 1998, 83.

50. Quoted in Banks, *The Writers*, 206.

51. F.X. Feeney, "The Game's The Thing: Game-Writing and Reinventing Story for Fun and Profit," *Written By*, June/July 2009, 24.

52. Ibid.
53. Steve Ince, "Game Writing Examples," Gamewriting.org, http://gamewriting.org/game-writing-examples/.
54. Aphra Kerr, *The Business and Culture of Video Games* (London: Sage, 2006).
55. Frampton's Twitch channel can be found at www.twitch.tv/quickybaby.
56. See, e.g., www.reddit.com/r/wow/comments/2i50f3/warlords_of_metzen/. This particular tradition also links Metzen to old-school *World of Warcraft* in-game "Barrens chat" jokes about Chuck Norris.
57. Cf. Henry Jenkins, *Fans, Bloggers and Gamers: Media Consumers in a Digital Age* (New York: New York University Press, 2007); and Brookey, *Hollywood Gamers*.
58. Adrienne Parks, "Terry Borst: Cowriter of *Wing Commander III & IV* Takes Flight," *Journal of the Writers Guild of America, West* (Feb. 1996): 32–33.
59. Mark J.P. Wolf, "Abstraction in Video Games," in *The Video Game Theory Reader*, ed. Mark J.P. Wolf and Bernard Perron (New York: Routledge, 2003), 47–65.
60. Brookey, *Hollywood Gamers*, 65.
61. Ibid., 34.
62. Banks, *The Writers*, 206–7.
63. Feeney, "The Game's the Thing," 25.
64. Ibid., 25, 50.
65. Raphael Chandler, "Organizing and Formatting Game Dialogue," Gamesutra.com, www.gamasutra.com/view/feature/130874.
66. Ibid., www.gamasutra.com/view/feature/130874/organizing_and_formatting_game_.php?page=2.
67. Stephen E. Dinehart IV, "Writing for 'Company of Heroes: Opposing Fronts,'" NarrativeDesign.org, http://narrativedesign.org/2008/07/writing-for-company-of-heroes-opposing-fronts/ (page removed).
68. Ibid.
69. Ibid.
70. Feeney, "The Game's the Thing," 50.
71. Ibid., 24.
72. Quoted in Denis Faye, "Pinboard Cowgirl," *Written By*, Feb./March 2010, 12.
73. Ibid.
74. Quoted in Oshry, "Getting in the Game," 53.
75. Quoted in ibid., 54.
76. Quoted in F.X. Feeney, "Games Player," *Written By*, Jan. 2009, 12.
77. Quoted in Oshry, "Getting in the Game," 54.
78. Quoted in Feeney, "The Game's the Thing," 51.
79. Quoted in Oshry, "Getting in the Game," 54.
80. Feeney, "The Game's the Thing," 10.
81. Quoted in Feeney, "Games Player," 52.
82. Parks, "Terry Borst," 34.

83. Quoted in Denis Faye, "Take 5: One Singular Sensation," *Written By*, Feb./March 2011, 22.
84. Ibid.
85. Wellenreiter, "Screenwriting and Authorial Control," 352.

CONCLUSION

1. Tips during Quickybaby's stream run to around $5 on average and happen every few minutes. Not infrequently, however, someone pays $20 to $30, and tips of over $100 are uncommon but not unheard of. Over the course of multiple five-hour streams the tip money adds up, but it is supplemental to advertising and subscription revenues for the streamer.

2. Quickybaby maintains a level of creative independence, despite receiving benefits of this kind from Wargaming. His review of the Sentinel was very negative; his criticisms intended both to warn fellow players against purchasing it in its current form and as a prompt to Wargaming to improve it before or after release.

3. See Clive Davies-Frayne, "ALT-SCRIPT: How Digital Filmmaking Destroyed Screenwriting," *Script*, March 13, 2015, www.scriptmag.com/features/career-features/alt-script-digital-filmmaking-destroyed-screenwriting.

4. By way of additional context, we have found it illustrative to conceptualize the media as still convergent, rather than "postconvergent." Although there is certainly an argument to be made that some media environments do exist in a postconvergent state, we believe that they are at the margins of the industry. At the obvious risk of being reductive, we are examining the broad development of a professional craft and the perspectives of its practitioners, not, for example, the technologies of embodiment in 3-D MultiUser Virtual Environments.

5. Sister Hibiscus, a.k.a. Sister Lotus or Shi Hengxia, is a Chinese Internet celebrity who became famous for posting about her thwarted educational and romantic aspirations beginning in 2005. She became an object of controversy because of her attitudes and an object of ridicule to some because of her apparent obliviousness to her own narcissism.

6. See Geekandsundry.com/shows/tabletop/.

7. See https://en.wikipedia.org/wiki/Satine_Phoenix.

8. "Creating the Viral Web Series," *Writers Store*, www.writersstore.com/creating-the-viral-web-series/.

9. See Henry Jenkins, *Textual Poachers: Television Fans and Participatory Culture* (London: Routledge, 1992).

10. The same could be said for many more conventional microbudget filmmakers, for that matter.

11. Harrison Jacobs, "We Ranked YouTube's Biggest Stars by How Much Money They Make," *Business Insider*, March 10, 2014, www.businessinsider.com/richest-youtube-stars-2014-3?op=1.

12. Quoted in Marc Graser, "Legendary Buys Felicia Day's Geek and Sundry," *Variety*, August 4, 2014, www.variety.com/2014/digital/news

/legendary-buys-felicia-day-geek-sundry-1201275126/. According to *Variety,* at the time of the acquisition Geek and Sundry reported 1.4 million subscribers to its YouTube network and Hulu channel and more than twelve million followers on social media.

13. Deloitte LLP, "Digital Democracy Survey: A Multi-generational View of Consumer Technology, Media and Telecom Trends," 10th ed., 11, www2.deloitte.com/content/dam/Deloitte/us/Documents/technology-media-telecommunications/us-tmt-deloitte-digital-democracy-executive-summary.pdf.

14. David Lieberman, "What Does It Mean To 'Watch TV'? It's Complicated—Survey," *Deadline Hollywood,* March 22, 2016, http://deadline.com/2016/03/deloitte-consulting-digital-democracy-survey-tv-watching-1201724587/.

15. "Viktor Kislyi NA Q&A," interview by GamesBeat, cited in Rita Sobral's (a.k.a. RitaGamer) *World of Tanks* blog *Rita's Status Report,* March 24, 2016, ritastatusreport.live/2016/03/24/4839/.

16. "#REHASH," *South Park,* season 18, episode 9, Comedy Central, broadcast Dec. 3, 2014.

17. Quickybaby streams at www.twitch.tv/quickybaby. His YouTube channel can be found at www.youtube.com/user/QuickyBabyTV. Here we use the term *professional* to signify that Quickybaby makes his living primarily from his own content creation and from the opportunities his entrepreneurial celebrity have earned him, such as paid commentating at Wargaming's eSports events. We do not imply that the surface production values of his streams and videos are consistent with the current technical specifications of broadcast television, for example. On his own terms, however, and within the context of the online streaming arena, Quickybaby is evidently concerned to provide material of the highest quality. Indeed, he makes the technical improvement of his personal computers and streaming equipment part of the interactive meta of his discussions. He even produces "build" videos for his fans when he upgrades his gear. Most recently, he requested feedback from his community about whether a new microphone was improving the sound quality of commentary on his videos.

18. For context, Wargaming reported more than one hundred million registered players of *World of Tanks* in 2014. Of course, the number of active players will be significantly fewer than that total, but the large size of the game's community of play can be appreciated from that figure. See (inter alia) Jef Reahard, "Wargaming Claims over 100 Million Registered Users," Engadget, August 13, 2014, www.engadget.com/2014/08/13/wargamings-cross-platform-portfolio-boasts-over-100-million-reg/. In 2015 Twitch announced that it had in excess of 1.5 million broadcasters and one hundred million visitors per month. Sarah E. Needleman, "Twitch's Viewers Reach 100 Million a Month," *Wall Street Journal,* Jan. 29, 2015, blogs.wsj.com/digits/digits/2015/01/29/twitchs-viewers-reach-100-million-a-month/. Quickybaby benefits from Twitch's Partner Program for popular streamers, which allows him a favorable split of advertising revenues.

19. PewDiePie has developed a limited crossover appeal as a kind of exemplar or "go-to" streamer for other media. As we noted above, PewDiePie appeared on *South Park*. He also appeared on the Clueless Gamer channel, playing and reviewing the new game *Far Cry Primal* with Conan O'Brien.

20. Frampton is still positive about his scholarly background despite the recent shift in his career path. He often offers detailed and supportive advice in discussion with his younger fans who are contemplating their own academic futures.

21. Known by their in-game identities, these collaborators have included QB's wife, PeppyPepper; his brother, Zaonce; his best friend, Ikzor, "The King of Norway"; fellow British streamer The Mighty Jingles; Wargaming EU employee Ectar; QSF team leader Roastedlemon; as well as fellow players, his Twitch chat moderators, and community members M4Real, Philippopoulos, Greenman, and many others.

22. *Laps around Dalaran* (podcast), FatBoss TV, www.youtube.com/playlist?list=PLu3dsh6Bc2HVOduLAyhI_t41Uof6FaTwj.

23. Tuskeh, "Professional Long-Form Guides," YouTube, www.youtube.com/user/tuskehgames/videos.

24. Wowhead, "Playlists," YouTube, www.youtube.com/user/Wowhead/playlists. The data miner and Wowhead manager, Perculia, joins Leeroy Jenkins in having her emergence reinscribed into the game, in this case with a gear item named after her: the epic ring "Perculia's Peculiar Signet."

25. Preach Gaming, YouTube, www.youtube.com/user/mikepreachwow.

26. For example, on April 7, 2016, QB showed his viewing audience the notes he had prepared for a recent YouTube video discussing in detail his perspective on why the "Rampage" game mode in *WoT* had failed.

27. TwitchCon Schedule, https://twitchstuff.3v.fi/twitchcon/.

28. For more information see, e.g., Dan Singer, "Twitch Fiction," *Experimental Television Lab*, http://etv.gatech.edu/2015/01/18/twitch-fiction/. *Twitch Plays Pokémon* was a 2014 experiment, conducted through a Twitch channel, to play a *Pokémon* video game via commands sent by users through Twitch chat.

29. Harry Mathias, *The Death and Rebirth of Cinema: Mastering the Art of Cinematography in the Digital Age* (Cardiff, CA: Waterfront, 2015), 295.

30. Loyola Marymount University, "Writing for the Screen," http://sftv.lmu.edu/academics/graduateprograms/writingforthescreen/; and Pepperdine University, "Master of Fine Arts in Writing for Screen and Television," https://seaver.pepperdine.edu/humanities/graduate/screenwriting/.

31. Here we make a broad distinction between the long-established prestige national film schools in Europe and Australia such as the Polish National Film School in Lodz and the National Film and Television School in the United Kingdom and those, such as the University of Westminster and Sheffield Hallam University, that have emerged in recent decades within the new university sector in the United Kingdom and elsewhere.

32. Thomas Kuhn, *The Structure of Scientific Revolutions*, 4th ed. (Chicago: University of Chicago Press, 2012).

33. University of Southern California, USC Cinematic Arts, http://cinema.usc.edu/writing/.

34. California State University, Fullerton, Department of Cinema and Television Arts, MFA in Screenwriting, http://communications.fullerton.edu/graduate_students/ (restricted access).

35. Sarah Mahan, *Facebook* discussion with Julian Hoxter, March 22, 2016 (written permission given to quote).

36. National University, "Master of Fine Arts in Professional Screenwriting," www.nu.edu/OurPrograms/School-of-Professional-Studies/Journalism-Film-and-Entertainment-Arts/Programs/MFAScreen.html.

37. Jennifer Hammett, one of our colleagues in the School of Cinema at San Francisco State University, is working on a book focused on short films for Rutgers University Press. Early drafts we have reviewed show that it promises to challenge the traditional structure placed on the short that are not actually found in compelling short films.

38. Not to be too defensive, Daniel Bernardi, although having been paid for screenwriting work, has never actually taught screenwriting. Julian Hoxter, a practicing screenwriter, teaches traditional story structure as well as scripting.

39. University of Texas at Austin, Radio-Television-Film, "Master of Fine Arts in Screenwriting," http://rtf.utexas.edu/graduate/mfa-screenwriting.

40. Neil Landau, *TV Outside the Box: Trailblazing in the Digital Television Revolution* (New York: Focal Press, 2016), 109.

Index

Aboud, John, 51–52
above-the-line workers, 12–13, 21–22, 81, 104
Abrams, J.J., 97
Abu Ghraib, 106
Abyss, The (1989), 93
academia, 11, 14, 219–20, 236, 242. *See also* film schools
Academy Awards, 120
action movies: *The Avengers* (2012) as, 94, 97–99; Black, Shane and, 28–29; as B movies, 68; conglomerate aesthetics and, 34; digital technologies and, 90; Eszterhas, Joe and, 28–29; formats and, 95–99; global markets and, 33; home video and, 146; Moreland, Robert and, 157; previsualization and, 94–95; redemptive endings and, 15–16; screenplays and, 90–93; spec scripts and, 71; spectacle and, 33–34, 90; studios and, 38; tentpole movies as, 71–72
active scene format, 205, 206*table*
Activision Blizzard, 186, 191, 210
Addica, Milo, 174
Adobe Premiere, 165
adolescent comedies, 2, 38
adventure films, 23, 71
advertising revenues, 57, 59–60, 111, 113, 114, 125, 225, 270n18
Afghanistan war, 106

AFI (American Film Institute), 5
Alcott, Todd, 159
Alice in Wonderland (2010), 72–73
Alien Isolation (game), 217
A-list writers, 42, 79, 82–84, 85, 86, 99, 241. *See also* individuals
Allen, Christian R., 140
Allen, Lindsey, 213
Alliance of Motion Picture and Television Producers. *See* AMPTP (Alliance of Motion Picture and Television Producers)
All in the Family (1971–79), 114
Alternative Screenwriting: Beyond the Hollywood Formula (Dancyger and Rush), 16
Altman, Robert, 27, 29
alt.screenwriters (column), 198–99
Amazon, 9, 49, 67, 113, 148
Amazon Studios, 67, 70
AMC, 114
American Pie 2 (2001), 68
AMPTP (Alliance of Motion Picture and Television Producers), 44–47, 49, 50–51, 53–54, 55, 57, 58–59, 152
amusement park rides, 23, 87. *See also* theme parks
Analyzing the Screenplay (Nelmes), 13–14
Anastasia (1997), 158
ancillary markets: character-driven dramas and, 36; comics and, 24, 37;

ancillary markets *(continued)*
digital technologies and, 58; Jenkins, Leeroy (character/meme) and, 183, 184; MBA (Minimum Basic Agreement) and, 44–45; media convergence and, 41; residuals and, 41, 45; revenues and, 67, 68; sexual content and, 170; *The Shield* (2002–8) and, 257n2; *Star Wars* (1977) and, 68–69; synergies and, 66; television and, 37; tentpole movies and, 62, 71–72, 73–74, 103; theme parks and, 66; toys and, 23, 66; video/games and, 23, 24, 36, 66, 183, 186; WGA strike (2007–8) and, 44, 50. *See also* cross-platform markets

Andrews, Brian, 94

Angelakis, Michael, 73–74

animation, 156–65; assignments and, 162; cable and, 160; Cartoon Network, 77; collaboration and, 161, 162–63; computer animation, 158–59, 160; conglomerates and, 158–59; convergence and, 156; crowd-funding and, 221; digital technologies and, 92; distribution and, 156, 159–60; DreamWorks Animation, 159, 161, 164; DVDs and, 160; economics and, 160; film schools and, 237; Fusco, John on, 161; Hollywood and, 158–59; home video and, 160; independent animation, 157, 158, 159, 160, 161, 163–64, 164–65; independent studios and, 160, 162–63; international markets and, 160, 161; Internet and, 156, 159–60, 161; major/studios and, 158–59, 162–63, 163–64, 165; Maras, Steven and, 164; markets and, 156–57, 158, 160; new/media and, 156–57, 158; online content/creators and, 156, 223; online distribution and, 159–60, 165, 221; outsourcing and, 159, 160; *Pacific Rim* (2013) and, 32; pipeline-free production model and, 160; Pixar and, 158–59; production and, 163–64; residuals and, 161, 263n49; revenues and, 160; screenplays and, 157, 158, 162–63; screenwriters and, 157, 160, 162; special-effects and, 92, 93; spec scripts and, 158; *Star Wars* (1977) and, 69; story/telling and, 158, 162, 163, 164; television and, 156, 161; tentpole movies and, 65, 71–72; 3-D and, 159; Vanguard Animation, 157, 160; *Variety* and, 163; video/games/writing and, 184, 205, 209–10, 212; Walt Disney Animation Studios, 72, 73, 263n50; WGA (Writers Guild of America) and, 55, 56, 161, 189; writing/drawing and, 163. *See also* Moreland, Robert; *individual titles*

Animation World Network (online magazine), 159

Animatrix, The (animated short), 9–10

Annenberg School for Communication and Journalism study (USC), 40

Annual Financial Report (2014) (WGA), 41

antiheroes, 103, 125

Ant Man (2015), 76

Antz (1998), 159

AOL–Time Warner, 67

Apple, 49–50

apprenticeship model, 9

Aquaman (2018), 78, 152

Arcadia Quest (board game), 183, 265n4

Aristotle, 15–16

Arndt, Michael, 69, 85

Aronofsky, Darren, 139, 142

Asian markets, 31, 32

assignments: animation and, 162; Gray, Pamela and, 149–50, 151, 153; A-list writers and, 83–84; new writers and, 60–61; spec scripts and, 100; studios and, 68, 88; sweepstakes pitching and, 78, 79–80; video/games writing and, 199; Writing Partners and, 85

Atlantic Monthly, 194

audiences: convergence and, 156; dramas and, 116; female audiences, 69–70, 154; four-quadrant audiences,

23, 69, 70; international audiences/markets and, 31, 32; Internet and, 114; ratings and, 114; Ryan, Shawn and, 115; sexual content and, 170; spectacle and, 72–73; television/showrunners and, 113–14, 114–15
August, John, 74, 82, 85
auteur theory, 12, 104, 107, 108, 262n13
authorship, 8, 13, 79, 141–42, 149, 161, 194, 200, 201–2, 203. *See also* copyright; IP (intellectual property); screenwriter credit
Authors League of America, 193
avant-garde cinema, 141
Avatar (2009), 31
A.V. Club, 127
Avellone, Chris, 200–201
Avengers, The (2012), 36, 37, 71, 87, 94, 97–99
Ayer, David, 119–20

backstories, 209, 213
Baghead (2008), 24
bake-offs, 151–52. *See also* sweepstakes pitching
Baldur's Gate (game), 202
Balio, Tino, 68, 263n36
Ballard, J.G., 241
Banks, Miranda, 13, 20–21, 22, 44, 149, 156, 190, 193, 203
Barbie (2017), 78
Barker, Cory, 110
Barthes, Roland, 104, 179, 245n8
Barton Fink (1991), 61, 62–64, 143
Basic Instinct (1992), 28–29, 174–75
Batman movies, 10, 23, 37, 38, 76–77, 217
Battleship (2012), 94
Battlestar Galactica (2004–9), 125
Bay, Michael, 35, 87, 94
Beacham, Travis, 32
Beaufoy, Simon, 69
Beaumont-Thomas, Ben, 139
Beauty and the Beast (1991), 158
Beef Sumo Show, The, 157, 164

Beer, Lindsey, 78
below-the-line workers, 12, 21–22, 52–53, 107–8, 115
Benchley, Peter, 68
Bendis, Brian Michael, 75
Benjamin, Robert, 145
Berg, Peter, 94
Berlinale Film Festival, 168
Berman, Alan, 52
Bernardi, Daniel, 83, 107, 115, 257n5
Bethesda Game Studios, 214
Beverly Hills Cop (1984), 81
BFA (Bachelor of Fine Arts), 238
Bicks, Jenny, 78
big-budget movies, 23, 31, 36, 99. *See also* blockbusters
Bigelow, Kathryn, 40
Big Lebowski, The (1998), 62
binge viewing, 114, 124, 226. *See also* streaming
BioWare, 186, 202, 211
Bird, Brad, 163
Black, Dustin Lance, 59
Black, Shane, 28–29, 94
blaxploitation films, 145
blind script deals, 86–87
Blizzard Entertainment, 182, 183, 185, 202, 266n21
blockbusters: character-driven dramas and, 36; independent cinema and, 144, 145; Jungian theory and, 15–16; as manic cinema, 34; multinational media companies and, 11–12; New Abnormal and, 70; redemptive endings and, 16; science fiction films as, 68; special-effects and, 34; storytelling and, 34; studios and, 38; tentpole movies and, 64
blogs, 51–52, 53, 110, 217, 251n56
Bloom, David, 160
Blouse Man, The (spec script), 150
Blue Sky Studios, 159
Blumhouse (production company), 146
Blu-ray, 44, 67
B movies, 64, 68, 70
board games, 223–24, 226, 236

276 / Index

Bochco, Steven, 109
Bogost, Ian, 189
Boon, Kevin Alexander, 13
Bordwell, David, 15
Borst, Terry, 198, 203, 212–13
Bourdieu, Pierre, 114–15
Bourne Ultimatum, The (2007), 80
Bowman, John, 50
box office, 10, 22, 30–33, 37, 67–68, 69, 74–75, 79, 248n5. *See also* domestic box office revenues
Brackett, Leigh, 40–41, 91
Bradbury, Ray, 182, 185–86
Brad Grey Television, 124
Braff, Zach, 139, 140, 142
brands, 71–72, 110, 114, 115–16, 117, 126, 134, 138, 257n1, 257n5
Bratz: Forever Diamondz, 205, 207–8
Brazil, Scott, 117
Breaking Bad (2008–13), 191–92
Brevoort, Tom, 37
Brillstein-Grey Entertainment, 124
Brinkman, Ron, 36
Broflovski, Ike, 228
Broken Steel (DLC), 214
Brontes and Rick, 170
Brookey, Robert Alan, 186–87, 194, 203
Brooklyn South (1997–8), 120
Brooks, James L., 114
Brosh, Allie, 224
Bruckheimer, Jerry, 73
Buckley, Dan, 75
budgets, 2, 36–37, 94, 108. *See also* big-budget movies; microbudget productions
Buffy the Vampire Slayer (1997–2003), 47–48, 106, 114, 116
Bujalski, Andrew, 166
Burke, Liam, 267n42
Burns, Scott, 80
business frame, 3, 4, 6–7, 11–12, 14, 28, 140, 164, 181, 242. *See also* Maras, Steven
Business Insider (website), 225
BUTT Magazine, 167, 264n57

cable: advertising revenues and, 125; animation and, 160; convergent cable, 137; convergent television and, 110; cultural legitimacy and, 191–92; digital distribution and, 58; dramas and, 23, 60, 116, 137, 220; FX Network and, 116–17, 123, 125; major studios and, 67; MBA (Minimum Basic Agreement) and, 44–45; mergers and, 67; *The Newsroom* (2012–14) and, 109; Parental Guidelines System and, 120; residuals and, 59; Ryan, Shawn and, 23; screenwriters and, 79, 221; *The Shield* (2002–8) and, 104, 108, 111, 122–23, 126, 220; social ills and, 191; *The Sopranos* (1999–2007) and, 125; Standards and Practices and, 113; television showrunners and, 108, 113, 114; 2014 negotiations (WGA) and, 59–60. *See also* individual networks
Caceres, Kurt, 133
Calderon, Wilmer, 133
Caldwell, John Thornton, 7, 14, 20–21, 28, 107, 108, 115, 126, 191, 242
California State University Fullerton, 239
Call of Duty (game), 227
Cameron, James, 31
Campbell, Joseph, 15
Cannes Film Festival, 24
Capital Cities/ABC, 67
capitalism, 10, 17–18, 19. *See also* hegemony
Captain America (2011), 36, 95
Carolin, Reid, 154
Carruth, Shane, 167
Cartoon Network, 77
Cassavetes, John, 146, 166
Cates, Gil, 57
CBS, 67, 115, 120, 124
CBS Films, 147
CCG (online collectible card game), 182
celebrities. *See* online celebrities
Chabon, Michael, 73

Chandler, Raphael, 204–5, 208
Chandler, Raymond, 194
Chandor, JC, 81
Chapman University, 236
character, 7, 11, 155, 168, 188, 200
character comedies, 38
character-driven dramas: ancillary markets and, 36; *The Avengers* (2012) and, 37; blockbusters and, 36; comic book movie genre and, 36, 37; females and, 147; *I Want Your Love* (2012) as, 171; mumblecore and, 166; screens and, 2, 70–71; *The Shield* (2002–8) and, 117; studios and, 33, 147; television and, 70–71, 220
characters, 212. *See also* Jenkins, Leeroy (character/meme)
Chase, David, 47–48
Chicago Tribune, 124–25
Chicken Big (Graves), 164
chick flicks, 154
Chiklis, Michael, 102, 105, 119, 121, 124
China, 31, 32, 237
Choose Your Own Adventure (novels), 233
Christopherson, Susan, 79, 190
Cinefex magazine, 94
cinema. *See* movies
CinemaScope, 31, 248n5
cinematization, 191, 197
circuit of culture, 19, 20, 47, 74, 115–16
class tensions, 42–43, 44, 53, 72, 235
Clements, Kim, 132–33
Close, Glen, 106–7
Cochran, Robert, 106
code, 185, 189, 200, 210, 211
Cody, Diablo, 78, 84
Coen brothers, 61, 62–64
coercion/consent, 10, 40, 242, 245n7
Cohen, David S., 263n50
collaboration: animation and, 161, 162–63; Mathews, Travis and, 167; movies and, 104; screenwriters and, 8, 74, 93, 155–56; story/telling and, 80; television/showrunners and, 83, 107–8, 155–56, 209; video/games/writing and, 200, 201–2, 209, 211; writers' collectives and, 84–86
Collider.com, 94
Columbia, 84, 85
Comcast, 67
comedies: adolescent comedies, 2, 38; character comedies, 38; film schools and, 238–39; Lear, Norman and, 114; new/screenwriters and, 23, 143; redemptive endings and, 15–16; sitcoms, 237, 238, 241; spec scripts and, 71; television comedies, 9; Universal Pictures and, 74. *See also* romantic comedies; *individual movies*; *individual shows*
Comedy Central, 120, 226
comic book franchises, 38. *See also* superhero franchises
comic book movie genre, 36–38, 74, 196, 267n42
comic book studios, 24. *See also individual studios*
Comic Con, 191
comics: ancillary markets and, 24, 37; Brosh, Allie, 224; cross-platform markets and, 37; cultural legitimacy and, 196; digital comic books, 224; Grant, Brea, 224; Hollywood and, 217; Jenkins, Leeroy (character/meme) and, 183; *Matrix* (1999) and, 9–10; National University and, 239; online content/creators and, 223; Phoenix, Satine, 224; screenwriters and, 8, 9, 196; *Secret Wars*, 37; *The Shield* (2002–8) and, 257n2; social ills and, 191; studios and, 24; superhero franchises and, 75; tentpole screenwriters and, 38; Whitta, Gary and, 187
Commish, The (1991–96), 124
common sense, 10, 73, 245n7
Company of Heroes series, 208
complex dramas, 23, 70. *See also* dramas; prestige dramas
computer animation, 158–59, 160

Computer Game Developers Conference, 195
Concrete Island (Ballard), 241
conglomerate aesthetics, 34–35
conglomerate media, 37, 236
conglomerates: animation and, 158–59; class tensions and the, 42–43; cross-platforms and, 44; digital distribution and, 55; economics and, 66; formulas and, 64; manic cinema and, 87; News Corporation, 116; new technologies and, 44; one-step deals and, 80; online content/creators and, 223; *The Player* (1991) and, 28; screenwriters/screenwriting and, 11, 66, 81, 99; studios and, 66; synergies and, 66–67, 74, 186; tentpole movies/paradigm and, 32, 61, 73, 74–75; transmedia marketing and, 10; video/games and, 186; Walt Disney Studios as, 73; WGA strike (2007–8) and, 46, 53, 54–55
conglomeration: creativity and, 29; cultural studies and, 18–19; *A History of the Screenplay* (Price) and, 14; Hollywood and, 242; political economy and, 17; screenwriters/screenwriting and, 10, 11, 29, 218–19; *Star Wars* (1977) and, 69
Conor, Bridget, 13, 28, 38, 88
consolidation, 29, 186, 198–99. *See also* media convergence; mergers
constraints/pressures, 2, 6, 9, 19, 38, 104
content creation. *See* online content/creators
controversial themes, 106–7, 109–10, 113, 116, 121, 123–24, 125, 133, 134
convergence: AMPTP (Alliance of Motion Picture and Television Producers) and, 58; animation and, 156; audiences and, 156; creativity and, 215; cultural studies and, 18–19; economics and, 43; European schools and, 237; film schools and, 235–41; interactive writing and, 194; Jenkins, Henry on, 58; labor and, 156; Loyola Marymount University and, 237; new media and, 187; online content/creators and, 234, 235; the paraindustry and, 238, 239; production and, 156; QB (Quickbaby) (Frampton, Will) and, 234; screenwriters/2.0 and, 3, 100, 186, 199–200, 223–24; screenwriting/craft and, 3, 8–9, 214, 218–19, 236, 237, 241, 243; scripting and, 219, 242–43; television and, 192; video/games and, 186, 187, 198, 199–200, 223; WGA (Writers Guild of America) and, 100, 190, 192; WGA strike (2007–8) and, 4, 42. *See also* media convergence
convergent cable, 137
convergent media: creativity and, 215; films schools and, 240; Internet and, 223; marketing and, 239; narrative and, 219, 223; online content/creators and, 226, 233; the paraindustry and, 236; QB (Quickbaby) (Frampton, Will) and, 228; screenwriters/2.0 and, 12, 101, 181, 185, 242; screenwriting and, 236; story/telling and, 220; television screenwriters and, 9; video/games and, 223; WGA (Writers Guild of America) and, 25, 185, 242. *See also* media convergence
convergent screenwriters, 3, 4, 16, 29, 42, 222, 235–36. *See also* screenwriter 2.0
convergent storytelling, 223
convergent television, 110, 113, 137, 220
Conviction (2010), 4, 147, 149, 151
Copland, Liesl, 57
Coppola, Francis Ford, 146
copyright, 112, 194. *See also* IP (intellectual property)
corporate media. *See* entertainment media corporations
corporate transmedia, 9–10
Counter, Nicholas, 46
Crackle, 113, 164, 240
craft guilds, 52–53, 53–54, 58, 59, 190, 236. *See also* DGA (Directors Guild

of America); WGA (Writers Guild of America)
Craig, Peter, 69
CRASH unit (LAPD), 106
Craven, Wes, 150
Creative Screenwriting magazine, 90
creativity: conglomeration/consolidation and, 29; convergence and, 215; DC Comics Universe (DCCU) and, 77; genres and, 2; independent cinema and, 144, 145, 179; Indiewood and, 139; Internet and, 215; Landgraf, John on, 102; major studios and, 67–68, 85; manic cinema and, 74; Marvel's Creative Committee and, 75–76; media industries and, 19; microbudget productions and, 165, 166; movies and, 71, 220; new writers and, 99; screenwriters and, 1, 2, 6, 8, 9, 16, 79, 80; screenwriting/manuals and, 6, 14; streaming and, 164; SVOD (Subscription Video on Demand) and, 103–4; television and, 60, 71, 103–4, 154–55; television screenwriters and, 104, 111, 113; television showrunners and, 104, 108, 113, 133–34, 220; tentpole movies/paradigm and, 61, 72, 103; transmedia storytelling and, 9; video/games and, 185, 187–88, 193, 194, 196, 214–15; WGA strike (2007–8) and, 51; women screenwriters and, 41; writers' collectives and, 85
credit. *See* screenwriter credit
crime dramas, 38, 68
Critic, The (1994), 45
"Critical Media Industry Studies: A Research Approach" (Havens, Lotz, Tinic), 20
Croods, The (2013), 161
cross-platform markets, 37, 73–74
cross-platforms, 9, 37, 38, 44
crowd-funding, 157, 165, 180, 221, 226
crowd-led/interactive storytelling, 233
Cruising (1980), 168
CSI (2000–2015), 115–16

CSU (California State University Fullerton), 239
cultural legitimacy, 191–92, 196–97
Curry, Gregory, 18

Daily Variety, 123
D'Alessandro, Federico, 94
Dancyger, Ken, 16
Darabont, Frank, 124
Dark Knight movies, 10, 217. *See also Batman* movies
Daurio, Ken, 70
Davis, J. Madison, 40
Davis, Judy, 63–64
Day, Felicia, 225
DC comic book movies, 37, 74
DC Comics Universe (DCCU), 76–78
DC Entertainment, 152
Deadline Hollywood, 45–46, 52, 59, 60, 78, 154
Deadwood (2004–6), 110, 125
Deborah Aquila Casting, 119
deconstruction, 16–17
Deloitte Consulting, 226–27
De Marle, Mary, 197
De Micco, Kirk, 161
Denby, David, 34–35, 80
Dent, Catherine, 120–21
Denton, Justin, 94
Depp, Johnny, 72–73
Despain, Wendy, 205, 207
Despicable Me movies, 70, 71
DGA (Directors Guild of America), 51, 53–54, 55, 56–57, 59
dialogue, 177, 182, 205–9, 211
Diamond, Reed, 117
Diamond, Ron, 159
DIC Entertainment, 159
Die Hard (1988), 33–34, 94
digital comic books, 224
Digital Democracy Survey, 226–27
digital distribution: accounting and, 57; cable and, 58; conglomerates and, 55; convergent television and, 110–11; DGA (Directors Guild of America) and, 55, 56–57; digital downloads and, 58; economics and,

digital distribution *(continued)* 55; Internet and, 16, 58; major/studios and, 57, 67; microbudget productions and, 24; monetization and, 113; online content/creators and, 217; ratings and, 114; revenues and, 49; streaming and, 58; SVOD (Subscription Video on Demand) and, 58; Twitch (platform) and, 58; WGA strike (2007–8) and, 49–51; YouTube and, 58. *See also* digital residuals; online distribution

digital downloads, 44, 49–50, 58, 186, 214, 218, 227, 250n41. *See also* streaming

digital media, 217, 219, 237

digital residuals, 41–42, 44, 46–47, 49–51, 53–54, 56–57, 58, 149, 189

digital technologies: action movies and, 90; ancillary markets and, 58; animation and, 92; big-budget movies and, 31; DVDs and, 41; economics and, 78; kinetics and, 99; labor and, 99–100; MBA (Minimum Basic Agreement) and, 58; microbudget productions and, 2, 24, 220; online content/creators and, 242; production and, 165; residuals and, 41, 44; revenues and, 78; screenplays and, 90, 92–93; screenwriters/screenwriting and, 9, 16, 22–23, 99–100, 220–21; special-effects and, 92–93; spectacle and, 33–34, 90; television and, 51, 137, 259n45; tentpole movies/screenwriters and, 65, 99; *United Hollywood* (blog) and, 52, 251n56; video/games and, 186; WGA (Writers Guild of America) and, 57, 58–59; WGA strike (2007–8) and, 44, 51, 60. *See also* digital distribution; digital downloads

Digital World (conference), 195

Dille, Flint, 211

Dinehart, Stephen E., IV, 208–9

Dinosaurs (1991), 158

Directors Guild of America (DGA), 51, 53–54, 55, 56–57, 59

discourse frame, 7, 14, 140, 242

Disney. *See* Walt Disney Company/Pictures

Disney (theme parks), 67, 73

distribution: advertising revenues and, 113; animation and, 156, 159–60; convergent/television and, 110–11, 113; independent animation and, 164–65; independent cinema and, 143, 144–45, 147; Internet and, 16, 159–60, 165; media convergence and, 49; microbudget productions and, 24, 165, 180; microdistribution, 225; MPAA (Motion Picture Association of America) and, 66; online content/creators and, 217, 225; streaming and, 44; SVOD (Subscription Video on Demand) and, 67; synergies and, 66; WGA strike (2007–8) and, 49. *See also* digital distribution; online distribution

distributor's gross, 51, 57

DiTerlizzi, Tony, 157

Divide, The (2014), 154, 155

Dixon, Leslie, 41

DLC (downloadable content), 214, 217, 218. *See also* digital downloads; streaming

documentaries, 4, 125, 141. *See also* *Interior. Leather Bar.* (2013)

domestic box office revenues, 30–31, 32, 33, 65–66, 69, 70, 72, 78

domestic markets, 68

downloading. *See* digital downloads

dramas: audiences and, 116; cable and, 23, 60, 116, 137, 220; cinema history and, 72; complex dramas, 23, 70; crime dramas, 38, 68; film schools and, 238–39; FX Network and, 9, 70, 115–16, 117; genres and, 70; HBO and, 9, 70, 110; independent cinema and, 147; independent dramas, 100–101; movies and, 60; prestige dramas, 2, 23, 38, 58, 147; screens and, 2, 70–71, 238; screenwriters and, 70–71, 148, 220; *The Shield* (2002–8) as, 23, 70, 137; spec scripts and, 71; studios and, 147, 153; tentpole movies and, 147. *See also* character-driven dramas; television dramas

Dreams on Spec (2007), 1–2, 3, 21

DreamWorks Animation, 159, 161, 164

drive-in circuit, 145

Druckmann, Neil, 196, 212

Duchovny, David, 258n26

Duke, Paul F., 80

Duncan, Jody, 94

Dunham, Lena, 24, 166, 180

Dunne, Philip, 194

Duplass, Jay and Mark, 24, 166–67

DVDs: animation and, 160; *Annual Financial Report* (2014) (WGA) and, 41; digital downloads and, 250n41; digital technologies and, 41; economics and, 33, 78; 80/20 formula and, 50; major studios and, 33, 67; MBA (Minimum Basic Agreement) and, 44–45; residuals and, 44, 49, 59; revenues and, 33, 136; sales and, 33, 250n41; sexual content and, 170; *The Shield* (2002–8) and, 124; video/games and, 186; VOD (Video on Demand) and, 146; WGA strike (2007–8) and, 136; women and, 70. *See also* home video

EA (Electronic Arts), 24, 186, 210

Ebert, Roger, 34, 139–40, 176–77

economics: animation and, 160; conglomerates and, 66; convergence and, 43; digital/online distribution and, 49–50, 55; digital technologies and, 78; domestic box office revenues and, 78; DVDs and, 33, 78; formulas and, 7; Hollywood and, 29–38, 41, 78; independent cinema and, 144, 145–46, 147, 148, 180; labor and, 41; low-budget genre and, 146; major studios and, 7–8, 66, 67–68, 78–79; manic cinema and, 74; masculinity economics, 126; multipart productions and, 72; online content/creators and, 223; screenwriters and, 1–2, 11, 29, 41, 42, 79, 87; screenwriting/craft and, 25, 41, 87; sexual content and, 170; *The Shield* (2002–8) and, 111; spec scripts and, 43; television and, 126; tentpole movies and, 70, 72–73, 74–75; video/games and, 195; WGA (Writers Guild of America) and, 39; WGA strike (2007–8) and, 43, 52–53, 54–55; writers' collectives and, 84–85. *See also* great recession of 2008; income

Edge Games, 200

Eglee, Charles H., 132–33

Eidos Montreal, 197, 202

80/20 formula, 50

electrocardiogram story/telling, 248n17

Electronic Arts (EA), 24, 186, 198, 210, 218

Elgato Game Capture HD60 Pro, 227

Ellis, Dave, 200, 211

EMEA [Europe, the Middle East, and Africa] region, 31

emergent game play, 184–85, 203

Emmys, 124

emotional action, 40

entertainment media corporations, 218, 225, 226, 227

entrepreneurialism, 24

Episode V: The Empire Strikes Back (1980), 91, 93

Erickson, Steve, 217, 222

Eszterhas, Joe, 28–29, 174–75

European cinema, 125, 146, 148, 248n17

European schools, 237, 271n31

Excellence in Television award, 106

Excel spreadsheets, 204, 205, 208

expanded television, 9, 23, 67, 70, 101, 107, 137, 220. *See also* convergent television; *individual networks*; *individual shows*

experimental cinema, 141, 166
experimental screenplays, 169–70
exploitation movies, 145

Facebook, 24
Fallout III (game), 214
fans: emergent game play and, 184; Jenkins, Leeroy (character) and, 183; online content/creators and, 225–26, 227, 228; QB (Quickbaby) (Frampton, Will) and, 217–18, 228–31, 232–33, 270n17, 271n20; scripting and, 223; SerB (Sergey Burkatovskiy) and, 202; *Teatime with Tuskeh* (Youtube show), 232; video blogs and, 227; video/games and, 185, 186, 214, 218; *World of Tanks (WoT)* (game) and, 232
Fantastic Beasts and Where to Find Them (2016), 253n20
Fantastic Four, The (franchise), 37, 71
fantasy films, 38, 94–95
Fantasy Flight Games, 10
Faraci, Devin, 75–76, 253n21
Fargo (1996), 62
Fast and Furious (franchise), 71
FatBoss TV, 232
Federal Communications Commission (FCC), 67, 110–11
Feeney, F.X., 204, 212
Feige, Kevin, 75, 76, 100
Feirstein, Bruce, 198, 210
females: character-driven dramas and, 147; chick flicks and, 154; female audiences, 23, 69–70; genres and, 41; Gray, Pamela and, 138, 180; Lifetime and, 116; major/studios and, 150, 153–54; roles and, 39–40, 69; *The Shield* (2002–8) and, 117–19, 122, 259n39; Sorkin, Aaron and, 109, 110; tentpole movies and, 69; video/games and, 69
festivals. *See* film festivals
Field, Syd, 15
Fierro, Adam, 102, 106
Fight Club (1999), 83–84
film. *See* movies

film and media studies, 12, 14, 15, 17, 18–19
Film Culture, 146
film education, 5–6, 12. *See also* academia; film schools; paraindustry
film festivals, 11, 24, 28, 38, 165, 168. *See also individual festivals*
filmmakers, 240
film schools, 235–41; animation and, 237; comedies and, 238–39; convergence and, 235–41; dramas and, 238–39; European schools and, 237, 271n31; *Final Draft* (software) and, 15; franchises and, 32; genres and, 32; higher education and, 5–6; media and, 237–38, 238–39, 241; narrative and, 238, 240; online content/creators and, 236, 240, 241; platforms and, 241; prestige films and, 24; screenplays and, 237, 238–39, 241; screenwriter 2.0 and, 240; screenwriting/craft and, 5, 25, 222, 223, 236–41; scripting and, 219, 238, 241; studio model transformation and, 22; television and, 236–37, 238–39; video/games and, 238–39. *See also individual schools*
film theory, 245n8
Final Cut Pro, 165
final cuts, 143
Final Draft (software), 15, 90
Final Draft Big Break (competition), 15
Financial Interest and Syndication Rules (fin-syn), 67, 110–11
Fine, Alan, 75
Finke, Nikki, 52, 59
Firefly (2002–3), 47–48, 125
First Amendment films, 116
first drafts, 80, 81
first-person shooter (FPS) games, 188, 211
Fiske, John, 18
Flash (animation program), 160
Fleming, Michael, 85
Forbes, 32, 68, 197

formats, 11, 15, 65, 95–98, 99–100, 166, 169–70, 204–6, 208, 256n70
formulas, 3, 5–6, 7, 8, 63–64, 80, 158
for-profit screenwriting workshops, 15
Foster, Ben, 191, 192, 266n21
Foucault, Michel, 141–42, 242
four-act structure, 222
four-quadrant audiences, 23, 69, 70, 170
Fox Broadcasting Company, 258n26
Fox Cable Networks Group, 111
FOX network, 106, 109
Fox Searchlight Pictures, 24, 139, 147
Fox Studios, 37, 84, 85, 159
Fox Television Studios, 119, 124, 125, 136
FPS (first-person shooter) games, 188, 211
Frameline festival, 168
Frampton, Tanya (a.k.a. PeppyPepper), 229, 271n21
Frampton, Will. *See* QB (Quickbaby) (Frampton, Will)
franchises: *Batman* franchise, 38; comic book franchises, 38; DC Comics Universe (DCCU) and, 77; film schools and, 32; *Ice Age* franchise, 159; international franchises, 31–32; *Lone Ranger* (2013) and, 73; major/studios and, 32, 68, 78, 100; Marvel franchises, 37, 69, 155; multipart productions and, 72; screenwriters and, 23, 74, 78; *Shrek* franchise, 159; *Spiderman* franchise, 38; *Superman* franchise, 38; *Toy Story* franchise, 158–59; *Transformers* franchise, 23, 34–36, 87, 186; Universal Pictures and, 74; video/games and, 186. *See also* superhero franchises; tentpole franchises
Franco, James, 168
free drafts, 79–80, 81, 82. *See also* unpaid work
freelance screenwriting, 22, 24, 88–90, 99, 151. *See also* spec scripts
French, Philip, 177

Friedkin, William, 168
Fuchs, Jason, 78
Full Moon, 146
Funny Ha (2002), 166
Furthman, Jules, 40
Fusco, John, 161
Futurama (1999), 45
FX Network: as brand, 115–16, 117, 126, 134, 138, 257n1, 257n5; cable and, 116–17, 123, 125; controversial themes and, 116; dramas and, 9, 70, 115–16, 117; HBO and, 116–17; males and, 138; Ryan, Shawn and, 115–16, 117, 134; *The Shield* (2002–8) and, 23, 48, 70, 102, 106–7, 111, 115, 116–17, 119–20, 122–24, 125–26, 134, 136, 259n36; Standards and Practices and, 111, 259n39; *The X-Files* (1993–2002) and, 258n26; youth sector and, 115, 137

games, 68, 223–24. *See also* video/games
games writing. *See* video/games writing
gaming, 58, 224, 232, 257n2. *See also* video/games; *individual games*
Gandolfini, James, 103
Ganz, Lowell, 83
Garden State (2004), 139–41, 144, 147
gatekeepers, 88–90, 100, 169, 190
gay films, 167, 168, 170–71. *See also individual films*
Geek and Sundry network, 223, 225–26
gender, 40, 106–7, 192. *See also* females; males
Generation Z, 226, 227
genres: creativity and, 2; domestic box office revenues and, 30–31; domestic markets and, 68; dramas and, 70; females and, 41, 69; film schools and, 32; formulas and, 64; four-quadrant audiences and, 69; Hollywood and, 23, 33, 64; independent cinema and, 145–46, 147; independent/screenwriters

genres *(continued)*
  and, 33, 74, 142, 153; international markets and, 68; low-budget genre, 145–46; major/studios and, 23, 33, 68; males and, 69, 70; manic cinema and, 34; marketing and, 16; new spec format and, 88; paraindustry and, 15–16; prestige films as, 24; production culture and, 19–20; screenwriting and, 23; *The Shield* (2002–8) and, 117, 259n36; spec scripts and, 71; spectacle and, 30–31, 70; superhero franchises and, 74; television/showrunners and, 114, 138; tentpole movies and, 68; Universal Pictures and, 74; video/games and, 188, 191, 208, 211. *See also individual video game genres*
Ghost Recon series (game), 204
Gilroy, Tony, 69
Girls (2012–17), 166
globalization, 10, 29, 32, 44
global markets, 2, 8, 19, 33, 242
Goggins, Walton, 102
Gold, Patrick, 70
Golden Globes, 124
Goldman, William, 79, 89, 144–45
Goldwyn, Tony, 149, 150
Goliath (2016), 70
Gomery, Douglas, 248n5
Gomez, Nick, 127, 133
Good Vibrations Indie Erotic Film Festival, 167–68
Gotham (2014–), 77
Gottlieb, Carl, 68
Graduate, The (1967), 139–40, 146–47
Grais, Michael, 34, 36
Gramsci, Antonio, 10, 40, 46, 57, 73, 242, 245n7
Grant, Brea, 224
Grant, David A., 119
graphic novels, 239
Graverobber Productions, 157, 164
Graves, Keith, 157–58, 164
Gray, Jonathan, 187–88

Gray, Pamela, 4, 24, 138, 142, 147, 149–56, 180, 181, 220
great recession of 2008, 43, 59, 67, 78, 87, 161
Green Lantern (2011), 96
Green Productions, 157
Griffith, D.W., 221
Gross, Larry, 89
gross point participation, 84–85
Ground Control (1998), 157
Guantanamo Bay, 106
Guardian, 139
Guggenheim, Marc, 213
Gunning, Tom, 253n15

Haigh, Andrew, 167
Hall, Stuart, 19–20
Halon Entertainment, 94
Hamm, Sam, 23, 37, 64
Hangover, The (2009), 23, 84
Hannibal (2013–2015), 23, 111
Happily N'Ever After (2006), 157
Happy Christmas (2014), 166–67
haptic effects/thrills, 35, 87, 91, 93, 99, 175, 196
Hardwick, Chris, 225–26
Harmon, David, 193
Harry Potter (2010 and 2011), 23, 72, 74–75, 186, 253n20
Hasbro, 68–69
Havens, Timothy, 20, 21
Hawks, Howard, 40
Hazelton, John, 57–58, 70
HBO: *Deadwood* (2004–6) and, 110; dramas and, 9, 70, 110; FX Network and, 116–17; *Girls* (2012–17) and, 166; *The Newsroom* (2012–14) and, 108–9; *OZ* (1997–2003) and, 110; screenwriters and, 60, 70; *The Shield* (2002–8) and, 111, 120, 124; *The Sopranos* (1999–2007) and, 103, 110, 124, 125; Sorkin, Aaron and, 23; television showrunners and, 113; *Togetherness* (2015) and, 167; TV-MA rating and, 120; viral videos and, 239; *The Wire* (2002–8) and, 70, 110

health benefits, 45, 59
Hearthstone: Heroes of Warcraft (game), 182, 183, 184, 185, 217, 265n1
hegemony, 10, 32, 33, 54–55, 144, 180, 245n7
Heinberg, Alan, 78
Hendrickson, Andy, 72–73
Hennig, Amy, 209–10
heroic monomyth, 15
Hero with a Thousand Faces, The (Campbell), 15
Herskovitz, Marshall, 81
Heyward, Andy, 159, 161
hierarchy, 22, 79, 193
high-art-vs.-low-art, 190, 191
higher education, 5–6. *See also* academia; film schools; paraindustry; *individual universities*
Hill St. Blues (1981–87), 105, 109, 110, 191–92
History of the Screenplay, A (Price), 14
Hoffman, Dustin, 150
Hollywood: accounting and, 50, 51, 57, 250n52; animation and, 158–59; capitalism and, 18; chick flicks and, 154; comics and, 217; conglomeration and, 242; economics and, 29–38, 41, 78; females and, 153–54; genres and, 23, 33, 64; global markets and, 2, 242; hegemony and, 32, 33; home video and, 33; independent filmmaking and, 140, 141; independent screenwriters and, 141; Indiewood and, 148, 179; international audiences and, 32; labor and, 241, 250n52; low-budget genre and, 146; manic cinema and, 87; microbudget productions and, 166; millenial manic and, 33; New Hollywood, 146–47; *A New Pot of Gold: Hollywood under the Electronic Rainbow, 1980–1989* (Prince), 12; online distribution and, 49; *The Player* (1991) and, 27–28; prestige dramas and, 147; revenues and, 145; screenwriters and, 27–29, 83, 87, 194, 222; screenwriting and, 61, 87; spec scripts and, 71; studio development paradigm, 11; tentpole movies and, 28, 70; transmedia marketing and, 10; video/games writing and, 187; WGA (Writers Guild of America) and, 3; women screenwriters and, 39–41. *See also* major studios; studios; WGA strike (2007–8)
Hollywood, the Dream Factory: An Anthropologist Looks at the Movie-Makers (Powdermaker), 38
Hollywood craft guilds. *See* craft guilds
Hollywood Renaissance, 146–47
Hollywood Reporter, 32, 34, 52, 72, 77, 78, 89–90, 134, 158
Holm, Ian, 139
Holt, Jennifer, 19–20
home video: action movies and, 146; animation and, 160; *Annual Financial Report* (2014) (WGA) and, 41; 80/20 formula and, 50; The Great Contraction and, 33; Hollywood and, 33; horror films and, 146; low-budget genre and, 146; major studios and, 67; mergers and, 66–67; residuals and, 44, 45, 49, 50, 57; science fiction films and, 146; screenplays and, 246n17; "A Warning for Our Next Great Screenwriters" (Ray) and, 8. *See also* DVDs
Homicide: Life on the Street (90's), 105, 117, 121
homophobia, 17–18, 106–7, 109. *See also* gay films
Hopper, Dennis, 146
Horder-Payton, Gwyneth, 102
Horn, Alan, 76
Horrible Experience of Unbearable Length: More Movies That Suck, A (Ebert), 34
horror films, 15–16, 38, 71–72, 145, 146, 188
Horton, Andrew, 14
housekeeping deals, 86–87

House of Cards (2013–), 23, 67, 70, 191–92
Howard, Ron, 86
how-to manuals/websites, 5, 15
Hoxter, Julian, 14, 25, 95–96, 166, 264n56
Hulu, 9, 49, 113, 148
Human Rights First, 106
Humpday (2009), 24
Hunger Games films, 7–8, 69, 72, 74–75
Hunt, Darnell M., 39
Hunt for Red October, The (1990), 94
Hyams, Peter, 92

IASTE (International Alliance of Theatrical Stage Employees), 52–53, 56, 161
Ice Age franchise, 159
ideology, 10, 11, 17, 245n7
Iger, Robert, 64
IGN.com, 76
I Hit It with My Axe (gaming web series), 224
IMA Expo, 195
Imagine Entertainment, 86
income: *Annual Financial Report (2014)* (WGA) and, 41; microbudget productions and, 166; movies and, 41; new media and, 235; online content/creators and, 225, 226, 234, 235; QB (Quickbaby) (Frampton, Will) and, 225, 269n1, 270n18; residuals and, 41; screenwriters and, 1–2, 9, 23–24, 41, 59, 78, 79, 86, 166, 220; streaming and, 219, 269n1; television and, 41, 220; video/games writing and, 192; WGA strike (2007–8) and, 59; women screenwriters and, 41
Incredibles, The (2004), 163
Independent (newspaper), 48
independent animation, 157, 158, 159, 160, 161, 163–64, 164–65
independent cinema, 139–81; animation and, 156–65; auteur theory and, 262n13; authorship and, 141–42; blockbusters and, 144, 145; creativity and, 144, 145, 179; definitions of, 142–44, 145, 146, 148, 156, 179; distribution and, 143, 144–45, 147; dramas and, 147; economics and, 144, 145–46, 147, 148, 180; final cuts and, 143; genres and, 145–46, 147; Gray, Pamela and, 150; hegemony and, 144, 180; horror films and, 145; independent gay cinema, 167; independent screenwriters and, 141, 142; major/studios and, 141, 143, 144–45, 147, 148, 180; media convergence and, 141, 143; microbudget productions/screenwriters and, 141, 148, 165–79, 180; MPAA (Motion Picture Association of America) and, 145; narrative and, 142, 143, 146; New Hollywood and, 146–47; new screenwriters and, 141, 143; paraindustry and, 144; reduction of, 2; scholarship and, 144; science fiction films and, 145; screenwriters/screenwriting and, 141, 143, 148–49; sexuality and, 168–78; story/telling and, 142, 144, 147; tentpole movies/paradigm and, 144, 147; textual analysis and, 24; Tzioumakis, Yannis on, 144, 148; WGA (Writers Guild of America) and, 148–49; *Wikipedia* and, 265n71; youth sector and, 145. *See also* individuals; *individual films*
independent contractors, 194
independent dramas, 100–101
independent filmmaking, 16, 24, 139, 140–41, 142, 145, 148
independent gay cinema, 167
independent screenplays, 24
independent screenwriters, 141, 142, 149, 150, 153, 155–56, 165, 179, 180–81. *See also* individuals
independent screenwriting, 11, 149
independent studios, 68, 160, 162–63
Indie 2.0, 148, 165
indie boom, 23–24, 140
Indiegogo, 226

indies, 149, 150, 220
Indiewood, 62, 139, 141, 142, 147, 148, 149, 165, 179, 220. See also independent cinema; *individual films*
industrial texts, 4, 24
industry lore/spin, 14, 21–22, 191
Insdorf, Annette, 144
intellectual property. See IP (intellectual property)
interactive/crowd-led storytelling, 208, 233, 234
interactive entertainment, 192, 199. See also interactivity; video/games
interactive media, 239, 246n17
Interactive Program Contract (IPC), 197–98
interactive television, 116
interactive video, 194
interactive writing, 192, 194, 195, 198–99, 212–13, 214
interactivity, 11, 203, 214, 217–18, 219, 233
Interior. Leather Bar. (2013), 168, 170, 264n56
International Alliance of Theatrical Stage Employees (IATSE), 52–53
international appeal/audiences, 23, 31–32. See also globalization; global markets
international box office revenues, 30–33, 69, 74–75. See also global markets
international distribution/exhibition, 66
international franchises, 31–32
international markets, 31, 32, 33, 68, 74, 160, 161, 170, 248n17. See also global markets
Internet: animation and the, 156, 159–60, 161; audiences and the, 114; convergent media and the, 223; creativity and the, 215; DGA (Directors Guild of America) and the, 56–57; digital distribution and the, 16, 58; distribution and the, 16, 159–60, 165; interactive television

and the, 116; labor and the, 52; ludisphere and the, 265n8; marketing and the, 114, 235; mergers and the, 67; microbudget productions and the, 24, 165; *The Newsroom* (2012–14) and the, 109–10, 113–14; as platform, 221; screenwriters and the, 11; streaming and the, 221, 227; television/showrunners and the, 113–14, 259n45; unions and the, 52; video/games and the, 184; viral videos and the, 222; WGA strike (2007–8) and the, 50–51, 51–52; Why So Serious teaser puzzles and the, 10. See also crowd-funding; online content/creators
Internet Movie Database (IMDb), 126
Internet shorts, 224
In Their Room (2009–present), 167–68
IP (intellectual property), 9, 10, 24, 49, 69, 194, 218, 223, 226, 229
IPC (Interactive Program Contract), 197–98
iPod, 49–50
Iraq war, 106
Iron Man 3 (2013), 94
Iron Man leveling, 184, 265n10
I Want Your Love (2012), 167, 168–69, 170–79, 264n56

Jace, Michael, 120–21
Jackson, Michael, 112
Jackson, Samuel L., 76
Jack the Giant Slayer (2013), 94–95
Jacobs, Gregory, 154
James, Caryn, 123
Jaws (1975), 68, 145
Jeffersons, The (1975–85), 114
Jendresen, Erik, 84–85
Jenkins, Henry, 16, 58, 203, 225
Jenkins, Leeroy (character/meme), 182–84, 185, 213, 222, 229, 265n4
Jenkins, Patty, 77
John Carter (2012), 73
Johns, Geoff, 77, 78
Johnson, Clark, 117

Johnson, Kenny, 102
Johnson, Richard, 19, 20
Johnson, Steven, 184
Jones, Duncan, 191
journalism, 109, 113–14, 187, 219, 223, 228, 236–37
Journal of the Writers Guild of America, West, 192, 194
Jungian theory, 15–16
Jurassic Park (franchise), 71
Justice League (2017), 77
Justified (2010–15), 115

Kamcord (platform), 233
Karns, Jay, 122
Kasdan, Lawrence, 90, 91
Katzenberg, Jeffrey, 159
Kaufman, George S., 62
Kellner, Douglas, 18–19
Kenner, 68–69
Kerr, Aphra, 201–2
Khouri, Callie, 40
Kickstarter, 157, 180. See also crowdfunding
Kinberg, Simon, 85
kinetics, 96–99, 126. See also manic cinema
King, Geoff, 147, 148, 165
Kislyi, Viktor, 227
Klasky, Neil, 132
Knight, Steven, 153, 154
Knoll, John, 69
Koepp, David, 83, 84
Kouf, Jim, 80
Kracauer, Siegfried, 98
Krim, Arthur, 145
Kristeva, Julia, 35, 249n24
Kruger, Ehren, 30, 35
Kuhn, Thomas, 238

labor: capitalism and, 10, 19; convergence and, 156; digital technologies and, 99–100; economics and, 41; *Hollywood, the Dream Factory: An Anthropologist Looks at the Movie-Makers* (Powdermaker), 38; Hollywood and, 241, 250n52; Internet and, 52; online distribution and, 50; production and, 18–19, 107; screenwriters and, 38, 80, 138; strikes and, 44; tentpole movies and, 11–12; video/games and, 198, 199; WGA (Writers Guild of America) and, 29, 190, 193, 235; WGA strike (2007–8) and, 42, 45, 50, 54, 80, 138
Landau, Neil, 114, 240–41
Landgraf, John, 102, 124, 257n1
Lane, Diane, 150
Langdell, Tim, 200
Laps around Dalaran (podcast), 232
Lara Croft: Tomb Raider (2001), 186
Last of Us, The (game), 196, 212
Latt, David, 52
Law and Order (1990–2010), 115–16, 121
LA Weekly, 140
Lawson, Richard, 109
layering, 93–94
Lear, Norman, 114
Lechte, John, 249n24
Lefler, Doug, 95
legacy media, 214, 219, 223, 224, 226, 236, 237–38, 240
Legendary Pictures, 225–26
Legendary Television and Digital Media, 225
lektonic representation, 35–36
Lender, Jay, 204
Lent, Michael, 256n70
Lerner, Michael, 63
Levine, Elana, 191–92
Li, Bingbing, 31
Lieblich Tipton, Darlene, 111–13, 132–33
Lie to Me (2009), 124
Lifetime network, 116
Liguori, Peter, 116–17, 119, 120
Lionsgate, 65, 74–75, 146, 157
Little Mermaid, The (1989), 158
Littleton, Claudia, 86–87
Littleton, Cynthia, 52, 54, 56, 57, 59
Lone Ranger (2013), 72–73
Looney Tunes: Back in Action (game), 204

Lord of the Rings, The, 186
Los Angeles City Council, 59
Los Angeles Police Department (LAPD), 106, 117
Los Angeles Times, 31, 70
Lost (2004–10), 125
Lotz, Amanda D., 20, 126, 259n45
low-budget films, 145–46, 148. *See also* microbudget productions
Loyola Marymount University, 237
LPs (Let's Play), 218, 230–31, 232, 233
Lucas, Chris, 159
Lucas, George, 15, 68, 69, 92, 93
Lucas, John, 84
LucasArts/Lucasfilm, 69
Lucy (2014), 74
ludic play, 185, 189
ludisphere/celebrity, 225–26, 228, 265n8. *See also* individuals

MacDonald, Scott, 169–70
machinima, 184
MacLaren, Michelle, 77
Mad Max (franchise), 71
Mad Men (2007–15), 114, 191–92
Magic Mike XXL (2015), 154
Mahan, Sarah, 239
major studios, 65–73; animation and the, 162–63, 163–64; box office and the, 67–68; cable and the, 67; Coen brothers and the, 62; conglomerates and the, 66; creativity and the, 67–68, 85; digital distribution and the, 67; domestic box office revenues and the, 65–66; DVDs and the, 33, 67; economics and the, 7–8, 66, 67–68, 78–79; females and the, 150; franchises and the, 68; genres and the, 23, 68; home video and the, 67; independent cinema and the, 145, 147; independent production/distribution and the, 62; mergers and the, 66–67; movie adaptations and the, 187–88; MPAA (Motion Picture Association of America) and the, 66; multipart productions and the, 72;

new technologies and the, 68; piracy and the, 68; prestige dramas and the, 2; revenues and the, 67; romantic comedies and the, 2; screenwriters and the, 68; streaming and the, 67; SVOD (Subscription Video on Demand) and the, 67; teen comedies and the, 2; tentpole movies and the, 2, 68, 70–72, 82–83; theme parks and the, 67; toys and the, 67; video/games and the, 67. *See also* Hollywood; studios; *individual studios*
males, 23, 69, 70, 116, 126, 138
Malin, Brenton J., 126
Mamet, David, 89, 115, 124
Mandel, Babaloo, 83
Man from U.N.C.L.E., The (franchise), 71
Mangan, Mona, 45
manic cinema, 34–37, 65, 74, 87, 100
Man of Steel (2013), 98
Manovich, Lev, 16
Maras, Steven: frames and, 3, 4, 5, 6, 7, 14, 140, 164, 181, 242; independent cinema and, 140, 142; *The Player* (1991) and, 28; *Screenwriting* (Horton and Hoxter) and, 14; *Screenwriting: History, Theory, and Practice*, 13; scripting and, 8, 95, 219, 226
Marcel, Kelly, 77
Margin Call (2011), 81
marketing, 9–10, 16, 108, 114, 165, 218, 235, 238–39
markets, 29–33, 156–57, 158, 160, 164–65, 220, 267n34. *See also* ancillary markets; global markets; international markets
Markus, Christopher, 95
Martinez, Benito, 120, 127, 133
Marvel Comics, 75
Marvel Comics Universe (MCU), 37, 74–75, 76, 77, 78, 100
Marvel franchises, 37, 69, 155
Marvel's Creative Committee, 75–76
Marvel Studios, 24, 36, 37, 69, 73, 74–76, 78, 94, 100

Marx, Christy, 198
Marxism, 16–17, 18, 46, 63, 79
Mary Tyler Moore (1970–77), 114
Massively Multiplayer Online Role Playing Game (MMORPG), 9–10, 182
Massive Multiplayer Online (MMO), 202, 217, 228, 230
master-scene screenplays, 88, 90, 92–93, 100
Mathews, Travis, 24, 142, 167–79, 180, 220, 264n56
Mathias, Harry, 234
Matrix (1999), 9–10
Matsushita, 66–67
Maude (1972–78), 114
Mayer, Vicki, 20–21
Mazin, Craig, 74, 81–82, 83, 153
MBA (Minimum Basic Agreement), 44–45, 50, 57, 58–59, 59–60, 189, 193, 235
McCarthy, Todd, 139
McClintock, Pamela, 86
McCreadie, Marsha, 40
McFeely, Stephen, 95
Mckee, Robert, 90
McLean, John, 45–46
McNary, Dave, 80
McQuarrie, Chris, 84–85
McTiernan, John, 94
MCU (Marvel Comics Universe), 37, 74–75, 76, 77, 78, 100
media: animation and, 156–57; convergence and, 187–88, 269n4; film schools and, 237–38, 238–39, 241; screenwriters and, 143–44, 242–43; screenwriting craft and, 222; WGA strike (2007–8) and, 43, 47, 54. *See also* new media
media convergence: ancillary markets and, 41; distribution and, 49; *Dreams on Spec* (2007) and, 3; *A History of the Screenplay* (Price) and, 14; independent cinema and, 141, 143; industry lore and, 22; Jenkins, Henry and, 58; residuals and, 41; screenwriters and, 3, 8,
23–24, 221; screenwriting/craft and, 8–9, 29, 185; WGA (Writers Guild of America) and, 4, 39. *See also* convergent media
media industries, 19, 20–21. *See also* new media
Media Industries: History, Theory, and Method (Holt, Perren), 19, 20
media production, 17, 21
membership. *See* WGA (Writers Guild of America): membership
mergers, 66–67, 158, 186, 198–99
Metzen, Chris, 202, 266n21
MFA (Masters of Fine Arts), 32, 236, 238, 239, 240
Michael Wiese Productions, 195
microbudget productions, 165–79; creativity and, 165, 166; digital technologies and, 2, 24, 220; distribution and, 24, 165, 180; experimental cinema and, 166; formats and, 170; gatekeepers and, 169; Hollywood and, 166; independent cinema, 141, 165–79, 180; indies and, 220; Internet and, 24, 165; marketing and, 165; minority filmmakers and, 24; screenwriters and, 2, 166; screenwriting and, 220–21, 241; social media and, 165; story/telling and, 24, 169, 180; tentpole paradigm and, 65; three-act screenplays and, 166; WGA (Writers Guild of America) and, 148, 165; women and, 24. *See also individual filmmakers; individual films*
microbudget screenwriters, 2, 11, 24, 101, 146, 148, 180. *See also* Mathews, Travis
microdistribution, 225
Microsoft, 199, 210. *See also* Excel spreadsheets
Midway Games, 210
Milk (2008), 59
Millard, Kathryn, 93
Millennials, 226, 227
Miller's Crossing (1990), 63

Million Ways to Die in the West, A (2014), 74
Minecraft (game), 218
mini-major studios, 65
Minimum Basic Agreement (MBA). See MBA (Minimum Basic Agreement)
Minions (franchise), 71
minorities, 24, 39–40, 118, 123–24
minority screenwriters, 39
Miramax, 139, 147, 148, 150, 170
misogyny, 17–18, 107, 153
Mitchell, John Cameron, 167
Mittell, Jason, 124
MMO (Massive Multiplayer Online), 202, 217, 228, 230. See also World of Tanks (WoT) (game)
MMORPG (Massively Multiplayer Online Role Playing Game), 9–10, 182
mobile devices, 221
monetization, 111, 113, 149
Monster's Ball (2001), 174–76
Monsters University (2013), 70
More, Scott, 84
Moreland, Robert, 22, 24, 138, 142, 149, 157–65, 167, 180, 221
Mortensen, Viggo, 150
Motion Picture Association of America. See MPAA (Motion Picture Association of America)
movie adaptations, 186, 187–88. See also *Warcraft* (2016)
Movie Magic Screenwriter (software), 90
movies: big-budget movies, 23, 31; B movies, 68, 70; collaboration and, 104; creativity and, 70–71, 220; digital technologies and, 51; dramas and, 60; exploitation movies, 145; income and, 41; MBA (Minimum Basic Agreement) and, 44–45, 193; minority screenwriters and, 39; online content/creators and, 223; political economy and, 17; residuals and, 41, 46–47, 57; screenwriters and, 8, 9, 221; television and, 116, 192, 193; video/games and, 186,

187–88, 266n22; women and, 39–41. See also action movies; blockbusters; tentpole movies
MP (system responses) speech, 208–9
MPAA (Motion Picture Association of America), 30, 31, 66, 68, 145
multinational media companies, 11–12
multipart productions, 72
multiuser dungeons (MUD), 200
mumblecore, 24, 166–67, 180, 220
mumbleporn, 171
"Mum" episode (*The Shield*), 126–33
Murdoch, Rupert, 116
Murphy, Terry, 246n18
Murray, Susan, 56
Music of the Heart (1999), 150

NakedSword, 170–71
narrative: Barthes, Roland and, 245n8; cinema of narrative integration, 221; conglomerate aesthetics and, 34–35; convergent media and, 219, 223; ensemble format and, 109; film schools and, 238, 240; film theory and, 245n8; independent cinema and, 142, 143, 146; interactivity and, 219, 233; *I Want Your Love* (2012) and, 177, 178; kinetics and, 98; ludic-paidiaic and, 189; manic cinema and, 34; MCU (Marvel Comics Universe) and, 75; online content/creators and, 233; Propp, Vladimir and, 245n8; QB (Quickbaby) (Frampton, Will) and, 217, 219, 230, 231, 232–33; screenwriters and, 100, 186–87; scripting and, 230; sexuality and, 168–69; *The Shield* (2002–8) and, 102, 124; spectacle and, 34–36; story/telling and, 12; streaming and, 219; superhero franchises and, 74; television screenwriters/showrunners and, 105, 110–11; tentpole movies and, 36, 100, 248n17; video/games and, 184, 185, 188, 195, 208, 210–11, 212, 213, 214, 222; video game writers and, 182, 186–87

Nash Bridges (1996–2001), 121
National Labor Relations Board (NLRB), 193
National Treasure (2004), 80
National University, 239
Naughty Dog Games, 196, 209
NBC, 111
Nelmes, Jill, 13–14
neoformalism, 17
Nerdist Industries, 225–26
Netflix, 9, 49, 58, 67, 70, 113, 148, 167, 226
network television: AMPTP (Alliance of Motion Picture and Television Producers) and, 44; convergence and, 192; mergers and, 67; monetization and, 111; online distribution and, 49; Parental Guidelines System and, 120; postnetwork era, 259n45; prestige dramas and, 23; ratings and, 115–16; reality television and, 56; residuals and, 59; screenwriters and, 59; *The Shield* (2002–8) and, 124, 125; Standards and Practices and, 111–13; story/telling and, 103, 111; synergies and, 67; television screenwriters and, 104; television showrunners and, 48–49, 104, 108, 114; tentpole movies and, 64–65; WGA strike (2007–8) and, 48–49, 53, 54–55
Neverwinter Nights (2002–6) franchise, 211
New Abnormal, 33, 55, 60, 70, 79, 147
New American Cinema, 146
New Hollywood, 146–47
Newman, Michael Z., 191–92
new media: alt.screenwriters (column) and, 198–99; Amazon as, 49; animation and, 158; convergence and, 187; convergent screenwriters and, 222; film schools and, 239; Hulu as, 49; income and, 235; markets and, 220; MBA (Minimum Basic Agreement) and, 58; Netflix as, 49; residuals and, 41–42, 47, 59; screenwriter credit and, 22; screenwriters/2.0 and, 9, 101, 181,

199, 220, 222; screenwriting/craft and, 185, 223; studios and, 57; transmedia and, 239; video/games and, 222, 223; WGA (Writers Guild of America) and, 3, 24–25, 55–56, 57, 149, 189, 190, 235; WGA strike (2007–8) and, 42, 43, 58, 59, 136
New Pot of Gold: Hollywood under the Electronic Rainbow, 1980–1989, A (Prince), 12
News Corporation, 66–67, 116
new screenwriters: assignments and, 60–61; big-budget movies and, 99; independent cinema and, 141, 143; new media and, 9; one-step deals and, 58, 82–83; reduced opportunities and, 3; spec scripts and, 89–90, 100; studios and, 88; WGA (Writers Guild of America) and, 29, 190; WGA strike (2007–8) and, 42
new spec format, 88, 90, 95–99, 100, 166, 209, 256n70
Newsroom, The (2012–14), 108–10, 113–14
new technologies, 11, 44, 68, 221, 234, 259n45. *See also* new media
New Yorker, 34
New York Times, 57, 123
Nickelodeon, 157
Nielsen ratings, 114. *See also* ratings
Nights and Weekends (2008), 24
9 Songs (2004), 176–77
9/11, 106, 117, 119
Nip/Tuck (2003–10), 115, 124
No Country for Old Men (2007), 62
Nolan, Christopher, 37, 76–77
noninteractive sequences (NIS), 204
Northern California Interactive Writers Caucus, 195
Nowalk, Brandon, 127
NPD Fungroup, 69
NYPD Blue (90's), 105, 121
NYU (New York University), 5

O'Brien, Kieran, 176
Obst, Lynda, 31–32, 33, 51, 53, 56, 60, 70

Odets, Clifford, 62
101 Dalmatians, 209
one-step deals, 58, 79–82, 82–83, 100–101, 104, 152–53
1.3.9. collective, 84–85
online celebrities, 225–26, 228–29. *See also* individuals
online collectible card game (CCG), 182
online commentary, 217
online/commercial degree programs, 239. *See also* paraindustry
online content/creators, 223–28; academia and, 219–20; animation and, 156, 223; blogs and, 217; broadcast series and, 232; celebrities and, 225–26, 228–29; comics and, 223; conglomerates and, 223; convergence and, 234, 235; convergent cable and, 138; convergent media and, 226, 233; digital distribution/technologies and, 217, 242; distribution and, 217, 225; economics and, 223; fans and, 225–26, 227, 228; film schools and, 236, 240, 241; gaming and, 232; income and, 225, 226, 234, 235; interactivity and, 233; IP (intellectual property) and, 223, 226; movies and, 223; narrative and, 233; the paraindustry and, 224, 236; screenwriters and, 101, 224; screenwriting/craft and, 25, 219, 223, 225, 235, 241; scripting and, 219, 223–28, 233, 234, 236, 242; *The Shield* (2002–8) and, 104; social media and, 217; story/telling and, 233; subscriptions and, 225, 226; *Tabletop* (board-game review show) and, 223; television and, 223, 226–27; WGA (Writers Guild of America) and, 219–20, 235; *Wikipedia* and, 217, 226; YouTube and, 225. *See also* individuals; QB (Quickbaby) (Frampton, Will); streaming
online distribution, 31, 49–51, 110–11, 146, 159–60, 165, 221, 240–41. *See also* digital distribution
online fan culture. *See* fans
online games, 218. *See also* video/games
online networks, 138, 141
online streaming. *See* streaming
online television, 9, 31, 137
Orange Is the New Black (2013–), 191–92
Oscillate Wildly, 170, 264n56
Oshry, Suzanne, 192
Ouellette, Laurie, 56
Outland (1981), 92
overall deals, 86–87
OZ (1997–2003), 110
Oz: The Great and Powerful (2013), 94

Pacific Rim (2013), 32–33, 34, 36
Pacino, Al, 168
paidiaic play, 185, 189
Palahniuk, Chuck, 83–84
Palumbo, Dennis, 1–2
Panser (a.k.a. Danielle Mackey), 228, 232
paraindustry: business frame and the, 3, 11–12; Campbell, Joseph and the, 15; convergence and the, 238, 239; convergent media and the, 236; film education and the, 5–6; freelance screenwriting and the, 88; gatekeepers and the, 90; genres and the, 15–16; independent cinema and the, 144; international franchises and the, 32; online/commercial degree programs and the, 239; online content/creators and the, 224, 236; practitioner frame and the, 3; prestige films and the, 24; scholarship and the, 15; screenplays and the, 15–16; screenwriter interviews and the, 4–5, 22; Screenwriters University and the, 15; screenwriting/craft and the, 5–6, 11, 14, 25, 90, 222, 242; scripting and the, 219; story/telling and the, 15, 99; studio model transformation and the, 22; video/games and the, 195, 211; web series and the, 224. *See also* film schools

parallel development, 77–78, 94
Paramount Communications, 67
Paramount Consent Decree of 1948, 88, 145
Paramount Pictures, 30, 65, 159
Paramount Vantage, 147
Parental Guidelines System, 120
Parents Television Council, 123
Paul, Cinco, 70
Pay Per View, 58
Pay TV, 227
Pearce, Celia, 265n8
Pencils Down campaign, 48
pensions, 45, 59–60
Pepperdine University, 236
Perculia, 232
Perlmutter, Isaac "Ike," 76
Perren, Alisa, 19–20
Petrie, Daniel, Jr., 81
PewDiePie (a.k.a. Felix Kjellberg), 227, 228, 271n19
Phantom Menace, The (1999), 93, 95
Phoenix, Satine, 224
piracy, 49, 68, 250n48. *See also* IP (intellectual property)
Pixar, 158–59, 163, 263n50
Planescape Torment (game), 200–201
platforms: accounting and, 57; animation and, 157; convergent screenwriters and, 3; film schools and, 241; Internet as, 221; screenwriting and, 24; tentpole/2.0/screenwriters and, 11, 38, 214; WGA (Writers Guild of America) and, 189, 190. *See also* new media
Platten, John Zuur, 200, 211
Playa Vista, 237
Player, The (1991), 27–29
player agency, 203
plot, 11. *See also* story/telling
podcasts, 224, 232
Poetics (Aristotle), 15
Polan, Dana, 125
political economy, 17–22
Poltergeist (1982), 34, 71
Poniewozik, James, 123
POP.com, 160

Portman, Natalie, 139, 140
postnetwork era, 259n45
Pounder, CCH, 119
Powdermaker, Hortense, 1, 7, 20, 38
practitioner frame, 3, 4, 6–7, 14, 28, 164, 181, 242
Preach Gaming (Youtube show), 232
Predator (1987), 94
Premium Video on Demand, 58
pressures. *See* constraints/pressures
prestige dramas, 2, 23, 38, 58, 147. *See also* complex dramas
prestige films, 24
previsualization, 30, 90, 93–95, 226
prewrites, 79–80, 82
Price, Steven, 13, 14
Primer (2004), 167
Prince, Stephen, 12–13
Prince of Persia: The Sands of Time (2010), 186
procedural rhetoric, 189
producers. *See* producers-writers; television showrunners
producer's gross, 50–51
Producers Guild of America, 81
producer's passes, 81, 82
producers-writers, 85, 135, 137, 221. *See also* television showrunners
production, 18–19, 21, 66, 79, 107, 136, 156, 163–64, 165. *See also* microbudget productions
production costs, 30–31
production culture, 7, 13, 19–21, 25, 87, 115, 126
Production Culture: Industrial Reflexivity and Critical Practice in Film and Television (Caldwell), 20, 126
production management, 47–48
Production Studies: Cultural Studies of Media Industries (Banks, Mayer, Caldwell), 20–21
Prometheus (2012), 96–97
Propp, Vladimir, 15, 245n8, 246n18
PS4 (game console), 227
Pseudo.com, 160
Pulp Fiction (1994), 143
Punch 21 Productions, 150

QB (Quickbaby) (Frampton, Will), 228–34; collaborators and, 271n21; convergence and, 234; convergent media and, 228; fans and, 217–18, 228–31, 232–33, 270n17, 271n20; income and, 225, 269n1, 270n18; interactivity and, 217–18; IP (intellectual property) and, 218; narrative and, 217, 219, 230, 231, 232–33; as online celebrity, 225, 226; Ryan, Shawn and, 138; as screenwriter, 218–19, 233; scripting and, 219, 230, 232–34, 242; story/telling and, 219–20, 234; streaming and, 217–18, 219, 229, 230–31, 233, 270n17; subscriptions and, 217, 269n1; Twitch (platform) and, 138, 202, 217, 225, 228, 229–30, 233, 268n55, 270n17, 270n18; Wargaming Public Co Ltd. and, 269n2, 270n17; *World of Tanks (WoT)* (game) and, 202, 217–20; YouTube and, 218, 228, 229–30, 232, 233, 270n17

QSF (Quickybaby's Special Forces), 229, 230–31

Quesada, Joe, 75

race, 17–18, 40, 106–7, 121, 126
radio, 221, 246n17
Rafferty, Terrence, 33
Raiders of the Lost Ark (1981), 90–91, 92
Raimi, Sam, 94
Ramos, Luis Antonio, 102
rape, 126–33
Rasulo, Jay, 73
Ratatouille (2007), 163
ratings, 22, 114, 115–16, 122–23, 125
Ray, Billy, 7–8
reality television, 55–56, 57, 121, 189–90, 192
real-time strategy games. *See* RTS (real-time strategy) games
redemptive endings, 15–16
Red Storm Entertainment, 204

Reilly, Kevin, 117, 120
Reitman, Ivan, 89
Reliance Big Entertainment, 86
Rescue Me (2004–11), 115
Resident Evil (2002), 186
residual-free windows, 57, 60
residuals: above the line talent and, 12–13; ancillary markets and, 41, 45; animation and, 161, 263n49; *Annual Financial Report* (2014) (WGA) and, 41; cable and, 59; DGA (Directors Guild of America) and, 54, 56–57; DVDs and, 44, 49, 59; home video and, 44, 45, 49, 50, 57; income and, 41; MBA (Minimum Basic Agreement) and, 44–45, 189; media convergence and, 41; movies and, 41, 46–47, 57; network television and, 59; new media and, 41–42, 47, 59; residual-free windows and, 57, 60; screenwriters and, 12–13, 83, 88; streaming and, 57, 59–60; television and, 41, 44, 46–47, 57, 59, 60; WGA strike (2007–8) and, 44–45, 46–47, 50, 53–54. *See also* digital residuals

revenues: ancillary markets and, 67, 68; animation and, 160; digital distribution/technologies and, 49, 78; DVDs and, 33, 136; Hollywood and, 145; major studios and, 67; screenwriters and, 44, 79, 136; streaming and, 49; WGA strike (2007–8) and, 44, 51, 136. *See also* advertising revenues; domestic box office revenues; international box office revenues

rewrites, 79, 81, 82–84, 99, 152, 241
Rhimes, Shonda, 47–48
Rhoda (1974–78), 114
Ride Along (2014), 74
Road to El Dorado, The (2000), 158
Robbins, Tim, 27
Rockwell, Sam, 149
Rodman, Howard, 45–46, 89–90
Rogue One: A Star Wars Story (2016), 10, 69, 187
Rokos, Will, 174

role-playing games. *See* RPG (role-playing games)
roles, 39–40, 69
romantic comedies, 2, 23, 38, 139, 154
Rosenblum, Bruce, 225
Rotten Tomatoes, 139
Rough Go, A (gameplay video), 182–83
Roundtable in Cyberspace, 192, 193–94
Roven, Charles, 77
Royal, Bert, 78
royalties, 194
RPG (role-playing games), 188, 200, 202, 211, 214
RTS (real-time strategy) games, 188, 202, 208–9
Rush, Jeff, 16
Russo, Rene, 41
Ryan, Maureen, 124–25
Ryan, Shawn: as auteur, 105–6; cable and, 23; FX Network and, 115–16, 117, 134; hierarchy and, 22; screenwriter interviews and, 4; *The Shield* (2002–8) and, 105–8, 109, 115, 121, 124, 126, 127, 130, 132–34, 259n36; Standards and Practices and, 113, 132–33; SVOD (Subscription Video on Demand) and, 114; as television showrunner, 104, 124, 133–38; *Timeless* (2016–) and, 124, 137; WGA strike (2007–8) and, 23, 48, 134–37

SAG (Screen Actors Guild), 53–54, 59
Salt, Waldo, 146
same-day series releases, 114
Sam's Club, 170
Samuel Goldwyn Writing Award, 150
Sandler, Kevin, 107, 115, 257n5
San Francisco State University, 40, 239
Saunders, Dusty, 105
Scheer, Paul, 224
Schmidt, Rohn, 117, 127, 133
scholarship, 5, 7, 12–17, 17–22, 124–26, 144, 185
Schulner, David, 136
Schulz, Ben, 182–83

science fiction films: as blockbusters, 68; Carruth, Shane and, 167; home video and, 146; independent cinema and, 145; kinetics and, 96–98; major studios and, 23, 38; Moreland, Robert and, 157; the paraindustry and, 15–16; spec scripts and, 71, 97; tentpole movies as, 71–72; Universal Pictures and, 74; video/games and, 188. *See also individual films*
science fiction franchises, 67
science fiction series. *See Firefly* (2002–3)
Scoggins Report, The, 71
Screen Actors Guild. *See* SAG (Screen Actors Guild)
Screen International (magazine), 70, 81
Screenplay, The (Field), 15
Screenplay: Authorship, Theory and Criticism, The (Price), 13
screenplay manuals, 15, 253n21
screenplays: action movies and, 90–93; analog effects and, 90–93; *Analyzing the Screenplay* (Nelmes), 13–14; animation and, 157, 158, 162–63; as concept sketch, 95–96; copyright and, 194; digital technologies and, 90, 92–93; experimental screenplays, 169–70; film schools and, 237, 238–39, 241; *Final Draft* (software) and, 15; formats and, 100, 205, 256n70; *A History of the Screenplay* (Price), 14; as industrial form, 14; interactive media and, 246n17; *I Want Your Love* (2012) and, 172–74, 177; kinetics and, 96–99; layering and, 93–94; manic cinema and, 34, 35; master-scene screenplays, 88, 90, 92–93, 100; Murphy, Terry and, 246n18; paraindustry and, 15–16; parallel development and, 77–78; previsualization and, 90, 93–95; production and, 21; screenwriters and, 16, 21; scripting and, 226; special-effects and, 90–93; studios and, 57–58; television and, 246n17;

tentpole movies/paradigm and, 65, 95; textual analysis and, 11, 16; three-act screenplays, 6, 15–16, 166, 222; video and, 246n17; video/games writing and, 213; web series and, 224; WGA (Writers Guild of America) and, 197; WGA West Registry and, 246n17. *See also* new spec format; spec scripts; tentpole screenplays

screenplay workshops, 15. *See also* paraindustry

screens, 2, 8, 41, 70–71, 238

Screen Writer (journal), 194

screenwriter 1.0, 2–3, 235. *See also* screenwriters

screenwriter 2.0: convergence and, 3, 186, 223–24; convergent media and, 242; Dinehart, Stephen E., IV as, 208; film schools and, 240; IP (intellectual property) and, 24; new media and, 199, 222; platforms and, 214; QB (Quickbaby) (Frampton, Will) as, 218; screenwriting craft and, 222; video/games and, 24–25, 186

screenwriter credit: franchises and, 78; free drafts and, 82; industry changes and, 149; new media and, 22; prewrites and, 82; residuals and, 83; rewrites and, 83–84; video/games and, 22, 197, 200, 201–2, 203; WGA (Writers Guild of America) and, 22, 83; as worker currency, 88

screenwriter interviews, 4–5, 21–22, 142

screenwriter rights, 13

screenwriters: as above the line talent, 12–13; adaptation and, 7, 11; alienation and, 78–87; animation and, 157, 160, 162; authorship and, 203; bake-offs and, 151–52; big-budget movies and, 23; box office and, 79; business frame and, 3, 4, 6–7, 181; cable and, 79, 221; capitalism and, 10; character and, 7, 11; class tensions and, 72;

collaboration and, 8, 74, 93, 155–56; comedies and, 23, 143; comics and, 8, 9, 196; conglomerates and, 66, 81, 99; conglomeration and, 10, 11, 29; Conor, Bridget and, 28; consolidation and, 29; constraints/pressures and, 2, 6, 9, 19, 38; convergence and, 100, 199–200; convergent media and, 12, 101, 181, 185; convergent screenwriters, 3, 4, 16, 29, 42, 222, 235–36; convergent television and, 220; creativity and, 1, 2, 6, 8, 9, 16, 79, 80; cultural legitimacy and, 196; DC Comics Universe (DCCU) and the, 77; definitions of, 8, 12; digital technologies and, 9; dramas and, 70–71, 148, 220; *Dreams on Spec* (2007) and, 1–2, 3; economics and, 1–2, 11, 29, 41, 42, 79, 87; fear-based working culture and, 151–52; first drafts and, 80, 81; formulas and, 3, 5, 7, 8, 80; franchises and, 23, 74, 78; free drafts and, 79–80, 81, 82; freelance screenwriting and, 88–90; genres and, 33, 74; Gramsci, Antonio and, 10; gross point participation and, 84–85; *The Hangover* (2009) and, 23; *Harry Potter* (2010 and 2011) and, 23; HBO and, 60, 70; health benefits and, 45, 59; hierarchy and, 79; higher education and, 5–6; high v low art and, 190; Hollywood and, 27–29, 83, 87, 194, 222; ideology and, 10, 11; income and, 1–2, 9, 23–24, 41, 59, 78, 79, 86, 166, 220; independent cinema and, 143, 148–49; as independent contractors, 194; independent filmmaking and, 140–41, 142; Indiewood and, 142; industry changes and, 149; interactivity and, 11, 214; international appeal and, 31–32; Internet and, 11; IP (intellectual property) and, 194; labor and, 38, 80, 138; layering and, 93–94; low-budget genre and, 146; major studios and, 68; manic cinema

screenwriters *(continued)*
and, 34, 74; Marvel Studios and, 75–76; media and, 143–44, 242–43; media convergence and, 3, 8, 23–24, 221; microbudget productions and, 2, 166; minority screenwriters, 39; movies and, 8, 9, 221; narrative and, 100, 186–87; network television and, 59; New Hollywood and, 146–47; new media and, 9, 101, 181, 220, 222; new spec format and, 99; new technologies and, 11; one-step deals and, 79–82, 152–53; online content/creators and, 101, 224; overall deals and, 86–87; parallel development and, 77–78; pensions and, 45, 59–60; platforms and, 11; *The Player* (1991) and, 27–29; plot and, 11; practitioner frame and, 3, 4, 6–7; prewrites and, 79–80, 82; producer's passes and, 81, 82; production and, 79; production culture and, 13, 87; QB (Quickbaby) (Frampton, Will) as, 218, 233; reality television and, 190; reduced opportunities and, 28, 29, 55, 68, 78; residuals and, 12–13, 83, 88; revenues and, 44, 79, 136; rewrites and, 79, 81, 82–84, 99, 152; screenplays and, 16, 21; screens and, 8; screenwriter 1.0, 2–3, 235; screenwriter interviews, 4–5, 21–22, 142; scripting and, 8, 242–43; self-promotion and, 5; special-effects and, 93; spec scripts and, 21, 89–90, 100; spectacle and, 36–37; story/telling and, 7, 11, 23–24, 33, 189; structure and, 11; studios and, 10, 57–58, 58–59, 60–61, 66, 68, 79–87, 88, 99, 156; superhero franchises and, 74; SVOD (Subscription Video on Demand) and, 148; sweepstakes pitching and, 77–78, 79–80, 104, 151–52, 254n31; television and, 8, 9, 60, 70–71, 83, 101, 154–56, 190, 220, 221; tentpole movies and, 3, 60–61, 70, 72, 82–83, 101, 153, 242; tentpole paradigm and, 11, 20, 65, 79, 141; tentpole screenwriters, 38, 65, 87, 93–94; *Transformers* movies and, 23; transmedia marketing and, 10; Twitch (platform) and the, 243; *United Hollywood* (blog) and, 152; unpaid work and, 81–82, 152–53; video/games and, 8, 9, 101, 181, 186–87, 188–89, 192, 194, 195, 198, 199–200, 203–4, 222; video/games writing and, 186–87, 210–13, 214–15; Warner Bros. and, 77; WGA (Writers Guild of America) and, 13, 29, 190, 193, 219–20, 235–36; WGA strike (2007–8) and, 43, 52, 53, 54–55; *Wikipedia* and, 8; women screenwriters, 39–41; *Wonder Woman* (2017) and, 77–78; *Writers: A History of American Screenwriters and Their Guild, The* (Banks), 13; writers' collectives and, 84–86. *See also* A-list writers; microbudget screenwriters; new screenwriters; screenwriter 2.0; screenwriter credit; screenwriting craft; television screenwriters; WGA (Writers Guild of America); WGA strike (2007–8); *individual screenwriters*

Screen Writers' Guild (SWG), 193, 194

Screenwriters University, 15, 224, 225

screenwriting: auteur theory and, 12; class tensions and, 235; conglomerates and, 11, 236; conglomeration and, 29, 218–19; convergence and, 218–19, 236, 237, 241; creativity and, 14; digital technologies and, 16, 22–23, 99–100, 220–21; economics and, 25, 41, 87; filmmakers and, 240; film schools and, 5, 25, 236–41; the future of, 235–36; genres and, 23; globalization and, 29; history of, 221; Hollywood and, 61, 87; independent cinema and, 141; industrial self-reflexivity and, 14; industry lore and, 22; *I Want Your Love* (2012) and, 172–74, 177, 178; Loyola Marymount University

and, 237; media convergence and, 29, 185; MFA (Masters of Fine Arts) and, 236, 238, 239; microbudget productions and, 220–21, 241; new media and, 185; online content/creators and, 25, 235, 241; paraindustry and, 5–6, 11, 25; platforms and, 24; post-craft and, 241; production culture and, 13, 25; QB (Quickbaby) (Frampton, Will) and, 218–19; scholarship and, 12–17; *Screen Writing: Texts and Scripts from Independent Films* (MacDonald), 169–70; scripting and, 219–20, 222, 223; *Scriptnotes* (podcast), 74; sexual content and, 172–75; spectacle and, 175; story/telling and, 10, 238; studios and, 61, 87; SVOD (Subscription Video on Demand) and, 148; television/showrunners and, 135, 137, 236; tentpole franchises and, 241; 3-D and, 30; unions and, 11; video/games/writing and, 186, 187, 196, 198, 218–19; WGA (Writers Guild of America) and, 149, 190, 192, 193; WGA strike (2007–8) and, 23, 135. *See also* freelance screenwriting; independent screenwriting
Screenwriting (Horton and Hoxter), 14, 25
screenwriting competitions, 15
screenwriting craft: academia and, 236, 242; conglomeration and, 29; convergence and, 3, 8–9, 214, 243; convergent screenwriters and, 222; definitions of, 221–23, 235, 242; film schools and, 222, 223; markets and, 220; new/media and, 222, 223; online content/creators and, 219, 223, 225; the paraindustry and, 14, 222, 242; *The Player* (1991) and, 27; screenwriters/2.0 and, 222, 242–43; *Screenwriting* (Horton and Hoxter) and, 14; television dramas and, 107; tentpole movies/paradigm and, 65, 243; video/games and, 181, 198, 214, 218–19; WGA (Writers Guild of America) and, 25, 219–20, 235, 242
Screenwriting: Creative Labor and Professional Practice (Conor), 13
screenwriting curricula, 5, 236–41
Screenwriting Expo (2004), 89
Screenwriting: History, Theory, and Practice (Maras), 13
screenwriting manuals, 5, 6, 15. *See also* self-help
screenwriting paraindustry. *See* paraindustry
Screenwriting Research Network, 13
screenwriting software, 15, 90
Screen Writing: Texts and Scripts from Independent Films (MacDonald), 169–70
Scrimshaw, Joseph, 224
Script Culture and the American Screenplay (Boon), 13
scripter 1.0, 235–36
scripting, 217–43; convergence and, 219, 242–43; digital media and, 219; fans and, 223; feature films and, 226; film schools and, 219, 238, 241; Maras, Steven and, 8, 95, 219, 226; narrative and, 230; online content/creators and, 219, 223–28, 233, 234, 236, 242; QB (Quickbaby) (Frampton, Will) and, 219, 230, 232–34, 242; Ryan, Shawn on, 135; screenplays and, 226; screenwriters and, 8, 242–43; screenwriting and, 219–20, 222, 223; video/games and, 222; web series and, 224; WGA (Writers Guild of America) and, 235
Script Magazine, 15
Scriptnotes (podcast), 74, 81–82
scripts, 108. *See also* screenplays; scripting
Scrubs (2001–10), 139, 140
Seata, Jennifer, 115
Second Life (game), 184
Secret Wars (comics), 37
self-help, 14, 16
self-promotion, 5
SerB (Sergey Burkatovskiy), 202

Sex, Lies, and Videotape (1989), 147
sexual content, 113, 122, 126–33, 146–47, 168–78, 259n39
sexuality, 121, 125
Shamama, Jack, 171
Sheldon, Lee, 210
Shelton, Lynn, 24, 166–67
Shield, The (2002–8), 102–38; ancillary markets and, 257n2; antiheroes and, 103; belief systems and, 109; below-the-line workers and, 107–8, 115; as brand, 110, 135; cable and, 104, 108, 111, 122–23, 126, 220; character-driven dramas and, 117; collaboration and, 107–8; controversial themes and, 106–7, 109, 121, 123–24, 125, 133, 134; as drama, 23, 70, 137; DVDs and, 124; Excellence in Television award and, 106; females and, 117–19, 122, 259n39; FX Network and, 23, 48, 70, 102, 106–7, 111, 115, 116–17, 119–20, 122–24, 125–26, 134, 136, 259n36; genres and, 117, 259n36; Golden Globe and, 124; HBO and, 111, 120, 124; kinetics and, 126; Liguori, Peter and, 116–17, 119, 120; Los Angeles Police Department (LAPD) and, 106, 117; masculinity economics and, 126; "Mum" episode, 126–33; narrative and, 102, 124; network television and, 124, 125; 9/11 and, 106, 117, 119; online content/creators and, 104; Parents Television Council and, 123; production culture and, 115, 126; ratings and, 114, 115–16, 122–23; reality television and, 121; Ryan, Shawn and, 105–8, 109, 115, 121, 124, 126, 127, 130, 132–34, 259n36; scholarship and, 124–26; screenwriter interviews and, 4; as *Shieldy*, 115, 122, 133, 134; *The Sopranos* (1999–2007) and, 124–26; as spec script, 105; Standards and Practices and, 111–13, 132–33, 259n39; story/telling and, 104, 125; TV-MA rating and, 120; WGA strike (2007–8) and, 48, 135–36, 137. See also individuals

Short, Thomas, 56
short films, 9, 240, 272n37
Showtime, 9, 113, 120
Showtime New Media, 159
Shrek franchise, 159, 164
Siegel, Tatiana, 82–83
SIGGRAPH (Special Interest Group on Graphics and Interactive Techniques), 72
Silverstein, Melissa, 154
Simon, David, 47–48
Simpsons, The (1989–), 45, 50, 114
Singer, Bryan, 94–95
Sins of the Father (television movie), 116
Sister Hibiscus, 223, 269n5
sitcoms, 114, 237, 238, 241. See also comedies
Sixteenth Street Baptist Church bombing, 116, 258n27
Slay the Dragon: Writing Great Stories for Video/games (Bryant and Giglio), 195
slug-line format, 169
Small Wonders (1995), 150
Smith, Dina, 50
Snyder, Daniel J., 1, 3
Snyder, Zach, 77, 78
Sobchack, Vivian, 98
social media: Facebook, 24; horror films and, 38, 146; microbudget productions and, 165; online content/creators and, 217, 223; screenwriting and, 11; WGA strike (2007–8) and, 45, 46, 51–52, 54
social problem films, 145
Soderbergh, Steven, 147
Solomon, Charles, 158
Son of a Beach (2000–02), 116
Sony Pictures Entertainment, 65, 66–67, 78, 84, 85, 157, 164
Sopranos, The (1999–2007), 23, 47–48, 103, 110, 123, 124–26, 191–92
Sorkin, Aaron, 23, 109–10, 114
South Park (1997–), 120, 227–28, 271n19
SP (storyline) speech, 208–9

Space Chimps movies, 157, 160, 161
Space Marines (1996), 157
special-effects, 33, 34, 36, 38, 65, 90–93
spec scripts: action/adventure movies and, 71; animation and, 158; assignments and, 100; comedies and, 71; dramas and, 71; economics and, 43; *Final Draft Big Break* (competition) and, 15; freelance screenwriting and, 88; gatekeepers and, 89; genres and, 71; Gray, Pamela and, 149–50; Hollywood and, 71; international appeal and, 32; A-list writers and, 79; one-step deals and, 58, 81; reduced opportunities and, 3, 23, 24, 100; science fiction films and, 71, 97; screenwriters and, 21, 89–90, 100; self-help market and, 14; *The Shield* (2002–8) as, 105; spec boom, 22–23, 29, 99–100; story and structure frame and, 5–6; studios and, 89–90, 100. *See also* new spec format
spectacle: action movies and, 33–34, 90; audiences and, 72–73; budget and, 36–37; China and, 31; digital technologies and, 33–34, 90; domestic box office revenues and, 72; genres and, 30–31, 70; international audiences and, 32; kinetics and, 98; narrative and, 34–36; screens and, 70–71; screenwriters/screenwriting and, 36–37, 175; story/telling and, 35, 98; tentpole movies/screenplays and, 35, 36–37, 95; *Transformers* franchise and, 34–36
Speier, Michael, 123
Spiderman movies, 38, 84
Spielberg, Steven, 68, 79, 143
Spink, J. C., 84
Spirit: Stallion of the Cimarron (2002), 161
sports, 116
Standards and Practices, 104, 111–13, 132–33, 259n39
Stanton, John, 73

StarCraft franchise, 202
Star Trek: The Next Generation, 150
Star Wars (games), 10, 202
Star Wars (movies), 10, 68–69, 71, 91, 92, 93, 95, 145, 187
Steig, William, 164
Steinberg, David, 68
Stern, Howard, 116
story and structure frame, 5–6, 6–7, 14, 35, 181, 242
storyboards, 95, 127, 161, 162, 212, 222, 226
story consultants, 15
story/telling: animation and, 158, 162, 163, 164; backstories and, 209, 213; blockbusters and, 34; collaboration and, 80; comic book movie genre and the, 37; convergent media and, 220; cross-platforms and, 38; DC Comics Universe (DCCU) and, 76–77, 78; electrocardiogram story/telling, 248n17; *Garden State* (2004) and, 140; independent cinema and, 142, 144, 147; independent filmmaking and, 16; interactive/crowd-led storytelling, 208, 233, 234; interactivity and, 214, 219, 233; *I Want Your Love* (2012) and, 172, 176, 177; kinetics and, 98; Marvel franchises and, 37; MCU (Marvel Comics Universe) and, 78; microbudget productions and, 24, 169, 180; mumblecore and, 166; narrative and, 12; network television and, 103, 111; new spec format and, 90; *The Newsroom* (2012–14) and, 109; online content/creators and, 233; paraindustry and, 15, 99; *The Player* (1991) and, 27–28; previsualization and, 90, 94; QB (Quickbaby) (Frampton, Will) and, 219–20, 234; *The Screenplay* (Field) and, 15; screenwriters and, 7, 11, 23–24, 33, 189; screenwriting and, 10, 238; sexual content and, 169, 172; *The Shield* (2002–8) and, 104, 125; special-effects and, 93; spectacle

story/telling *(continued)*
and, 35, 98; *Star Wars* (1977) and, 69; streaming and, 233; studios and, 81, 100; superhero franchises and, 74, 75–76; television and, 39, 103, 138; television showrunners and, 48, 104, 105, 113, 133, 155; tentpole movies and, 37, 72–73; transmedia storytelling, 9, 16, 208; video/games and, 181, 188–89, 194–95, 196, 198, 200, 203, 209–11, 212–13, 214, 222; video/games writing and, 209, 212; web series and, 224; WGA (Writers Guild of America) and, 219–20; WGA strike (2007–8) and, 43; WOW (*World of Warcraft*) and, 266n21. *See also* narrative

Strand Releasing, 168

streaming: consumption and, 227; creativity and, 164; digital/distribution and, 44, 58; Duplass, Jay and Mark and, 167; games industry and, 227; income and, 219, 269n1; independent animation and, 164; interactivity and, 219, 233; Internet and, 221, 227; major studios and, 67; narrative and, 219; online content/creators and, 225; QB (Quickbaby) (Frampton, Will) and, 217–18, 219, 229, 230–31, 233, 270n17; residuals and, 57, 59–60; revenues and, 49; story/telling and, 233; television dramas and, 188–89; video games industry and, 227. *See also* online content/creators; online distribution; Twitch (platform)

Streep, Meryl, 150

Street Fighter (1994), 186

strikes, 18–19, 27, 44, 56. *See also* WGA strike (2007–8)

Strong, Danny, 69

Strong, Tara, 164

structure, 11, 238

student films, 141

studio model transformation, 22

studios: action movies and, 38; AMPTP (Alliance of Motion Picture and Television Producers) and, 44; animation and, 158–59, 163–64, 165; assignments and, 68, 88; bake-offs and, 151–52; blaxploitation films and, 145; blockbusters and, 38; character-driven dramas and, 33, 147; comics and, 24; digital distribution and, 57; Directors Guild of America (DGA) and the, 54; dramas and, 147, 153; 80/20 formula and, 50; females and, 153–54; film festivals and, 38; formulas and, 64; franchises and, 32, 78, 100; gatekeepers and, 89; genres and, 33; hierarchy and, 79; independent cinema and, 141, 143, 144–45, 147, 148, 180; independent screenwriters and, 153; Indiewood and, 179; international franchises and, 32; markets and, 29–33; mini-major studios, 65; new media and, 57; one-step deals and, 80–82, 152–53; online distribution and, 31; production company partnering and, 38; production costs and, 31; reality television and, 57; residual-free windows and, 57; screenplays and, 57–58; screenwriters and, 10, 57–58, 58–59, 60–61, 66, 68, 79–87, 88, 99, 156; screenwriting and, 61, 87; spec scripts and, 89–90, 100; story/telling and, 81, 100; television showrunners and, 48–49; tentpole movies and, 28, 64–65, 70–72, 72–73, 74–75; tentpole paradigm and, 11, 65, 78; 3-D and, 30; 2011 negotiations (WGA) and, 58–59; video/games and, 24; WGA strike (2007–8) and the, 43, 45, 48–49, 53, 54–55, 60, 87; Whedon, Joss on, 53; writers' collectives and, 84, 86. *See also* conglomerates; major studios; MPAA (Motion Picture Association of America)

subscriptions, 217, 225, 226, 269n1

Subscription Video on Demand. *See* Netflix; SVOD (Subscription Video on Demand)

Suicide Squad (2016), 77

Sundance Film Festival, 16, 24, 139, 147, 148, 167, 168
Sundance-Miramax boom, 170
Sunderland, Craig, 132
Super 8 (2011), 97
superhero franchises, 67, 69, 74–78, 186
Superman franchise, 38
Super Mario Brothers (1993), 186
Surnow, Joel, 106
Sutherland, Kiefer, 106
Sutter, Kurt, 126, 127, 130, 132, 133
SVOD (Subscription Video on Demand), 58, 67, 103–4, 113, 114, 148, 226
Swanberg, Joe, 24, 166–67
Swank, Hilary, 149
sweepstakes pitching, 77–78, 79–80, 104, 151–52, 254n31
SWG (Screen Writers' Guild), 193, 194
SXSW (South by Southwest), 166
synergies, 66–67, 74, 186

Tabletop (board-game review show), 223–24, 226, 236
Tankfest, 228–29. *See also* QB (Quickbaby) (Frampton, Will); *World of Tanks (WoT)* (game)
Tarantino, Quentin, 143
Tassi, Paul, 197
TBS, 117
Teamsters, 48, 59, 135
teamwork, 11. *See also* collaboration
Teatime with Tuskeh (Youtube show), 232
teen comedies, 2, 38
Teen Titans Go (television), 77
television: alt.screenwriters (column) and, 198–99; ancillary markets and, 37; animation and, 156, 161; audiences and, 113–14; big-budget movies and, 31; box office and, 248n5; character development and, 155; character-driven dramas and, 70–71, 220; collaboration and, 83, 155–56; convergence and, 192; convergent television, 110, 113, 138, 220; creativity and, 60, 71, 103–4, 154–55; cultural legitimacy and, 191–92, 196; digital technologies and, 51, 137, 259n45; distribution and, 110–11; economics and, 126; European schools and, 237; Excellence in Television award, 106; film schools and, 236–37, 238–39; gender and, 192; genres and, 138; Gray, Pamela and, 149–50, 154–56, 181; income and, 41, 220; interactive television, 116; Internet and, 113–14, 259n45; Jenkins, Leeroy (character/meme) and, 183; Marvel Studios and, 76; MBA (Minimum Basic Agreement) and, 44–45; minority screenwriters and, 39; movies and, 116, 192, 193; online content/creators and, 223, 226–27; online television, 9, 31, 138; Parental Guidelines System and, 120; political economy and, 17; postnetwork era and, 259n45; residuals and, 41, 44, 46–47, 57, 59, 60; screenplays and, 246n17; screenwriters and, 8, 9, 60, 83, 101, 154–56, 190, 220, 221; screenwriting and, 137, 236; social ills and, 191; Standards and Practices and, 111; story/telling and, 39, 103, 138; strikes and, 44, 55; SVOD (Subscription Video on Demand) and, 67; teamwork and, 11; Television Writers Association (TWA), 193; University of Texas at Austin and, 240; WGA (Writers Guild of America) and, 154–55, 192–93; WGA strike (2007–8) and, 55; women screenwriters and, 39–40. *See also* cable; expanded television; Lionsgate; network television; reality television; *individual networks; individual shows*
television comedies, 9
television dramas: complex dramas, 23; cultural legitimacy and, 191–92; four-act structure and, 222; FX Network and, 9, 115–16; screenwriters and, 9,

television dramas *(continued)*
60, 70–71, 220; screenwriting craft
and, 107; streaming and, 188–89;
television showrunners and, 110. *See
also individual shows*
television movies, 116
television networks. *See* network
television
television screenwriters, 9, 83, 104,
110–11, 113, 114, 211, 213, 238
television showrunners, 102–38;
audiences and, 114–15; below-the-
line workers and, 107–8; as brands,
110, 114; cable and, 108, 113,
114; circuit of culture and, 115;
collaboration and, 107–8, 209;
controversial themes and, 113;
creativity and, 104, 108, 113, 133–
34, 220; genres and, 114; HBO and,
113; Internet and, 114; marketing
and, 108; narrative and, 105;
network television and, 48–49,
104, 108, 114; production and, 136;
screenwriting and, 135; Standards
and Practices and, 104; story/telling
and, 48, 104, 105, 113, 133, 155;
studios and, 48–49; television
dramas and, 110; University of Texas
at Austin and, 240; WGA strike
(2007–8) and, 42, 47–49, 134–37;
Wikipedia on, 102, 104; Writers
Guild of America (WGA) and,
134–35. *See also* individuals
Television Will Be Revolutionized, The
(Lotz), 126
Television Writers Association (TWA),
193
Televisuality (Caldwell), 20
tentpole franchises, 30, 32, 71–72, 77,
152, 241
tentpole movies, 62–101; action movies
as, 71–72; as amusement park ride,
34, 35; ancillary markets and, 62,
71–72, 73–74, 103; animation and,
71–72; blockbusters and, 64; box
office and, 74–75; brands and, 71–72;
conglomerates and, 61, 74–75;
creativity and, 61, 72; cross-platform
markets and, 73–74; definitions of,
62, 64–65; digital technologies and,
99; dramas and, 147; economics and,
70, 72–73, 74–75; electrocardiogram
story/telling and, 248n17; exhibition
and, 70; females and, 69; films
schools and, 241; genres and, 68;
Hollywood and, 28, 70; horror films
as, 71–72; independent cinema and,
144; kinetics and, 98, 99; labor and,
11–12; lektonic representation and,
35–36; major studios and, 2, 68,
70–72, 82–83; as manic cinema,
34, 35, 87, 100; Marvel Studios and,
36; MCU (Marvel Comics Universe)
as, 74–75; narrative and, 36, 100,
248n17; network television and,
64–65; previsualization and, 90;
science fiction films as, 71–72;
screenwriters and, 3, 60–61, 70, 72,
82–83, 101, 153, 242; screenwriting
craft and, 65, 243; spectacle and, 95;
Star Wars (1977) and, 69; story/
telling and, 37, 72–73; studios and,
28, 64–65, 70–72, 72–73, 74–75;
superhero franchises as, 74; 3-D and,
30; time pressures and, 94; video/
games and, 186; Warner Bros. and,
74–75; WGA (Writers Guild of
America) and, 13, 242; *Wikipedia*
and, 62, 64–65. *See also* tentpole
franchises
tentpole paradigm: ancillary markets
and the, 74; animation and the, 65;
conglomerates and the, 32, 73;
creativity and the, 103; independent
cinema and the, 147; independent
screenwriters and the, 142;
international audiences and the,
32; microbudget productions
and the, 65; new screenwriters
and the, 141; online writing and
the, 65; screenplays and the, 65;
screenwriters and the, 11, 20, 65,
79, 141, 142; screenwriting craft and
the, 65; studios and the, 11, 65, 78;

Universal Pictures and the, 73–74; video/games and the, 65
tentpole screenplays, 35, 36–37, 58, 93
tentpole screenwriters, 36–37, 38, 65, 87, 93–94
Terminator films, 71, 93
Terriers (2010), 124
Terry, Frank, 160
textual analysis, 7, 11, 16, 17–22, 24, 240
Thalberg, Irving, 27, 28
That's My Bush (television show), 120
Thelma and Louise (1991), 40
theme parks, 66, 67, 73, 87. See also individual theme parks
third-person shooter (TPS) games, 202
Thomas Crowne Affair, The (1999), 41
Thompson, Anne, 40
Thorburn, David, 125
3-D, 30–31, 159, 248n5, 263n36, 269n4
three-act screenplays, 6, 15–16, 166, 222
thriller films, 23, 28–29, 38, 70, 71
Thunder Pig (2002), 157
Thurman, Uma, 41
ticket sales, 30. See also box office; domestic box office revenues
Time (magazine), 123
Timeless (2016–), 124, 137
Tinic, Serra, 20
Tiny Furniture (2010), 24, 166
TNT, 117
Todd, Deborah, 187, 195, 198, 209
Togetherness (2015), 167
Tolkin, Michael, 27, 28, 29
Tomb Raider (game), 202
Tomita, Tamlyn, 120
Toole, Anne, 210–11, 212
Toro, Guillermo del, 32
torture, 106
Total Recall (1990 and 2012), 87
Total War: Arena (game), 217
toys, 23, 36, 66, 67, 68–69, 70, 257n2
Toy Story franchise, 158–59, 263n36
TPS (third-person shooter) games, 202
Trade Chat, 228, 232
Training Day (2001), 119–20

Transformers franchise, 23, 34–36, 87, 186
Transformers movies, 30, 31, 33, 34–36
Transformers: The Game, 200
transmedia, 239, 241
transmedia marketing, 9–10
transmedia storytelling, 9, 16, 208
True Blood (2008–14), 125
Truth about Cats and Dogs, The (1996), 41
Tuskeh, 232
TV Academy film writing internship, 150
TV-MA rating, 120
TWA (Television Writers Association), 193
20th Century Fox, 65, 116, 258n26
24 (2001–10), 106
Twilight: Breaking Dawn (2011 and 2012), 72
Twitch (platform): digital distribution and, 58; QB (Quickbaby) (Frampton, Will) and, 138, 202, 217, 225, 228, 229–30, 233, 268n55, 270n17, 270n18; screenwriters and, 243
Twitch Plays Pokémon, 233
2011 negotiations (WGA), 58–59
2014 negotiations (WGA), 58, 59–60
Tzioumakis, Yannis, 144, 148

UCLA (University of California at Los Angeles), 5, 6, 32, 39, 57, 149, 240
Uhls, Jim, 83–84
unions, 10, 11, 38, 41, 45, 52–53, 190, 198. See also craft guilds; labor; Teamsters; WGA (Writers Guild of America); WGA strike (2007–8)
Unit, The (2006–9), 115, 124, 136, 261n63
United Artists, 145
United Hollywood (blog), 52–53, 251n56
United Showrunners group, 47–49
United States, 236–37
Universal Pictures, 65, 67, 73–74, 146
Universal Studios (theme park), 67

universities, 238. *See also* film schools; *individual universities*
University of California at Los Angeles (UCLA), 5, 6, 32, 57, 149, 240
University of Southern California (USC), 5, 40, 238–39
University of Texas at Austin, 240
unpaid work, 79–80, 81–82, 152–53
Upstream Color (2013), 167
USA (network), 117
Utvich, Michael, 192–93, 194

Valiant (2005), 160
Vanguard Animation, 157, 160
Vanity Fair, 109
Variety: animation and, 160, 163, 263n50; *Garden State* (2004) and, 139; one-step deals and, 80, 81, 82–83; a shingle and, 86; Sony Pictures Entertainment and, 84; WGA strike (2007–8) and, 51, 52; writers/producers and, 85
variety shows, 116
Verbinski, Gore, 73
Verrone, Patric, 45, 47, 52, 161, 190
Vestron, 146
VHS/video. *See* home video
Viacom, 67, 159, 226
video blogs, 223, 227, 228
video/games, 182–215; active scene format and, 205, 206*table;* agency and, 203; alt.screenwriters (column) and, 198–99; ancillary markets and, 23, 24, 36, 66, 183, 186; animation and, 184; authorship and, 200, 201–2, 203; backstories and, 209, 213; characters and, 212; code and, 185, 189, 200; collaboration and, 200, 201–2, 211; Computer Game Developers Conference, 195; conglomerates and, 186; consolidation and, 186; convergence and, 186, 187, 198, 199–200, 223; creativity and, 185, 187–88, 193, 194, 196, 214–15; cultural legitimacy and, 196–97; dialogue and, 182, 205–9, 211; digital technologies and, 186; Digital World, 195; DVDs and, 186; economics and, 195; emergence and, 184–85; emergent play and, 203; Excel spreadsheets and, 204, 205, 208; fans and, 185, 186, 214, 218; females and, 69; film schools and, 238–39; FPS (first-person shooter) games, 188, 211; franchises and, 186; genres and, 188, 191, 208, 211; IMA Expo, 195; interactive writing and, 194, 212–13; Internet and, 184; IP (intellectual property) and, 194; Iron Man leveling, 184, 265n10; Jenkins, Leeroy (character/ meme) and, 182–84; labor and, 198, 199; LPs (Let's Play) and, 218; ludic play and, 185, 189; ludology, 184; major/studios and, 24, 67; males and, 69; manic cinema and, 34; market for, 267n34; marketing and, 218; *Matrix* (1999) and, 9–10; mergers and, 186; meta and, 265n1; movies and, 186, 187–88, 266n22; MP (system responses) speech, 208–9; multiuser dungeons (MUD), 200; narrative and, 184, 185, 188, 195, 208, 210–11, 212, 213, 214, 222; new media and, 222, 223; new screenwriters and, 143; new spec format and, 209; online content/ creators and, 223; paidiaic play and, 185, 188–89; paraindustry and, 195, 211; procedural rhetoric and, 189; QB (Quickbaby) (Frampton, Will) and, 217–20; RPG (role-playing games), 188, 200, 202; RTS (real-time strategy) games, 188, 202, 208–9; scholarship and, 185; screenwriter 2.0 and, 24–25, 186; screenwriter credit and, 22, 197, 200, 201–2, 203; screenwriters and, 8, 9, 101, 181, 186–87, 188–89, 192, 194, 195, 198, 199–200, 203–4, 222; screenwriting/craft and, 181, 186, 187, 196, 198; scripting and, 222; social ills and, 191; SP (storyline) speech, 208–9; *Star Wars* (1977) and, 68–69; story/telling and, 181, 188–89, 194–95, 196, 198, 200,

203, 209–11, 212–13, 214, 222; superhero franchises and, 186; teamwork and, 11; tentpole movies/paradigm and, 65, 186; tentpole screenwriters and, 38; TPS (third-person shooter) games, 202; unions and, 198; updateable nature of, 213–14; video blogs and, 227; virtual worlds and, 184; VUP (viewer/user/player role) and, 208; WGA (Writers Guild of America) and, 24–25, 190–91, 192, 193–94, 195–99, 201, 211, 235; WGA strike (2007–8) and, 50–51; Whitta, Gary and, 187. *See also* gaming; individuals; MMORPG (Massively Multiplayer Online Role Playing Game); video games industry; video game writers; *individual games*

video games industry, 193, 194–95, 196, 198–99, 200, 204, 214, 222, 227, 235

video/games writing, 199–213; active formats and, 204–5; animation and, 205, 209–10, 212; authorship and, 201–2, 203; code and, 210, 211; collaboration and, 209; creativity and, 214–15; cultural legitimacy and, 196–97; design and, 185; Excel spreadsheets and, 204, 205; fan/player responses and, 214; flexibility and, 209–10, 211; formats and, 204–5, 208; Hollywood and, 187; income and, 192; narrative and, 182; passive formats and, 204; screenplays and, 213; screenwriters and, 186–87, 210–13, 214–15; screenwriting/craft and, 187, 196, 214, 218–19; story/telling and, 209, 212; television screenwriters and, 211, 213; Videogame Writing Award, 196–97; WGA (Writers Guild of America) and, 187, 210; *Written By: The Magazine of the Writers Guild of America, West* and, 187, 192, 196, 198, 199, 204, 210, 212

video game writers, 182, 185, 186–87, 195, 196, 197

Videogame Writers Caucus (VWC), 195, 196, 197, 198, 199, 211

Videogame Writing Award, 196–97

Video on Demand. *See* VOD (Video on Demand)

viewer/user/player role (VUP), 208

Village Roadshow, 150

Villanueva, Annabelle, 33–34

viral videos, 239

virtual worlds, 184, 185

Vivendi Games, 186

vlogs, 223, 227, 228

VOD (Video on Demand), 113, 146, 227

Vogler, Christopher, 15

Vudu (online streaming service), 164

VUP (viewer/user/player role), 208

VWC (Videogame Writers Caucus), 195, 196, 197, 198, 199, 211

Wagstaff, Christopher, 248n17

Walk among the Tombstones, A (2014), 74

Walk on the Moon, A (1999), 147, 150, 153

Wall Street Journal, 73

Walmart, 164, 170

Walt Disney Animation Studios, 72, 73, 263n50

Walt Disney Company/Pictures: animation and, 158; *The Avengers* (2012) and, 37; digital distribution and, 49–50; Lucasfilm and, 69; as major studio, 65, 67; mergers and, 67; Miramax and, 147, 150; Pixar and, 159; tentpole movies and, 64; *Written By: The Magazine of the Writers Guild of America, West* and, 198–99

Walt Disney Studios, 73, 74, 253n22. *See also* Marvel Studios

Walt Disney World, 73

Walter, Richard, 6–7, 8, 32

Warcraft (2016), 183, 186, 191

Wargaming Public Co Ltd., 202, 227, 229, 269n2, 270n17, 270n18. *See also* World of Tanks (WoT) (game)

Warlords of Draenor (game), 183–84
Warner, Jack, 1, 2, 3
Warner Bros., 58, 65, 74–75, 76, 77, 84–85, 119–20, 152
"Warning for Our Next Great Screenwriters, A" (Ray), 7–8
Warren Script Application (software), 90
Washington, Denzel, 120
Washington Post, 154
Watchmen (2009), 217
web series, 224–25, 238–39
Weitz, Chris and Paul, 69, 159
Wellenreiter, Michael, 188, 212–13, 214
Wells, Audrey, 41
Wells, John, 59, 84–85
westerns, 68, 71, 74, 161, 188
West Wing, The (1999–2006), 109, 191–92
WGA (Writers Guild of America), 38–42; AMPTP (Alliance of Motion Picture and Television Producers) and the, 59, 152; animation and the, 55, 56, 161, 189; *Annual Financial Report* (2014), 41; convergence and the, 100, 190, 192; convergent media and the, 25, 185, 242; convergent screenwriters and the, 29, 235–36; digital residuals and the, 51, 58, 149; digital technologies and the, 57, 58–59; economics and the, 39; hierarchy and the, 79, 193; Hollywood and the, 3; independent cinema and the, 148–49; independent screenwriters and the, 149; industry changes and the, 149; IPC (Interactive Program Contract) and the, 197–98; labor and the, 29, 190, 193, 235; media convergence and the, 4, 39; membership and the, 4, 13, 39, 42, 47, 55–56; microbudget productions and the, 148, 165; new media and the, 3, 24–25, 55–56, 57, 149, 189, 190, 235; new screenwriters and the, 29, 190; online content/creators and the, 219–20, 235; platforms and the, 189, 190; producer's passes and the, 82; reality television and the, 55–56, 189–90, 192; screenplays and the, 197; screenwriter credit and the, 22, 83; screenwriter interviews and the, 22; screenwriters and the, 13, 29, 190, 193, 219–20, 235–36; screenwriting/craft and the, 25, 149, 190, 192, 193, 219–20; screenwriting craft and the, 235; screenwriting/craft and the, 242; scripting and the, 235; story/telling and the, 219–20; sweepstakes pitching and the, 152; television/showrunners and the, 134–35, 154–55, 192–93; tentpole movies and the, 13, 242; TWA (Television Writers Association) and the, 193; 2011 negotiations and the, 58–59; video/games and the, 24–25, 187, 190–91, 192, 193–94, 195–99, 201, 210, 211, 235; Videogame Writing Award and the, 196–97; VWC (Videogame Writers Caucus) and the, 195, 198; *The Writers: A History of American Screenwriters and Their Guild* (Banks) and the, 13; writers' collectives and the, 86; *Writers Reports*, 39. *See also* WGA strike (2007–8); WGA West (WGAW); *Written By: The Magazine of the Writers Guild of America, West*
WGA East, 44–45, 250n42
WGA strike (1988), 56
WGA strike (2007–8), 41–55; agendas and the, 42; AMPTP (Alliance of Motion Picture and Television Producers) and the, 44–47, 49, 50–51, 53–54; ancillary markets and the, 44, 50; blogs and the, 51–52, 53, 251n56; circuit of culture and the, 47; class tensions and the, 42–43, 44, 53; conglomerates and the, 46, 53, 54–55; convergence and the, 4, 42; craft guilds and the, 53–54; DeadlineHollywoodDaily.com (Deadline.com) and the, 52; DGA (Directors Guild of America) and

the, 57; digital distribution and the, 49–51; digital residuals and the, 149, 189; digital technologies and the, 44, 51, 60; Directors Guild of America (DGA) and the, 53–54; distribution and the, 49; DVDs and the, 136; economics and the, 43, 52–53, 54–55; hegemony and the, 54–55; income and the, 59; Internet and the, 50–51, 51–52; labor and the, 42, 45, 50, 54, 80, 138; Los Angeles City Council and the, 59; media and the, 43, 47, 54; membership and the, 42, 47, 50, 51, 189; network television and the, 48–49, 53, 54–55; new media and the, 42, 43, 58, 59, 136; one-step deals and the, 104; overall deals and the, 87; Pencils Down campaign, 48; reality television and the, 56; residuals and the, 44–45, 46–47, 50, 53–54; revenues and the, 44, 51, 136; Ryan, Shawn and the, 23, 48, 134–37; SAG (Screen Actors Guild) and the, 53–54; screenwriters and the, 43, 52, 53, 54–55; screenwriting and the, 23, 135; *The Shield* (2002–8) and the, 48, 135–36, 137; social media and the, 45, 46, 51–52, 54; story/telling and the, 43; studios and the, 43, 45, 48–49, 53, 54–55, 60, 87; sweepstakes pitching and the, 104; television/showrunners and the, 42, 47–49, 55, 134–37; transmedia marketing and the, 10; unions and the, 45, 52–53; *United Hollywood* (blog) and the, 52–53; United Showrunners group and the, 47–49; *Variety* and the, 51, 52; video/games and the, 50–51; writers' collectives and the, 86. *See also* 2011 negotiations (WGA); 2014 negotiations (WGA)
WGA West (WGAW), 39–40, 41, 44–46, 59, 81, 82, 195, 246n17, 250n42. *See also Written By: The Magazine of the Writers Guild of America, West*

Wheaton, Will, 223, 226, 236
Whedon, Joss, 37, 47–48, 53, 87, 94, 97–99, 114, 125
Which Lie Did I Tell? More Adventures in the Screen Trade (Goldman), 144
Whitaker, Forest, 106–7
Whitta, Gary, 69, 183, 187, 210
"Why So Serious" (online puzzles), 10
Wikipedia: independent cinema and, 265n71; Indiewood and, 139, 141, 179; Jenkins, Leeroy (character/meme) and, 183; online content/creators and, 217, 226; Phoenix, Satine and, 224; screenwriters and, 8; strikes and, 27; on television showrunners, 102, 104; tentpole movies and, 62, 64–65; video game writers and, 182, 186
William Morris Endeavour Entertainment, 57
Williams, John H., 164
Williams, Linda, 177
Wilson, Keith, 180
Wimmer, Kurt, 41
Windus, Arthur, 94–95
Wing Commanders (game), 212–13
Winship, Michael, 45
Winston, Hilary, 78
Winterbottom, Michael, 171, 176–77
Wire, The (2002–8), 47–48, 70, 110, 125, 191–92
Wired (magazine), 93
Witcher, The (game), 210
Wolf, Mark J. P., 203
women, 24, 39–41, 69–70, 192. *See also* females
women screenwriters, 39–41
Wonder Woman (2017), 77–78, 152
Woolverton, Linda, 72–73
World of Tanks (*WoT*) (game), 202, 217, 218, 228–31, 232, 265n1, 270n18. *See also* QB (Quickbaby) (Frampton, Will)
World of Warcraft (WOW), 182–84, 185, 191, 202, 229, 232, 265n2, 266n21

Wowhead Weekly (Youtube show), 232
Wright, Edgar, 76
Wright, Micah, 197, 204, 209
writer-producers, 85, 135, 137, 221. *See also* television showrunners
Writers: A History of American Screenwriters and Their Guild, The (Banks), 13
Writers Co-op, 84–86
Writers Guild of America. *See* WGA (Writers Guild of America)
Writers Journey: Mythic Structure for Writers, The (Vogler), 15
Writers Reports, 39
Writers Store, 15, 224
writing/drawing, 163
Writing Partners, 85
Written By: The Magazine of the Writers Guild of America, West: alt. screenwriters (column) and, 198; Bird, Brad and, 163; Gray, Pamela and, 149; special effects and, 36; video/games and, 187, 192, 196, 198, 199, 204, 210, 212; VWC (Videogame Writers Caucus) and, 211

X-Files, The (1993–2002), 106, 116, 258n26
X Wing (game), 10

Yahata, Craig, 115
"You Gotta Be Dumb If You're Gonna Be Tough," (Wade), 231
Young, David, 46, 47, 54, 82, 190
Your Sister's Sister (2011), 166–67
youth sector, 23, 24, 67, 115, 138, 145, 191
YouTube: digital distribution and, 58; Jenkins, Leeroy (character) and, 184; Mathias, Harry and, 234; Metzen, Chris and, 202; monetization and, 149; online content/creators and, 225; QB (Quickbaby) (Frampton, Will) and, 218, 228, 229–30, 232, 233, 270n17; *Teatime with Tuskeh* and, 232; *Wowhead Weekly* and, 232; YouTube series, 232

www.ingramcontent.com/pod-product-compliance
Lightning Source LLC
Chambersburg PA
CBHW021337230426
43666CB00006B/322